THE FACTORY OF GRIEVANCES

Patrick Buckland

The Factory of Grievances

Devolved Government in Northern Ireland 1921-39

GILL AND MACMILLAN, DUBLIN
BARNES & NOBLE BOOKS, NEW YORK
(a division of Harper & Row Publishers, Inc.)

First published 1979 by
Gill and Macmillan Ltd
15/17 Eden Quay
Dublin 1
with associated companies in
London, New York, Delhi, Hong Kong,
Johannesburg, Lagos, Melbourne,
Singapore, Tokyo

Published in the U.S.A. 1979 by
Harper & Row Publishers, Inc.
Barnes & Noble Import Division

SBN 7171 0954 2 (Gill and Macmillan)
ISBN 0-06-490752-X (Barnes and Noble)

Origination by Joe Healy Typesetting, Dublin
Printed and bound in Great Britain by
Redwood Burn Limited
Trowbridge & Esher

To Pat and to my Mother and Father

Contents

Preface

This book, based largely upon hitherto unavailable cabinet and departmental papers, is the first attempt to examine through the eyes of the regional government the formative period in the history of the new region of Northern Ireland created by the 1920 Government of Ireland Act. Originally it started life as a political biography of James Craig, Northern Ireland's one and only Prime Minister between the wars, but it soon became clear that circumstances, colleagues, civil servants and the constitution as much as Craig determined what the government did and, more frequently, did not do. It therefore seemed more appropriate to present a study of the processes of government in Northern Ireland, an analysis of the way in which the regional government did actually govern, identifying and responding to problems and making decisions in face of the many constraints placed upon its freedom of action.

The choice of the period 1921–39 was partly determined by the availability of official records. It was (and remains) the only extended period of peacetime government for which adequate documentation is available from official sources, first under special dispensation and then under a recently introduced but still restrictive thirty-year rule. The main justification for selecting the first twenty years was, however, the realisation that they constituted a crucial period in the development of Northern Ireland. During these years the pattern of government and politics was so firmly established that by the late 1930s it was unlikely to be fundamentally altered except by political or economic revolution.

Initially, too, the book was favourably disposed both to partition, as the most practical way of reconciling the apprehensions of Ulster Unionism with the aspirations of Irish nationalism, and to regional government, in view of the many limitations of British rule in Ireland in the nineteenth and early twentieth centuries. The preference for partition survived both the research and writing, but, for reasons which should become clear, the preference for regional government turned to distaste and despair about the desirability of parliamentary devolution in the United Kingdom in general and in Northern Ireland in particular.

Acknowledgments

My biggest debt is once more to the staff of the Public Record Office of Northern Ireland. I am particularly indebted to the Keeper, Mr Brian Trainor, for permission to use and reproduce extracts from the Northern Ireland cabinet and departmental papers, and to Dr Peter Smyth for the friendship and professional assistance which eased my way through an often daunting forest of files. Thanks are also due to Mrs S. Hughes, in charge of inter-library loans in the Sydney Jones Library, University of Liverpool, and to Mr T. Hamilton, the parliamentary Librarian at Stormont, both of whom made printed sources more readily available. I am grateful to Viscount Craigavon for permission to quote from the diary of the first Lady Craigavon; to Mrs R. Dingwall for permission to consult and quote from the diaries of her father and mother, Sir Wilfrid and Lady Spender; and to Dr S. Elliott and Dr J. Whyte of the Queen's University of Belfast, Miss S. Greenlees, formerly of the New University of Ulster, and Dr J. F. Harbinson of the Northern Ireland Polytechnic, for allowing me to consult the unpublished works listed in the bibliography. I wish to acknowledge the financial assistance given by the Wolfson Foundation and my own university, the University of Liverpool, and to thank the University of Manchester for electing me to a Hallsworth Fellowship in Political Economy for the session 1977—78, thus giving me the freedom to complete my research. Finally, for helpful advice on both writing and presentation, I am grateful to Mr Harvey Cox, my friend and colleague at the University of Liverpool, Mr Colm Croker, my editor, and to the anonymous (but obviously discerning!) reader who recommended publication.

ABBREVIATIONS

D.O.R.A.	Defence of the Realm Act
I.R.A.	Irish Republican Army
M.P.	Member of Parliament
P.R.	Proportional representation
R.I.C.	Royal Irish Constabulary
R.O.I.A.	Restoration of Order in Ireland Act
R.U.C.	Royal Ulster Constabulary
U.A.O.S.	Ulster Agricultural Organisation Society
U.D.C.	Urban District Council
U.F.G.D.A.	Ulster Fruit-Growers' Defence Association
U.F.G.M.A.	Ulster Fruit-Growers' Marketing Association
U.F.U.	Ulster Farmers' Union
U.P.A.	Ulster Protestant Association
U.U.C.	Ulster Unionist Council
U.U.L.A.	Ulster Unionist Labour Association
U.V.F.	Ulster Volunteer Force

NOTE ON TERMINOLOGY

For the sake of quick and easy identification, a number of terms have been used which might offend the purist. Professor F. S. L. Lyons's excellent example in *Ireland since the Famine* has generally been followed in the spelling of such words as 'labour', 'nationalist' and 'nationalism'. A small initial letter has been used when referring to general matters connected with the needs and demands of labour and of Irish nationality, but initial capitals have been used for 'Labour' and 'Nationalist' whenever it seemed necessary to identify a specific party and its supporters, the latter referring to the heirs of the old Irish Parliamentary Party in Northern Ireland. The government in London was often described by Ulster Unionists as the 'imperial government', and this practice has been adopted to distinguish the London government, its ministers and civil servants from other governments and their ministers and officials. Although the six counties of Northern Ireland constituted only two-thirds of the historic province of Ulster, the epithet 'Ulster', widely used by contemporaries, has been used with discretion, as has the term 'province' to describe the area of Northern Ireland. Finally, Sir James Craig, created Viscount Craigavon of Stormont in 1927, has for convenience been referred to throughout by his surname.

Introduction:
The Trouble with Partition

In Northern Ireland we claim that we have the biggest shipyard, the biggest ropeworks, the biggest linen manufacturers and the biggest tobacco factory in the world; I am afraid there is one other factory in which we could probably claim that we or the Free State are the largest manufacturers – namely the factory of grievances. I am not at all sure that this particular factory isn't the most paying one in the Province.[1]

So wrote Sir Wilfrid Spender in December 1939 after twenty years experience as a senior civil servant in Northern Ireland. His jaundiced appraisal provided a sad contrast to the optimism shown during the first speeches in the new Northern Ireland parliament in June 1921, when much was said about the creation of a model state securing prosperity and justice for all classes and creeds. 'At all events, Sir,' James Craig, the first Prime Minister, told the Speaker,

I myself and my colleagues are at the disposal of the people of Northern Ireland. We have nothing in our view except the welfare of the people. Our duty and our privilege are from now onwards to have our Parliament well established, to look to the people as a whole, to set ourselves to probe to the bottom those problems that have retarded progress in the past, to do everything that lies in our power to help forward developments in the town and country. . . . We will be cautious in our legislation. We will be absolutely honest and fair in administering the law.[2]

Even sadder is the reflection that Spender's jaundiced view rather than Craig's initial optimism fairly summed up Northern Ireland's experience of regional government in the inter-war years.[3] Far from creating a new and equal society, the government seemed to spend its time responding to a whole range of real or imagined grievances, often of the pettiest kind, for which it was held responsible. The grievances most widely publicised by contemporary and later critics of Ulster Unionism were those of the substantial Catholic/nationalist majority, who complained of discrimination and oppression. But it was not the minority's grievances that Spender primarily had in mind when he wrote of the grievance factory. Even more trying for the government were the grievances of its supposed supporters, who were far from united behind and contented with their Unionist government, except on the question of partition. Northern Ireland was, indeed, a difficult and unsatisfying place to govern, especially for an administration in such close touch with the people and with so limited powers. That Craig and his colleagues were 'at the disposal of the people' was far from being an advantage.

Herein lay the fundamental weakness of the 1920 Government of Ireland Act, which partitioned Ireland and Ulster and established in the six north-eastern counties (Antrim, Armagh, Down, Fermanagh, Londonderry and Tyrone) a regional government and parliament.[4] The fundamental weakness lay not in the fact of partition. Irishmen were divided before partition. The political, social, religious and economic development of Northern Ireland had produced by the early twentieth century two powerful but opposed political movements, Irish nationalism and Ulster Unionism. Partition merely recognised this division. Nor did the fundamental weakness lie in the six-county borderline, adopted after much discussion among members of the imperial government and after consultation with Ulster Unionist leaders. Any boundary between North and South would have caused some economic dislocation and been contrary to either nationalist or Unionist wishes. The six-county border at least had the merits of following existing administrative boundaries and of being acceptable to the majority of Ulster Unionists. With Protestants comprising 66 per cent of the population, the six counties constituted the largest area of Ulster with a safe Unionist majority.[5] Rather, the fundamental weakness of the 1920 act lay in the type of government it established in Northern Ireland.

The decision to set up a government and parliament in the North as well as in the South of Ireland was not based upon any long-term consideration of the benefits or otherwise the six counties would derive from regional government. Instead, it sprang from the imperial government's anxiety to extricate itself from Ireland in face of a strident Irish Republicanism, but in a way which would redeem past pledges to Ulster Unionists that they would not be coerced into accepting Dublin rule, and yet also be relatively acceptable to Irish nationalists by appearing to foster Irish unity.[6] The result was that the governmental structure established in Northern Ireland was ill-thought-out and the new regional government and parliament were given responsibility without real power.

Indeed, the constitutional arrangements of the 1920 act seemed deliberately designed to restrict the new regional authority's freedom of action and power of development. It was true that the new authority was given control over purely local affairs. The parliament had the power to make laws on matters relating exclusively to Northern Ireland, such as trade, industry and agriculture, law and order, education, social services and minor taxes. Yet this power and freedom was more apparent than real.

In the first place, the regional authority had to share much of the responsibility for the administration of transferred services with the well-entrenched and largely unco-operative local authorities it inherited. In the second place, the right of citizens to religious freedom and the rights of certain institutions were written into the constitution. Section 5 of the 1920 act prohibited the legislature from making laws interfering with religious liberty or equality, and, except for certain purposes, from acquiring compulsorily the property of religious denominations or educational institutions, even on payment of compensation.

Thirdly, certain vital powers were retained by Westminster. The Northern Ireland parliament was unable to legislate in respect of either 'excepted' or 'reserved' services, which remained the preserve of the imperial parliament. 'Excepted' matters consisted of those on which uniformity throughout the United Kingdom was considered essential, such as the Crown, peace and war, the armed forces, treaties with foreign states, trade with any place outside Northern Ireland, currency and trade marks. The 'reserved' services included the Supreme Court of Northern Ireland, the registration of deeds, the postal service, stamp designs, savings banks and certain highly important taxes. The distinction between these two types of services lay in the imperial government's original desire to encourage the two parliaments envisaged in the 1920 act to achieve Irish unity: the intention was to reserve certain topics until the Southern and Northern parliaments united, when the reserved powers could be transferred to the new all-Ireland assembly. As a result, these services were financed differently. Northern Ireland was required by section 23 of the 1920 act to make a contribution, commonly called the 'imperial contribution' or simply 'the contribution', towards imperial liabilities and expenditure; but the imperial government deducted from reserved taxation the cost of reserved services in Northern Ireland.

Finally, sovereign power was reserved to the imperial parliament. The Northern Ireland parliament was by law subordinate. All acts passed at Westminster extended to Northern Ireland unless it was excluded expressly or by implication, for, like every other part of the kingdom, Northern Ireland was subject to the rule of the United Kingdom constitution that the parliament at Westminster was legally supreme. This subordinate status was specifically enshrined in section 75 of the 1920 act, which stated that

Notwithstanding the establishment of the Parliaments of Southern and Northern Ireland . . . the supreme authority of the Parliament of the United Kingdom shall remain unaffected and undiminished over all persons, matters, and things in Ireland and every part thereof.

These powers and limitations remained substantially unchanged in the inter-war years, with only minor modifications in 1922, 1928 and 1932.[7]

Given the degree of community tensions in Northern Ireland, the ban on religious discrimination and the reservation of sovereign power to Westminster did provide the imperial authorities with an opportunity to supervise the administration of certain transferred services touching potentially explosive issues, but successive imperial governments preferred not to take advantage of such powers. Of the limitations inherent in the structure of government, those which most constricted the regional government were the need to share power within Northern Ireland with local authorities and the lack of financial control.

Local authorities were not only numerous but they also had a very narrow conception of their responsibilities. Their main preoccupation was not the development of services but to keep rates to the minimum. Even more inhibiting was the regional authority's limited financial powers. While it controlled, at least formally, most of its expenditure, it controlled only a small proportion (between 10 and 20 per cent) of its revenues. It could neither impose nor collect customs duties, major excise duties, income tax or surtax, any tax on profits or any general tax on capital. These taxes were reserved to the imperial parliament, which imposed and collected them at uniform rates throughout the United Kingdom. The taxes transferred to the Northern Ireland parliament were comparatively minor ones, such as motor vehicle tax and death duties; and although it could grant relief from income tax and surtax, it could do so only at the expense of the Northern Ireland treasury. Not only was Northern Ireland's revenue dependent upon general imperial fiscal policy, but so also was the regulation of its economic life. Such matters as currency devaluation, tariff protection and trade agreements were beyond the competence of the parliament and government of Northern Ireland, although they were essential to the development of regional economic policies.

The most serious defect of the three-tier system of government established in Northern Ireland was, then, the uncomfortable position the regional government occupied between an imperial authority with an exacting Treasury and a multitude of parsimonious local authorities. These imperial and local perspectives were often at variance with the regional perspective, and thus severely restricted the Northern Ireland government's will and capacity for developing satisfactory regional policies.

The consequences of this basic defect were aggravated by the circumstances in which the new regional authority had to operate. In the first place, the nature of Northern Ireland politics and society could not fail to affect the operations of government. The area of Northern Ireland is rather less than that of Yorkshire, while in the inter-war years its population of some 1¼ million was almost evenly divided between urban and rural areas. The exposure and accessibility of government ministers in such a small and intimate society were inimical to long-term and overall planning, as was the underdeveloped state of political thinking there. The history of Northern Ireland in the late nineteenth and early twentieth centuries had been distinguished by sectarian conflict and had not made for political maturity. In particular, Ulster Unionists were ill-equipped to assume the responsibility for running the new government. The whole structure and ethos of Ulster Unionism had been based upon a single object – determined opposition to Home Rule – and no constructive philosophy had been developed over the years of struggle to equip Ulster Unionists to govern a state they had neither expected nor wanted.

Secondly, Northern Ireland's economic structure and position within the larger United Kingdom economy had implications for the nature and capacity of government. They committed the government to certain lines of policy and expenditure, particularly in respect of the major cash social services. They created almost intractable social and economic problems, and yet also prevented the government from taking any imaginative, let alone effective, action to tackle the most serious of these problems – a rate of unemployment which was always much higher than the United Kingdom average and which became the highest in any region of the kingdom.

Thirdly, government in Northern Ireland was further conditioned by events in the South. Although it had provided for the creation of two equal parliaments in Ireland, the 1920 act never operated in the twenty-six counties that would have constituted Southern Ireland. Instead, the 1920 act was superseded there by the Anglo-Irish Treaty of 6 December 1921, which conferred dominion status on what became the Irish Free State, which in 1937 became Éire. Although by the Anglo-Irish Treaty and, more specifically, by the border agreement signed on 3 December 1925 by the imperial government and the two Irish governments, the Free State government formally acknowledged the existence of the border, Southern Irishmen never renounced their claims to the North. They occasionally sought to supervise the treatment of the minority there and more frequently demanded the reunification of Ireland. What is more, dominion status conferred wider powers of economic management than those available to the Northern government. The Southern government used those powers in a way which increasingly excluded

Northern Ireland manufacturers and traders from their traditional Southern market and which provided invidious comparisons between its vitality and the apparent lethargy of the government of Northern Ireland. This element of unhealthy competition between North and South provided a further obstacle to the formulation and development of regional policies in the interests of the Northern Ireland community as a whole.

The coincidence of these constricting circumstances with a constricting constitution did produce in Northern Ireland Spender's 'factory of grievances', sheltered in what Professor R. J. Lawrence has described as 'not a half-way house, but a lean-to'.[8] Having responsibility without real power, the new regional government sought to maintain the loyalty of its supporters in face of mounting tension and discontent within those sections of the community which comprised the Unionist Party. It did so by developing an informal style of government inimical to long-term and overall planning and by discriminating in favour of Protestants and Unionists in respect of education and representation and, to a lesser extent, governmental employment and law and order. The imperial government took few steps to remedy the deficiencies of government in Northern Ireland. It was largely content to observe processes which undermined the essential unity of the United Kingdom. Admittedly, despite some strains, Northern Ireland's formal constitutional position within the United Kingdom remained unchanged, but there was scarcely equality of treatment within the United Kingdom. Material standards of living were in general lower in Northern Ireland than elsewhere in the United Kingdom, while the civil rights of the Catholic/nationalist minority were restricted. Northern Ireland's experience in the inter-war years, therefore, indicates some of the causes of the troubles that at present beset Northern Ireland and demonstrate some of the limitations of devolved government British-style.

To demonstrate the processes of government in Northern Ireland, this book is divided into three parts. Part One describes in general terms the framework of decision- and policy-making, emphasising the constraints placed upon the regional government. Parts Two and Three illustrate the interaction of these various factors, not by relating a detailed history of Northern Ireland, but by examining specific episodes or policies. Part Two stresses the powerlessness of the regional government to develop distinctive policies on financial, social and, agriculture apart, economic matters. Part Three examines questions relating to the minority. It shows how a tendency towards discrimination on matters of law and order developed almost accidentally out of the confused troubles of the years 1921–22, but how, in respect of education and representation, discrimination became an integral part of government policy. In all, the book presents not only an analysis of the operation of regional government in the inter-war years, but also an argument against parliamentary devolution.

Part One

1

The Regional Government

Whatever else it lacked, Northern Ireland did not lack institutions of government. For such a small area, it possessed an elaborate structure of government with its three tiers — the imperial government at Westminster, congeries of local authorities, and the new regional government. Responsibility rested mainly on the regional government, which consisted of an executive, backed by an army of civil servants and answerable to a two-chamber elective assembly. The Northern Ireland parliament, however, was little more than a cipher, and whatever real power the regional government had lay with the executive and civil service.

1

The executive consisted of the Prime Minister's Department and six other departments with clearly defined responsibilities. This arrangement had been drawn up between February and May 1921, largely by Sir Ernest Clark, then Assistant Under-Secretary in Northern Ireland, in consultation with Craig, the Prime Minister elect, and senior officials of the Irish Office, but with only a perfunctory reference to local opinion. Clark's task had not been an easy one.[1] Under the Union the powers of government in Ireland had been distributed among some thirty different departments, and the problem was how these powers could be most efficiently grouped in Northern Ireland without producing too many office-holders in parliament. Costs were a secondary consideration.

The number of ministries suggested varied between five and eight. Clark's original scheme suggested five ministries,[2] but Adam Duffin, an ageing Liberal Unionist, after discussing a revised version of Clark's original scheme with the Belfast Chamber of Commerce, suggested the establishment of eight ministries.[3] Clark rejected this suggestion because he thought that 'The *minimum* workable ministry is already unduly large in proportion to the number of the Party (whatever it may be) that is for the time being in power. Assuming a majority of 12, (majority party consisting of 32), then a quarter of them are ministers; or if the Party had a bare majority (27 or 28), the position would be even worse.' Moreover, an increase in the number of ministries would mean either increased costs or, as Clark pointed out, 'If you keep your expenditure constant, you reduce your individual remuneration, and are, therefore, less likely to get the best permanent officials.'[4] This anxiety to keep to a minimum the number of ministries created problems about their functions. There was at first general agreement that there should be ministries for Health and Local Government (combined), Agriculture and Education, but there was agreement on little else. Of course, a Ministry of Finance or Treasury was essential, but should it take on some functions normally associated with the Home Office? Or should it also act as a Ministry of Commerce? Alternatively, should there be a combined Ministry of Labour and Commerce? The answers to these and other questions gradually emerged during discussions in the spring of 1921 between Craig, Clark and Irish Office officials when administrative convenience was weighed against political expediency. Thus, when the scheme of government was announced towards the end of May, the Ministry of Health and Local Government had disappeared, a Ministry of Home Affairs had been created, and Labour and Commerce emerged as separate departments. The final list of departments was: the Prime Minister's, Finance, Home Affairs, Education, Labour, Agriculture and Commerce, the last two being headed by a single minister until 1925.[5]

The number of government departments was a source of vocal complaint during the early years of the state, especially since ministers were given political understudies in the shape of parliamentary secretaries,[6] and the Ministry of Commerce was denounced as unnecessary and positively harmful to industry.[7] Yet the Northern Ireland departments were grouped together more efficiently than under the Dublin Castle system, and it is difficult to see how the number of departments could have been reduced without jeopardising major interest groups and creating undue tensions within departments. Certainly Sir Edward Archdale found himself with conflicting loyalties when he was responsible for both Agriculture and Commerce. As Minister of Agriculture he opposed a scheme to encourage flax-growing as unprofitable to the farmers, but as Minister of Commerce he felt bound to support a scheme which would render the linen industry less dependent upon supplies of imported flax![8]

More important than the administrative structure were the men who operated it. Northern Ireland's governmental machine was operated by a surprisingly small number of individuals in the inter-war years. Between 1921 and the outbreak of war in 1939 twelve individuals served in the Northern Ireland cabinet, some continuously. Craig was Prime Minister from 1921 until his death in November 1940. Sir Richard Dawson

Bates remained at Home Affairs until 1943. John Miller Andrews was Minister of Labour until 1937, when he became Minister of Finance, a post which he combined with the premiership for a short while after Craig's death. Other members of the original cabinet also showed remarkable staying power. Admittedly, the 7th Marquis of Londonderry served as Minister of Education only until 1925, when he returned to British politics; but Hugh McDowell Pollock soldiered on until his death in 1937 as Minister of Finance; and Sir Edward Mervyn Archdale combined Agriculture and Commerce until 1925 and then carried on with just Agriculture until 1933, shortly before his death. Ministers who joined the cabinet subsequently also showed a tendency to stay in office. James Milne Barbour was Minister of Commerce, unpaid, from 1925 until 1941, when he became Minister of Finance. Sir Basil Brooke, who became Minister of Agriculture in 1933, changed to Commerce in 1941 before beginning in 1943 a twenty-year stint as Prime Minister. The 8th Viscount Charlemont, Londonderry's successor as Minister of Education, served from 1925 until 1937. It was true that his successor, John Hanna Robb, lasted a mere five years, resigning to become a county court judge, but he had been the junior minister since 1925. Indeed, Robb's long apprenticeship was indicative of stability or stagnation at the junior minister level. Thus Herbert Dixon, later 1st Baron Glentoran, remained Parliamentary Secretary to the Ministry of Finance and Chief Whip until 1941, when he became Minister of Agriculture.

Long service meant an ageing as well as an experienced government. The average age of the cabinet in 1921 was 54 years: Pollock was 69; Archdale 68, Andrews and Craig both 50, Bates 44, and Londonderry 43. In the early 1930s, therefore, the cabinet contained in Pollock and Archdale two octogenarians, and even their disappearance did not radically alter the ageing tendencies of the government. In 1938 the average age of the cabinet members was 62: Milne Barbour was 70, Andrews and Craig both 67, Major David Graham Shillington (Minister of Labour for a few months in 1937–38, when he was succeeded by the long-serving junior minister, John Fawcett Gordon) 66, Bates 61, Robb 50, and Brooke 50. Health was just as important as age. In this respect Craig, Bates, Pollock and Shillington were badly served, being subject to repeated and incapacitating illnesses, although in Pollock's case this may simply have been old age.

Ministers shared another characteristic apart from growing old together. They were socially unrepresentative, being drawn from the upper reaches of Ulster society. The first cabinet consisted of three landowners, two of whom had substantial business interests; two men with wide business experience, one of whom also owned land; and one solicitor. The junior ministers fell into the same category. Admittedly, two were workingmen, one of whom became, very much later, a cabinet minister, but the other five parliamentary secretaries were a noble land-owner who was also chairman of a large railway company, three men with substantial business connections, and a barrister. The list of ministers did indeed 'read like an executive committee of Northern industry and commerce'.[9]

Yet, while not representative of Ulster society, members of the government were *of* Ulster society. They had been born and educated there. They earned their livings there, retaining their business interests when in office. They identified themselves with Ulster's problems and the preoccupations of the Protestant community, particularly by their involvement in the Ulster Unionist resistance to Home Rule. Born in Bangor in 1852 and educated at a local primary school, Pollock eventually became managing director of Shaw, Pollock & Co. Ltd, Belfast flour importers, a director of the Belfast Rope Works, a harbour commissioner and president of the Belfast Chamber of Commerce. Andrews, born in Belfast in 1871 and educated at the Belfast Royal Academical Institution, became chairman of the family firm ot linen manufacturers, J. M. Andrews & Co. Ltd, a director of the Belfast Rope Works and of the Belfast and County Down Railway Co., and was also involved in the affairs of the county where he owned land, being a member of the Down County Council. On the other side of the province, Archdale, despite being educated at Knight's Naval School, Portsmouth, and serving in the navy for some fourteen years, became almost totally identified with the affairs of Co. Fermanagh, where he had been born at the family home, Rossfadd, in 1853. He owned and farmed land there, represented the county at Westminster for many years, and was vice-chairman of the County Council. So attached was he to his county that it was only with difficulty that he managed to bring himself to attend cabinet meetings in Belfast. Just how closely ministers had been identified with Ulster Unionists' resistance to Home Rule was indicated by the fact that Bates, a solicitor who had been born in Belfast in 1877 and educated at Coleraine Academical Institution, was secretary to the Ulster Unionist Council (U.U.C.) from 1905 until his appointment as Minister of Home Affairs in 1921.

Long service, age and background combined to give ministers two characteristics which augured ill for the future of Northern Ireland: limited vision and a defensive political stance.

In the main, ministers were competent but limited. They lacked imagination and adaptability. The Union and the maintenance of partition represented their basic platform, and they tended to view questions connected with the constitution, such as voting systems and the administration of justice, from a narrow Ulster Unionist viewpoint, with scant regard for wider interests or long-term benefits. Other matters they approached with a pragmatism tinged by a fear of socialism, a strong prejudice in favour of *laissez-faire,* and an economic fatalism in which Providence played a dominant role. Such a limited perspective was at least understandable. Most ministers had been drawn into politics for one reason and one reason only — to maintain the Union. It was true that the experience and responsibility of government did help to broaden their outlook, but this educational experience was limited by their involvement in the local community. Since ministers were closely integrated into the local community, they were continually exposed to a local point of view. As Andrews told Craig during one of the recurrent campaigns by the Protestant clergy against the 1923 Education Act, 'Already the Protestant pulpits are being used for defending what is called "Protestant rights". I had myself to listen to two lengthy harangues on the subject on Sunday last in Little's church at Castlereagh'.[10] Furthermore, born in the second half of the nineteenth century in a relatively buoyant economic environment, ministers had absorbed very limited and traditional views on the proper sphere of government.

This is not to say that there was always unanimity amongst members of the government. Although a unanimous front was presented in public, there were often disagreements over priorities as ministers took up postures appropriate to their departments. Industry and Agriculture were sometimes at loggerheads,[11] and throughout the inter-war years there was a running battle between the Ministry of Finance and the main spending departments, a battle which sometimes reflected a muted conflict between capital and labour. Andrews's endeavours to extend social services invariably met with opposition from Pollock and his officials, obsessed with the need to balance the budget and keep on good terms with the imperial Treasury and suspicious that labour was being pampered at the expense of employers.[12] There were, too, differences of opinion on questions relating to the Northern minority and to the Free State. Bates and Dixon were always inclined to take a hard line on such questions; but Pollock, described by one English official as 'better informed and more intellectual than his colleagues',[13] and, to a lesser extent, the compassionate Andrews, were capable of taking a wider view.[14]

Such disagreements were, however, over emphases rather than fundamentals. The constitutional and related issues were paramount, upon which neither Pollock nor Andrews pressed their broader views. On all other matters ministers shared conservative social, economic and financial views. Andrews's quarrel with Pollock was not over whether there should or should not be a balanced budget, but over who should balance it — the Northern Ireland taxpayers and ratepayers or the imperial Treasury.[15] There was general agreement that the state should play a minimal role and that private enterprise should be encouraged.

There was a reluctance to innovate and a tendency to follow British examples.

The second and related characteristic was a defensive political stance, a pronounced political timidity. Lacking the self-confidence born of generations of governing and experience of the rough-and-tumble of parliamentary politics, and being very closely identified with their followers and local communities, ministers tended to be extremely sensitive to any form of criticism. Thus the formation in July 1923 of the Ulster Reform Association, a short-lived organisation financed by the drink trade and vocally critical of the government, caused panic among inexperienced ministers. Police reports of its private meetings were forwarded to Craig, then in England, who was told by the Chief Whip that 'I will have this new Association well watched & get a few of the right sort into it'.[16] Such sensitivity often reduced the government to following opinion rather than leading it.

Bates was the extreme case of political timidity. It was only with great difficulty that Craig had persuaded him to submit in 1921 to the turmoil of a parliamentary election, and the mantle of high office never sat lightly on his shoulders. Londonderry was quite right when he remarked in January 1922 that Bates's 'previous work was no training for the duties of Home Secretary and his support and standing in the Six Counties was not high enough to give him that general support and confidence which are such factors in successfully controlling a Government office'.[17] All too often was Bates reduced to indecision or inaction in face of any public outcry. His refusal in 1927 to suspend the Belfast Corporation after revelations of corruption in housing contracts conveniently illustrated both the government's fear of socialism and its capacity for avoiding decisive and possibly unpopular action. As he explained to Craig,

> The Corporation is not a Socialistic body notwithstanding all its defects. With an industrial population such as we have it may be that, if the workers were deprived of any control over corporation affairs, they might revert to Socialism. . . . Bad and all as the Corporation is, I can easily visualize a far worse condition of affairs under the control of a Socialistic majority.[18]

Craig and Londonderry, who served as acting Prime Minister during Craig's absences, did not necessarily share these characteristics. Both had held office in Britain and would have continued their political careers there but for the establishment of Northern Ireland. Moreover, Londonderry's family did have a tradition of governmental service, a fact which Londonderry emphasised by aping his controversial ancestor, Castlereagh, wearing 'a high black stock over his collar and a very tightly-fitting frock coat', and not looking 'as if he belonged to this century at all. In manner he is a little bit the Lord Curzon type, and stands very much on his dignity'.[19] Londonderry's perspective was thus somewhat broader than that of his colleagues. He did not, for example, share conventional Ulster views on the limited role and capacities of women, successfully opposing a proposal to change the law regarding, and thereby virtually eliminating, women jurors. Women, he insisted 'should be educated up to their duties'.[20] This was the sole victory in Londonderry's apparent campaign to educate his colleagues. He unsuccessfully advocated a conciliatory approach to questions of law and order,[21] but was most disappointed when he found that the religious provisions of his Education Act, which he had confidently thought would solve the problem of religious education, were being undermined by noisome and noisy Orangemen and Presbyterians, whom, he confessed to Craig, 'I never have understood'.[22] Had he spent more time in Northern Ireland, he might have come to understand and to have influenced decisions more effectively. As it was, he divided his time between his substantial British interests and his ministerial duties in Northern Ireland. He was never at home in the latter role.[23] Having refused Bonar Law's offer of the Air Ministry in 1922 because Craig wanted him to stay on until the boundary question had been settled, Londonderry became so anxious to leave Northern Ireland that in November 1925 he sought appointment as a mere under-secretary at the Foreign Office. 'I can remain on in Ireland,' he rather disingenuously told Austen Chamberlain, then Foreign Secretary, 'although I am not at all certain that I should be altogether a benefit to Northern Ireland'.[24] He did resign as Minister of Education in December 1925, but had to wait until 1928 for a seat in the imperial cabinet – as First Commissioner of Works.

Craig stood a much better chance of broadening his colleagues' outlook. He provided almost a complete contrast to Londonderry. The youngest son of a recently enriched whiskey millionaire, his broad figure and red face might have cast him in later days as the prototype of Colonel Blimp, but in fact he was a modest, humane, good-humoured and imperturbable man, with a personal charm that few could resist. Having served in the South African War, he entered parliament in 1906 as M.P. for East Down. He quickly made his mark as a resolute and expert draftsman to Irish bills, and held junior office at Westminster from 1916 to 1921 (as Treasurer of the Household, 1916–18, at the Ministry of Pensions, 1919–20, and at the Admiralty, 1920–21). It was he who made the practical plans for Ulster Unionists' resistance to the Third Home Rule Bill before the First World War, and he was the obvious choice as Ulster Unionist leader, and thus first Prime Minister of Northern Ireland, when the ill and ageing Sir Edward Carson resigned the leadership in February 1921.[25] He quickly established himself as the dominant figure in Northern Ireland politics, the un-rivalled leader of the Ulster Unionists. Even when Craig's power and health had so obviously deteriorated by 1938 that the permanent head of the civil service suggested that he should be persuaded to resign, Andrews refused on the grounds that Craig's popularity made him indispensable.[26]

It was true that Craig's ideas were hardly original. He agreed that the Union and the maintenance of partition were the fundamental issues, and he did share the widely held views on the limited role of government in economic and social matters. However, his experiences in British politics, his close contacts with leading British politicians, and even his prolonged absences from Northern Ireland, gave him a different perspective from his colleagues. This broader, more tolerant perspective showed Craig at his best during the first two troubled years of the state, when, despite the reservations of his colleagues, he maintained contact with Southern leaders and was the only member of his government capable of even contemplating the possibility of a united Ireland in his lifetime.[27] The breakdown of his agreements with Collins in 1922 and the civil war in the South caused him to revise this opinion, but by the late 1920s he was evidently able to consider (at least when far away from Ireland, in Australia) the possibility once more.[28]

There were, then, indications that Craig could have asserted himself with effect. The fact was that he did not choose to assert himself or to develop long-term plans for the province. Instead, he adopted a style of leadership which compounded his ministers' limitations and country's natural disadvantages and which militated against efficient government. He liked to see Northern Ireland as one large happy family with himself as the benevolent and popular father-figure and head. This imagery comes over time and again in his speeches. Thus on 6 November 1931 he told a conference of farmers and retailers summoned to resolve an acrimonious dispute about milk prices:

> In such a small area as ours it is a much happier position of affairs if we are able to arrange our differences ourselves, and the public are very much more satisfied when we are able to do so. . . . Outside our area of Ulster the daily reports in the bigger Press in London and so on are a very great hurt to us here. . . . I place more reliance upon a settlement tonight than I can tell you. . . . I make a strong appeal to both sides. . . . Lady Craigavon is anxious that we should go for tea and I think we will adjourn for that purpose.[29]

Such an image of Northern Ireland and such a style of leadership gave considerable freedom to ministers. Although inclined at times, especially as he got older and more infirm, to interfere with the routine affairs of different departments, he would tolerate no criticism of his ministers, let alone dismiss them.[30] The result was that when differences of opinion arose between departments, matters were allowed to drift[31] or unsatisfactory compromises arranged.[32] Craig's style of leadership also meant accessible government. He was all too ready to receive correspondence and deputations on any matter and encouraged his ministers to be equally accessible. Just how accessible government could be was illustrated by the tours of the counties Craig undertook in the 1920s. On these tours he would sometimes admonish the government's critics, as in February 1927 when he defended a Stewartstown potato inspector against the complaints of local farmers.[33] Sometimes he would simply offer encouragement, and for this reason the recently created but bickering Donaghadee Urban District Council was included in the 1928 itinerary in the hope that 'a few words of encouragement from the Prime Minister' would wake the squabbling councillors to 'a proper realisation of the dignity of their office'.[34] Most often, however, the Prime Minister would listen to local grievances and problems and hand out largesse. Thus the result of the 1927 tour, during which Craig received sixty-five deputations and talked to at least twenty individuals, was an impressive list of promises of government aid.[35]

Such an open style of government had its advantages. It made possible a two-way flow of information between government and people, and it could circumvent bureaucratic procedures, enabling speedy decisions to be made. As one grateful local newspaper put it,

> The visit of Lord Craigavon to Cookstown on Wednesday was memorable as the first visit of any Premier to our district in his official, as distinct from his party position. He came as the Premier, prepared to hear anything that the people had to say, and to judge on the spot. It is particularly gratifying to the ratepayers of the Rural and Urban districts to know that when his attention had been called to the injustice which existed in regard to the upkeep of the road from Orritor quarry to Cookstown railway station, which would have baffled the efforts of the Councils to have remedied through the ordinary channels, when it would have been strangled with red tape by permanent officials, his Lordship (with the assent of the Minister of Home Affairs, in whose department it was), swept the red tape aside in a regal fashion and uttered his fiat — let it be done from this very day. That, in itself, justified our expectations from his visit, and we are grateful alike for the manner of doing it as for the act itself.[36]

Nevertheless, Craig's personal style of government did not necessarily make for good government. The desire to conciliate local interest groups made difficult the development of long-term and consistent policies. A deputation could easily persuade Craig to alter cabinet decisions, as was the case with the continuation of a subsidy to the Londonderry and Lough Swilly Railway Co.[37] Moreover, Craig's almost promiscuous reception of deputations from Protestant groups complaining about 'disloyal' elements within the government service helped to create the impression that the government was hostile to the interests of the Catholic minority.[38] These defects became more obvious as the years went by. The quality of leadership deteriorated and government policy became more directionless. When faced with problems and criticisms, Craig preferred to forestall his critics by gestures rather than by attempting solutions, as over housing policy in June 1933.[39] Moreover, he crudely tried to shift attention from bread-and-butter issues by appeals to Protestantism and loyalty. The anti-Catholic and pro-Protestant speeches of 1933–34 may have been a reflex response to increased Southern Catholic rhetoric,[40] but the calling of a general election on the border issue in February 1938 was simply a way of breaking the growing influence of the Progressive Unionists.[41] By 1934 Craig even seemed to be losing touch with reality, thinking that he could solve the problems of the Belfast shipyards or settle issues with the imperial government by means of 'little personal conversations' with shipping magnates and imperial ministers.[42]

In fact, by the summer of 1938 the government of Northern Ireland was simply drifting along. According to the permanent head of the civil service and Ministry of Finance, there was 'an entire absence of clear thinking and co-ordination'. The Prime Minister was 'so unwell that he cannot do more than an hour's concentrated work' and 'prefers to make quick hasty decisions rather than go fully into a question with his colleagues'. The Minister of Home Affairs 'is much more ill than is generally known' and thus 'seems incapable of giving his responsible officers coherent directions on policy'. The Minister of Labour 'is so ill that everyone knows he will not return'. Then there was the Minister of Commerce 'who is abroad at a time when his Department is being subjected to violent criticism & whose officials can never depend upon'; a Chief Whip 'whose Dr told me should retire for his own sake, but who does not wish to do so till certain ambitions are satisfied'; and a Cabinet Secretary who 'has been advised to retire on medical grounds'. The result was that

> Cabinet meetings seldom take place now, and the most important decisions are announced without any indication that they are the result of mature consideration, and very often the Ministers most concerned seem to be unaware of what is happening until an announcement is made in the Press.[43]

2

Ailing or healthy, ministers were served by a civil service which was one of the growth sectors of the Northern Ireland economy. The total number of staff in post (excluding labourers, cleaners and part-time employees) was 2,103 on 1 April 1932 and 3,113 six years later, about one-third of whom belonged to the higher, the administrative grades.[44] The first recruits were the permanent heads of department, appointed by the ministers responsible. Clark reluctantly agreed to remain in Northern Ireland to head the Ministry of Finance; the Secretaries of Home Affairs, Education and Agriculture were drawn from Dublin Castle, and those of Commerce and Labour from the imperial civil service; the Cabinet Secretary was an English soldier and not a professional civil servant. In addition, a number of experienced officials were borrowed for a short period from the imperial ministries to help get the new Northern departments off the ground.[45] For the rest, it had been hoped that there would have been a substantial transfer of civil servants from Dublin Castle, but officials were slow to apply for Northern postings. The delay in the setting up of the civil service committee, envisaged in the 1920 act to arrange for the transfer of civil servants, certainly suggested, as senior Northern Ireland officials complained,[46] obstructionism in the South, but there were probably other reasons for the poor response to the Northern government's requests for staff, such as conservatism, dislike of an industrial city and doubts about Northern Ireland's future. Whatever the reasons, only a small proportion of the Northern Ireland civil service came from Dublin. For example, by January 1924 the Ministry of Home Affairs had a staff of 187, of whom only 42 had been transferred under the 1920 act, all of them volunteers.[47]

Thus, despite frequently reiterated complaints that it was manned by Southerners and Englishmen at the expense of Ulstermen, the bulk of the civil service was from the start recruited locally. As was to be expected on the setting up of a new government, a number of early appointments were 'political', the most conspicuous instance being Craig's nomination of Spender as Cabinet Secretary.[48] Nevertheless, the majority were recruited by a specially established Selection Board which tried to apply the entrance criteria of the imperial civil service. The main considerations influencing the board were 'the suitability and qualifications of the candidate and the satisfactory references as to character and loyalty which he could produce';[49] but there was also, for example, in the Ministry of Home Affairs a policy to 'secure Ulstermen provided – and this is not an unreasonable proviso – a competent man to fill the position can be found'.[50] Competence did not necessarily entail experience, with the result that the early years of the Northern Ireland civil service were something of an adventure. One Dublin volunteer, a lawyer from the Land Commission who transferred to the national insurance section of the Ministry of Labour, was stimulated by the change, finding that, contrary to his expectations, 'Except for the head of the section and three Englishmen, who will be leaving at the end of the month as they are here on loan, every man in the place is a newcomer not only to the work but also to the service'.[51] His only problem of adjustment was his use of the semi-colon in official letters, but, he happily reported, 'On my explaining there was nothing sinister or Papistical about it, it was allowed to pass.'

The rate of turnover of senior civil servants was, as with ministers, very low, the result being that the service was dominated by a small group of officers. Most of them were extremely well qualified, competent and, with one possible exception, upright, as were their staffs, for a high standard of entry was insisted upon. Admittedly, the educational tests for entry to the Royal Ulster Constabulary (R.U.C.) were somewhat lower, but the rejection of large numbers of applicants whose sole testimonial was their Protestantism was indicative of the desire to secure competent personnel.[52]

The biggest weakness of the Northern Ireland civil service and police force was that they were largely identified with one section of the community. A recurrent loyalist complaint was the allegedly high proportion of 'disloyal elements' in the government service, but, considering the long-term interests of the province, the real trouble was exactly the reverse. Although Catholics comprised one-third of the population, they never even remotely looked like securing a similar proportion of posts in the government service. Figures compiled in 1943 by the Ministry of Finance to evaluate allegations of a Catholic takeover of key posts showed that Catholics comprised only 5.83 per cent of the administrative class and analogous technical grades, there being 37 Catholics and 597 Protestants. Moreover, there were no Catholics at all among the 55 permanent and assistant secretaries and analogous technical officers, the highest grades in the civil service.[53] And these figures evidently represented a deterioration in the Catholic position from the early 1920s. Spender told the Cabinet Secretary in November 1934 that since he had taken over the Ministry of Finance in 1925 'no Roman Catholic has entered the Administrative ranks of our Service, although had one succeeded in passing the Examination he would have been accepted'; and just over a year later he told a persistent Orange correspondent that since 1925 there had been a considerable diminution in the number of Catholics in the senior ranks, although there had been no discrimination against them. In the lower ranks of the civil service the proportion of Catholics was, Spender estimated in 1934, somewhere in the region of 10 per cent.[54]

Catholics fared marginally better in the R.U.C. In July 1936 they comprised 17.12 per cent of the entire force, there being 488 Catholics and 2,361 Protestants. Among the higher ranks, however, the proportion was slightly lower, 16.36 per cent, for there were only 9 Catholics among the 55 officers who held the rank of district inspector and above. Once again, Catholic participation had declined since the early 1920s, for 535 Catholics had been serving in the force in January 1924.[55]

Discrimination was not, as was so often alleged, the sole reason for the low proportion of Catholics in government service. A lower level of educational attainments among Catholics may have prejudiced their chances of entry into and promotion within the civil service and police force. Moreover, the hostility of Catholics and nationalists towards the new state may have made those qualified reluctant to administer and police it. Spender certainly believed that 'There were strong indications that the Roman Catholic hierarchy did not encourage any of their co-religionists to enter our Service but rather the reverse'.[56]

On the other hand, the government of Northern Ireland must take a good deal of the responsibility for the failure to attract Catholic recruits. It was certainly not the government's original intention to have an overwhelmingly Protestant governmental service. When planning the structure of the civil service in 1921, Clark had raised with Craig the question of reserving a proportion of posts for Catholics, but there is no record of a quota being decided upon.[57] There was, however, a hope that all creeds would join the government service. In August 1921 the Ulster Ex-Servicemen's Association protested to Craig against the appointment of a Catholic as the permanent head of the Ministry of Agriculture (although he had, in fact, been appointed only as head of one of the branches of the ministry). The protest was submitted to the cabinet. After Archdale had explained that the civil servant in question, although a Catholic, was also a loyalist whom he had known personally for twenty years, he was authorised to reply that 'The Government intended to enrol members of all creeds in their Staff provided their loyalty was unquestioned and it was hoped Southern Ireland would be equally broad-minded'.[58] Selection procedures reflected these good intentions and seem to have been devoid of religious discrimination. There seems no reason to doubt the first chairman of the Selection Board when he wrote in 1924 that the board had not regarded 'the question of religious belief of essential importance in interviewing candidates and deciding upon appointments to the Service'.[59] It was true that when entrance requirements were considered by the cabinet in 1926, Bates would have liked to have placed a ban on Catholics; but the various loyalty and employment safeguards which were adopted were directed against Free State residents rather than Northern Catholics. The administrative grade was recruited through the imperial Civil Service Commission; otherwise entrance was by open competition among United Kingdom residents.[60]

By contrast, religion was taken into account in recruitment to the police. One-third of the force was to be reserved for Catholics if they so wished.[61] Although this quota was criticised by some Unionists as introducing sectarianism into the police force,[62] it was intended as a gesture of reassurance towards Catholics as well as being sound common sense. As Lieutenant-Colonel Wickham, the first Inspector-General of the R.U.C., tartly retorted in reply to quite ill-founded allegations that his force was full of disloyal Catholics, 'It is quite useless to expect to obtain any information from the R.C. areas unless there are R.C. Police and R.C. Detectives. The efficiency of the Force suffers at present from a lack of R.C. Police'.[63]

Despite initial good intentions and fair selection procedures, the government did little to attract Catholic recruits. On the contrary, ministers did much to deter potential applicants and discourage serving officers. Quite simply, they could not bring themselves to trust Catholics with key posts. In 1924 there were only four Catholics in the Ministry of Home Affairs and, Watt, the Permanent Secretary, assured Spender, 'They are not in any way employed on confidential work'.[64] In 1934 Bates refused to use the telephone for any important business, after learning, 'with a great deal of surprise, that a Roman Catholic Telephonist has been appointed to Stormont'.[65] The telephonist was transferred. Bates, who regarded all Catholics as potential if not actual traitors, was only the most extreme in his suspicions. Pollock and Milne Barbour apart, all ministers were ready to believe that Catholics were a source of trouble, and were thus inclined to believe the allegations made by their extreme supporters. Throughout the 1930s the religious beliefs of the Chief Establishment Officer, a Ministry of Finance official, gave cause for concern. Spender, who found the question distasteful, was first forced to investigate the matter in December 1935 and was relieved to be able to report that although the officer's wife was a staunch Catholic, 'Her own views are those of a strong Unionist and she comes of a family which for four generations at any rate has given service in one of His Majesty's Forces, and her traditions are Loyalist in character'.[66] Spender's assurances seem to have been accepted, but when this officer died in September 1940 and was buried as a Catholic, Spender felt obliged to write to the cabinet secretariat an extraordinary note in his own defence:

> Allegations have been made that in view of the fact that ——— was buried as a Roman Catholic the assurances given by me and others in this Ministry on the subject in the past have been proved incorrect. It is very natural that the Whip's Office should have this impression in the circumstances. The facts however are that last year, up to the time of his illness, ——— had no intention of reverting to the Roman Catholic Church, and as late as last autumn he discussed the

matter of his religious faith quite frankly with me. In February last, when still suffering from his great illness, he was persuaded by his family to take the step and it was only then that he changed his denomination. It is true that on his return he did not inform me of the change as I think he ought to have done, but I am quite satisfied that it did not in any way prevent him from carrying out quite loyally the fair and discreet policy which we have tried to observe on this very vexed question. Perhaps if Lord Glentoran or Hungerford should raise the matter with the Prime Minister you would take an opportunity of making the facts known. You may have noticed that the Presbyterian Minister attended his funeral.[67]

Clearly, then, it was not easy to be a Catholic in government service. Catholics in the police force and civil service could expect very little encouragement from ministers. Rumours about their so-called disloyalty, often maliciously started by self-interested individuals, were taken up by Protestant organisations and all too often treated seriously by Craig. At the beginning of 1924 a deputation from the Ulster Protestant Voters' Defence Association, a group consisting largely of Belfast Orangemen, protested to Craig against the alleged preference given to disloyal Catholics in government posts at the expense of loyalists, making some obviously outlandish observations. Yet, instead of sending this unrepresentative clique away with a flea in its ear, Craig ordered an investigation in several departments, the correspondence relating to which dragged on for several months. Not surprisingly, the Inspector-General of the R.U.C. complained to the Ministry of Home Affairs against this 'effort to bring unfair influence to bear on the detriment of R.C. members of the Force', which militated 'against efficiency as it tends to undermine the confidence of the men in their superiors'.[68]

Spender, who was Cabinet Secretary in 1924, resented this implied criticism of the Prime Minister,[69] but ten years later he found himself echoing Wickham's sentiments with a vengeance. The occasion was a sustained attack by the Orange Order against a Stormont estate worker alleged to be a dangerous Sinn Féiner but in reality a loyal Catholic with a distinguished war record and known personally to the Prince of Wales, whose horse he had looked after in the war. Spender was so incensed at this 'vile persecution', especially since the Prime Minister was treating the Orange complaints seriously, that he told the Cabinet Secretary that

If the Prime Minister is dissatisfied with our present system [of recruitment], I think the only course would be for the Government to come out in the open and to say that only Protestants are admitted to our Service. I should greatly regret such a course, and am quite convinced . . . that we are getting loyal service from all those who have entered our Service.[70]

Spender's anger reflected both the limits of the civil servant's influence in Northern Ireland and the crucial way in which the Northern Ireland civil service differed from the imperial civil service on which it was modelled.

In many respects the nature of regional government, involving as it did many, if not mainly, questions of detail, gave civil servants ample scope to run the country. The able, well-informed and enthusiastic George Scott Robertson, Permanent Secretary of the Ministry of Agriculture in the 1930s, took full advantage of his ministers' prolonged absences from Belfast to dominate agricultural policy and administration,[71] and Wilfrid Spender exercised a powerful influence throughout the government and civil service. An Englishman and an army officer, Spender had been one of the organisers of the Ulster Volunteer Force, had served with the 36th (Ulster) Division, had acted as 'Soldiers' Friend' at the Ministry of Pensions in London, and had returned to Northern Ireland in 1920 to organise the Special Constabulary in Belfast. He had been reluctant to accept Craig's offer of the post of Cabinet Secretary, because he and his wife were unsure as to whether they wanted to settle in Northern Ireland and because he realised that the appointment of an 'outsider' would (and did) arouse considerable resentment among Ulstermen and, perhaps, the regular civil service. However, having decided to accept the post, he proved a quick learner. He picked up the ropes of running a cabinet secretariat during a two-day apprenticeship with Sir Maurice Hankey at the Cabinet Offices in London, and at critical times he acted almost as a minister without portfolio.[72] The cabinet records were never more complete than under his aegis, and for that reason it was a pity that in 1925 he succeeded Clark as Permanent Secretary of the Ministry of Finance and head of the civil service when the latter became a colonial governor. At the Ministry of Finance, where he remained until 1944 and kept a detailed financial diary, Spender somewhat belied his name. He proved himself to be a rigorous 'economist', intent on keeping expenditure and taxation as low as possible, not only in the interests of economic and financial stability but also in the interests of his good relations with the imperial Treasury. His views on the legitimate and fruitful sphere of government expenditure did expand in the late 1930s in face of persistently high unemployment,[73] but he never came to accept Keynesian economics. 'I think the world quite mad,' he wrote on 12 January 1939 to the Treasury, where Keynesian views had begun to penetrate. '. . . My views on economics are quite too old fashioned for modern conditions, & I am even fool enough to believe one ought to live within one's income'.[74] So enthusiastic were Spender and his subordinates to stamp down expenditure in other departments that on one occasion Andrews felt obliged to complain to Craig about the Ministry of Finance's obstruction of the government's programme of unemployment relief works. Pollock, Andrews reckoned, 'is quite of our opinion but . . . is blocked by those who ought to be told that it is their duty *immediately* to carry out the views of the Cabinet'.[75]

Nevertheless, in the last analysis, the civil servants could only be as effective as their political masters – or as effective as their political masters would allow. They provided information, they advised and even cajoled, but ultimate responsibility rested with the politicians, and they often chose to disregard both advice and established bureaucratic procedures.

Civil servants could do little to influence policy and administration in respect of such sensitive issues as the border, security and the fate of loyalty and Protestantism. It was true that on such issues the views of leading civil servants differed little from those of the ministers or the Unionist population at large. Spender, for instance, was an ardent Unionist with a cordial dislike – if not contempt – for the South and its politicians,[76] while Watt of Home Affairs shared the Unionist view that special crimes legislation should not be invoked against loyalist offenders.[77] Nevertheless, they and civil servants in general did have a different perspective. They did not regard themselves as party men and liked to see themselves as acting impartially and in the long-term interests of the community as a whole. They considered it their duty to look at questions in the round and did not always agree with the views and methods of their political chiefs. All they could do, however, was to offer advice, which was frequently ignored, not only on such general questions as the position of Catholics within governmental service, but also on specific matters, such as the decision to make 12 July, Orange Day, a public holiday. Ministry of Home Affairs officials thought that such a declaration would be both unnecessary and provocative, but their minister, Bates, took the matter to the cabinet who decided that the Twelfth should be a public holiday.[78] The same process was evident in education, where not only matters of general principle, such as the control of schooling,[79] but also matters of detail, such as the dropping of a history textbook commenting favourably on English and Irish Home Rulers,[80] were determined by the attitude of Protestant and Unionist pressure groups.

A disregard of civil service advice and of bureaucratic processes was a general feature of government in Northern Ireland. While Andrews complained about the baneful influence of the Ministry of Finance, Spender was struck by how little control his ministry and minister had over government expenditure compared with the imperial Treasury. Despite efforts to follow 'the high British standards', Spender found himself confessing to Treasury officials in 1933 that 'Owing to our own peculiar local circumstances pressure was sometimes brought to bear on the Ministry of Finance by the Prime Minister and others in a way that would not happen in . . . the Treasury'.[81] Indeed, in the 1930s Northern

Ireland civil servants, except those attached to the Ministry of Agriculture, were becoming increasingly demoralised by the way in which government was conducted. Rebuked by his minister in 1934 for failing to refuse categorically the demands of one deputation, Spender retorted that 'We had been so often overruled by the Prime Minister's decisions that we did not feel justified in assuming a non possumus attitude'.[82] Northern Ireland's civil servants were in no position to compensate for the limitations of their ministers or to alter fundamentally the pattern of government.

3

The parliament of Northern Ireland consisted of a House of Commons of 52 members and a Senate of 26 members. Its size had been prescribed by the 1920 act, but it was Craig who determined that procedures should be based upon the imperial model – with one or two important modifications, such as ministers, although eligible to vote only in the House of which they were members, being able to speak in both Houses. Despite its elaborate protocol, it was very much a part-time affair, usually meeting for only a couple of months each year and seeming to exist largely to endorse government policy.[83]

In a sense, this part-time and almost passive role was forced upon parliament by its limited powers. Not only were its powers severely limited by the 1920 act, but its voice was further strangled by the convention that it should not even discuss any of the 'excepted' or 'reserved' services. There may have been some advantage in allowing members to let off steam on matters handled from Westminster, but successive Speakers interpreted the constitutional position very narrowly. What occasioned the Nationalist withdrawal from parliament in 1932 was the Speaker's refusal to permit, during the budget debate, discussion of the Post Office, a service run by Westminster, usually at a loss, but paid for by the Northern Ireland taxpayer. Nationalist frustration was summed up in Joseph Devlin's outburst against the ruling:

> It is obviously a sham and a farce being Members of Parliament elected by the people to discuss public expenditure . . . if our rights and liberties are to be so circumscribed that we are not permitted to discuss them. I for one will take no part in this sham discussion.[84]

Others shared this sense of frustration, for there was more than a suspicion that the government invoked such self-denying conventions to avoid unwelcome criticism, as over the controversial Anglo-Éire agreements of 1938.[85]

Even, however, in respect of services clearly within its competence, the Northern parliament exercised little initiative. There were few private members' bills and even fewer private members' bills that impinged on the interests of the province as a whole.[86] The legislative programme was determined by the government, often following British examples and usually after consultation with or pressure from interested outside bodies. Parliament existed to endorse decisions made elsewhere. This was as much true of issues affecting the province as a whole, such as amendments to the 1923 Education Act (which arose out of consultations between the Prime Minister and the Ministers of Education on the one hand and the Orange Order and representatives of the Protestant churches on the other),[87] as of issues primarily affecting particular areas, such as fruit marketing legislation (hammered out between the government and conflicting trade interests).[88] Only on rare occasions did M.P.s make a positive contribution to policy. When the government was itself divided, as over the size of houses eligible for subsidy, a strong expression of opinion in the House could determine the issue.[89] Opposition in either House, actual or anticipated, could also influence the government's programme. Certain measures were withdrawn, either because of anticipated outright opposition, as with the Betting (Juvenile Messengers) Bill, which was not proceeded with in the Senate in 1930,[90] or because the House was divided against itself, as with a bill dealing with market tolls, where in the late 1930s the conflicting interests of farmers and market authorities were reflected in parliament.[91]

Decisions to bow to the opinion of the House by abandoning a measure were taken by the cabinet, but the decision as to whether or not to accept amendments in the House often depended upon the courage of the minister in charge of the measure in question. In May 1924 the Junior Minister of Home Affairs, rather than risk the defeat of the government, preferred to accept a Commons amendment which complicated the Public Libraries Bill by giving majority representation on committees to rural district councils whereas the county councils provided the cash.[92] On the other hand, Pollock usually believed that firmness paid in face of a potentially recalcitrant House, as in October 1933 when he successfully defied the vigorous protests of Unionist M.P.s against a measure which required local authorities to pay stamp duties just as local authorities in Britain had long done.[93] It was true that at the beginning of a tense session in March 1937 Pollock did have to make a concession — on the Cabinet Secretary's salary — to secure a supplementary vote on the Prime Minister's salary. Yet such a cliff-hanger was probably unique. It was the product of particular circumstances, for the House was, according to Spender, 'in a very ugly temper', partly because of the incompetence and timidity of the Chief Whip, and partly because of resentment at the government's failure to consult it over the appointment of a new Deputy Speaker and at the prolonged absences from Ireland of the Prime Minister, the Ministers of Agriculture and Home Affairs and the Speaker.[94] Generally the government was sensitive to opinion in the House, but the fact remained that parliament was normally content to play second fiddle and follow the government's lead. The main reasons for this quiescence were the political composition of parliament and M.P.s' limited perception of their role.

Throughout the inter-war years the party of government, the Unionist Party, had a substantial majority in both Houses. For instance, of the 52 members of the Commons, 40 official Unionists were returned in the 1921 general election, 32 in 1925, 37 in 1929, 36 in 1933, and 39 in 1938. Successive general elections thus gave the government an overall majority of 28, 12, 22, 20 and 26 respectively, a majority upon which the government could confidently rely.*[95] In the first four parliaments, that is between June 1921 and February 1938, when there were 771 divisions in the Commons, a handful of Unionists voted against the government on only 95 occasions.[96]

The size and reliability of the government's majority owed much to the large Protestant majority in Northern Ireland, the importance of the constitutional issue, and the policies pursued by the government. They also owed something to organisation and the system of representation. In the early 1920s Ulster Unionism was still very efficiently organised throughout the province. It had a network of constituency associations and a central body, the U.U.C., which acted as an umbrella for most Unionist and Protestant organisations.[97] The need for comprehensive organisation might have persisted had not the system of representation been altered. The results of the 1925 general election, the first and only proportional representation (P.R.) election held under 'peacetime' conditions, suggested that this system might have widened the field of political debate, encouraged new alignments and weakened the hold of official Unionism. However, the abolition of P.R. in time for the 1929 general election reasserted and stereotyped the overwhelmingly Unionist majority,[98] against which the Opposition parties and groups which sat in parliament after 1925 could make little headway.

Nationalists were, when they condescended to sit, the largest Opposition group in parliament.[99] Until 1938, when they contested only nine seats and won eight, nationalists of various shades could usually rely upon returning eleven or twelve members to the Commons. For the first general election, in May 1921, they were divided into supporters of

*The Senate, which was elected by proportional representation by members of the Commons, was never an independent force in decision- and policy-making in Northern Ireland. Its historian has rightly concluded that its record as 'a revising Chamber has not been outstanding. . . . The permanent government majority has not exerted itself to impart to the Chamber those qualities of unfettered judgment and judicial temperament that are requisite in Upper Houses. . . . The truth is that where legislation of a party controversial nature is concerned there is no Upper House in Northern Ireland but, rather, a second Lower House.' (Magill, pp. 354, 361.)

the old Irish Parliamentary Party and Republicans, but after the Sinn Féin split over the Treaty they were divided into three factions, the old-style Nationalists being the most numerous. At first, all nationalists boycotted the new parliament. For a few months after 1922 some Catholics and nationalists did consider recognising the new state and taking their seats, but nothing came of these discussions, partly because of the inability of the Northern government to follow a consistently conciliatory policy, partly because of divisions within the nationalist community itself, and partly because of continued nationalist hopes that Northern Ireland would disappear as a result of the Boundary Commission. Republican M.P.s never did take their seats, but in 1925, when it became clear that the border would remain, two Nationalists entered parliament, and by 1927 they had been joined by the other eight. At first they were not organised as a party, but in May 1928 they did take steps towards organisation when a National League was formed. With the formation of this league, Nationalists did seem prepared to make the best of a bad job and to accept partition as an accomplished fact.

The Northern Ireland Labour Party was the only other coherent group in the Commons.[100] Since 1885 Labour in the North had been engaged in political activity, and Ireland's first ever local Labour party was formed in Belfast in 1892, affiliating in the next year to the newly formed British Independent Labour Party. Belfast Labour's most successful intervention in local elections had occurred in 1920, when, under P.R., thirteen Labour councillors had been returned, but, in respect of parliamentary elections, Northern Labour was hindered by being part of the Irish Labour Party, anxious to avoid election contests until the national issue had been settled. Thus only Independent Labour candidates contested four seats in the 1921 Northern general election, and all were roundly routed. Eventually Northern Labour leaders took the initiative, and in March 1924 the Belfast Labour Party called a conference of its two divisional parties and its twenty affiliated trades unions, which resulted in the formation of the Northern Ireland Labour Party. The new party's first efforts at parliamentary electioneering seemed to augur well: in the 1925 general election all three candidates were returned. Subsequent elections, however, starkly revealed the weakness of the party. Only one of its five candidates was returned in 1929, the three M.P.s of 1925 being defeated – a fate shared by two Independent Labour candidates. In the 1933 general election two of its three candidates were returned, but in 1938 only one of its seven candidates was successful, although a sitting Labour member who had been expelled from the party in 1934 successfully stood as an Independent Labour candidate. The five N.I.L.P. M.P.s, who sat in the House at one time or another in the inter-war years, were all trades unionists and Protestants. They drew their support from the central area of Belfast, around the docks, although the Nationalist decision to put up fewer candidates in 1938 did enable the unopposed return of the N.I.L.P. candidate for South Armagh.

The manifest weakness of the Labour Party in the industrial parts of Northern Ireland cannot be attributed simply to the divisiveness of sectarianism. Certainly one of the causes of the weakness of the Labour Party was its failure to take a stand on the question of partition. Its first constitution skirted the issue and enabled the party to be attacked by both Unionists and nationalists. Moreover, its socialist programme, which called for immediate socio-economic reform, could not be a vote-winner. On the one hand, the Catholic Church roundly condemned socialism as incompatible with Catholicism, a condemnation made the more plausible by the Protestantism of Labour candidates. On the other hand, its major demands, nationalisation apart, were frequently pre-empted by the Unionist government's commitment to a step-by-step policy with Britain in respect of the major social services, and by Andrews's conciliatory approach to trades unions. These made a Labour party almost irrelevant in Northern Ireland. The major battles on behalf of the working classes there were fought out in Britain, and the fruits of the Labour movement's victories in Britain were simply transferred to Northern Ireland by the Unionist government. Government policy stunted the growth of the Labour Party in Northern Ireland, not by sectarian appeals but rather by buying off potential opposition with major cash social services on British lines. Yet the Northern Ireland Labour Party was not wholly irrelevant to the processes of politics and government. Its very existence provided the government with an incentive to continue to cater for the special needs of the industrial working-class electorate.

In addition to representatives of the main political parties, there was always after 1925 a handful of unattached M.P.s.[101] The way had been prepared for these independents by the shock return in a by-election in West Belfast in May 1923 of an Independent Unionist, specialising in the problems of ex-servicemen and critical of the high level of unemployment in Northern Ireland. In the 1925 general election the candidate of the Unbought Tenants' Association, an organisation formed by farmers who had not purchased their holdings, was returned for Co. Antrim to speed up the completion of land purchase. This member survived only one parliament, but Independent or unofficial Unionists were a feature of all parliaments after 1925. Independent Unionists contested four seats in 1925 and won all four, one member being returned for two constituencies, but they won only three out of ten in 1929, three out of eight in 1933, and three out of 22 in 1938. Altogether, six Independent Unionists sat in the Commons at one time or another in the inter-war years, three sitting for only one parliament, one sitting for two parliaments, another for three, and the sixth sitting in four of the inter-war parliaments. Such Independent Unionists are best described as party rebels, dissatisfied with the official Unionist Party's procedures for selecting parliamentary candidates, as in the case of Thomas Henderson, a painter and decorator, Orangeman and a founder member of the Ulster Unionist Labour Association (U.U.L.A.), who had met a chilly reception when originally offering himself as an official Unionist to the Shankill selection committee. The chairman, when confronted by this small and rather shabbily dressed housepainter, is alleged to have asked: 'And who is this?'[102] Henderson did not bother to wait for the selection meeting. Instead, he went out to show the local association exactly who he was – winning and holding the seat for over twenty years and becoming the most long-winded member of the House.

Despite the persistence of Independent Unionist candidatures and the return of a number of M.P.s, there was never an Independent Unionist party, nor a distinctive Independent Unionist policy. The nearest approach to an organised and coherent Unionist opposition to the official party occurred in 1938 with the formation of the Progressive Unionist Party.[103] Organised by William John Stewart, the millionaire Unionist M.P. for the Westminster constituency of South Belfast, to contest the 1938 election, its platform combined a call for more government initiative on such matters as housing with a demand for less government intervention in rural areas. Despite a good deal of publicity, however, none of the new party's twelve candidates, who dramatically increased the usual number of unofficial Unionist candidatures, were returned. The short-lived Progressive Unionist challenge apart, any Independent or unofficial Unionist organisation or policy centred upon the personality of individual candidates or members. John William Nixon, who had been dismissed from the R.U.C. for making an inflammatory speech on the border question and who sat as an Independent Unionist for Woodvale from 1929 until his death in 1950, was on the right of the Unionist Party. On the other hand, James Woods Gyle, a publican and wine merchant who represented East Belfast in the 1925 parliament, was to the left. As with the Labour Party, the very existence of Independent Unionists, particularly as they were returned mainly for working-class constituencies in Belfast, may have helped to focus the government's attention on working-class demands; and their return in 1925 certainly did confirm the government's fears of the fissiparous tendencies of P.R.[104]

It was not simply the existence of a large Unionist majority that helped to explain the relative unimportance of parliament in Northern Ireland. More important was the fact that most M.P.s had little to contribute. Taken as a whole, M.P.s were almost as socially unrepresentative as members of the government, invariably middle-aged and older and usually much involved in their local communities.[105] As such, they had a limited perception of their role. Most considered themselves primarily as representing their immediate constituents and were most at ease in the House when presenting a very local view of issues. 'Coming as I do from a farming constituency where most of the farmers are very small producers,' Major George William Panter, Unionist M.P. for Mourne, told the House during the second reading of the 1939 Bacon Industry Bill, 'I must admit quite frankly that I have examined the Bill almost entirely from their point of view'.[106] This preoccupation was understandable in a society such as Northern Ireland, where members were well known and were expected to act as brokers between their constituents and government departments. Certainly constituents seemed to believe that representatives in a regional parliament were of more use than their former representatives at Westminster. Devlin told the House in 1929 that when he had been a member of the imperial parliament he did

> not get twenty letters a month from my constituents asking me to look into their grievances, but since I came into this Parliament I receive on an average thirty letters a day, because there are questions of unemployment, old-age pensions, widows' pensions, and other matters which so closely touch the lives and conditions of the people day by day.[107]

There was much to be gained from this close contact between constituents and M.P.s, a close contact emphasised by the very local and specific nature of parliamentary questions, but the result was that M.P.s lacked an independent role and showed a marked reluctance to accept responsibility. When urging the postponement of the 1936 Eggs Marketing Bill, Hugh Minford, the Unionist M.P. for Antrim, reckoned that it was not for him to judge the merits of the measure, but rather that 'It is up to the Minister to meet all the parties concerned and see exactly what is required'.[108] As the debates on housing legislation underlined,[109] timidity was not confined to members of the Unionist Party, but it was most consistently challenged by a Unionist, Mrs Dehra Parker, M.P. for Londonderry City and County from 1921 until 1929 and for South Londonderry from 1932 until 1960. She, along with Devlin, had the most elevated concept of a member's role. Members should represent not merely their constituents, nor any sectional interests, but should act independently for the good of the community as a whole. Criticising Minford's plea for delay and consultation over the Eggs Marketing Bill, she argued that

> When we come to this House we do not come with the intention of submitting ourselves into the hands of the general public and expecting to be dictated to by interests outside. I must say that

some remarks made by the hon. Members sounded as if we were going to put ourselves in the hands of outside people who would tell us whether we should or should not vote for this measure. Personally, I think we ought to exercise our own judgement.[110]

That, at any rate, was the theory, but when it came down to specifics Mrs Parker's perspective narrowed and her practice fell short of her ideal.[111]

Members' responsiveness to local considerations and limited conception of their role had a number of consequences for the nature and relative unimportance of parliament. They help to explain why relatively few farmers sought to enter parliament: they could easily nobble their M.P.s. They also help to explain the essential amateurishness of members of both Houses, who, despite some conspicuous exceptions, were generally, and often embarrassingly, ill-informed. Lastly, they made party labels irrelevant. It was true that a real rift existed between Unionists and Nationalists on matters relating to religion, the constitution and partition, but on all other issues there was a marked coincidence of views. On such other issues the real line of division lay not between the parties but between M.P.s representing Belfast and those sitting for the rest of the six counties.

The irrelevance of party divisions on issues other than the most sensitive is not surprising in view of the similarity of the social bases of the two major parties. The majority of M.P.s sat for rural constituencies and were socially unrepresentative, even in Belfast. It was true that the official Unionist Party did attempt to broaden the basis of its representation in the city, but this experiment was not persevered with. The U.U.L.A., founded in June 1918 to counteract the widely held impression that Ulster Unionism was the preserve of property-owners and to represent Labour views within the party, was allotted three candidates in the 1918 general election and six in the first election to the Northern Ireland parliament. All these candidates were elected, but their return did little to alter the outlook of the Ulster Unionist parliamentary party. Not only did such working-class candidatures arouse considerable resentment among other sections of the party, but the working-class M.P.s themselves revealed little ability and were unable to transcend their Unionist and Protestant origins. Apart from the occasional piece of class rhetoric, U.U.L.A. M.P.s said much the same things as the rest of the party and soon disappeared from parliament.[112] It was also true that, in an effort to increase its support in Belfast, the National League adopted an impressively broad programme and a marked socialist rhetoric.[113] The League aimed not only to unite Ireland and secure justice for nationalists, but also to foster co-operation amongst all creeds and classes; and its election manifesto in 1929 demanded an end to unemployment, the raising of the school-leaving

age, increased and earlier old-age pensions, town planning, slum clearance, and public utility works to relieve unemployment. Its actions
and social composition, however, belied its words. Nationalist M.P.s
and organisers were the Catholic middle classes – publicans, lawyers
and businessmen – who acted in close alliance with the clergy, and the
League's true priorities were starkly revealed in the contest with the
Labour Party for the Falls division of Belfast in the 1929 general election. In that contest the National League defined its position. Despite
its manifesto, it was neither a socialist nor a radical nor a nationalist
party, but rather 'a Catholic party claiming to represent the Catholic
population without distinction of class or politics but therefore in practice representing the Catholic Church and the Catholic middle class'.[114]

While religion did divide M.P.s, other interests did unite them in
sentiment if not in the lobbies. Whatever their parties, the majority
of M.P.s shared a pronounced distrust of state activity and state expenditure, and a fierce determination to defend local interests, be they
those of different sorts of farmers, carriers in Belfast, the local magistracy, rural district councils or the Belfast Corporation. The overwhelming impression from a reading of parliamentary debates is that,
religion and the constitution apart, the only difference between most
Unionist and Opposition M.P.s was that while neither were enthusiastic
about government policies, the former voted for the government and
the latter did not. The prevailing conservatism of the House was only
partially modified by the existence of a small lobby demanding improved social welfare, because owing to personal and sectarian rival-
ries, this lobby possessed only an occasional coherence. The longest-
serving U.U.L.A. M.P., William Grant, a shipyard worker, active trades
unionist, M.P. for North Belfast and then Duncairn, may have divided
against the government on twenty-six occasions in the 1925 parliament,[115] usually in company with the Labour Party, but he took care
all the time to reassert his identity as a Protestant and Unionist.

Both the party composition of the House and the limitations of its
members help to explain why it was never highly regarded by the
government as part of the policy-making process. Devlin used to complain bitterly that the government, having welcomed Nationalists'
participation in parliament, then proceeded to ignore and insult them.
'You had opponents willing to co-operate,' he told Craig in March
1932. 'We did not seek office. We sought service. We were willing to
help. But you rejected all friendly offers. You refused to accept co-
operation'.[116] Like most of Devlin's remarks, this was an exaggeration
both of the government's offence and of his party's potential contribution to government. It was true that Craig and Bates could have shown,
on occasion, more courtesy in face of Nationalist complaints about discrimination; and certainly some concessions should have been possible

on such issues as the renewal of the Special Powers Act,[117] and some spontaneous generosity shown in financing Catholic schools.[118] Yet it was also true that other ministers were both frank and courteous on matters relating to their departments, that Devlin seemed to enjoy his cups of tea with Andrews in the parliamentary refreshment room, and, above all, that Nationalists had little to offer. Their participation in parliament seemed only conditional. Ultimately committed, at least in theory, to the achievement of an autonomous united Ireland, they refused to act as an official Opposition and in the 1930s periodically withdrew from the House. They swept out dramatically in 1932, after which they adopted a policy of 'creeping abstentionism'.[119] Their participation depended not solely on the attitude of the Northern government, but also on changes in Irish politics generally. De Valera's return to power in the South in February 1932 posed sharply once again the question of the future of the border.[120] When in parliament most Nationalists contented themselves with denunciations of the government and with moving either the rejection of government measures or wrecking amendments cutting across the principle of such measures. Only one or two, such as Richard Byrne and Patrick O'Neill, representing Falls and Mourne respectively, did try to consider social and economic measures on their merits and come to terms with the details. When they did so, their suggestions were usually met by the government in the same spirit as it met similar amendments from other parts of the House, amendments being accepted only if they fitted in with predetermined government policy.[121]

And this was the root of the trouble. Devlin's complaint may have been primarily about the limited role of the Nationalist Party, but it was also a complaint about the limited role of the Northern Ireland parliament. Policies and decisions were made elsewhere — with interested parties outside parliament. If M.P.s were so responsive to local and outside interests, why then should not the government in such a small society itself directly consult with such interests? This was certainly the lesson to be drawn from an early clash between Craig and one of his backbenchers. In April 1922 one of the Unionist M.P.s for Fermanagh and Tyrone, James Cooper, a company director from Enniskillen, infuriated Craig by denouncing in the Commons the latter's recent peace pact with Collins,[122] and then apologising privately afterwards. His constituents' intense opposition to the pact, he said, had left him with no alternative. Craig's enraged wife recorded in her diary:

What makes me so raging is the lack of guts of them all, none of the people who really heartily approve of his [Craig's] action have the courage to get up and say so. . . . It makes one wonder whether they are worth someone slaving themselves almost to death for.[123]

2

The Other Tiers of Government

Although the regional executive may have been supreme within its own tier of government, its freedom of action was severely circumscribed by the existence and attitude of the two other tiers. The devolution of government arranged by the 1920 act involved only a partial rearrangement of government within Northern Ireland. It merely slipped the new regional authority in between existing central and local authorities, expecting that the new authority should act in most respects as a smaller-scale Westminster. Beyond the fact that the distribution of powers between Westminster and Northern Ireland had been the subject of much discussion and calculation, little thought had been given as to how far the role of the regional government and parliament should differ from that of their imperial counterparts. No consideration had been given to the distribution of power within Northern Ireland and the extent to which the new regional authority could legitimately take full responsibility for services hitherto administered by local authorities. The result was that the government of Northern Ireland found itself uncomfortably sandwiched between the imperial government with its exacting Treasury and parsimonious local authorities, neither of which had a consistent interest in the development of regional policies.

1

Responsibility for the administration of transferred services was shared between the new authority and over seventy local authorities, most created by the Local Government (Ireland) Act of 1898, which democratised Irish local government, and the rest under earlier legislation relating to municipal corporations (1840), the Poor Law (1847) and towns improvement (1854). Although there were some changes in status after 1921, as a few urban district councils became incorporated and town commissions became urban district councils, the basic pre-partition structure of a multitude of local authorities remained. In

1938 there were six county councils, two county borough councils, three borough councils, thirty urban district councils, thirty-two rural district councils, three town commissions and twenty-seven Boards of Guardians. As if these pre-partition authorities were not sufficient, soon eighteen regional education committees were established under the provisions of the 1923 Education Act. Such local authorities administered a wide range of services, including poor relief, medical treatment, public health, roads and education, under the supervision of the Ministry of Home Affairs, except for the local education authorities (the county and county borough councils) and their regional committees, which were under the auspices of the Ministry of Education.[1]

Although modelled on the British system, Northern Ireland's differed from it in one important respect – finance. There was a marked contrast between Northern Ireland and Britain in the distribution of public 'domestic' (as imposed to 'imperial') expenditure between rates and taxes. Rate-borne public expenditure was much lower in Northern Ireland than in Britain. In 1927–28 rates in Northern Ireland bore only 19 per cent of total public 'domestic' expenditure, while rates in Britain bore 42 per cent; and two years later the percentages were 14 and 39 respectively.[2]

This inequality of rate burdens was due largely to the historical development of the education and police services in Northern Ireland.[3] The cost of these services was shared almost equally between the state and local authorities in Britain, but it was borne almost entirely by the state in Northern Ireland. Although most pronounced in Belfast, this discrepancy was general throughout the six counties. Under the Union education and the police had been centrally financed and controlled, and it was difficult to escape from these precedents in Northern Ireland. There had never been any demand for locally controlled police forces, as in Britain; on the contrary, the need was for a regionally controlled force, towards whose cost only two local authorities made a contribution, and that only a small, and in the case of Belfast a disputed, one. In 1930–31 the net cost of the police force was £1,079,000, of which only £25,120 (or 2.33 per cent) was contributed by local authorities (£25,000 by Belfast and £120 by Londonderry city).[4] As regards education, the 1923 Education Act, which remodelled the education system in Northern Ireland, attempted to give some satisfaction to the long-expressed demand for local control of and responsibility for education by establishing local education authorities and providing for rate contributions towards its cost. Nevertheless, by maintaining a close supervision of the system, by paying teachers' salaries, and by making grants to the local education authorities, the state continued to be the main source of educational finance. In 1930–31 the net cost of education to public funds was £2,174,000. The local authority contribution was theoretically £250,000 (or 7 per cent), but, owing to derating, the actual contribution was £92,000 (or 4.23 per cent).[5]

Finance apart, the system of local government was distinguished by two characteristics. In the first place, local authorities were frequently party battlegrounds and sources of patronage. Since its democratisation in 1898 local government in Northern Ireland, as in the South, had been conducted on party lines, there often being bitter election contests between Nationalists and Unionists. The introduction of P.R. for local elections may have broadened the field of political debate in some areas in the 1920 elections, but it also deepened Unionist and Nationalist rivalry, since, much to Unionists' disgust, Nationalists had been able to gain control of a number of marginal councils. The abolition of P.R. for local elections in 1922 and the consequent redrawing of electoral areas increased Nationalist resentment and stereotyped the composition of local councils with either built-in Unionist or built-in Nationalist majorities, and each council used its powers and patronage in the interests of the majority party. In many places, indeed, 'the intensity of political rivalry threatened to obscure the object of local government'.[6]

The second characteristic was conservatism and lack of dynamism. Since their creation most local authorities in the North of Ireland seem to have regarded their main function as keeping rates as low as possible and limiting services accordingly. Such conservatism may have been partly a consequence of scale, for many rural and urban districts were small and impoverished, and partly a consequence of inadequate co-ordination;[7] but it was largely a consequence of a lack of appreciation of the importance of providing services. For instance, by the time of partition, that is after twenty years of democratic local government, twenty-five of the sixty-four county borough and district councils had taken no measures to prevent tuberculosis, thirty-eight had done nothing about maternity and child welfare, only one authority had begun to feed needy schoolchildren, and only one had made arrangements (which were not fully operative) for their medical inspection.[8] Nor did local authorities show much enthusiasm for extending their activities after partition. The phrases 'criminally foolish' and 'pure rubbish' summed up the Unionist majority's hostility to any proposals for extending Belfast Corporation's financial liabilities, despite a housing shortage and widespread distress in the early 1930s.[9] According to the evidence submitted by the various local authority associations to a government inquiry into financial relations between the state and local authorities, 'The only item in regard to which they anticipate that some expansion is permissible is in respect of educational expenditure'.[10] That it was lethargy as much as problems of finance that governed local authority action or inaction was underlined by the failure of rural district councils to build labourers' cottages, even though money presented no pressing problems for several years.[11]

The inadequacies of this system of local government were soon acknowledged by the government, and in 1924 a departmental committee was established to inquire into local government administration. The publication of its findings three years later may have alarmed local authorities, but the majority report was hardly sweeping and never challenged the conventional division of responsibility between local authorities and parliament.[12] Even then, the report was shelved, so that, despite some adjustments, the structure and essential attitudes of local government were substantially the same in 1939 as they had been in 1921, perhaps with the difference that under regional government local authorities had even less incentive to enterprise.

Confused thinking on local government finance hardly encouraged local authorities to adopt a more dynamic view of their functions. On the one hand, derating both complicated local authority finance and limited the rateable capacity of local authority areas.[13] Government grants did provide some compensation, but local authorities were reluctant to assume additional burdens which would fall on a diminished number of ratepayers, especially when in the later 1930s government grants-in-aid were stabilised or slightly reduced as part of a drive to save money and to bring financial relations between the state and local authorities more into line with those obtaining in Britain.[14] On the other hand, at the same time the government encouraged local authorities to look to the state for aid. Spender much objected to the policy of giving special consideration to local authorities, particularly since he thought that they signally failed to appreciate how more generously they were treated by the government than their British counterparts. Craig, unmoved by Spender's protests, remained susceptible to local authority pressure, instructed the Ministry of Finance to provide a surplus for 'special local purposes', and evidently enjoyed what he called 'the policy of "distributing bones"'.[15]

A restricted view of the proper role of the state and parliament may have been one reason for this accommodating attitude to local authorities. Northern Ireland ministers and civil servants subscribed freely to the concept of private enterprise, and after private enterprise they favoured action by the local authorities. State responsibility was to be avoided wherever possible. These views were not peculiar to Northern Ireland, but they were held with particular force there because of the sad history of local government under the Union. It was generally held in Unionist circles that administration had been too centralised under the Union and that local initiative and responsibility had been discouraged; hence the state of Ireland in the early twentieth century. The government of Northern Ireland was determined not to repeat that mistake. It wanted to develop local responsibility, and thus one of its first major legislative achievements was to decentralise the administration of education, sharing responsibility between a Ministry of Education, county and county borough councils and regional education boards.[16] It did not seem to matter that some of these new boards were too small to operate efficiently and attract men of calibre; and no thought was given to the view that the regional parliament itself might have provided an adequate means of involving local people with the administration of education. The limited political imagination of the inter-war period could conceive of the Northern parliament only as a miniature Westminster, having the same relationship to local authorities as obtained in Britain. This view was constantly being reinforced by the anxiety of imperial Treasury officials to ensure that the Northern Ireland ratepayer was not being unduly subsidised by the United Kingdom taxpayer.[17]

Political theory may have helped to justify the traditional division of responsibility between the state and local authorities, but it was largely fear and a sense of powerlessness that prevented the government from forcing local authorities to face up to their nominal responsibilities. It was true that the government did suspend Nationalist-controlled local bodies which refused to recognise its authority in 1921–22, and later suspended one Labour, one Nationalist and one Unionist local authority – the first for squabbling incompetence, the others for corruption.[18] Such decisiveness was rare and the product of particular circumstances. Generally the newly established government was wary of upsetting bodies which had become entrenched in the lives of the local communities and identified with political parties. As Craig warned the Junior Minister of Home Affairs during a disagreement with Belfast Corporation over housing policy, 'We always have to bear in mind that the City represents in many respects one-half of Northern Ireland and therefore requires careful handling'.[19] The basis of Belfast's political influence was obvious, but other local authorities also felt able to stand up to the government. Not only were individual councils quick to inform the government of their views, but the various types of local authorities had representative organisations equally quick to publicise their members' views. For example, the Association of Rural District Councils was always quick to defend the position of these much-criticised bodies as against the county councils, and, as amendments to the Public Libraries Bill showed, the rural district councils had their sympathisers in parliament.[20]

Whether political theory or political reality determined the government's approach to local authorities, the consequences of that accommodating attitude were clear. Local authorities were encouraged to postpone action in the hope of getting government money and took credit for any government assistance, while at the same time resentment was created among those authorities not given similar treatment.

Reviewing a long list of financial promises made to local authorities by Craig during his 1927 tour, Spender complained that the government did not reap the benefit of such largesse and suggested instead that

> If at the end of each financial year the Government were to consider whether there were any available balance in hand and were then to expend the money *themselves* to the best advantage, the results would be far more beneficial to the Province and would redound to the credit of the Government, whereas at present the Local Authorities . . . get most of the benefits of the savings made by the Government.[21]

There was much truth in Spender's complaint. The government's responsiveness to local authorities did not make for efficient, prompt or economical government, while it did blur lines of responsibility.

That the government's attitude did not necessarily make for economical administration was indicated by the loose and sometimes lax supervision exercised by the Ministry of Home Affairs over local authorities. Although Spender was a bit of a prig on matters of finance and morals, it is difficult not to sympathise with his regret that Ministry of Home Affairs inspectors had not been the first to uncover corruption in Belfast housing contracts in the early 1920s,[22] or with his amazement at the ease with which the architect of the Co. Down Regional Education Committee had been able in the early 1930s to embezzle money from schoolbuilding contracts.[23] Such episodes did reflect upon the system of local government audit operated by the Ministry of Home Affairs, the ministry responsible for local government. There was a good deal of truth in Spender's observation that laxity was the result of the intertwining of regional and local government, with too many M.P.s and members of the government having positions on local authorities and too many leading men acting irresponsibly by simply signing statements put before them by permanent officials. An alternative, originally suggested by Clark and Spender, would have been to have made the Comptroller and Auditor-General responsible for the local government audit, but Craig had rejected this suggestion on the grounds that such an audit might have been 'too rigid'.[24]

Nor did the government's accommodating attitude to local authorities make for prompt government. Rather it created further expectations and delays, for any project involved long financial arguments. Belfast Corporation's unsuccessful appeal to the Judicial Committee of the Privy Council to prevent the government from shifting more of the cost of education to the rates[25] was only the most dramatic instance of a constant conflict in Northern Ireland as to who should finance what. Local authorities outside Belfast displayed just as much tenacity as Belfast Corporation.

The case of Portstewart harbour provided a convenient illustration of the contrast between the appearance of satisfying promptitude entailed by Craig's style of government and the reality of delay and discontent.[26] During his tour in 1927 Craig had visited Portstewart harbour and had promised a grant of £350 to remove the rocks which were making the entrance perilous to fishermen. The grant was approved by the cabinet on 1 March 1927, immediately after the Prime Minister's return, and was included in the 1927–28 estimates. However, by May 1928 work had not yet begun and Craig received a letter of protest from the local Church of Ireland minister, who complained of the delay and observed: 'Our men are all loyal supporters of the Government but I fear their loyalty is being shaken by the tardy methods of meeting their demands'.[27] The delay was not the government's fault, since the appropriate authority, through which the matter had to be handled, was the Londonderry County Council. A first cause of delay was the fact that the work had not been included in the County Council's original programme for the year 1927–28. This difficulty was overcome when the work was sanctioned at the Council's annual meeting on 16 July 1927, but a further cause of delay soon arose when the contractors engaged for removing the rock also wanted the contract for larger harbour improvements which were then being contemplated by the Council. Londonderry County Council thereupon attempted to get the government to bear the whole cost of all the harbour works, and a prolonged correspondence ensued, the government offering only 50 per cent of the cost of the larger works. For these reasons Craig's promise could not be redeemed until August 1929, after the government had purchased a dredger and rock-breaking machine for use in all Northern Ireland harbours.

Finally, the government's financing of a new Londonderry bridge summed up all the defects of working through Northern Ireland local authorities.[28] The rotting and rusting Carlisle Bridge, open to traffic since 1863, was deemed unsafe and inadequate to handle twentieth-century traffic, and the idea of building a new bridge was first mooted in November 1923 by Londonderry Corporation, who wanted the cost shared between the city, Londonderry and Tyrone County Councils and the government. At first the government decided to pay about £100,000, roughly 40 per cent of the cost, and hoped Londonderry city would then drop the controversial idea of contributions from the county councils. Gradually, however, Londonderry Corporation also dropped the idea of its own contribution. After many meetings and deputations between representatives of the Corporation and the Prime Minister, the government came to assume full financial responsibility for the bridge itself, though not the approach roads, an obligation almost forced upon it by the Corporation's threat to abandon essential waterworks if government aid for the bridge was not forthcoming. Moreover, expectations were encouraged elsewhere, for, Bates told the House in May 1931, misconceptions about the extent of government aid to the Corporation in respect of the bridge was 'often used by other local authorities in making claims on us for preferential treatment'.[29]

Not only did the negotiations show the influence of local authorities on the government, but they also showed how spheres of responsibility became easily blurred. Although the Ministry of Home Affairs was the responsible department, most of the negotiations were carried on between the Town Clerk and Mayor of Londonderry on the one hand and Craig on the other. This meant many loose ends. Craig, when visiting Londonderry, would promise in general terms that the government would bear the whole cost of the bridge, but then officials of the Ministries of Home Affairs and Finance would exclude certain items, which would necessitate further negotiations between the Prime Minister and Londonderry officials. Moreover, individuals or groups objecting to the design of the bridge or the prospect of tolls being charged sought meetings with the Prime Minister. Not surprisingly, Spender on one occasion mistakenly wrote to Blackmore in the belief that the Cabinet Secretary was in charge of the negotiations. Such a situation produced duplication of effort. Nominally the bridge was the responsibility of the Londonderry Corporation, and its officials formally carried out all the negotiations with outside firms; but since the bridge was financed from the Road Fund, the Ministries of Finance and Home Affairs inspected the plans and selected the tenders. This duplication of effort also provided opportunities for buck-passing. The local authority was able to point critics in the government's direction, while ministers were able to tell critics that Londonderry Corporation was the responsible authority and that the government was merely acting as its agent. It is hard to resist the conclusion that the work might have been more speedily and economically carried out if the Board of Works had assumed direct responsibility for the bridge from the start, thus avoiding consultants' charges, time-consuming negotiations and much duplication of effort.

2

The top tier of government — Westminster — virtually set the limits of decision- and policy-making in Northern Ireland. The 1920 act, by reserving ultimate sovereignty to Westminster and distributing powers between Northern Ireland and Westminster, not only limited the former's powers but also laid it especially open to British influence. Bills had to be submitted to the Home Office, which took this opportunity to circulate them to the relevant imperial ministries, which would often offer detailed comments on technical and administrative matters. All Northern Ireland bills had to receive the royal assent. Most importantly, the bulk of Northern Ireland's revenue was imposed by Westminster and Northern Ireland's expenditure was subjected to an annual scrutiny by Treasury officials. In view of the large amount of power retained by Westminster, Northern Ireland was allotted thirteen representatives in the United Kingdom parliament, elected on the same franchise as the rest of the kingdom. The Westminster parliament, however, exercised little initiative in relations between Northern Ireland and Great Britain, usually being content to register agreements arrived at between the two governments.

Normally eleven of the thirteen Northern Ireland M.P.s were Unionists. Superior in birth and education to the general run of their counterparts in the Northern Ireland parliament, the Ulster Unionist M.P.s had their own organisation at Westminster, complete with chairman, secretary and whip.[30] In most matters their views differed little from those of the rank and file of the Conservative Party. On matters affecting Northern Ireland, however, they mainly took their cue from the home government, which seems to have tried to have kept a tight rein on them, instructing them what to say and, more frequently, what *not* to say.[31] The remaining Northern Ireland M.P.s at Westminster were opponents of partition, the combined constituency of Fermanagh and Tyrone alternating between Republicans and Nationalists. Abstentionism also affected nationalist representation at Westminster, but when nationalists did take their seats they proved constant critics of the Northern government.[32]

Neither group of Northern Ireland M.P.s made much impact upon the imperial parliament. This was partly because all Westminster M.P.s were precluded from discussing matters which fell within the jurisdiction of the Northern Ireland parliament, and partly because most British M.P.s had no consistent interest in Northern Ireland. This is not to suggest that the Westminster parliament was always oblivious to events in the North. Some Labour and Liberal M.P.s were always hostile to Ulster Unionism and particularly critical of the administration of law and order – even to the extent of insisting on seeing a sinister sectarianism in juvenile crime there, despite the fact that such crime presented a problem throughout the United Kingdom.[33] Other British M.P.s were more anxious to see that devolution did not bestow upon Northern Ireland financial and economic benefits greater than those enjoyed by Britain.[34] Such opinion did occasionally, even decisively, influence imperial policy towards Northern Ireland. Resentment at the confinement of Cahir Healy, the Sinn Féin M.P. for the Westminster constituency of Fermanagh and Tyrone, prompted both Conservative and Labour leaders to insist on his complete freedom;[35] and fear of the wrath of the Public Accounts Committee disinclined the Treasury to repeat certain expedients to help balance Northern Ireland's budget.[36] Above all, the imperial government was always anxious to avoid introducing, especially in the 1930s, any even potentially controversial legislation concerning Northern Ireland for fear of raising the whole question of Anglo-Irish relations.[37] For its part, the government of Northern Ireland was always concerned that there should be no adverse criticism of its administration and was always at pains to meet fully and courteously any criticism offered by British members of the Westminster parliament.[38]

Nevertheless, what determined relations between Northern Ireland and Britain was not the views of either parliament, but the views and actions of a small group of ministers and senior civil servants. This pattern had been determined in the early years when relations were fluid and Craig spent much of his time in Britain, interviewing ministers and senior civil servants, at first defending Northern Ireland's position during the Treaty negotiations and then trying to obtain financial and other aid towards the maintenance of law and order. In these early years Craig proved himself an accomplished negotiator, often able to withstand the threats and blandishments of leading imperial politicians, particularly those of Lloyd George.[39] Craig continued to have great faith in his ability to advance Northern Ireland's interests by direct and personal contact with imperial ministers, a belief which he used to justify his prolonged sojourns at Cleeve Court, Streatley-on-Thames. As he told Pollock, whom he left in Northern Ireland to handle the consequences of the coal strike in May 1926, 'I go to Town to-morrow for an important Dinner at which I shall meet a mixture of the Leaders here, including your friend Philip Snowden: in this and other ways I keep in touch with what is going on and if there is anything of interest to relate I will let you know at once'.[40] Indeed, Craig at times acted less as Northern Ireland's Prime Minister than as its ambassador in Britain. His colleagues at first met their British counterparts less frequently, but always tried to ensure that they appreciated Northern Ireland's special interests. Thus, when the first Labour government came to power, Pollock had an interview with the new Chancellor, Snowden, to explain the basis of Northern Ireland's finances and then a less formal interview on the boundary question with the Colonial Secretary, J. H. Thomas.[41]

More regular than ministerial contacts were contacts between civil servants. Partly because of their often highly technical nature, most matters of common concern were hammered out by the civil services meeting as equals – or so Northern Ireland civil servants liked to think.[42] Civil servants had considerable freedom in arranging relations between the two governments. Only in the event of deep disagreements between

Northern Ireland and imperial departments, or on a very few matters of high policy, were the politicians brought into play to do other than rubber-stamp arrangements made by officials.[43] More often than not, however, by the 1930s officials, particularly those from the two treasuries, preferred to reach compromises among themselves, for example over the question of the North's share of new import duties, a tendency which did not always best serve Northern Ireland's interests.[44]

Relations between these small groups of ministers and officials were sometimes strained, for the interests of their two governments were by no means identical. Such were their different perspectives on some fundamental questions that the 1920 settlement was on occasion subject to severe stress.

Potentially disruptive differences arose over foreign economic policy, controlled by Westminster. In the inter-war years Northern Ireland farmers and industrialists felt that they would have benefited from protection, but until the 1930s the prevailing philosophy at Westminster was one of *laissez-faire* in respect of both agriculture and industry. With the dismantling of wartime controls, the imperial government reverted to its traditional posture of minimal interference with agriculture; and although industry, or certain sections of it, did receive a degree of protection under the 1921 Safeguarding of Industries Act, this ostensibly protectionist measure was administered in a free-trade spirit. Admittedly, Northern Ireland did benefit when, in face of world depression, the imperial government took steps to protect British agriculture and industry against the dumping of foreign manufactures and produce at abnormally low prices in the world's one great free-trade market. Temporary measures in the winter of 1931 foreshadowed the permanent protectionist policy implemented in the following February with the Import Duties Act. This represented a dramatic change in imperial economic policy, but its benefits to domestic producers were limited, partly by the necessity to maintain trade agreements with foreign countries which provided substantial markets for British manufactures, but mainly by imperial sentiments. Such sentiments led the imperial government to conclude at the Imperial Economic Conference in the summer of 1932 the one-sided Ottawa agreements, under which dominion foodstuffs and other products continued to receive substantial preference in the United Kingdom market.[45] Northern Ireland's particular interests had to be discussed within this general and often restrictive framework.

A second, and the most potentially disruptive, conflict of interests between the Northern Ireland and imperial governments was the latter's policy towards the South of Ireland. Ulster Unionists' determination not to accept Dublin rule but to maintain Northern Ireland, governing it in their own way and endeavouring to protect regional interests, often conflicted with broader imperial policy. The different Northern

Ireland and imperial perspectives were clearly evident in 1938, when, in the imperial government's settlement of outstanding issues with the Éire government, Northern Ireland's economic interests had eventually to be subordinated to a wider imperial policy of international conciliation.[46] More dramatic was the conflict in 1921–22, when the imperial government sought to extricate itself from Ireland in face of the rise of Irish Republicanism. Highly placed critics in the imperial government and civil service felt that the Northern Ireland government's attitude to partition and questions affecting law and order and the minority would upset the Irish settlement, while Northern Ireland ministers and civil servants feared that the imperial government would sell Northern Ireland out to the South, or at least fail to defend it against nationalist aggression.[47]

The third and most persistent area of conflict was finance. The financial provisions of the 1920 act were unrealistic and inequitable, allowing Northern Ireland insufficient revenue to meet increasing and usually necessary expenditure. The result was that Northern Ireland ministers and officials had to go on repeated begging expeditions to London either to persuade the imperial government to revise the financial provisions of the 1920 act or to arrange for various *ad hoc* payments to tide them over difficult periods. For its part, the imperial government and particularly the Treasury looked upon Northern Ireland's repeated claims with a jaundiced eye, suspecting that Ulstermen were trying to sponge off the British taxpayer while enjoying considerable regional autonomy. Even when the justice of the North's claims were admitted, help was given only after long bargaining and only under strict conditions.[48]

Considering the possible occasions for friction, relations between Northern Ireland and Britain were on the whole harmonious. Neither government was willing to push disagreements to the point where the 1920 settlement might have collapsed. The government of Northern Ireland had every interest in maintaining a settlement which provided imperial cash and protection as well as a bulwark against a united Ireland. The imperial government, in turn, was unwilling to undertake once more direct responsibility for the administration of Northern Ireland. Admittedly, the Northern Ireland government felt more comfortable when a Conservative government was in power in London,[49] but Labour ministers were equally, and on occasion more, accessible and cordial.[50]

Cordiality and accessibility did not imply equality. Northern Ireland was the subordinate authority, and its subordination was underlined by the financial provisions of the 1920 act which, by reducing ministers and officials almost to mendicancy, induced in them a pathetic anxiety to avoid, as Pollock once said, 'irritating the Chancellor or making him think we want to oppose him in what he considers necessary'.[51] Such dependence upon and subordination to Westminster could not fail to affect the nature of policy and politics in Northern Ireland. Not only did it involve secrecy and restrict public participation in policy-making; it also limited policy and administrative options. Of course, Ulster Unionists were predisposed to toe the British line on many issues, but their chances of developing distinctive policies suited to their regional requirements were further limited by the large degree of power and influence reserved to Westminster.

Most obviously, the government of Northern Ireland was prevented from taking certain measures to encourage economic development. Serious attempts to develop agriculture and improve agricultural marketing had to await a slight extension of powers in 1928[52] or the imperial government's change from free trade to protection in 1931–32.[53] Similarly, the failure of attempts in the 1920s to invoke the Safeguarding of Industries Act left the linen industry exposed to unrestricted foreign competition until the change of imperial policy in the early 1930s.[54] Such limited power and influence often meant that the government of Northern Ireland had to look for other ways of rewarding its supporters and maintaining credibility. Thus Londonderry city was continuously in receipt of special government grants in the inter-war years and achieved notoriety with the alleged gerrymandering of local government boundaries in 1936; but this was all that the government could do for a politically sensitive area suffering from a decline in the shirt trade and, more obviously, from Free State economic policy, both matters beyond its competence.[55] The government's limited powers and influence thus rendered difficult, if not impossible, the development of long-term and comprehensive policies for the region and the community as a whole.

Less obvious and less precisely stated was Westminster's influence upon transferred services. Westminster thought that Northern Ireland's transferred services should be run in the interests of and in conformity with the United Kingdom as a whole, whereas Northern Ireland ministers were often conscious of the peculiar needs of the province. These different perspectives often provoked sharp disagreements between Westminster and Belfast during which the limits of Britain's ability or willingness to interfere in Northern Ireland's affairs were starkly demonstrated. The Westminster government signally failed to influence decisively policies on sensitive questions involving Protestant susceptibilities and the position of the Catholic minority. Having abandoned its attempts to prevent the abolition of P.R. in local elections in 1922, Westminster made no effort to dissuade the Northern Ireland government from abolishing it in parliamentary elections in 1929; and the Home Office made only a half-hearted effort to secure a reconsideration of the Education Amendments Bills of 1925 and 1930, which, it was thought, contravened the 1920 act by virtually endowing Protestantism.[56] Moreover, on some economic matters pressure from Westminster failed to persuade the government of Northern Ireland to conform to British practices. For instance, the English Ministry of Agriculture favoured voluntary marketing schemes, but its Northern Ireland counterpart insisted that conditions there made compulsion essential.[57]

In other respects fear of British opinion did exercise an influence upon government attitudes and policy in Northern Ireland. Once having mastered their ministries, most ministers did not like to appear to the outside world simply as partisan politicians.[58] Thus, even where Protestant and Unionist susceptibilities were concerned, they were not wholly unresponsive to the promptings of the imperial government. Such promptings might not have been able to alter a basic line of policy, but they could secure mitigation. In deference to the opinion of the imperial government certain local elections were postponed from 1923 until 1924;[59] and after the Home Office had pointed out that it might have to hold up the 1930 Education Bill if there was a Catholic outcry against it, the cabinet adopted a more accommodating attitude on the question of grants to voluntary schools.[60] On economic matters, too, the government of Northern Ireland was inclined to minimise the effects of departures from British practices, as over the continuation of loans guarantee facilities after their withdrawal in Britain.[61]

More importantly, and more consistently, financial considerations intensified the Unionist preference for copying Britain and often seemed to nullify some of the advantages of devolution. The 'step-by-step' policy in the major cash social services adopted in 1922 soon became the cornerstone of Northern Ireland's financial relations with Britain, absorbing most of its budget and pre-empting a potentially fruitful source of debate.[62] If some policies were rendered almost inevitable by the nature of Northern Ireland's financial relationship with Britain, the formulation of others was often dominated by financial considerations. In the provision of such services as housing, public health and education Northern Ireland demonstrably lagged behind the rest of the United Kingdom, but the question that often overrode all others was, not what would be in the best interests of Northern Ireland, but what would be acceptable to the imperial Treasury.[63]

Finance was the main key to what influence Westminster could exercise over Northern Ireland affairs. In 1922 Craig, despite pressure from his ministers, reached agreement over Special Constabulary finance before attempting a showdown with the imperial government over its withholding of the royal assent to the Local Government Bill.[64] His instinct was right. Later on both Labour and Conservative governments did make their support for special votes for Northern Ireland in the

Westminster parliament conditional upon changes, albeit minor, in the administration of justice.[65] And it was pressure from the Treasury, which would otherwise have refused to help balance Northern Ireland's budget in the early 1930s, that gave the government the courage to incur the wrath of taxpayers, ratepayers and local authorities alike by proceeding with revaluation and an education levy.[66]

Just how frequently such blackmail could have been used to mitigate some of the more controversial aspects of Unionist policy, it is difficult to say. What can be said, however, is that such pressure was exceptional and of limited application. The only constant and overriding concern of Westminster in the administration of transferred services was to see that Northern Ireland did not enjoy home rule at Britain's expense and equip herself with services superior to those existing in the rest of the United Kingdom. Such financial control was, on the whole, acceptable to the Northern Ireland Ministry of Finance, which believed that Northern Ireland should, as far as possible, stand on its own financial feet. But for the imperial government to have gone further and tried to influence controversial legislation which had the full support of the Northern Ireland government and a significant body of Ulster Unionists would have jeopardised the 1920 settlement in Northern Ireland. Quite simply, Westminster's influence over Northern Ireland was limited by the lack of an alternative government there. Craig could have resigned and handed the troublesome six counties back to an imperial government anxious to end its involvement in Ireland.

3

Further Constraints

Policy and administration in Northern Ireland were not determined
simply within the formal framework of government. Circumstances
created as many problems for and constraints on the regional government as did the constitution. Firstly, Northern Ireland's position as an
integral yet the most disadvantaged part of the United Kingdom economy
meant that economic and social problems, particularly the problem of
unemployment, constituted, relatively speaking, a more serious challenge
in Northern Ireland than in Great Britain. Moreover, it also meant that
the government of Northern Ireland was almost powerless to take steps
to regenerate the economic life of the province or even develop a distinctive economic and social policy. Secondly, the proliferation of pressure and interest groups was an inescapable fact of political life in
Northern Ireland. In this highly politicised and localised society any
and every issue could call forth some more or less representative group
seeking the ear, and sometimes the whole body and soul, of the administration. Thirdly, politics and policies were conditioned by the existence and activities of the Southern Irish state. In particular, Southern
irridentism and economic policy served to complicate and devalue the
processes of government in Northern Ireland. These three circumstances conspired to limit still further the Northern Ireland government's capacity and will to formulate, let alone develop, long-term
regional policies in the interests of the whole community.

1

Northern Ireland 'is not a separate economy at all but an undifferent-
iated part of a single economic system embracing the whole of the
United Kingdom': so wrote Isles and Cuthbert, the two leading experts
on Northern Ireland's economic problems.[1] This economic interdependence with Britain was evident in a number of ways. Most of Northern
Ireland's trade was with the rest of the United Kingdom: in 1935, for
example, 84 per cent of its exports (by value) were sent to Britain.[2]

Economic institutions were either unified with those in Britain or run on parallel lines: of the seventy registered trades unions operating in Northern Ireland in 1935, no fewer than fifty-seven, accounting for 87.5 per cent of total trades union membership, had their headquarters in London or Edinburgh.[3] Industries, too, operated on a United Kingdom basis. Not only did some 40 per cent of the value of any shipbuilding undertaken in Belfast accrue to Britain, largely on account of raw materials,[4] but British labour was often imported for certain finishing processes, leading one Labour M.P. to complain in May 1936 that he 'could take you to parts of a ship in the finishing end, and you would think you were in Scotland, while in another part you would think you were in the Midlands of England, and then I could take you to persons following the same occupations at our labour exchanges'.[5]

Northern Ireland was, however, a small, and the most disadvantaged, region of the larger United Kingdom economy. Its most obvious disadvantage was its dependence upon three main industries – agriculture, linen and shipbuilding. Agriculture played a greater role in the Northern Ireland economy than it did in the British. Whereas in the United Kingdom as a whole only 6.2 per cent of gainfully occupied persons were engaged in agriculture, in Northern Ireland the proportion was 26 per cent of the total labour force and as high as 30 per cent of the male working force.[6] Industrial production was dominated by linen within a thirty-mile radius of Belfast and shipbuilding within Belfast. Of the 156,834 persons employed in undertakings covered by the 1924 census of production, 81,198 (or 51.77 per cent) were employed in linen and textile finishing, and 17,219 (or 10.98 per cent) in shipbuilding and mechanical engineering.[7]

This traditional dependence upon a narrow range of industries created many problems in the inter-war years, when all three were on the defensive.[8] Agriculture was adversely affected by the world-wide decline in the prices of primary produce and by fierce foreign competition in the British market. The overexpansion of world trade caused a fall in the demand for new ships, with the results that the Belfast shipyards were always working at less than half capacity, that one yard, Workman, Clark & Co., closed down in 1935, and that the rate of unemployment in shipbuilding and engineering never fell below 13.3 per cent (in February 1930) and was once as high as 64.5 per cent (in December 1932).[9] The decline in linen was permanent, brought about by the introduction of new fibres, high tariffs in the United States, the best customer, and the development of the industry overseas where production costs were lower. In 1927, for example, the volume of exports of linen piece goods and of yarn represented 40 per cent and 70 per cent respectively of the 1913 figures. Consequently, employment within the industry fell from 86,762 in 1924 to 61,000 in 1935; and the long-term decline combined with shorter-term cyclical movements to produce a rate of unemployment ranging between 6.2 per cent (in October 1927) and 56.3 per cent (in July 1938).[10]

The effect of the decline of the two great industrial staples was felt by other industries, with the result that in the inter-war years Northern Ireland's rate of unemployment was significantly higher than that of Britain as a whole. It was true that certain areas in Britain, dependent on a single industry such as shipbuilding or coal, did experience unemployment as great and greater than that in Northern Ireland, but such areas were the responsibility of a government with much greater resources than those available to the government of Northern Ireland. The number of Northern Ireland's unemployed reached a peak of 101,967 in July 1935, but the relative position was worst in 1938. In February 1938, when 92,000 were registered as out of work, the percentage unemployed among insured industrial workers was 29.5 in Northern Ireland, as compared with 23.8 in Wales, the highest British figure, and 12.8 for Britain as a whole.[11] The social consequences of this high rate of unemployment, the hardship and the suffering, are too universally realised to need stressing, but they were highlighted by dramatic protests in the autumn of 1932, mainly against the parsimony of the Belfast Board of Guardians, which culminated in rioting.[12]

The alleviation of this chronic unemployment problem, either by reviving the old industries or by attracting new ones, was rendered difficult by the fact that costs of production were higher in Northern Ireland than elsewhere in the United Kingdom. This was partly a result of Northern Ireland's industrial structure, which, shipbuilding apart, was characterised by the existence of a large number of small firms, each of which cherished its independence.[13] Such a structure had its advantages, particularly as family firms were, perhaps, less ready to shut down and more willing to draw upon reserves to survive periods of depression. Nevertheless, there were disadvantages, the most obvious being high costs of production, as in the bacon industry, which was having to meet formidable Danish competition. The price paid for the convenience of a large number of small curers,[14] in contrast to the large scale of production carried on in Denmark and Britain, was inefficiency. It helped to explain why the pig producer in Northern Ireland received only 60 per cent of the bacon price, whereas the percentages for Britain and Denmark were 71.9 and 78.1 respectively.[15]

Even when, as in the case of the linen and hemp industry, the average size of establishments was larger in Northern Ireland than the United Kingdom as a whole, the existence of a large number of fiercely competitive small units made it difficult for the industry to adjust to changed conditions. The industry contained a number of processes: flax merchanting, spinning, yarn merchanting, weaving, bleaching, dyeing and finishing, and the marketing of the final product. Some of the larger concerns combined all processes from the raw materials stage to that of the finished product for sale to distributors in Britain or overseas, but the greater number of undertakings specialised in one or other of the processes, there being in the 1920s about fifty spinning, about a hundred weaving, and over eighty merchanting firms. The difficulties arising from the existence of so large a number of competitive undertakings was spelled out in 1928 in the report of a committee appointed by the trade to investigate 'the basic causes of the present difficulties of the Irish linen industry'. The most obvious consequences of what the committee called *'the present disjointed organisation of the industry'* were high costs of production, uneconomic working, and a costly and inefficient marketing system which in the 1920s led to suicidal price-cutting.[16]

While Northern Ireland's industrial structure raised costs of production in existing industries, its natural disadvantages increased costs for both existing and prospective industries. Poor natural resources meant that raw materials had to be imported, and the cost of transport did help raise costs of production above those of British firms.[17] Coal, for instance, was an important basic raw material used in most industries, for which Northern Ireland was entirely reliant upon imports from Britain. Since Northern Ireland was situated furthest away from the coal-producing areas than most industrial centres in Britain, additional transport and handling costs meant that the average cost of industrial coal to firms in Northern Ireland was much in excess of the corresponding average for Britain. In 1935 the percentage excess in the shipbuilding and engineering, linen and hemp, butter and cream, and earthenware and china trades was 36.1, 43.4, 66.7 and 95.1 respectively.[18]

Agriculture also distinguished the Northern Ireland economy from that of the rest of the United Kingdom.[19] Not only did the relative importance of agriculture differ, but the nature of farming also. In the first place, the structure of output was different. More important than the fact that Northern Ireland was more reliant on livestock and livestock products such as milk and eggs, were the different emphases within both arable and pastoral farming. Potatoes were a more important crop throughout Northern Ireland, but in Britain there was a distinct pattern of regional specialisation. On the other hand, the cultivation of wheat was less important in Northern Ireland. Certain areas of Britain, especially along the east coast, had long specialised in wheat-growing and had come to constitute a powerful lobby; but in Northern Ireland little wheat was grown, and that of a different quality, much of it being unsuitable for milling because of a high moisture content. Thus, whereas England derived some 5 per cent of its agricultural income from wheat, the figure for Northern Ireland was a mere 0.0015 per cent. In respect of livestock, too, there were crucial differences. Northern Ireland specialised in the production of store cattle, leaving the fattening to be completed in Britain; and whereas in Northern Ireland 70 per cent of milk produced was used for manufacturing purposes and only 30 per cent went on to the liquid market, the proportions were reversed in Britain. Finally, Northern Ireland agriculture produced more than could be consumed by the home market, and thus the surplus had to be exported. By contrast, farmers in Britain produced for, and could scarcely satisfy, the home market, supplying in the inter-war years less than half the home demand for meat, less than a tenth of the demand for butter, and less than two-thirds of the demand for eggs.

The structure of farm-holdings was also different in Northern Ireland. The predominant form of agricultural organisation there was the small family farm, owned and worked mainly by the farmer himself and members of his own family, and employing outside labour (if at all) only at busy seasons of the year. With the completion of land purchase in the 1920s, nearly all the holdings, which numbered 105,215 in 1926 and 93,842 in 1938, were owner-occupied, in contrast to the rest of the United Kingdom, where most holdings were rented and the proportion occupied by owners was only some 13 per cent. The small family farm was not peculiar to Northern Ireland. There were many such farms in Britain and the South of Ireland, but the proportion was highest in Northern Ireland. In 1937 37.9 per cent of holdings in Northern Ireland were under 15 acres and 82.7 per cent below 50 acres. In England and Wales and in the Free State 62.5 per cent and 76.1 per cent of farms were below 50 acres. Correspondingly, Northern Ireland had a smaller proportion of large farms. Only 4.4 per cent of its farms exceeded 100 acres compared with 20.9 per cent in England and Wales and 8.8 per cent in the Free State.

The prevalence of the small family farm meant very little specialisation. Although Northern Ireland did specialise in a broad sense in livestock and livestock products, the actual system on most farms was based upon a range of enterprises. Few farms derived their total income from one livestock enterprise, and the typical pattern was a small range of products contributing to total receipts, with one supplying the greatest proportion but that varying from farm to farm. Such diversity made much economic sense. It enabled the fullest use to be made of available land and labour; it spread risks; and it made for a more even income flow throughout the year.[20] Moreover, the small family farm did make for stability in the countryside. It was certainly arguable that what helped Northern Ireland agriculture to weather the most difficult years of the inter-war depression was the widespread existence of such farms, for, as a contemporary analysis of farm accounts concluded, the most successful farms had been those 'on which the bulk of the work was done by family labour due, in the main, to the attention given to detail and willingness to work very long hours when necessary'.[21]

Nevertheless, the prevalence of small farms did present a number of problems. Such problems may have helped to dictate lines of agricultural policy, but they also rendered difficult its realisation.

The first and most obvious problem was that of maintaining a sufficient cash income. A survey of forty smallholdings made by the Ministry of Agriculture in 1929 showed that none had a sufficient surplus to pay an agricultural labourer's wage to the farmer, and the situation changed little before the Second World War, as was amply demonstrated by an analysis of eleven of the farm accounts meticulously kept between 1930 and 1937 by the ministry.[22] Since it is likely that only the more progressive farmers kept systematic accounts, and since the survey farms were considerably larger than the average, the net income of these farms was probably above the average for the province as a whole.

This preoccupation with cash flow largely determined farmers' attitudes towards agricultural policy. At least rents had been negotiable with the landlord in times of falling prices, but after land purchase most of the farmers' cash payments were to public bodies – rates to local authorities and land annuities to the state. Farmers therefore tended to think in the short term and see agricultural policy in terms of cash relief, demanding relief from rates and later from land-purchase annuities, agitating for cheap loans, and objecting to any government activity which might increase either costs of production or the level of taxation. Concerned to maintain an already low level of income, the Northern Ireland farmers' almost instinctive response to any fall in agricultural prices was to demand a reduction of taxes or rates, to which was later added a demand for guaranteed prices, rather than to try to increase earning power by more efficient production and marketing.[23] It was instructive that at a representative meeting of producers and curers, called by the Ministry of Agriculture in March 1932 to discuss the proposed reorganisation of the pig and bacon industry in the United Kingdom, only one representative, a farmer, spoke of the need for increased efficiency, to see 'what is the lowest price we can take and still make the thing a passing success'. The rest were concerned with 'what is the highest price we can simply screw out'.[24]

Standards of production and marketing were a second problem presented by the prevalence of small mixed farms. It was difficult for one man to 'keep abreast of technical developments or resolve the difficulties inherent in several distinct enterprises which compete for attention'.[25] Moreover, partly because of the almost legendary conservatism of the Ulster farmer and partly because of the cost of modernisation, farms in Northern Ireland were not generally as well equipped as those in Britain, either with farm buildings or with the more elaborate kinds of machinery. 'It is no exaggeration to say', reported an Agricultural Enquiry Committee in 1947, 'that in many parts of Ulster to-day farmers and labourers are working with implements that show little if any advance on those in use a century ago. This applies not only to tillage and other farming implements but to the condition and equipment of farm buildings'.[26]

Nor were farmers very willing to try to overcome the disadvantages of small-scale production and marketing by systematic co-operation. The co-operative movement, inaugurated in Ireland in the later nineteenth century, had made headway only in relation to creameries, and even then only a small proportion of farmers belonged to such co-operatives. Moreover, the creamery movement came to lack vision, imagination and a taste for new ventures, and, more importantly, it had only a tenuous hold on its members' loyalty and little control over their activities. The organising body in Northern Ireland, the Ulster Agricultural Organisation Society (U.A.O.S.), formed in 1923 from among the Northern members of the parent Irish Agricultural Organisation Society, was, for example, unable to control the pricing policies pursued by the various creameries in the 1920s. There had been a good case for concerted action to maintain prices, and in 1926 forty-seven of the society's creameries set a price for the sale of butter; but by 1931 only twenty-three were still operating the schedules set by the voluntary ring.[27] As regards other agricultural produce, marketing was characterised by the existence of a long chain of dealers between the producer and the consumer. Northern Ireland had, for instance, more cattle dealers per head of cattle than either Britain or the Free State.[28]

The results were all too evident in the state of produce and its marketing in the early 1920s. There were, of course, centres of excellence, and some farmers were anxious to modernise. Moreover, much depended upon the accidents of geography and location. Whereas small farms of good land with accessibility to centres of dense population provided better incomes and were prosperous, those of poor land in remote areas often provided little more than a subsistence livelihood, the general standard of farming being higher in the best parts of Counties Down, Antrim and Londonderry. Nevertheless, efforts at improvement were likely to be jeopardised by the continuance of bad practices. Although cattle occupied pride of place in Northern Ireland agriculture, relatively few farmers paid much attention to good breeding.[29] Anxious to cut costs, and having little interest in the final product since cattle were produced for store and passed on elsewhere to be fattened and finished, many farmers were content to have their cows served by inferior bulls, the 'scrub bull', described in 1922 by Archdale, the Minister of Agriculture, as 'more like a goat than a bull'.[30] Not only did such carelessness give the Northern Ireland cattle a bad name, but the existence and freedom of inferior bulls jeopardised attempts at improvement by threatening the purity of neighbouring herds. The egg trade, too, was marred by the marketing of stale, ungraded and dirty eggs. The stale eggs might have been the result of a long marketing chain or their holding back by producers and dealers anticipating a rise in prices. The marketing of dirty eggs was, however, simply the result of bad and avoidable farm practices – dirty nests and dirty yards. 'I think the hen that would lay a dirty egg', Archdale told critics of egg marketing regulations in 1926, 'would be worthy of a medal'.[31]

Such deficiencies were all the more in need of remedy in view of increasing competition in Northern Ireland's main market, Britain, to which most of its agricultural surplus was exported. With the cutting off of foreign supplies during the First World War, Ireland's agricultural trade with Britain had boomed, and Irish producers, North and South, had abused their near monopoly by demanding high prices for inferior produce. They themselves paid the price after the war, when the import of foreign foodstuffs was resumed. It was not simply that increased competition forced down prices, but that consumers preferred to buy the well-packed, graded, high-quality goods sent from such countries as Denmark. The fall in the demand for Irish eggs was just one example of the fate that could befall Northern Ireland produce in the early 1920s. Between 1921 and 1923 the number of eggs exported from Northern Ireland fell by 212,000 great hundreds (a great hundred comprising 120 eggs), from 3,492,000 to 3,280,000, and even more significantly the wholesale price per great hundred fell from 24s 2d to 15s. From commanding top rates in the English market in 1921 Northern Ireland eggs had fallen to third or fourth place by 1923.[32] To survive, let alone prosper, agriculture in Northern Ireland needed to modernise both the methods of production and the marketing of produce.

Perhaps Northern Ireland's economic disadvantages as compared with the rest of the United Kingdom are best summed up in two calculations undertaken by Isles and Cuthbert: private civilian income per head, and the income and employment multipliers. The average income per head in Northern Ireland in the late 1930s was substantially lower than in the United Kingdom as a whole: £64.7 as against £111 in 1939, that is, 58.3 per cent.[33] The income and employment multipliers were also low in Northern Ireland. Since most of Northern Ireland's industries produced goods for export, Northern Ireland had to import its raw materials, capital equipment and consumer goods, and imports usually exceeded exports by some 4 per cent in the 1920s and 12½ per cent in the 1930s.[34] This excess reflected such a high marginal propensity to import that the multiplier effect of either government expenditure or industrial expansion was limited. Increased incomes resulted not in an increased demand for home-produced goods but in a demand for extra imports so that, as Isles and Cuthbert pointed out, 'The stimulus which their production offers to income (and employment) accrues outside the province and has no effect within; the stimulus to a growth of domestic income is lost just as effectively as if the money spent in importing the extra goods were saved'.[35] As Isles and Cuthbert further remarked, the lowness of the income and employment multipliers both summarised and stressed the salient features of Northern Ireland's economy: its position as the smallest region of a unified economy, its paucity of natural resources, its high costs of production, its dependence on a few manufacturing industries producing for export, and its reliance upon imports.[36] Such considerations both presented the regional government with problems and restricted its power to solve them.

2

The range of pressure and interest groups was more limited in Northern Ireland than in the rest of the United Kingdom. There was, as Professor Lawrence has observed, 'certainly no organised campaign' nor 'any sustained movement of public opinion' against 'poverty, unemployment, ill health, poor housing, inadequate roads, indifferent education' and 'the limitations imposed on the legislature'.[37] Nevertheless, within their different horizons Northern Irishmen did have such strongly held views that pressure groups were an integral part of the process of government. The tendency was encouraged by, and sometimes worked to the advantage of, the government, which liked to consult interested parties both to gain information and carry and educate opinion. Often, however, the agitation of pressure groups would simply prove irksome and embarrassing, providing only a further obstacle to government initiative and the development of regional policies.

Political parties did not contribute much to the process of government. Their function was to organise voters, and rarely did they act as channels of communication between the electors and the government. Only over the abolition of P.R. in local elections in 1922 was pressure from Unionist constituency associations general enough to prompt a government response. After this the party organisation was consulted only rarely by the government, for example, over schemes for parliamentary redistribution.[38] What was true of the Unionist Party was even more true of the other and less well-organised parties. At least part of the explanation for the relative unimportance of party organisations was the availability of other channels of communication, not only the partisan local authorities but also a wide range of religious and economic pressure groups and organisations.

In God-fearing and church-going Northern Ireland the most persistently vocal pressure groups were those interested in religious or quasi-religious and moral issues. Here Protestants clearly outstripped Catholics in respect of influence on government. The guardian of Catholic interests in Northern Ireland was the Catholic Church, but its hostility towards the state meant that the hierarchy never became involved in the process of government and a distinctly Catholic viewpoint emerged only on educational matters.[39] By contrast, groups purporting to defend the interests of Protestantism abounded and were ever anxious to enter into dialogues with ministers and officials. The heads of the three major Protestant denominations – Presbyterian, Church of Ireland and Methodist – had easy access to the government, yet the political influence of clergymen alone was limited. To influence the government they needed the backing of a significant section of the laity. Fear of the General Assembly of the Presbyterian Church could sometimes provoke a limited response from the government, as over housing policy in 1933,[40] but, as the various agitations against the 1923 Education Act showed, the support of the Orange Order was necessary to achieve a more wholehearted response.[41]

Originating in the rural tensions of North Armagh in the 1790s, the Orange Order soon became an integral part of the social and political life of Ulster.[42] By the twentieth century it was estimated that some two-thirds of adult male Protestants belonged to the Order, organised hierarchically into lodges on a district, county and provincial basis. Dedicated to maintaining the Protestant religion and the Protestant ascendancy, the Order had historically been identified with Unionism. Although Orangeism was not synonymous with Unionism, and although its importance to Unionism has sometimes been exaggerated, the Order did play a significant role in holding together the Unionist movement in the North. With its marches, its sashes and banners and its bands, particularly 'those thudding, evocative drums, it has provided the Ulster Unionist with much of the colour and drama of his creed. Each year the Twelfth of July is a gigantic exercise in catharsis which serves to give the kind of identity to what otherwise would be a variegated and much fragmented Protestantism.' Moreover, the Order acts as 'a link between different sections of society – small farmers, aristocratic landlords, linen magnates and shipyard workers – all can enter it on the same basis of equality. As a social emollient, therefore, no less than as a stimulus to patriotic emotions, the Orange Order has been essential to the structure of Unionism'.[43] Not surprisingly, therefore, Orangemen felt themselves to be a power in the land, confident that the government would respond to any of their demands. It was a confidence derived partly from a sense of mission in their historic role in the maintenance of Protestantism and Unionism, and partly from the support they were thought to be able to mobilise at elections and the demonstrations of opinion they knew they could organise each July.

The Orangemen's confidence was not misplaced. It was true that their self-esteem took a knock in 1932, when Craig publicly described the U.U.L.A. as 'the most wonderful organisation in Ulster',[44] but they need not have worried. Even on a matter of such fundamental importance to working men as unemployment, it was the Orange Order and not the U.U.L.A. that prompted the fullest and most respectful response from the government, which tried to justify its record.[45] The Order was, indeed, the pressure group the government feared most. Ministers were ever anxious to settle sensitive issues before the July demonstrations could subject them to denunciation from platforms throughout the province. This is not to suggest that the Order was constantly involved in politics. Its very structure prevented that, but there were two issues upon which the Order could be relied to take a stand in the inter-war years: the safeguarding of Protestantism in the educational system, and the supposed infiltration of Catholics and 'disloyal elements' not only into the civil service and the police but also into the province as a whole. The mere suggestion of Orange criticism on these issues was sufficient to provoke a response from the government to forestall agitation, if only by gestures of reassurance that the state and Protestantism were safe. In fact, ministers and leaders of the Order had a mutually profitable relationship. Leaders of the Order enjoyed being taken into ministers' confidence, and in return they could use their influence and the disciplinary procedures of the Order to protect the government. Thanking Spender for frankly explaining to him the true and limited role of Catholics in the civil service in December 1935, one leading Orangeman wrote: 'A section of our people . . . are prepared to swallow any falsehood. I have been fighting it behind the scenes for twelve months'.[46]

This not to say that the Order's influence was unlimited. On issues obviously involving Northern Ireland's image in, and relationship with, Britain, broader considerations of policy overrode fear of the Orangemen's wrath. Because he had the full support of Belfast Orangemen, one police officer, District Inspector J. W. Nixon of East Belfast, later the Independent Unionist M.P. for Woodvale, was able to organise an Orange lodge within the R.U.C. and rule the roost in his district. He showed, in the words of the Minister of Home Affairs, 'strong party feeling which is unbecoming in a police officer' and allowed to develop in his district the feeling that 'there is only one law and that for the Protestants, and in consequence the Protestant hooligan is allowed to interpret in his own fashion the laws of the country'.[47] However, in January 1924 he overstepped the mark by making a provocative speech on the border question, which was still under review, saying that Belfast loyalists would come to the aid of the border counties at any time. The case aroused widespread interest in Britain and concern among ministers and senior officials. Since it was impossible to secure witnesses to proceed against Nixon by court of inquiry, he was dismissed by an administrative order, despite threats by Orange lodges to campaign against the government at future elections for supposedly sacrificing Nixon to please Catholics.[48]

Obviously the success of any pressure group depended upon the issues involved and the nature of its support, and the government showed itself particularly sensitive to the nuances of opinion, as the temperance reformers discovered to their cost. The temperance reformers were the most persistent of the many single-minded guardians of morality in Northern Ireland. They liked to attribute all the world's evils to the demon drink. In so far as they had a united policy it was local option, but this demand only thinly disguised a strong preference for complete prohibition. Temperance reformers were well organised and vocal, they had the support of the temperance lodges of the the the Orange Order, and they represented 'a partial expression of the Calvinistic Puritanism which is characteristic of so much religion in Ulster'.[49] The temperance lobby could thus not be ignored by parliamentary candidates or by government ministers who came into office committed to a degree of temperance reform. However, that reform had to be strictly limited. Not only were publicans an interest group to be considered, but many Ulstermen were fond of a decent tipple. The 1923 Licensing Act was, accordingly, a moderate measure which pleased neither publicans nor ardent temperance reformers. It did, however, represent an adequate enough measure for most Ulstermen. On the one hand, the Ulster Reform Association, said to have been financed by the trade, quickly petered out. On the other hand, temperance reformers were convincingly defeated when they attempted to launch a concerted attack upon the government in the 1929 general election.

The 1929 general election provided a telling illustration of the conditions for the success or otherwise of a pressure group in Northern Ireland politics. At the time two groups of clergymen were agitating on two separate issues: education and temperance. The United Education Committee of the Protestant Churches of Northern Ireland, led by what the Minister of Education regarded as an unholy trinity of clerical troublemakers, wanted a further amendment of the 1923 Education Act to protect Protestant interests. The other group of clergymen demanded local option. The government gave way to the education agitators to prevent the matter from becoming a major election issue, but resisted the demands of the temperance reformers. Whereas the former had the backing of the entire Orange Order, the latter had the support of only part of the Order – the temperance lodges. Moreover, whereas the government could not effectively or safely discount the demand to safeguard Protestantism within the education system, it could with some confidence counter the views of the temperance lobby. Not only did many so-called local optionists reveal themselves in their true prohibitionist colours, but their campaign could be represented as an attack upon the state. Craig was quick to rebut such libels on Northern Ireland and its citizens as '17,000 drunkards in Ulster' and '20,000 children deprived of food and affection in Belfast'. Northern Ireland had, he countered, a temperance record second to none, and 'It is rather a scandal for certain persons to paint the character of Ulstermen as black as they do. I have not banged the door on negotiations, but I am not going to be dragooned'.[50] Craig's political instinct proved correct. Despite all the publicity and threats of splitting the Unionist vote to let Republicans in, local optionists contested only three seats and their low poll (9,776, or 25.5 per cent, of the 34,635 votes cast in the three constituencies) bore out Craig's contention that the movement had no real popular backing. Never again did temperance reformers mount such a determined and concerted attack upon the government. Although the movement remained active, the government was content to meet it by stating its own record on temperance.

Less spectacular but just as numerous were the economic interest and pressure groups reflecting the diverse elements of Northern Ireland's economic life. The small-scale nature of trade and industry was reflected in the proliferation of employers' organisations, representing not only different trades and industries but also different sections of particular trades and industries, as in linen, where all the different processes had their own separate associations. It was thus difficult to speak of an employer's viewpoint, but employers did share an almost unbounded faith in private enterprise, were concerned at the level of taxation and were often interested in tariff policy. Such general views as did exist could be expressed through the chambers of commerce and trade and through the Belfast Reform Club, the last being a convenient corner for putting ministers informally on the rack.[51] Employees, by contrast, were less thoroughly organised. In the inter-war years the level of unionisation in Northern Ireland was always lower than in the United Kingdom as a whole: in 1935 some 36 per cent of insured male workers belonged to trades unions, whereas the percentage for the whole kingdom was 41.[52] Moreover, a certain complicated divisiveness was caused by the fact that a couple of large unions had their headquarters in Dublin and were accordingly suspect. Nevertheless, certain key industries, such as shipbuilding and transport, were heavily unionised, and, with the threat of unemployment constantly looming, trades unionists did find it easy to agree upon certain basic policies, particularly in respect of the maintenance of social services, policies which could be expressed not only through individual unions but also through trades councils. Furthermore, the fact that most trades unionists belonged to unions with headquarters in Britain enhanced not only their status but also their expectations. British standards had to apply in Northern Ireland industry.[53]

On only one occasion did the government experiment in general participation in the formulation of industrial policy. In the hope of eliciting contributions towards the solution of Northern Ireland's economic problems, Andrews, as Minister of Labour, and the Lord Mayor of Belfast called together in June 1925 one of the most representative and influential conferences ever held in Belfast. Convened to inquire into the causes of unemployment and to suggest remedies, its personnel comprised some members of all parties in parliament and the Corporation, representatives of the chambers of commerce and trade and of the Belfast local employment committee and other public bodies, together with some of the most prominent employers and trades unionists in the shipbuilding, linen, engineering, building and transport industries. The conference in turn appointed a general purposes subcommittee and several specialist subcommittees to consider in detail the shipbuilding and engineering industries, the linen industry and the building trade. The reports of these subcommittees, which were adopted by the general conference, proved of some moral support to the government, but made little contribution to the development of an economic policy. They recognised that the causes of unemployment were almost wholly due to circumstances over which the government had no control, and their recommendations amounted to little more than an endorsement of the policies which different government departments had been pursuing or had declared their intention of pursuing.[54] Henceforth, despite much public and parliamentary pressure, the government eschewed the idea of general conferences, which it regarded as unnecessary. There was no need, Andrews wrote on one occasion, for special conferences of businessmen to enable them to put their views before the government, for 'We are always willing and ready to receive them, and, in point of fact, Northern Ireland being, comparatively speaking, such a small place, we are constantly meeting them in our daily pursuits both private and public'.[55]

This was all too true. From the start it was evident that the government intended to keep in close touch with the business community. Most ministers had business interests and subscribed to the view that the generation of wealth and prosperity depended almost solely upon the employers, to whom the government had a special if ill-defined duty. The only businessman whose advice the government was unwilling to consider was W. J. Stewart, whose plans for economic recovery in the 1930s included housing schemes and the construction of a tunnel

linking Northern Ireland with Scotland. At first the government tried
to outmanoeuvre him on housing, then buy him off under the loans
guarantee scheme, but finally Craig crushed him by calling a general
election in 1938 in which Stewart's Progressive Unionists were routed.[56]
In general, however, ministers and their departments were eminently
accessible. The Ministry of Commerce always intended to have an
office in the centre of Belfast within easy reach of busy entrepren-
eurs,[57] and at times the ministry must have seemed like a public thorough-
fare as it answered queries and tried to serve Northern Ireland's trade
and industry. Where lesser mortals were considered inadequate, the
Prime Minister was usually available to meet important and representative groups.[58]

The government as a whole was less enthusiastic about the other side
of industry – labour. Labour was recognised as important factor and
electoral fodder, and ministers did acknowledge a certain obligation to
cater for the interests of the working class. But they were less ready to
receive the views of working-class organisations than they were to listen
to employers. Of the various working-class organisations it was the
trades unions which became most closely associated with the process
of government. Craig may have welcomed in 1922 the support of the
U.U.L.A. as a 'very representative and important body' and described it
ten years later as 'the most wonderful organisation in Ulster', containing 'the cream of our working classes' and 'so many influential Trades
Union Leaders'.[59] Nevertheless, it was to the trades unions rather than
the U.U.L.A. that the Ministry of Labour turned for a true representation of working-class views. In this respect Andrews as Minister of Labour more than made up for his colleagues' lack of enthusiasm by consulting trades unionists on the work of his ministry and ensuring that
labour was adequately represented on important government committees. When the Ministry of Commerce suggested that two labour
representatives would suffice on a proposed commission to inquire into
Northern Ireland's natural resources, 'since it was capital alone and not
labour that contributes to development', Andrews insisted, eventually
successfully, upon increased trades union representation. What is more,
Andrews did not confine himself to consulting 'tame' trades unionists
from the U.U.L.A., but was happy to work with such 'socialists' as Sam
Kyle, a Protestant member and later Irish secretary of the Amalgamated Transport and General Workers' Union, and leader of the Labour
Party and of the Opposition in the Commons from 1925 to 1929. Kyle
was, Andrews reckoned, 'not a bad sort of fellow and . . . carries a lot
of weight with the independent labour party, the members of which are
far more numerous in Northern Ireland than is generally realised'.[60]

The agricultural community was far more vociferous than the industrial community. Since most farms relied on family labour, agricultural

labourers were in a minority among the rural population, and they were accordingly badly organised and had little sense of separate identity. Farmers were, however, very aware of their place in the natural order of things and were never slow to make their views known. Three matters were capable of arousing general interest – transit costs, rates and annuity payments – but otherwise Northern Ireland agriculture was distinguished by its diversity, either by product or by problems, such as drainage, disease or customs difficulties. Agriculture was a very local affair. Although the Ulster Farmers' Union (U.F.U.)[61] and the U.A.O.S. did operate on a broad provincial basis, there also existed various organisations to foster particular interests. There were associations of pig breeders, egg producers, etc.;[62] there were co-operative creameries with local allegiances;[63] and local branches of the U.F.U. often acted on behalf of particular local interests or would focus attention on particular grievances, especially complaints about Ministry of Agriculture regulations.[64]

Perhaps because of the deep conservatism of the agricultural community, 'the inertia and . . . active obstruction which met every proposal for better methods',[65] the government realised from its inception the necessity of involving farmers in the decision-making process. How necessary wide consultations were was underlined by the outcry against the Fruit Marketing Bill in 1930, which had to be postponed for a year while support was organised.[66] This was an experience Craig was anxious not to repeat,[67] and thus in the 1930s the Ministry of Agriculture was even more careful to consult all interests in the very early stages of any proposed change. For example, in March 1932 a meeting of representatives of the pig and bacon industries was arranged to discuss the opportunities created by the reorganisation of the industry in Britain. Representatives of the U.F.U., the Ulster Curers' Association, the U.A.O.S., the Royal Ulster Agricultural Society and the Fermanagh Pig Breeders' Association, along with the chairmen of the county committees of agriculture, were assured by Craig, not wholly accurately, that the government sought not compulsion but 'help from you as practical men'.[68]

The government was always sensitive to outside opinion and ever anxious to conciliate. Agitation was never ignored. The progress of any movement of discontent was anxiously watched by ministers and officials, who usually responded. Sometimes the response may have been merely a gesture to thwart criticism, as over housing policy in 1933.[69] Sometimes discontented but interested parties were given by ministers a full and confidential explanation of the reasons for government action or inaction, as over Workman, Clark & Co.'s complaint in December 1930 that it was not to be given the steel work for the new Londonderry bridge.[70] Usually, too, the government was circumspect in its response to demands relating to reserved services or Westminster legislation applicable to Northern Ireland. Ever anxious not to offend imperial politicians and officials, the government never supported uncritically the demands of any pressure group. Instead, ministers and officials tried either to head off agitation, as over the question of land-purchase annuites in the 1930s,[71] or to ensure that demands were presented in a manner most likely to win support at Westminster, as over amendments to the Wheat Quota Bill in 1932.[72] How important it was to ensure that Ulstermen presented their case with due care was underlined in February 1925 by the short shrift the Conservative Home Secretary, Sir William Joynson-Hicks, gave to a deputation of tenant farmers critical of the imperial bill to complete land purchase in the North. Hardly had the farmers opened their case when, in the words of Dixon, the Chief Whip, who had set up the meeting, Joynson-Hicks 'suddenly fell on them and simply tore them', saying that 'Englishmen, including himself, were tired of paying money to Irishmen and if they did not like the Bill the best thing they could do, would be to get out of the room, as he was busy!'[73]

More often than not, however, where a demand was clearly articulated by a more or less representative group, and where it was constitutionally within its power to do so, the government generally liked to satisfy that demand. Only very rarely did it resist such a demand, and this was usually in respect of agriculture, for the Ministry of Agriculture proved more tough-minded than other departments. Its perseverance with much-criticised marketing schemes, despite the reservations of other ministers, underlined the fact that accessibility in a small society was a two-way process, since ministry officials were well aware of their critics' limitations.[74] This relative resoluteness on agricultural marketing was, however, notable for being the exception rather than the rule.

The rule was to oblige, and this rule created difficulties when equally clear but opposed views were expressed by interested parties. Usually the government managed to see both sides of the question and tried to arrange a compromise, as in the dispute between milk producers and sellers over prices in November 1931. To end a damaging milk strike Craig prolonged a meeting of representatives from the U.F.U., the Belfast Co-operative Society and the Belfast Retail Dairymen's Association until an agreement was reached.[75] When, however, opposing parties proved intransigent, the government was in a quandry. On occasion, as in 1938 with the extension to Northern Ireland of recent British factory legislation, the government did decide to favour one side rather than another. The linen employers strongly opposed any further restriction on the hours of work of women and young people, which, they argued, would render the industry still less competitive, but the trades unions and some M.P.s were equally strenuously opposed to any watering-down of the British legislation.[76] The government's decision to ignore the employers' representations showed a great deal of political realism. Indeed, on most matters affecting major social security benefits and factory legislation, the government considered it wise to follow British practice, despite the laments of employers about the burden of taxation and factory legislation. Often, however, the balance of political and other advantages was not so obvious, and in these circumstances the government shrank from taking the initiative and preferred instead to let the disputed matters drift, as over the question of market tolls in the 1930s, when market authorities and farmers could not reach agreement,[77] and over the question of the co-ordination of road and rail transport in 1939–40, when the demands of farmers and the railway companies proved incompatible.[78]

Devolved government in Northern Ireland was in leed responsive and accessible government, but it is another matter as to whether responsiveness and accessibility were in the long-term interests of the province. The existence and volubility of so many pressure groups, and the government's willingness to be guided by them, presented yet another obstacle to government initiative and the formulation of other than short-term policies. The regional government either subordinated its views to those of a pressure group, as over education[79] and agricultural rating relief,[80] or, as over the rationalisation of the linen industry,[81] waited upon events.

3

The activities of the Southern Irish state and some of its subjects were yet another factor conditioning politics and policies in Northern Ireland. While a working relationship was eventually established between the two governments, even to the extent of allowing Southern officials to inspect Southern eggs passing through the port of Belfast on their way to Britain,[82] there was always a sense of competition between them, and the majority of Northerners entertained a less than cordial dislike for the South. Two issues in particular served to complicate the process of government in the North: Southern attitudes to partition, and Southern economic policy.

The border question went through three phases in the inter-war years.[83] In the years 1921–25 it was possible to regard the existence of Northern Ireland as still open to question. This feeling of insecurity was worst in 1922, with the threat of the Boundary Commission, border raids and conflict in Belfast, activities connived at by certain leading Free State politicians. By June 1922 Michael Collins may have been disclaiming any intention of forcing the North into a union, but the facts remained that, engaged in a civil war with Eamon de Valera and the Republicans, he was not in full control of the South, and that he was anyway committed to unification as 'our final goal'.[84] The years 1925–31 were a period of relative quiescence, with the border agreement of December 1925, W. T. Cosgrave's peaceful government and de Valera's acceptance in 1927 of the role of constitutional Opposition. The third period, from 1932 onwards, was fraught with tension. Dissatisfaction in the South with Cosgrave's government had shown itself violently in clashes between rival armed gangs, including the Irish Republican Army (I.R.A.), and constitutionally in de Valera's advent to power. After a general election in February 1932 he and his Fianna Fáil party were able to form a minority government, but a snap election held the following January gave him a small overall majority. This latter victory may well have 'made for a central stability in [Southern] Irish political life',[85] but by confirming de Valera's personal ascendancy it created problems elsewhere.

De Valera was a devout Catholic and was committed, at least in theory, to Republicanism and a united Ireland. He vaunted the Catholicism of the South, moved towards a Republican constitution, indulged in anti-partition rhetoric and tried to wring concessions from the imperial government. His intentions were clear from the moment of his return to power. It was, perhaps, unfortunate for Northern politics that this return was shortly followed by the holding in Dublin of the Eucharistic Congress, a spectacular demonstration of Catholic devotion and power held in a different country every four years, and that during the accompanying celebrations de Valera chose to insult the Governor-General, the Crown's representative in the Free State, by acting as ceremonial as well as actual head of state.[86] Catholic and Republican Ireland did indeed seem to be on the march. De Valera succeeded in persuading the imperial government to abandon the Treaty ports and won financial and economic concessions in the Anglo-Éire agreements of April 1938,[87] while in the previous December a new constitution had come into operation in what was thenceforth called Éire. Among other things, the new constitution proclaimed the Catholicism of the South by recognising the 'special position' of Catholic Church and giving legal force to its teaching on such matters as the family, most obviously by the prohibition of divorce. It also formally claimed Northern Ireland as an integral part of Éire, asserting that the national territory consisted of the whole island of Ireland, its islands and its territorial seas, although the *de facto* position of Northern Ireland was also acknowledged.[88]

De Valera's actions and rhetoric were accompanied by, and may have encouraged, a revival of I.R.A. hopes and activities. However, the strong measures he eventually took against terrorist groups soon isolated the I.R.A. in the South, but this very isolation simply turned I.R.A. eyes towards the North and Britain.[89] A raid on the Armagh army barracks, planned for the summer of 1937, had to be cancelled at the last moment owing to leaks of information, and in November 1938 the I.R.A.'s attack on imperial customs houses did as much harm to its members as to the border posts. Nevertheless, the thought behind the attacks rather than their efficiency caused alarm among Ulster Unionists, whose fears were further heightened in January 1939 when, after its demand for the complete withdrawal of British troops and officials from all parts of Ireland had been ignored, the I.R.A. launched a bombing campaign in Britain. The I.R.A. had not, of course, the blessing of de Valera's government, but Ulster Unionists held the Southern government at least morally responsible for I.R.A. activities. Many of the recent statements of de Valera and his colleagues had, Andrews as acting Prime Minister told Neville Chamberlain, then imperial premier, 'encouraged the members of the I.R.A. to believe that now that they have got rid of Britain in Éire all they have to do is to fight on and they will get Ulster'.[90]

Assertions of Southern claims to Northern Ireland had serious repercussions on the nature of government and politics there. They helped to polarise feelings and fossilise attitudes.

The majority of Northern Irishmen had no intention of joining in a united Ireland ruled from Dublin. Ulster Unionists had always been wary of the South and of Irish nationalists. Indeed, one of their reasons for opposing Home Rule had been apprehension of the future of Ireland and themselves in particular under Home Rule. The Anglo-Irish war had turned these fears into hatred. Henceforth Ulster Unionists wanted no contact whatsoever with the South. On 5 May 1921 Craig had a clandestine and fruitless meeting in Dublin with de Valera, and on his return to Belfast, where news of the meeting had leaked out, he and his wife were, as Lady Craig put it, 'met by various palefaced, nervy, agitated people, all thinking he had made a fearful mistake'.[91] Loyal wife that she was, she 'let fly' at those who doubted her husband's integrity, but suspicion of the South and its politicians prevented Craig making any more direct contact with Southern leaders until after the Treaty of December 1921. When he did resume direct negotiations, his supporters and colleagues were less than enthusiastic, as the cool reception given to the Craig–Collins peace pact of 30 March showed.[92] The civil war in the South enhanced this dislike and distrust. Although it was true that with the boundary settlement of December 1925 feelings did die down, suspicions remained and there was a feeling that Cosgrave's moderate government in the South was simply sapping away the foundations of the settlements of the early 1920s. In fact, there was almost a feeling of relief when de Valera's return to power once more clarified issues. 'In short, as I see it,' Londonderry, then an imperial cabinet minister, wrote to Craig on 2 February 1933, we are now faced by the more or less open opposition of a De Valera government instead of the somewhat doubtful friendship of a Cosgrave government, whose very existence and good will would probably depend entirely upon the concessions they could get from us.[93]

This viewpoint, shared by many Ulster Unionists, reflected the widely held opinion that there was no such thing as a reliable nationalist. The only change Ulster Unionists would contemplate was the fiscal reunion of the British Isles, something, Pollock thought, 'in the nature of a Customs Union, by which all tariffs between the two countries [the United Kingdom and the Free State] would be removed'.[94]

Consequently, Southern claims and action against the North were largely responsible for the siege mentality that is often said to have characterised Ulster Unionism. Ulster Unionists were often in fear of being swallowed up by the South and often doubtful whether imperial governments and British opinion would withstand Southern agitation. After the Treaty settlement it was unlikely that any imperial government would put undue pressure upon Northern Ireland to join with the South, although it would not stand in the way of unification. As soon as the new Éire constitution came into force on 29 December 1937 the imperial government issued a statement taking note of the new constitution but, at Craig's suggestion, firmly repudiating Southern claims over the North.[95] Such reassurances were not sufficient for Ulster Unionists or their government, which constantly sought for more emphatic declarations of solidarity, especially with the onset of the bombing campaign. It would be 'most helpful' in allaying public anxiety and preserving peace in Northern Ireland, Andrews told Chamberlain at the beginning of the campaign, if the imperial government would make 'some definite public statement' to the effect that it 'fully recognises Northern Ireland's constitutional right to remain part of the United Kingdom, and will, should occasion arise, give us any necessary assistance'.[96]

This siege mentality expressed itself most clearly in attitudes towards the administration of law and order. A sense of the need to defend the state from attack not only caused the government to maintain a large and armed regular police force, the R.U.C., backed by an armed reserve, the controversial Ulster Special Constabulary; it also encouraged the government to retain the equally controversial Special Powers Act. Anti-partition activities in the South were closely watched in the North, and events in the South largely governed security policy in Northern Ireland.[97] It is difficult to assess the justice and efficacy of Northern Ireland security policy. It certainly did help to alienate the minority, but, on the other hand, the existence of the Special Constabulary was regarded as essential reassurance to loyalists in the border areas, inclined to panic and take the law into their own hands.[98] Moreover, the existence of the Special Powers Act did enable the police to respond swiftly to curb terrorist activity, as in 1938, when internment was used to disorganise the Belfast brigade and Northern divisions of the I.R.A. and secure hostages against the good behaviour of nationalists generally.[99]

The administration of law and order may have been a divisive issue, but it was at least defensible. Less defensible, although understandable in purely party terms, was the rhetoric used by ministers in response to events in the South, particularly after de Valera's return to power. Ministers sought to calm the consequent apprehensions aroused among Protestants and Unionists in the North by asserting, especially in 1933 and 1934, the Organeism and Protestantism of the North. Such rhetoric was a response to a particular situation and to de Valera's Catholic rhetoric and should not necessarily be regarded as evidence that the government as a whole regarded Catholics and nationalists as second-class citizens. Replying to one Nationalist critic of the use of the epithet 'Protestant' to describe the Northern parliament, Craig argued:

> The hon. Member must remember that in the South they boasted of a Catholic State. They still boast of Southern Ireland being a Catholic State. All I boast of is that we are a Protestant Parliament and a Protestant State.[100]

Nevertheless, such speeches, or rather selected parts of them, became notorious, giving Northern Ireland's opponents a powerful propaganda weapon and serving to discredit the government in the eyes of the Northern minority.[101] Furthermore, the operation of the new Éire constitution helped to limit the field of political debate among Unionists by giving Craig an opportunity to undermine growing discontent with his government's policies on housing and unemployment. By calling a general election in February 1938 on the border issue, he was able to increase his majority and rout the Progressive Unionists, the 'wreckers', as he called them, who vainly pleaded that their plans for economic and social advance were compatible with the maintenance of the constitutional status quo.[102]

The passivity or otherwise of Southern claims over the North not only affected Ulster Unionists and government policy; it also affected, both directly and indirectly, the attitude of Northern nationalists to Northern Ireland. The effects were, in part, indirect since nationalist attitudes were in some degree determined by Unionist attitudes, but the effects were also direct because the minority was reminded that it was part of a larger nationalist community. It is likely that Collins's insistence in 1922 on supervising the government of Northern Ireland and representing nationalists there did much to intimidate and deter those nationalists and Catholics who wanted to collaborate with the new government,[103] while it is beyond dispute that the prolonged controversy over the Boundary Commission kept alive nationalist hopes that Northern Ireland would collapse, so that most nationalists boycotted the Northern government and parliament.[104] It is significant that after the border agreement most nationalist M.P.s took their seats in the Northern parliament. It is equally significant that with de Valera's return in February 1932 they soon withdrew from parliament and concentrated once again upon the question of partition.[105] John Henry Collins, the Nationalist M.P. for South Down, once a regular contributor to parliamentary debates, withdrew with the rest of his colleagues in May 1932, and by January 1933 he was making election speeches in the South on behalf of Fianna Fáil and looking, as he said, 'for guidance to the great leader of the Irish people, Eamon De Valera'.[106]

Economic matters were the second source of complication. Free State economic policy and development often threw the limited powers of the government of Northern Ireland into sharp and unflattering contrast.[107] The Free State did attempt to develop itself economically by taking advantage of all the powers it possessed as a dominion, particularly in respect of tariff policy. Unlike Northern Ireland, the Free State had been given control over customs, and in April 1924 a policy of selective protection was inaugurated, at first tentatively but gathering momentum annually. The advent to power of de Valera's government, however, wrought a dramatic change in customs policy. Fianna Fáil's preference for more thoroughgoing protection was strengthened by the outbreak of an economic war with the United Kingdom.[108]

De Valera insisted on retaining in the Free State the money due to the imperial government from Southern tenant purchasers in respect of holdings purchased under the imperial Land Acts. Since this financial question was linked with a constitutional question – the oath of allegiance to the Crown taken by members of the Free State parliament – it provoked a sharp reaction from the imperial government, which accused de Valera of violating the Anglo-Irish Treaty. Twenty per cent *ad valorem* duties, known as the special duties, were imposed in July 1932 on Free State agricultural produce entering the United Kingdom with the object of recovering the money withheld by the Free State. Even more severe counter-measures were taken by Dublin against United Kingdom exports. The list of high and often prohibitive duties was so extended by this retaliation and the general tariff policy pursued by de Valera's government that within a few months the Free State had become one of the most heavily protected countries in the world.

Not only were imports controlled, but financial incentives were also offered to home producers. Cheap-money facilities for industry and agriculture had their parallels in the North, but the Free State system of subsidies and bounties, particularly for agriculture, was more comprehensive than anything in the United Kingdom. To outsiders, at any rate, there could be no more profitable life than to farm in a country where a creamery could receive for each hundredweight of butter government aid by way of a 31s subsidy and a 51s 6d export bounty.

The economic policy of the Free State had obvious implications for Northern Ireland. Most obviously, the imposition of customs and package duties,* and of a minimum duty on each consignment of dutiable goods, meant that certain sections of Northern Ireland traders and manufacturers found themselves outpriced in and often excluded from their former markets in the South. Thus by 1926 Northern Ireland biscuits were rendered uncompetitive by the combination of the 6d package duty and a customs duty of 3d per pound.[109] Nor did Free State economic policy just simply involve the loss of the Southern market. It also meant increased competition within the Northern Ireland market. Not only were Free State manufacturers able to dump their products in the North, but British firms, finding their products excluded from the Free State market, began to concentrate upon the Northern Ireland market, 'undercutting prices' and 'utilising ingenious advertising schemes'.[110]

The more generous the Free State incentives and the more comprehensive and prohibitive its tariffs, the wider became the aggrieved area of Northern Ireland trade. By 1933 the agricultural community was seriously concerned about the dumping of Irish butter in the United Kingdom. Other dominions were also dumping butter, but Northern Ireland agricultural opinion focused upon the effects of Free State exports, which were selling for 70s per cwt and helping to force down the price of Northern Ireland butter from 90s to 72s.[111] Millers were also affected. Since the spring of 1926, when a duty of £2 10s per ton had been imposed upon oatmeal entering the Free State, Northern Ireland millers had been complaining about falling trade with the Free State, and their complaints were increased by further changes in 1932 and 1933. In September 1932 a duty of £6 per ton – equivalent to 100 per cent *ad valorem* – was imposed on wheat offals, while an act of 1933 withdrew the duty but prohibited the import of wheat offals except under licence – the licences evidently being issued only to Free State millers. Not surprisingly, the wheat offal trade collapsed.[112] Just how wide an area of Northern Ireland trade and industry was affected by Free State economic policy, and how greatly that policy cut back Northern Ireland imports, was underlined by figures prepared in 1938 by the Ministries of Agriculture and Commerce, when urging the imperial government to secure free trade with Éire. Trade across the land boundary from

---

*What was colloquially called the 'package duty' was a customs entry duty of 6d on all classes of goods, irrespective of quantity and whether of a dutiable class or not.

Northern Ireland to the Free State, valued at £7.4m in 1924, had fallen to £5.4m by 1929, and to £1.6m in 1936.*[113] Such figures cannot, of course, as Dr David Johnson has rightly pointed out,[114] be taken as precise indicators of the effects of partition and Free State policy upon trade between the North and South and upon the Northern economy. Nevertheless, they did provide a rough guide for contemporaries and constituted a source of grievance among Ulster Unionists.

Southern economic policy thus produced both economic and political problems in Northern Ireland. Profits were reduced, and it was said by the middle of 1933 that the dairying industry was on the verge of collapse owing to falling prices.[115] Employment opportunities were reduced. Employment in biscuit manufacturing fell so that by the spring of 1926 two Londonderry factories were working only at one-third capacity, employing 83 instead of 250 hands, and a Belfast firm, which before protection had employed 700 hands, was employing only 300.[116] On the whole, whatever the efficacy of its policies, the Free State was able to create the impression of vitality. According to disgruntled Northern Ireland millers, Free State action on behalf of its millers had produced a flourishing milling industry. By 1933 the milling capacity of the Free State industry was said to have been about 300 sacks per hour compared with 100 in Northern Ireland, and Southern millers were able to export their surplus cheaply to the North.[117] Not surprisingly, some firms threatened to transfer their businesses to the

---

*The first and last items of each of the five pages on one schedule showing, among other things, the value of United Kingdom exports to the Free State across the land boundaries in the years 1924, 1929 and 1936 and the restrictions imposed by the Free State were as follows:

Product	Value in £s of exports from U.K. to I.F.S. across land boundary			Restriction or duty imposed by I.F.S. government
	1924	1929	1936	
Biscuits	100,812	15,114	–	Import only under licence
Linen handkerchiefs	30,583	50,296	10,626	60% *ad val.*
Damask table linen	13,330	15,909	3,758	40% *ad val.*
Shirts and collars	210,734	41,872	2,697	40% *ad val.*
Hosiery	201,595	111,591	12,172	40% *ad val.* (generally)
Paper bags	14,981	14,361	248	$33\frac{1}{3}$% *ad val.*
Cardboard boxes	3,282	5,674	7,222	$33\frac{1}{3}$% *ad val.*
Wire and wire mfrs	17,741	15,372	967	$10-33\frac{1}{3}$% *ad val.*
Maize products	692,287	473,299	5	Import only under licence
Oilseed cake and meal	82,063	76,019	4,711	Import only under licence

(5 Mar. 1938, P.R.O.N.I., CAB 9R/60/2)

Free State, a transfer which would not only increase unemployment in the North but also highlight the advantages of the Free State. The consequences of Free State economic policy upon the milling and baking trades of Londonderry would, according to the Unionist Mayor of the city in March 1926, 'have the effect on others, which the Free State have always been aiming at, of making loyalists feel "What is the use of staying under a Government that either don't care a d--n for our interests, or at any rate can't protect them".'[118]

In fact, the government did not need reminding of the danger that the Free State might appear a more attractive proposition than the North. This is why Andrews was particularly anxious when in the 1930s the question arose of the Free State's payment of the land-purchase annuities. He was concerned lest concessions made by the imperial government would enable the Free State to sustain a lower rate of income tax yet develop its social services, thus beguiling the younger generation in Northern Ireland. As he told Craig in June 1932,

> If the Free State, in addition to being relieved from any [imperial] contribution, is relieved to some extent of their existing financial liabilities it will simply mean that they will be able to continue to have a lower Income Tax than in the United Kingdom, and, further, they will be able to improve their social services, probably in some respects better than ours. A Bill has already obtained a second reading and is, I am informed, sure to become law to reduce the age for blind persons' pensions from 50 years to 35 years, and also to make much easier the conditions for the receipt of old age pensions.
>
> If the Free State were enabled to continue this policy into other services, it will ultimately have a very unsettling effect upon some of our people. We can absolutely trust, as you know, the older members of our community, but among the younger ones is where a danger lies.[119]

Yet, alive though it was to such problems, the government was powerless to take effective action. It had, as the Permanent Secretary of the Ministry of Commerce, W. D. Scott, pointed out, 'no counter argument in the shape of retaliatory measures to advance as an inducement in persuading the sister State to adopt a more friendly tariff'.[120] Nor could it reserve even the Northern Ireland market, let alone the United Kingdom market, for Northern Ireland and British producers to compensate for their exclusion from the Southern market. Such matters were the preserve of Westminster. As Scott resignedly commented on the complaints of Londonderry millers,

> The position therefore reduces itself to this, that we must accept the fact that the Free State can, by imposing a duty on such articles as oatmeal, derive from their action the same advantages in their own

market as are enjoyed by other protective countries. Not only so, but . . . the protection of the home market will in certain cases . . . . enable the Free State manufacturers to dump goods in Northern Ireland at a price with which local manufacturers find difficulty in competing. Unpleasant as it may be to have to make such an admission, there is no disguising the fact that unless we can persuade the Imperial Authorities to adopt a system of retaliation or make use of other methods of inducing the Free State to adopt a policy less inimical to our commercial interests, both of which methods are matters of major policy, there is no way in which we can satisfactorily meet the complaint of the Londonderry millers.[121]

In the 1920s it was felt futile to try to persuade free-trade imperial governments to adopt retaliatory measures against the Free State, but with the change in imperial fiscal policy late in 1931 and the onset of the economic war, the government of Northern Ireland was constantly asking for special measures against Free State imports into the United Kingdom. Sometimes, as over pig quotas, the requests were granted, but not when, as over butter in 1933 and the Anglo-Éire trade agreement in 1938, Northern Ireland and imperial interests were in conflict.[122] A second line of approach was to seek from the imperial government financial and other compensation to offset the effects of Southern economic policy and any financial concessions made to the South. This was the line eventually adopted in the discussion leading up to the Anglo-Éire settlement of April 1938, which ended the economic war. Having failed to persuade the imperial government to agree only to trading terms favourable to Northern Ireland, Craig said that he could accept the settlement only if the North received, to quote one Treasury official, 'as large a financial bribe as possible'.[123]

Free State economic policy, then, did have a significant effect upon the operations of government in Northern Ireland. Unable to negotiate directly with the Free State and even attempt to arrange a satisfactory commercial agreement, and anxious to avoid the impression of impotence, the government of Northern Ireland was forced to find other ways of advancing Northern Ireland's interests, satisfying its supporters and maintaining its own prestige. Some measures by pandering to the whims of local Unionists, as in the gerrymandering of Londonderry city, served to reinforce sectarian divisions. Other measures, such as the handing out of doles, combined with a reliance upon British goodwill and financial concessions to hinder the development of overall and long-term policies suited to the needs of the province. The partition question had similar effects, so that, taken together, Southern attitudes to partition and Southern economic policy made even more unlikely the success of the devolution experiment in Northern Ireland.

Part Two

4

Impotence (1): Finance

The distribution of financial power and responsibility between Northern Ireland and Britain and within Northern Ireland hardly made for prompt and effective government. The history of financial policy in the inter-war years was not a story of a search for a policy and structure suited to Northern Ireland's needs, but instead a story of repeated wranglings over who should finance what, during which the regional government found itself under contradictory pressures from the imperial Treasury and its own local authorities. The outlines of this story have been tellingly revealed by Professor R. J. Lawrence in his book, based on printed materials, *The Government of Northern Ireland: Public Finance and Public Services, 1921–1964.* However, it has taken the recently opened Northern Ireland archives to bring home just how the delibitating financial provisions of the 1920 settlement reduced the government of Northern Ireland to impotence.

1

The most obvious limitation on the regional government was its lack of control over revenue.[1] Its revenue was derived from three main sources: transferred revenue, special payments by the imperial Treasury, and reserved revenue. Transferred revenue, that controlled by the Northern Ireland parliament, usually represented at most some 20 per cent of total revenue. It was derived mainly from such minor taxes as death and motor vehicle duties, the two most profitable;* but there were also some useful non-tax sources, particularly land-purchase annuities – a free gift from the imperial government.† Special payments from the imperial Treasury were always variable, so that the bulk of Northern

---

*The other transferred taxes were stamp duties, entertainment duties, certain excise licence duties (other than those on certain manufactures, such as wines, spirits, tobacco, sugar and matches, where the duty varied with the production of the goods) and mineral rights duties.

†Other non-tax transferred income was derived from interests and dividends, church temporalities, fees and casual receipts.

Ireland's income, some 70–80 per cent, was derived from reserved revenue. Reserved non-tax revenue, mainly from the Post Office, was insignificant compared with the revenue derived from reserved taxes: customs and excise duties (other than transferred excise licence duties), income tax and surtax, excess profits duty, and corporations profits tax.

The level and nature of these reserved taxes was determined not by the needs or taxable capacity of Northern Ireland but by those of the United Kingdom and Empire as a whole and Britain in particular. Northern Ireland's Minister of Finance was not consulted beforehand by the imperial Chancellor of the Exchequer about his budget, and at the beginning of each financial year the Ministry of Finance anxiously awaited the imperial budget so that Northern Ireland's share of reserved revenue for that year could be provisionally determined by the Joint Exchequer Board, which was composed of a chairman appointed by the Crown and one member from each of the imperial Treasury and the Northern Ireland Ministry of Finance. Although estimates of expenditure for any financial year were prepared during the second half of the preceding year, realistic estimates of likely revenue were not available until after the Chancellor had announced any tax changes in his budget, and the calculations were made not by the Ministry of Finance but by imperial revenue departments, which persistently underestimated Northern Ireland's share of reserved taxation. The completion of the Northern Ireland budget was thus often a last-minute and very hurried affair.

This sense of uncertainty might have been more tolerable had the financial provisions of the 1920 act guaranteed Northern Ireland sufficient revenue. This was not, however, the case. The imperial government responsible for the act, Lloyd George's coalition, had affected to believe that Northern Ireland's revenue would be sufficient to allow it a surplus of £2.5m annually to develop its services over and above the existing levels. This optimistic view had been based upon estimates in a white paper published in May 1920.[2] According to these estimates, in the financial year 1920–21 Northern Ireland would receive a total of £16.5m. Of this £16.5m, it was estimated that a total of £6.3m would be spent on transferred and reserved services, leaving £10.2m for a contribution towards imperial services and a surplus for development. The advisory committee appointed by the U.U.C. to discuss financial provisions with the imperial government had thought these figures unrealistic and based on an untypical year,[3] but Ulster Unionists had eventually become reconciled to the imperial government's proposals because of public and private assurances that the new Irish parliaments would be treated not only with justice but also with generosity. The financial provisions of the bill had been 'settled in no niggling spirit', the minister in charge of the measure had told the Commons at Westminster on 22 October 1920. 'They are generous, and sufficient to enable the two Parliaments to enter upon their duties without fear that their efforts will be stultified by want of money'.[4] This optimism was misplaced. In 1922–23 Northern Ireland's revenue was almost £3m below the white paper estimate, and always remained well below it until 1938–39.[5] The explanation was simple – a dramatic fall in revenue from reserved taxation.

In the late 1930s Northern Ireland benefited from increased imperial taxation imposed to finance the rearmaments drive, but in the 1920s the tendency was to reduce the high level of war taxation. Tax cuts were announced in successive budgets. Some taxes were abolished altogether: excess profits duty in 1921 and corporation tax in 1924, although revenue from outstanding claims continued to trickle in into the 1930s. Other taxes, particularly those on tea, sugar, beer and income were lowered.[6] Moreover, the yield of taxation was lower in Northern Ireland than in Britain, largely because Northern Ireland was more severely affected by industrial depression and unemployment than Britain taken as a whole.[7] Had reserved taxation been distributed on a population basis, this difference would have been ironed out; but this was not the procedure envisaged by the 1920 act.[8] Northern Ireland's share of reserved taxation depended upon the amount of revenue generated there. Revenue from income taxes was attributed according to the area in which the recipient of the income resided, while revenue from customs and excise duties was attributed to Northern Ireland on the basis of the consumption of dutiable goods there. In Great Britain the falling tax returns of the depressed areas were to some extent offset by the increased revenue derived from the more prosperous midlands and south-east. No such compensation was to be found in Northern Ireland, whose revenue difficulties were still further increased by changing social habits, particularly the decline in the consumption of spirits. The yield of taxation per head was therefore significantly lower in Northern Ireland than in the rest of the United Kingdom, as, for example, in 1929–30:[9]

	Northern Ireland	Great Britain
Customs and excise	£3 4s	£5 4s
Income tax	£2 3s	£5 6s
Surtax	6s	£1 5s

A combination of depression, changing social habits and, above all, cuts in the rates of taxation reduced Northern Ireland's revenue from reserved taxation by 29 per cent between 1922–23 and 1930–31, from £11m to £7.5m, both figures being well below the white paper estimate of £14.7m.[10]

Not only did the government and parliament lack control over Northern Ireland's inadequate revenue; they also lacked effective control over expenditure. In theory, the latter should not have been the case. Northern Ireland's parliament did have formal control over most of its expenditure, which fell under four main heads: the consolidated fund services, the supply services, reserved services, and the imperial contribution.[11] Expenditure under the last two heads was beyond Northern Ireland's control. That on the reserved services was authorised by the imperial parliament, and the cost chargeable to Northern Ireland was certified annually by the Joint Exchequer Board. The Joint Exchequer Board also determined, at least in theory, the amount Northern Ireland should contribute towards the cost of excepted or imperial services as defined in the 1920 act. Expenditure on reserved services usually represented between 15 and 17 per cent of total expenditure, but the percentage represented by the imperial contribution fell rapidly in the 1920s – from almost 50 in 1922–23 to almost 5 by the end of the decade, when it became merely nominal. Expenditure on transferred services therefore came to constitute the bulk (between 70 and 80 per cent) of Northern Ireland's total expenditure. Expenditure on consolidated fund services, consisting principally of certain permanent charges on the treasury,* usually comprised only some 10 per cent of the total. Thus Northern Ireland's main expenditure was on the supply services.† Expenditure on these services was authorised annually by parliament on the basis of estimates prepared towards the end of each calendar year by the different administrative departments and subsequently approved by the Ministry of Finance.

The reality was somewhat different. Control over expenditure was limited, and the regional government and parliament could not make decisions independently. In the first place, the pace of government

---

*The original charges were: the Road Fund; sinking funds to perpetuate terminable revenues received from land-purchase annuities and church temporalities and to provide for interest accruing on Ulster Saving Certificates; reserve funds in respect of capital liabilities; interest on saving certificates and temporary borrowing; the salaries of the Speakers of the Houses of Parliament and the Comptroller and Auditor-General; and the expenses of returning officers at elections to the Northern Ireland parliament. To these original permanent charges were later added issues relating to a special rating relief suspense account, housing requirements under the Irish Soldiers' and Sailors' Land Trust, and the Loans Guarantee Acts.

†It was the practice in Northern Ireland to present for public consumption supply expenditure under four heads: administrative departments; social services, listed as pensions, state insurance, education, agriculture, grants to local authorities, and unemployment relief grants; justice and police; and other services, such as parliament, surveys and public works, fisheries, harbours and railways.

spending was set by the imperial government, whose example the Northern government felt obliged to follow. The step-by-step policy had originally applied to the major cash social services under the control of the Ministry of Labour, but it quickly came to mean that Northern Ireland should not lag behind Britain in granting financial boons to its citizens. Such a policy imposed considerable strains, as was all too evident in the case of unemployment insurance. Northern Ireland's unemployment insurance scheme, which had been separated from the British scheme in 1921 as part of the devolution of responsibility, remained identical with Britain's, benefits in both countries being paid at the same rates from separate Unemployment Funds financed by employers, employees and the respective treasuries. Yet Northern Ireland was able to keep up with Britain only by building up a massive debt. By 1925, when 24 per cent of its insured population were out of work compared with 11 per cent in Britain, the deficit on the Northern Ireland Unemployment Fund was £3.6m, which was an enormous sum for an area whose domestic budget was then less than £6m.[12] It was the same with what Pollock, the Minister of Finance, called the 'ghastly mistake' of derating.[13] The decision to follow Britain in derating all agricultural land in 1929 overnight turned the government into the largest ratepayer in the country![14]

The regional authority's control over expenditure was further compromised by the structure of government and the nature of Northern Ireland politics and society. The cost of maintaining law and order proved unexpectedly high in the early years.[15] Many services were financed by grants-in-aid to local authorities or voluntary bodies, the initiative resting with the recipients. The appropriate ministry could withhold approval of schemes and urge delay if economies were desired, or it could offer exhortations if action was needed, but the government was invariably in the position of having to respond to local initiatives, which often consisted, as Pollock once put it, of 'presenting a pistol at the Head of the government, demanding financial assistance at very short notice'.[16] Moreover, in such a small community, where ministers were eminently accessible and lacked (particularly the Minister of Finance) the prestige and mystique of their British counterparts, the scope for financial planning was limited. All too often government financial policy, especially when it involved economies, was thwarted by a whole range of very local and often petty considerations. As Pollock wryly told the Commons in June 1929, the words 'economy' and 'retrenchment' were 'as sweet as honey to the multitude, and as bitter as gall to the individual. I cannot even discharge a redundant junior official without my life being made a burden'.[17]

The following of British example thus combined with various local considerations to commit the Northern Ireland government to expenditure far in excess of the white paper estimates. Although the cost of reserved services stabilised at below the estimate (some £1.7m as against £2.2m), the cost of transferred services soared above the original figure of £4.1m, being £5m in 1922–23 and £9.5m in 1930–31.[18] What is more, this increased expenditure occurred at a time when revenue fell far below expectations. So rapidly and consistently did revenue and expenditure pull in opposite directions that, except for a few years in the late 1920s, the government of Northern Ireland was in constant dread of a budget deficit. Never at any time did it contemplate leaving the budget unbalanced. Pollock was an utterly orthodox Minister of Finance who regarded a deficit as betokening not only political and financial but also moral bankruptcy. Instead, he stressed the importance of a balanced budget for achieving both financial stability and national progress.[19] The government was therefore forced to try to balance its budget by a number of expedients. Since, however, its scope for making economies or raising extra revenue was strictly limited, it had no alternative but to seek imperial aid.

2

These 'repeated begging expeditions', as Andrews once called them,[20] began in November 1921 and continued in one form or another, with a break between 1926 and 1929, almost to the outbreak of the Second World War. At first Craig played the leading role in financial relations between Northern Ireland and Britain, as he persuaded successive imperial governments to finance, in whole or in part, the Special Constabulary in the early 1920s,[21] but gradually the permanent officials of the Ministry of Finance bore the brunt of financial negotiations with the Treasury.[22]

That they did so was probably to Northern Ireland's advantage. It was true that there was a tendency for officials to compromise and present agreed solutions to their respective ministers, and that Spender, when Permanent Secretary of the Ministry of Finance, was ever anxious not to disrupt 'the friendly relations that exist between Treasury officials and ourselves'.[23] It was, however, also true that there was a terrier-like quality about Ministry of Finance officials, especially when faced with a deficit, and they were more competent and no more prone to compromise than ministers. They certainly had more grasp of detail, and during meetings with their British counterparts they could defend and explain Northern Ireland's position and at the same time appraise imperial financial policy.[24] Such discussions had more sense of direction and precision than did meetings involving ministers. In the 1930s particularly, Pollock's eighty years weighed very heavily upon him. During discussions with Treasury officials he was inclined to talk in very general terms about the deficiencies of the North's finances and about what Britain owed it, and often had to be brought back to the immediate matter in hand.[25] And meetings between ministers, at which no officials were present, served only to create further problems when nobody seemed to know what exactly had been decided.[26] Moreover, officials did have a permanent professional interest in Northern Ireland's finances, whereas their political bosses were essentially part-time and had their normal lives to run, Craig in particular being increasingly disinclined to allow Northern Ireland's financial problems to interfere with his private plans.[27]

At one time or another during its many begging expeditions the government of Northern Ireland suggested three ways in which the imperial government could help to balance the budget. The first was to secure the North's long-term financial future by a revision of the financial provisions of the 1920 act, which would give Northern Ireland sufficient revenue to enable it to match British expenditure without incurring additional regional taxation. In the 1930s this idea was expressed in the demand for a 'minus contribution', by which was meant that the Treasury should make good any deficit in the Northern Ireland budget. Although there was not, as Craig at one time liked to maintain, any legal basis for it in the 1920 act,[28] a good case could nevertheless be made out for a minus contribution. And it was Andrews, when Minister of Labour, who made out the best case.

Andrews had no patience with the view held by Pollock and others that Northern Ireland ought to stand on its own financial feet.[29] Northern Ireland was not, he argued, 'an autonomous State, but simply a subordinate legislature on which had been devolved certain limited powers of local legislation and administration'. In particular, it was not financially independent of Britain: 'On the contrary, our financial arrangements almost automatically follow those made by the British Chancellor, whether up or down, and our reserved taxes – about 90% of the whole – are actually levied and collected by the United Kingdom Government which also settles the subject and amount of taxation.' In such circumstances Northern Ireland should experience neither a lower standard of services nor additional regional taxation. As citizens of the United Kingdom, 'our people are entitled to the same social advantages as our fellow subjects in other parts of the Kingdom', and 'equal taxation per head of the population and equal contributions to our Social Services ought to produce exactly similar benefits throughout the Kingdom'. Justice demanded that Britain should help Northern Ireland to maintain standards. Northern Ireland had 'gladly' handed over large surpluses to the Treasury in the past and 'would willingly do so again'. The imperial government should therefore help Northern Ireland out of difficulties which were largely the result of 'the initiative of the United

Kingdom Government in remitting War Taxation and introducing Contributory Pensions and Derating'. In fact, the United Kingdom virtually owed Northern Ireland a living. The contention was that Northern Ireland should never suffer financially for having a parliament that few people had wanted. The vast majority of the people of Northern Ireland 'never desired to be governed otherwise than from Westminster, and the only motive for accepting a Parliament of our own was to assist Great Britain to settle the Irish question'. Had the six counties remained under direct rule from Westminster, Andrews concluded,

> We would have been under existing conditions a debtor part of the Kingdom, just as Wales is probably today. It is inequitable that our people should be put in a worse position than their fellow-subjects in any other area of the United Kingdom as a consequence of the devolution of local services; provided that the devolved local services are conducted with prudence and economy.

The second, but from Northern Ireland's point of view less satisfactory, way in which Britain could relieve the former's financial problems was by reamalgamating the Unemployment Funds. The wisdom of separating these funds had been questioned by both imperial and Northern Ireland officials in 1921,[30] but it was not until 1925 that the Northern government first pressed seriously for reamalgamation.[31] The grounds for doing so were summed up in a memorandum submitted to Craig by Andrews in November 1924. Andrews listed seven main 'reasons why Northern Ireland should be assisted by Great Britain':

(*a*) No allowance for financing unemployment made in White Paper which set out the financial relations between Great Britain and Northern Ireland.

(*b*) But for the Government of Ireland Act, 1920, the problem would never have arisen. No justification for Northern Ireland workers being asked to suffer in a domestic matter of this kind because of their acceptance of a Parliament at the bidding of Great Britain and against their own wishes.

(*c*) Northern Ireland industries are part and parcel of industries organised on a United Kingdom basis, e.g. shipbuilding, engineering, making-up trades, etc.

(*d*) Workers largely in the same Trades Unions as those of Great Britain, employed under the same industrial conditions and moving regularly between the two areas.

(*e*) Causes of unemployment in Great Britain and Northern Ireland identical and beyond the power of the Northern Ireland government to control, i.e., international trade conditions resulting from the Great War.

(f) Unjust to throw financial burden of unemployment on Northern Ireland as it would be to cut the Clyde or Sheffield district out of the rest of Great Britain and ask them to bear their own unemployment, which they would be equally unable to do.

(g) On financial grounds Northern Ireland too small an area for a self-contained Unemployment Fund; too dependent upon two export trades, linen and shipbuilding with no sufficient proportion of steady industries with generally good employment.[32]

The third and least satisfying forms of aid were *ad hoc* payments or arrangements. In the early 1920s assistance was sought towards specific items of expenditure, such as unemployment insurance or the Special Constabulary,[33] but in the early 1930s the Treasury was also asked to co-operate in juggling with the imperial contribution and the residuary share, so that the former would diminish and the latter increase.[34] Such juggling, having to be executed from year to year, offered no long-term solution to Northern Ireland's financial difficulties, but did have the advantage of being susceptible to agreement between the two treasuries and not requiring legislation. It was possible because of the way in which Northern Ireland revenue from reserved taxation was determined. At the beginning of each financial year that share was estimated by the Inland Revenue and customs authorities, and the North's imperial contribution and residuary share of reserved taxation was provisionally fixed by the Joint Exchequer Board, which determined the final amounts two years later when complete sets of accounts were available, but which could in the interval revise its provisional figures. At all these stages the size of the imperial contribution and residuary share could be subject to dispute between the Ministry of Finance and the Treasury. The outcome of any contested submission, never certain, was likely to be even more uncertain in the early 1930s, when some fundamental issues affecting financial relations were raised. While it was true that Northern Ireland did have claims to make against the imperial Treasury, such as its so-called 'hidden contribution',*[35] it was also true that the Treasury could advance counter-claims, particularly in respect of the lower proportion of rate-borne public expenditure in the North. The Treasury could therefore help to relieve Northern Ireland's financial

*These claims varied from time to time, and in the 1930s included the fact that Northern Ireland was receiving no share of the special duties imposed during the economic war, from which Northern Ireland suffered (so it thought) more than the rest of the United Kingdom. The main claim was, however, Northern Ireland's 'hidden contribution' in the form of estate duties on British parts of assets of deceased Northern Ireland residents, stamp duties on Northern Ireland securities registered in Britain, and the profits of Bank of England notes circulating in Northern Ireland. Under the provisions of the 1920 act such revenue, worth some £600,000 a year, accrued to the Treasury without being considered part of the imperial contribution.

uncertainty by agreeing to a low imperial contribution, including the revision of past contributions, and by agreeing that if (whether because of inaccurate estimates of revenue or subsequent changes in rates of taxation) the actual revenue attributable to Northern Ireland should exceed the original estimates, the surplus should not be retained by the imperial Treasury to swell the imperial contribution but should be credited to Northern Ireland. If the two treasuries presented joint recommendations to the Joint Exchequer Board, Northern Ireland's revenue would be increased and a degree of uncertainty decreased.

The imperial government's response to Northern Ireland's importuning was largely determined by Treasury officials. Craig's view that Northern Ireland's claims were less sympathetically received when Philip Snowden was Chancellor in a Labour government[36] was based upon prejudice rather than fact. The imperial line on the North's financial claims was fundamentally consistent, and successive Chancellors seem to have accepted entirely the advice of their officials. Certainly direct negotiations between ministers did not result in concessions beyond those outlined by Treasury officials.[37]

Treasury officials did not share Andrews's view of the imperial government's obligations to Northern Ireland. Although by the late 1930s some leading Treasury officials had been converted to Keynesian economics, in the formative years of financial relations between Northern Ireland and Britain the Treasury had a narrow view of government expenditure in general and an even narrower view of its responsibilities towards Northern Ireland in particular.[38] In the early 1920s the predominating advice was given by Otto Niemeyer, Deputy Controller of Finance and the Treasury's representative on the Joint Exchequer Board. He disliked Craig's informal methods of conducting business and his demand that the imperial government should spend millions of pounds on the Special Constabulary, over which it had no control. 'Sir James Craig', he noted for the Chancellor, Sir Robert Horne, on 26 May 1922, 'rather humorously says that the last thing in his mind is to escape the obligations of the 1920 Act. But under that Act the *whole* obligation for Specials is on the Ulster Exchequer!'[39] Niemeyer was, in fact, one of that band of politicians and civil servants virulently critical of the government of Northern Ireland and suspicious that Ulster Unionists would enjoy the benefits of local autonomy at the expense of the British taxpayer. 'Incredible if they were not in black and white' was his comment on Craig's proposals in November 1922 for an adjustment of financial relations.[40]

Such hostility had softened by the 1930s with a change of officials. The two Treasury officials most concerned with Northern Ireland in the 1930s, S. D. Waley, Principal Assistant Secretary, and Sir Richard Hopkins, the Second Secretary, did develop a more sympathetic understanding of the difficulties arising from Northern Ireland's position as a distressed area with limited powers of taxation and no room to make economies except by reducing the level of social services below that prevailing in Britain. Waley fully appreciated the 'obvious political objections' to such economies, since the North had been 'separated from the U.K. by no desire of her own'.[41] They recognised that the imperial government did have some obligation to assist Northern Ireland. Explaining to the Chancellor, then Neville Chamberlain, that the North merited help in avoiding an anticipated deficit of over £1m in 1933–34, Hopkins wrote:

> This is not due to extravagance on their part. On the whole I think it could be said that they have economised pretty well. The fact is that they copy all our legislation and that therefore we set their general standard, and for better or worse in times like these that standard means bankruptcy for a small country which is suffering terribly from unemployment.[42]

This more accommodating approach probably owed much to the friendly relations which Spender and his senior officials had developed with Treasury officials such as Waley and Hopkins. Waley believed that he and Spender had a common aim, 'to give N.I. a real motive for economy & remove the pauper taint',[43] and both sets of officials cooperated to bring home to Northern Ireland ministers the need for strict and economical administration.[44] To that end carefully worded prearranged letters were sent to Pollock, and interviews were arranged with the Chancellor, especially with Craig in mind. For, Hopkins warned Chamberlain in preparing him for one such meeting, 'Lord Craigavon, in discussions of this kind, is very inclined to assume that decisions are in his favour, unless it is made unusually clear what the decisions are'.[45]

Yet although relations between Northern Ireland and the Treasury were friendlier in the 1930s than they had been in the 1920s, the Treasury line on Northern Ireland's claims did not fundamentally change. It was believed that Northern Ireland should try to stand on its own financial feet and should make a contribution towards the cost of imperial services, a view even reinforced by the imperial government's own budgetary crisis in 1930–31,[46] which meant that the Treasury was anxious to exploit to the full existing sources of revenue rather than hand out money.[47] On all financial questions in the inter-war years, imperial budgetary needs were paramount, and Northern Ireland's problems had to be placed within the context of broader imperial policy.

The imperial government thus turned Northern Ireland's order of priorities upside down. It was reluctant to undertake any long-term financial commitments in Northern Ireland. The furthest it went towards a revision of financial relations was when Bonar Law's Conservative government agreed in 1923 to refer the matter to arbitration. The arbitration committee, headed by Lord Colwyn, the chairman of the Joint Exchequer Board, issued two reports.[48] The first recommended a lowering for 1923 and 1924 of the imperial contribution of £7.9m provided for in the 1920 act. The second report devised a formula to determine the contribution in subsequent years. The committee recommended that expenditure on necessary services should rank as the first charge on Northern Ireland's revenue, and that the imperial contribution should be based on the difference between revenue and actual and necessary expenditure. The contribution was thus reduced from a first charge of almost £8m to a residual charge. The committee also recommended that *per capita* expenditure in Northern Ireland should increase at the same rate as in Britain. Although regarded by some Treasury officials as a spendthrift's charter,[49] the Colwyn Award was not a licence for free spending in Northern Ireland. Necessary expenditure was not to include spending on services that did not exist in Britain or were superior to services there; and account had to be taken not only of average standards in the two countries but also 'any lower general level of prices, of wages, or of standards of comfort or social amenity which may exist in Northern Ireland as compared with Great Britain'.[50]

As a result of the Colwyn Award, the contribution acted as a buffer between rising expenditure and falling or stable revenue. Domestic spending increased throughout the 1920s at the expense of the contribution, which gradually dwindled away. This happy state of affairs lasted until 1930–31, when the contribution all but disappeared[51] and led to the formulation of the demand for the minus contribution. Yet the imperial government refused to consider any further formal change in financial relations. A minus contribution was dismissed as unthinkable,[52] especially since it would require legislation and have implications for relations with the Free State. In fact, de Valera's return to power in 1932, and the development of the financial dispute between his and the imperial governments, made the Treasury reluctant to meet publicly and openly Northern Ireland's claims for a permanent adjustment of financial relations. The imperial government had justified allowing Northern Ireland, unlike the Free State, to retain land-purchase annuities on the ground that the North made a contribution to imperial services; but if the North were given a subsidy as well, Waley argued, 'We should certainly appear to be dealing harshly with the Irish Free State in insisting on the payment of the land annuities at the present time'.[53] Only as part of the price of Northern Ireland's acquiescence in the Anglo-Éire settlement of 1938 did the imperial government eventually accept, and then only in principle, the idea of a minus contribution.[54]

Nor was the Treasury prepared to make a less radical permanent adjustment by agreeing to the amalgamation of the Unemployment Funds. Its objection to doing so was largely financial – it would unjustifiably increase contributions by the state, employers and employees in Britain[55] – but in public the refusal was wrapped up in more principled terms. Reamalgamation, Chamberlain told the House at Westminster in 1936, would be 'contrary to the whole spirit of the Act of 1920, which was that the social services should be administered by Northern Ireland and not by Whitehall'.[56] All that the imperial government would concede was, in effect, a partial reamalgamation of the funds under the Unemployment Reinsurance Agreements of 1926 and 1936. The measure of relief given by these agreements did enable Northern Ireland to keep benefits and contributions at British rates without being waterlogged by debt. Under the first agreement, the extent to which Northern Ireland could increase its deficit on its Unemployment Fund was limited: as from 1 October 1925 the Northern government undertook to provide an 'equalisation' payment sufficient to make the deficit per head of the insured population equal to the corresponding deficit on the British fund; and if in any one year Northern Ireland's equalisation payment per head of population exceeded the corresponding British payment, the imperial Treasury was to meet three-fourths of the excess.[57] This arrangement did result in substantial payments by the Treasury in the late 1920s, but it was far from ideal. It gave the imperial government the option of withdrawing if its payments to Northern Ireland exceeded £1m in any year; and it left Northern Ireland with responsibility for the large debt incurred before the agreement, for normal state contributions to the fund, and, as a safeguard against profligate administration, for part of the equalisation payments. Moreover, when by 1931 the original agreement had ceased to work in Northern Ireland's favour, the Treasury only reluctantly and under stringent conditions agreed to its modification – just in time to help Northern Ireland present balanced budget estimates for 1935–36.[58]

The usual method of helping Northern Ireland out of its financial difficulties was, therefore, through a series of *ad hoc* arrangements. Such arrangements both limited the Treasury's commitment and provided an opportunity to supervise the North's financial administration. In the 1920s, therefore, there were special votes for the Special Constabulary, an unemployment relief grant as part of the Craig–Collins peace pact of March 1922, and some less formal arrangements to help Northern Ireland's Unemployment Fund in 1921–22.[59] In the 1930s grants continued to be made for specific purposes, particularly agricultural subsidies,[60] but in the early 1930s the Treasury did also help Northern Ireland from year to year by accepting some reassessment of the provisional residuary share. To this end, for example, 'a hidden reserve of £300,000' was made in the 1933–34 imperial budget.[61] Like the Northern Ireland government, the Treasury had good reason for preferring agreed submissions to the Joint Exchequer Board. There was always the possibility that in a contested case the board would declare in Northern Ireland's favour, especially in respect of 'hidden contributions', which would not only increase the imperial government's liabilities but would also have implications for imperial policy towards the Free State. Compromise, Hopkins told the Comptroller and Auditor-General in justifying one of these agreed submissions in 1933, was preferable to a contested case in which 'we had much to risk and little to gain'.[62]

Even then, however, the path was not smooth. The hands of Treasury officials were still tied by law, constitutional practice and the possible implications of any concession for imperial policy towards the Free State. Thus, for fear of 'stultifying the whole case for their imposition',[63] the Treasury was unable to take a convenient way of helping Northern Ireland in 1933 by allowing it a share of the special duties imposed to compensate for the land-purchase annuities withheld by de Valera. The Treasury had also to bear in mind the attitude of the Comptroller and Auditor-General and the Public Accounts Committee. After the former had queried an arrangement to credit Northern Ireland in 1933 with some £400,000, Hopkins was reluctant to undertake similar adjustments in the following year. 'It was no light matter', he insisted to Spender, 'for him to have to try and justify these private arrangements between the two Governments'.[64]

Not only was help strictly limited, it was also, as the financial negotiations of the early 1930s underlined, given on conditions and only after long and hard bargaining. During this bargaining the details of Northern Ireland's finances were closely examined to ensure that Ulstermen were not enjoying higher standards of government expenditure at the expense of the British taxpayer. The relatively low use made of the Road Fund for general treasury purposes, the amount given for relief works, the extent of reserves, the building up of sinking funds, and the alleged generosity of agricultural derating were all subject to criticism; but two items particularly bothered Treasury officials and Chancellors: valuation and the financing of police and education. Since Northern Ireland's local authorities bore proportionately less of the cost of education and police than did their British counterparts, the United Kingdom taxpayers were, in effect, subsidising Northern Ireland ratepayers to the tune, Treasury officials estimated, of between £500,000 and £900,000 a year.[65] Moreover, because of an obsolete valuation, the yield of Schedule A income tax was less than it might have been. There had been no general revaluation of the six counties since 1852, apart from Belfast, which had been completely revalued in 1906.[66] The infrequency of general revaluations contrasted with the practice in the rest of the United Kingdom, where revaluations were undertaken every five years and did result in marked differences between assessed and actual values.

Such major discrepancies in valuation and the financing of police and education enabled the Treasury to maintain that Northern Ireland was demanding equal benefits without bearing equal burdens.[67] Although prepared to admit that Northern Ireland's special circumstances justified, at least temporarily, differences in police finance,[68] the Treasury was always insistent that there should be a speedy revaluation of the province to increase the yield of income tax and that more of the cost of education should be borne by the rates.[69] This was the price of Treasury co-operation in helping Northern Ireland to avoid a budget deficit in the early 1930s: it demanded that Northern Ireland's financial practices should be brought more into line with those in Britain, even though such changes would raise a storm of protest in the North.

3

Even this brief impression of the way in which Northern Ireland's finances were arranged underlines both the impotence of the regional government and the possibilities for friction between it and the imperial government. Northern Ireland's financial problems were viewed from such different perspectives that the imperial government not only rejected all Northern Ireland's requests for long-term amendments of financial relations, but also imposed conditions when conceding to requests for short-term assistance. Even in the comparatively affluent years 1926–29 the interpretation of the Colwyn Award led to frayed tempers,[70] and the detailed discussions of the early 1930s led Craig to complain that there was 'a complete misunderstanding among officials on the other side of the true position' in thinking that 'our accounts were as much subject to the scrutiny of the Treasury as those of the Admiralty or any other Department in London. This was quite wrong. Ulster was a Province and had its own elected Government'.[71]

Yet these different perspectives and consequent irritations did not lead to any disruption of the 1920 settlement. On the whole the government of Northern Ireland toed the Treasury line. The reasons for such acquiescence lay in the very nature of Ulster Unionism and in disagreements among members of the cabinet.

Very much aware and proud of Northern Ireland's place within the United Kingdom and British Empire, Northern Ireland ministers were ever susceptible to appeals to the wider interests of kingdom and Empire. In 1931 officials of the two treasuries had been in dispute as to whether, as a result of higher taxation imposed in Snowden's September economy budget, Northern Ireland's provisional residuary share should be increased by £300,000, for which no provision had been made in the imperial budget. The dispute dragged on for so long that Pollock eventually appealed to the Chancellor, by then Chamberlain, but in a cleverly worded reply the latter refused to go beyond the £150,000 previously suggested by his officials·

> The difficulties of your position are so akin to my own that you may be sure that I appreciate them fully and I shall be quite ready to agree to a considerable increase in the Provisional Residuary Share in response to your request. I am sure that you on your side will be ready to take steps which you would not contemplate at a more normal time in order to assist me in securing that our Budget should be effectively balanced with an adequate surplus. That result, seeing how our currency is placed, is of paramount importance to every part of the United Kingdom. I hope, therefore, that you will see your way to agreeing that the increase should be £150,000, in which case we should not oppose the application.[72]

A Unionist government could scarcely resist such an appeal to patriotism. On 7 January 1932 Pollock accepted the compromise, for, he told Chamberlain, both he and Craig agreed 'without hesitation that the interests of the Imperial Budget are paramount in the present crisis'.[73]

This way of handling business by a series of compromises was far more acceptable to Pollock than pressing for a minus contribution, and of all the ministers it was Pollock who assumed most responsibility for financial relations. Andrews, the most vehement and persistent advocate of a permanent settlement on the basis of a minus contribution, was, when Minister of Labour, only occasionally involved in financial negotiations with the Treasury, while Craig, who sympathised with Andrews's view, had neither the time nor inclination to devote himself consistently to sorting out his government's financial problems. Pollock's ascendancy as Minister of Finance from 1921 until April 1937 thus made for harmonious relations with the Treasury because he preferred to seek short-term solutions. He was convinced of neither the necessity nor the desirability of establishing the principle of a minus contribution.

Pollock's main objection to the idea of a minus contribution was a stubborn conviction that Northern Ireland should live off its own resources. This conviction was surprising in view of persistent difficulties in assessing revenue, which depended almost entirely on the imperial budget, and in determining expenditure, which was largely dependent upon British examples. Such difficulties and uncertainty did not lead him to accept Andrews's argument that Britain should therefore contribute to the balancing of Northern Ireland's budget. Rather,

Pollock openly told senior imperial officials, such as the Permanent Secretary of the Home Office, that 'In view of the fact that Ulster had been given its own Government within the Empire and a contribution of £700,000 a year towards its expenditure, he personally could not contemplate the idea of Ulster coming to Great Britain as a beggar asking for a minus contribution'.[74] Additional taxation, he later told Andrews, was 'preferable to appearing as mendicants on Britain's bounty' and 'the disgrace attendant on the insolvency of the Province, and the reflection cast upon us as a business Government that we are unable to manage our own affairs'.[75]

Moreover, Pollock refused to admit that Northern Ireland had a long-term financial problem. He believed instead that, for example, the difficulties he experienced in balancing the budget in the early 1930s were the result of only temporary causes – world trading conditions in general and in particular the economic war, which he largely blamed for the North's diminishing trade and revenue.[76] Ministry of Finance officials did not share this optimism. They were less hopeful of an imminent and sustained economic recovery in the North, particularly since they believed that Pollock exaggerated the adverse effects of the economic war and paid too little attention to the probability that on balance the North had gained from the virtual elimination of Free State agricultural competition in the British market.[77] Pollock's officials also believed that revenue and expenditure would continue to pull in opposite directions. Any improvement in conditions, particularly if it occurred in Britain, would lead to a reduction in taxation, while it was certain that the future would see the expansion of state activity, particularly in respect of social services and education. Even though they enlisted the aid of Treasury officials,[78] Spender and his colleagues could not shift their minister from the optimistic view which coloured his attitude in negotiations with the Treasury. Before one meeting at the Treasury on 3 January 1934 Spender recorded in his diary: 'Mr Pollock told me . . . that I must not take too pessimistic a view of the future with trade improving and the consequent increase in our revenues'.[79]

Thus it was that during discussions at the Treasury as to how Northern Ireland could avoid a deficit of between £350,000 and £950,000 in 1934–35 Pollock disregarded a prior government decision to press for a minus contribution. At a conference at Stormont Castle on 15 December 1933, attended by Craig, Andrews, Pollock and their senior officials, it had been decided to press for a permanent adjustment of the financial provisions of the 1920 act so as to end Northern Ireland's recurrent financial uncertainty.[80] Yet the discussions at the Treasury three weeks later revolved not around the question of a permanent settlement but around the balancing of the 1934–35 budget by a number of expedients. This was Pollock's doing. 'I have given an undertaking to the Prime Minister', he told Hopkins, 'that we must balance next year's budget, and I am primarily concerned with coming to some arrangement by which that promise can be carried into effect'.[81] He felt able to take this line because his peculiar optimism about Northern Ireland's long-term financial prospects was touchingly reinforced by his conviction that Craig would — so Pollock told Spender — be able to relax and enjoy the six-week cruise he was soon to begin if he could be assured that 'he need no longer worry about next year'.[82]

The government of Northern Ireland not only tolerated the rejection of its major financial demands; it also agreed to pay the price demanded for what assistance the Treasury was prepared to give. Most notably, it tried to bring Northern Ireland's financial system more into line with Britain's by undertaking revaluation and by compelling local authorities to contribute a larger share of educational expenditure. Yet it did so against its better judgment. It was not just the fear that these measures would be unpopular in Northern Ireland, coming at a time when the official inquiry into financial relations between the state and local authorities had reported that the level of taxable capacity had been reached and the level of rateable capacity almost so.[83] There were also some legitimate doubts as to the intrinsic merits of attempting to conform to British practices. In particular, it was argued that conditions were not comparable and necessitated different systems. Not only were the systems of valuation and education finance legacies of the Union, but also Andrews contended that

> We were handed over Northern Ireland in a condition much behind standards in Great Britain, with regard to school buildings, police barracks, Labour Exchanges, prisons, the condition of our roads, sanitary arrangements, water supplies, etc., all of which arrears must be gradually overtaken unless it is held that Northern Ireland is to be permanently behind British standards, which suggestion ought never to be agreed to by us.[84]

In fact, education and police apart, government grants to local authorities were generally proportionately lower than in Britain.[85]

The Valuation Acts Amendment Bill, providing for quinquennial revaluations, the first to be completed sometime in March 1935, was introduced into the Commons on 24 November 1931.[86] When introducing its second reading a few days later, Pollock tried both to minimise its likely effects and to explain its urgent necessity. On the one hand, he dismissed 'unworthy' and 'disheartening' suspicions that the bill was some 'deep-laid scheme to compass the undoing of the people'.[87] On the other hand, as he himself said, he 'very succinctly in three separate points' summed up the case for revaluation:

> The first is: — We must pass this Measure in this Parliament, or have it

forced upon us at Westminster. That is definite. The second is:— We have always claimed equal rights and equal services with the rest of the Kingdom. Can we logically repudiate Britain's right to claim from Northern Ireland the same conditions in respect of revaluation as obtains in Britain? The third is:— Serious anomalies and injustices have arisen in Northern Ireland from the long spell of disregard of these conditions. Is there any logical argument against their removal?[88]

The reaction against the measure was as fierce as the government had feared.[89] Revaluation was opposed by every local authority and representative trade organisation. It was generally recognised that it would certainly increase the incidence of taxation and probably increase the burdens of ratepayers, since ratepayers had to contribute towards its cost and since it could lead to a reduction of government derating grants. Moreover, there was considerable resentment that the measure had been forced upon the North by Westminster and a widespread feeling that the government should have resisted such baneful pressure. In the stirring words of one member of Belfast Corporation:

> I say, if the Members of the Northern Government are not in a position to act as elected buffers against the impregnable walls of Westminster, then push them out of our way, and let us do on behalf of the finances of Northern Ireland what we did in the past when we shouldered a rifle on behalf of the Empire.[90]

Indeed, Nationalists made much of this reaction to turn the debate on revaluation virtually into a vote of confidence not merely in the government but in Northern Ireland as well.[91]

It was a trying period for the government, but it stood firm on the principle of the bill. It knew that it could rely upon its backbenchers to rally round in support of what was, in effect, a vote of confidence — and rally round all but four of the backbenchers did.[92] Yet while sticking to the principle of the bill, the government was as conciliatory as possible over such details as appeals procedures[93] and did try to reassure local authorities and ratepayers. The leader of the local authorities' campaign against revaluation, in return for dropping his opposition, wanted either its limitation to income tax purposes or a guarantee that government derating grants would remain unaltered. Pollock did not give way on either of these points, for he did hope to make some savings, but he did accept an amendment suggested by Down County Council to the effect that 'Nothing will be done to impose any unjust burden upon any County Council, or any body concerned with the imposition of rates'.[94]

The government was more reluctant to take the more pointed step of shifting more of the burden of educational expenditure onto the rates. Craig and Pollock had agreed to do so in May 1933, as part of a deal with the Treasury to juggle with past imperial contributions, but they had balked at doing so at the last moment.[95] However, in response to continued Treasury nagging, if not disdain,[96] the cabinet decided at the end of April and the beginning of May 1934 to levy an education rate of 6d in the £ for 1934–35 and 1s for subsequent years. It was a gesture rather than a serious attempt to emulate Britain, for, as Pollock explained, 'If we only made an attempt to equalise Northern Ireland's rating burdens with those in Great Britain . . . we would receive most sympathetic treatment [from the Treasury]'.[97] The education levy, announced in his budget speech on 16 May 1934 and incorporated in a Finance Bill the following day,[98] was justified by Pollock on much the same ground as he had justified the Revaluation Bill nearly three years earlier.

As expected, the levy was as unpopular as revaluation. In some respects the Ministry of Finance had only itself to blame. The levy first applied to a financial year for which estimates had been made and rates struck, and was imposed without prior consultation with local authorities, contrary to the practice of the Ministry of Home Affairs, which was forever in consultation.[99] More importantly, there were objections to the levy itself. M.P.s were once more unimpressed by the argument that it was necessary to conform to British practices: Midgley, the Labour M.P. for Dock, argued that conditions were not comparable since Northern Ireland's educational system had to make up for 'a hundred years of neglect'.[100] It was also argued by M.P.s of all parties that the levy would retard educational development by causing cutbacks, particularly in such undramatic but necessary areas of educational expenditure as the provision of free meals and books. As Mrs Parker, the Unionist M.P. for South Londonderry and former chairman of the regional education committee in a 'very poor' area of the county, warned,

> Some of our poorer districts will definitely have to face this problem in an even more economical manner than they have done in the past. . . . It is a sad day for education in the country districts, and I do wish that the Minister had found some other way rather than this way of dealing with the matter.[101]

Pollock was unmoved. He was quite familiar with the historical argument against the levy and was far from sympathetic to the notion that further economies might be effected. He therefore persisted with the measure, refusing all amendments and relying upon the support of such members as Mrs Parker who, though critical, was, she told the House, 'naturally going to support the Government'.[102] Indeed, Pollock was at first pleased with the apparent relative lack of vehement opposition to the levy,[103] but it soon came under attack outside parliament, particularly from the two county boroughs of Londonderry and Belfast.

Belfast began an aggressive campaign against the levy, which, it was estimated, would double the city's existing expenditure on education. Such an increase was unacceptable, not only because Belfast's contribution would be proportionately much larger than that of the rest of the country (since the levy did not apply to derated hereditaments which abounded in the countryside), but also because Belfast Corporation and its supporters reckoned that the levy had 'nothing to do with education' but was simply a device to enable the government to balance its budget.[104] Pollock denied such allegations which he saw as doing 'great injury and discredit' to the government, arguing that other less difficult and more unpleasant expedients could have been adopted if all that had been required had been a balanced budget.[105] There was a germ of truth in both assertions but no desire to compromise. After an unsuccessful attempt to amend the Finance Bill the Corporation decided to contest the legality of the levy by petitioning the Governor for a reference to the Judicial Committee of the Privy Council under section 61 of the 1920 act – the only time the constitution was challenged in this way.[106] The Corporation's contention that the levy was substantially the same in character as Schedule A or B income tax and thus *ultra vires* under section 22 of the 1920 act was rejected by the Law Lords, one of whom aptly commented: 'Income tax, if I may say so, is a tax upon income.' The Corporation had no legal alternative but to accept the ruling, but the case marked the nadir of its uneasy relationship with the government in the inter-war years.

Londonderry Corporation's response to the education levy was to use it as a lever to win further government aid for the city.[107] At the beginning of February 1935 the Unionist Mayor wrote to Pollock reminding him of a promise Craig had evidently given that the government would assist the city in any difficulties created by the new levy. Spender recorded in his diary that the Mayor 'did not wish to adopt the same attitude as Belfast in criticising the Government on the education rate, but . . . they must expect special financial help' to avoid increasing the rates from their then present level of 19s 6d in the £.[108] At first the Ministry of Finance disputed the figures presented by the Mayor, but in a telephone conversation with the latter on 22 February 1935 Pollock did commit the government to make good any increase in the rates:

> We want to see you through by normal arrangements, and possibly later on we may be able to juggle things so as to help you. We do not want any formal arrangement, on account of other people, but the Government will see you through as far as they can.[109]

The upshot was a series of concessions on revaluation and unemployment relief grants, culminating in a direct subsidy in 1936 of £28,000.

4

Craig's promise to Londonderry city to offset the effect of the education levy on rates underlined the absurdity of a financial system which was geared to nobody's needs and interests. The unsatisfactory financial provisions of the 1920 act forced the government of Northern Ireland to go cap in hand to the imperial Treasury and then to respond to British views on financial administration. Such a response would have been the more justified had it resulted in a permanent adjustment of financial relations between Northern Ireland and Britain and within Northern Ireland itself. This did not happen. It was true that Northern Ireland's budget was always balanced in the inter-war years, but only by a series of what Hopkins called 'fudges' and 'wangles' and 'dodges and devices' giving 'gifts and subventions within the ambit of the Government of Ireland Act so as to save the Northern Ireland Government from coming openly on the dole as Newfoundland did'.[110]

In this process Northern Ireland paid a price for having a separate existence and at the same time trying to conform, if only in principle, to British practices. This was evident in the consequences of revaluation and the education levy. They embroiled the government with local authorities and heightened the longstanding controversy over the proper division of financial responsibility between taxpayers and ratepayers. The result was to hinder the development of all those services which depended upon local initiative. Services, such as housing, relief works, drainage, harbour improvements, hospitals and the treatment of lunatics, hung fire as the regional and local authorities discussed interminably their relative contributions, and as local authorities refused to take advantage of what powers they had without further government aid, and as the government constantly looked over its shoulder at the Treasury.

The close connection between the slowing down in the development of social services and the financial reforms of the early 1930s was underlined by the fate of education, the financing of which had been the source of so much controversy. Although much had been done since 1921 to retrieve education from the morass into which it had sunk under the Union, by 1939 Northern Ireland's educational system was 'still a generation or more behind most of England and Wales' in the provision of accommodation and such services as scholarships, free books and stationery, and free meals and clothing for necessitous children, who in rural areas often ate nothing but dry bread throughout the day.[111]

The financial wranglings of the 1930s contributed to this underdevelopment in two ways. Firstly, there was, as critics of the education levy had warned, a slowing down in the rate at which local authorities took advantage of the powers available to them under the Education Acts, enabling them to provide, for example, free meals and books to needy children.[112] Secondly, the government would offer nothing but exhortations. The Ministry and Ministers of Education would have liked to have been more generous to both local authority and voluntary schools, but even as late as 1939 the cabinet was unwilling to depart from the balance established in the early 1930s. By then Catholic school managers were finding it difficult to raise funds locally for building or extending schools, while most local authorities were receiving maximum grants from the government.[113] Robb, the Minister of Education and Leader of the Senate, who had been the junior minister from 1925 until 1937, was impressed by the arguments put forward by the Roman Catholic Clerical Managers' Association and the Association of Northern Ireland Education Committees. He therefore urged the cabinet on 15 May 1939 that 'In the interests of education generally more generosity should be shown not only towards Local Authorities in connection with Transferred Schools but also towards those who control Voluntary Schools'.[114]

Robb's proposals were not unreasonable. Education services were underdeveloped in Northern Ireland. Since 1936 denominational schools in Britain had been eligible for larger building grants than those available in Northern Ireland under the 1930 Education Act.[115] And by 1939 Northern Ireland was paying an imperial contribution of over £1¼m.[116] Nevertheless, the proposals were quickly squashed by Andrews, who since his appointment as Minister of Finance in April 1937 had sufficiently absorbed Treasury notions. Not only was he reluctant to raise once more the controversial question of denominational education,[117] but he also objected to reopening the whole question of the financing of education, pointing out that

> The British Treasury, which had made generous concessions to us in other directions during recent months, would look with disfavour on any additional expenditure being thrown on the Northern Ireland Exchequer as proposed.[118]

Andrews's view, which had Craig's support, prevailed. It was decided that 'The whole question should be postponed for further consideration in a year's time, if the Minister of Education then wished to resubmit the matter.' A marginal note on the Cabinet Office's working copy of the minutes, dated 3 January 1940, reads: 'This is unlikely to be raised now in view of the war'.[119]

The fate of educational expenditure was merely one aspect of that many-faceted and recurrent financial problem which cribbed and confined the regional government. It had to try to match expenditure in Britain, yet its lack of independent financial resources not only brought it into conflict with local authorities but also made it almost subservient to the imperial Treasury. Northern Ireland's financial structure thus militated against any long-term and comprehensive, let alone adventurous, regional planning.

5

Impotence (2): Trade and Industry

An equally overwhelming impression of impotence is apparent in economic policy. The government of Northern Ireland had formal responsibility for questions relating to trade and industry in Northern Ireland and was generally held responsible by all sections of the community for the encouragement of economic activity. It was constantly in touch with leaders of industry and was, too, as Andrews, the Minister of Labour, said, 'always ready . . . to remedy their grievances if possible and to do anything in our power to help them'.[1] The trouble was that the government's power to help was strictly limited.

The limitations on the government's power to assist trade and industry and to develop a regional economic policy stemmed partly from the limited vision of ministers and civil servants; partly from confused responsibility, for although the Ministry of Commerce was nominally responsible for assisting trade and industry, all other departments, except the Ministry of Education, had a finger in the pie; partly from the problems created by a small and accessible political system which inhibited the government rather than stimulated it to immense activity and long-term planning; and partly from Northern Ireland's financial problems. The root causes of this impotence lay, however, in Northern Ireland's constitutional and economic position. The government's powers to regulate and develop economic life were restricted by the 1920 act, while its range of manoeuvre was further circumscribed by Northern Ireland's economic circumstances. The country's position as the most disadvantaged region of the United Kingdom economy was further complicated by its long border and trading relationship with the Free State. The disadvantages accruing from these constitutional and economic limitations outweighed the advantages to be derived from a system of regional government. On occasion, the usually cited advantages of accessibility, speed of decision-making, effective representation of regional needs to the central authority, and a general responsiveness to local and regional wishes and needs, all worked in Northern Ireland's favour. Yet such occasions were more than offset by the government's inability either to develop its own economic policy to protect existing and attract new industries or to influence effectively imperial policy on matters relating to trade and industry.

1

The most obvious restriction placed upon the regional government's handling of trade and industry was the need to work within the limited confines of the 1920 act. The main powers of economic management, particularly control over external trade and foreign economic policy, were reserved to Westminster. Northern Ireland's capacity for independent action was, therefore, narrowly circumscribed, and many of its economic problems had to be settled within the general framework of imperial policies determined by Westminster.

So constricting did the government of Northern Ireland find the 1920 act that by 1926 it began to press for a limited extension of its powers. The initiative came from the Ministry of Agriculture, which had quickly found its efforts to improve the agricultural trade with Britain hampered by constitutional niceties. The trouble was that section 4(1)(7) of the 1920 act prevented Northern Ireland from making laws in respect of trade outside its own territory, which meant that it could not easily regulate and thus improve the quality of its exports to the rest of the United Kingdom. At first, with the 1924 Eggs Marketing Act, this limitation was circumvented by carefully framed legislation which avoided mention of the export trade,[2] but this ingenious method was considered impracticable in respect of other produce, particularly the potato trade, which sorely needed regulation to shore up its sagging reputation in Britain. The Ministry of Agriculture thus urgently pressed the cabinet to seek 'only a very slight extension' of the existing powers of the Northern Ireland parliament to enable the regulation and inspection of consignments intended for outside markets.[3]

The ministry's sense of urgency was not shared by the imperial departments to whom the matter was referred. The subject was first raised in June 1926, but a long period of silence succeeded by protracted discussions meant that almost two years passed before Northern Ireland obtained satisfaction. The delay was caused partly by the dilatoriness that characterised the Home Office's dealings with Northern Ireland, especially when other imperial departments (in this instance the Ministry of Agriculture, the Board of Trade and the Foreign Office) were also involved, but largely by the reluctance of imperial officials to meet Northern Ireland's claim. This reluctance stemmed from a certain distaste for the compulsory nature of the proposed potato marketing scheme,[4] but mainly from an almost innate fear of conceding any control over exports which might interfere with imperial foreign economic policy and commercial treaties.[5] Not until January 1928 was the Permanent Secretary of the Home Office, Sir John Anderson, persuaded that the rights of the imperial parliament could be adequately safeguarded.[6] Then the adjustment was swiftly made in the Northern Ireland (Miscellaneous Provisions) Act of the same year. The crucial provision for agricultural marketing was clause 2, which removed the restriction on the compulsory grading of agricultural produce for the British, Free State and Isle of Man markets.[7] Even then there was always the suspicion that certain measures, such as the 1930 Fruit Marketing Bill,[8] exceeded these extended powers. Although the Home Office was eventually prepared to turn a blind eye to such possibilities, the need to seek clearance for measures, the constant discussions with imperial officials, and the dilatoriness of imperial departments, all involved a delay in presenting legislation. Thus the 1929 Marketing of Dairy Produce Bill was delayed for over four months and reached M.P.s only a few minutes before its second reading.[9] Nevertheless, the extension of powers did encourage a rash of measures regulating the marketing of potatoes (admittedly a year later than planned), meat, dairy produce and fruit.

The government made no similar effort to extend its control over Northern Ireland's wider export trade or over imports. Northern Ireland's inability to control imports was often a matter of regret among Unionists and a constant source of criticism and derision among nationalists, who liked to point to what the Free State could achieve with its wider powers, including the power of protection.[10] The government, however, firmly set itself against any further extension of its powers and showed no anxiety to control customs and excise. Rather, it considered that there were positive advantages in their control by Westminster. Central control, asserted Pollock, the Minister of Finance, was 'one of the great safeguards of the preservation of the complete unity of the kingdom'.[11] Moreover, it also reflected the fundamental fact that Britain was Northern Ireland's main trading partner, against whom Northern Ireland would have no wish to use any sanctions. Finally, Milne Barbour, the Minister of Commerce, reckoned that Northern Ireland lost nothing by central control of customs, since it had the 'power of expressing our views and making representations to the imperial parliament at Westminster who have the imposition of duties within their power and in their special care'.[12]

In public members of the government may have expressed themselves content with their influence, but in private some were well aware of and chafed at their limited influence and at the way in which they thought that Northern Ireland's particular interests were ignored at Westminster. It was true that Northern Ireland could influence imperial policy on some matters of detail, but when Northern Ireland interests were at variance with British or imperial interests or prevailing thinking at Westminster, little headway was made. There was often a large difference between imperial and Northern Ireland perspectives, but Craig was unwilling to bridge the gap by exploiting to the full any political leverage that his government might have had. Potentially disruptive conflicts of interest were thus always settled in the imperial government's favour without precipitating a constitutional crisis or jeopardising the 1920 settlement.

In the late 1930s the Northern government and the Ministry of Commerce in particular liked to boast of the way they had helped the linen industry by representing its interests in the negotiations leading up to the Anglo-American trade agreement in 1938.[13] Yet such achievements in trade negotiations did not erase the failures in the 1920s when various sections of the linen industry failed to secure protection under the Safeguarding of Industries Act.[14] The sense of grievance widely felt in Northern Ireland at the Board of Trade's rejection of the industry's applications for the imposition of duties on linen imports was well summed up by Devlin when in October 1930 he told the government:

> If you want protection you will not get it because you are asking the English people to protect your goods at the expense of their own. . . . You will not get it for linen as long as they are trying to save cotton and artificial silk in England.[15]

This view came easily to the leader of a party which reckoned that ever since the twelfth century Irish trade and industry had been subordinated to English interests; but on this occasion it was shared by Andrews, who was disgusted that the expressed wishes of the majority of employers and employees in a key Northern Ireland industry had been overruled by a handful of well-entrenched free traders in England. 'Our linen trade', he complained to Craig, 'is more important to us than even the coal industry is to Great Britain, to help which various exceptional measures have been and are being taken'.[16] Craig, however, simply refused to allow his government to become directly involved in such a potentially contentious issue. On the contrary, as he told his cabinet after one meeting with imperial ministers, he had 'agreed not to cause embarrassment to the Imperial Government by pressing the matter in the meantime'.[17]

It was the same story with Northern Ireland's trade with the South. The government found itself able to do little to safeguard the North's economic interests *vis-à-vis* the South. Once again, it could influence matters of detail, as over the amendment in 1932 of the imperial government's Wheat Quota Bill, to ensure that those interested in trade with the South were not unduly hampered by United Kingdom legis-

lation. Yet on broader policy matters, such as the Anglo-Éire negotiations in 1938, imperial views and interests took precedence.

The 1932 Wheat Quota Bill, designed to maintain the price of wheat,
was financed by a levy on flour.[18] Its chief beneficiaries were the wheat
farmers of eastern England, but for reasons of policy the government of
Northern Ireland agreed to the North's inclusion in the measure, although it was inappropriate to Northern Ireland conditions and aroused
considerable criticism.[19] The most vocal critics of the measure in
Northern Ireland were the millers and bakers. With their various trade
associations, they were a well-organised group, which had long suffered
from the effects of Free State tariff policy. Their traditional Southern
market had been restricted and competition had been intensified within
the Northern Ireland market, and they thought that the Wheat Quota
Bill would increase their difficulties.[20] Their main concern was that the
levy on flour, by raising the cost of flour by 2s 6d per sack, would
render Northern Ireland bread and buns dearer than Free State produce, thereby jeopardising exports to the Free State, then valued at
£200,000 per annum, and enabling Free State bakers to compete more
successfully in the Northern market, especially in the border areas. The
millers' and bakers' preferred solution was the exclusion of Northern
Ireland from the bill; but as a second best they wanted it so amended
as to allow a remission of the levy in respect of bread exported. On 11
March 1932, therefore, a deputation of milling and baking interests
throughout Northern Ireland (including Devlin, who was a director of a
Belfast bakery) put their case against the bill to Milne Barbour, as Minister of Commerce the minister responsible for trade.[21]

Milne Barbour dismissed as impractical and impossible their demand
for the exclusion of Northern Ireland from the bill, but he was impressed by the arguments in favour of amendment, not surprisingly in
view of his ministry's appreciation of 'how important it is to the City
of Derry that we should gain our point in regard to exported bread'.
His ministry therefore readily acted not merely as broker between the
imperial authorities and the millers and bakers but as advocates of the
latters' case. It was arranged for a senior ministry official to accom-
pany (and control, since the millers' leader still preferred exclusion) a
small deputation of millers and bakers who went to London on 14
March 1932 to put their case to Northern Ireland's Westminster M.P.s
and the English Ministry of Agriculture. There then began a series of
negotiations involving local trade associations, the Northern Ireland
Ministries of Commerce and Agriculture, the Ulster Unionist Party at
Westminster and the English Ministry of Agriculture, in which Northern
Ireland civil servants played the key role. The discussions were not at
first easy, but perseverance told in the end. Concessions were eventually
made to meet not only the case of a remission of the levy on exported

bread but also a technical difficulty relating to the Londonderry bread trade. The Belfast and Londonderry millers were delighted at the outcome of this 'series of prolonged and delicate negotations', and so was the Ministry of Commerce. And well they might have been, since the concessions obtained for a very specialised interest had entailed amendments at both the report stage and third reading of a highly contentious measure. It is difficult to imagine that such amendments would have been forthcoming had there been no devolution of government and Northern Ireland millers and bakers had been left to present their own case to the imperial authorities.

By contrast, the government of Northern Ireland had little influence on broader policy matters. Where there was a conflict between Northern Ireland and British or imperial interests, and where the protection of Northern Ireland interests jeopardised imperial policy, Northern Ireland ended up by making sacrifices for the greater good. The limitations of Northern Ireland's ability, and willingness, to persuade the imperial government to run risks to protect Northern Ireland's trading interests *vis-à-vis* the South were clearly evident during the discussions which led up to the Anglo-Eire agreements of April 1938.

By the beginning of 1938 both the Éire and imperial governments were anxious for a settlement of the many outstanding issues in dispute between them. The economic war had seriously dislocated the Southern Irish economy, while a significant section of the imperial government, including Neville Chamberlain, the Prime Minister since May 1937, Malcolm MacDonald, the Dominions Secretary, and Oliver Stanley, the President of the Board of Trade, were anxious to demonstrate that conciliation could be a useful force in international politics. The talks began in London, with an Irish delegation under de Valera facing a British team led by Chamberlain.[22] The latter's anxiety to reach a settlement greatly assisted the negotiations, enabling the basis of an agreement soon to be reached largely on Éire's terms. While the Éire government could make no headway on the ending of partition, it gained most and gave away least in the three agreements signed on 25 April 1938 and published on the following day. By the first agreement the imperial government, without obtaining a defence agreement in return, gave up control of the naval bases Britain had retained in the South under the Anglo-Irish Treaty of 1921; the second agreement effectively ended the economic war and obliged the imperial government to make considerable financial concessions to Éire; and the third was a comprehensive trade agreement, giving most Éire goods free entry into the United Kingdom market but allowing United Kingdom goods less than free access to the Éire market.* Taken as a whole, the out-

* Comprising nineteen articles and six schedules, the agreement in general allowed Éire goods to be admitted into the United Kingdom free of customs

come of the negotiations was, MacDonald admitted, 'not a good agreement on paper', but he hoped that it would 'open a new chapter in Anglo-Irish relations and that our generosity would have its effects in Ireland'.[23] Chamberlain put it in an even wider perspective, reckoning that 'in this kind of agreement what was not included was sometimes more important than what was', and attaching 'great importance to the psychological effect of the conclusion of another Treaty of a pacific character following the Italian agreement'.[24]

This triumph for conciliation had almost been jeopardised by the government of Northern Ireland. During these negotiations there arose a serious conflict between Northern Ireland and imperial interests over the proposed trade agreement. So serious was the difference that the whole talks would have foundered had it not been for Craig's readiness to subordinate Northern Ireland's interests in face of imperial blandishments and bribes.

The Northern Ireland government had not been, and had not wished to be, directly represented in the negotiations,[25] but throughout had been able to make clear to imperial ministers and officials that Northern Ireland had special interests at stake which required special attention. The special interests it stressed were a rectification of the consequences of the South's economic and financial policies. In January 1938 Craig forwarded to Samuel Hoare, the Home Secretary, a memorandum showing how 'very grievously' Northern Ireland had been affected by Southern economic policies and 'how much more acutely we, with a long boundary dividing us from the South, have felt the repercussions, compared with our fellow citizens in other parts of the United Kingdom'. The memorandum therefore urged 'most earnestly' the need to secure concessions from the South which would 'help to revitalise certain features of our industrial life' and the adoption of measures 'to safeguard our industrialists against the influx of goods across the land boundary from a highly protected market'.[26]

These requests were taken seriously by the imperial cabinet, which from the start of the negotiations considered it essential that Northern Ireland should accept whatever agreements should emerge from the negotiations. This sensitivity had nothing to do with Northern Ireland's enhanced strategic importance once the Southern Irish ports had been surrendered, but to the political influence it was thought Northern

duties, subject to certain provisions for the quantitative regulation of agricultural products. Reciprocally, the Éire government guaranteed the right of free entry for certain classes of United Kingdom goods which were not subject to duty at the date of the agreement, and also undertook to remove or modify the duties on certain other classes of goods. The method adopted was that existing protective duties should be reviewed by an Éire prices commission to give United Kingdom producers opportunity for reasonable competition but at the same time affording adequate protection to Éire industries.

Ireland could exercise in Britain. MacDonald reckoned that any pronounced dissatisfaction in Northern Ireland with imperial policy towards the South could have serious repercussions in the House at
Westminster.[27] Moreover, if the usually reliable and trustworthy Spender
is to be believed, Hoare was ready not only to champion Northern
Ireland's interests but also to use any Northern Ireland opposition to
an agreement to break off negotiations which he regarded as giving too
much away to Éire.[28] He thus continually emphasised to his cabinet
colleagues that 'Politically . . . it was important to obtain a trade agreement so satisfactory that Northern Ireland would not stir up agitation
in Parliament against handing back the ports'.[29] Chamberlain, however,
was more concerned about criticism of the trade agreement, for he
reckoned 'the man in the street' would care less about the defence and
finance agreements than the trade agreement, which 'affected his
pocket'.[30] This consideration, as Hoare pointed out, only made it the
more necessary to secure Northern Ireland's agreement.[31]

During the negotiations, therefore, the fostering and safeguarding of
Northern Ireland's economic interests became a high priority, and the
Northern government was consulted at every stage on commercial questions.[32] At first it was hoped that Northern Ireland products would benefit
along with British products in a reciprocal, almost free-trade, agreement
between the United Kingdom and Éire, but it quickly became clear that
Éire would not consent to free trade with the United Kingdom, lest its
infant industries be crushed by well-established British industries. The
second line of approach was, therefore, to work out some special concessions for Northern Ireland, particularly free trade between the North
and South. This attempt was backed up by strong words, Chamberlain
on one occasion addressing 'some well chosen words to the Éire ministers', making it 'clear that there could be no question of handing back
the ports unless something was done for Northern Ireland and that perhaps there would be no trade agreement, and no finance agreement
either'.[33] Such strong words did not, however, have the anticipated
salutary effect. The Éire negotiators were willing to refer proposals to
the full cabinet in Dublin, but the most that was offered was an immediate reduction of duties on certain goods to be selected by the government of Northern Ireland. The objection seems to have been that as
long as the Northern government treated its minority unjustly, the Éire
government saw no reason to give it free entry to the Southern market.[34]

This concession was not sufficient for the government of Northern
Ireland. It wanted at the very least free trade between North and South
within a year. Any other arrangement, especially the 'inequitable, unacceptable and indefensible'[35] arrangement envisaged in the draft trade
agreement, would simply further weaken the ailing Northern economy
by placing 'in the hands of the Government of Éire the means of bring-

ing further economic pressure on Northern Ireland'.[36] Such an arrangement would, Craig told Chamberlain,

> raise for us serious political difficulties. It will be argued that the disloyal part of Ireland is getting a substantial advantage at the expense of the loyal portion, and really there would be no answer because the proposed agreement provides the Free State with a powerful economic and industrial weapon which could and, I am convinced, would be used to the detriment of our already sorely harassed industries.[37]

Two courses were considered by the government of Northern Ireland in face of Éire's unwillingness to make the concessions it sought. One was to accept the agreement and seek compensation from the imperial government – some 'tangible advantages for undertaking a risk which is bound to have a very disturbing effect both politically and economically'.[38] What form these 'tangible advantages' should take was discussed from mid-February onwards.[39] The second course open to the Northern government was to oppose the agreement publicly. Compensation would alleviate some of Northern Ireland's difficulties, but it would not make equitable a fundamentally unfair settlement. From the beginning of March, Andrews and Brooke, then Ministers of Finance and Agriculture respectively, considered resignation and public opposition, an action in which they were assured of the Governor's support.[40] Such an action followed by a general election would, according to Blackmore, the Cabinet Secretary, focus British attention on the agreement and create a crisis in Britain. In face of such a prospect the imperial cabinet would not have run the risk of persevering with an Irish settlement, for, MacDonald told his colleagues on 16 March 1938, 'If nothing could be obtained which would commend itself to Northern Ireland, it would be necessary to realise that the negotiations had broken down, perhaps for a long time'.[41]

This eventuality the imperial government was not prepared to accept. MacDonald and the Chancellor of the Exchequer, Sir John Simon, egged on by his officials, considered Northern Ireland's fears exaggerated and its demands outrageous. 'Are we never to be allowed by Ulster to come to terms with the South?', asked the Permanent Secretary at the Treasury, a lifelong critic of Ulster Unionism. 'Is the tail always going to wag the dog?'[42] Chamberlain, the Prime Minister, was, however, willing to recognise the honesty and sincerity of Northern Ireland's views. He also argued that to force an agreement on the North would both expose his government to the 'bitterest opposition' from Northern Ireland and its British supporters and nullify any advantage to be gained from improved relations with the South.[43] From the middle of March,

therefore, imperial ministers concentrated less upon winning concessions from Éire, but on persuading Northern Ireland to accept the
commercial agreement whatever its limitations. Chamberlain successfully appealed to Craig, who duly responded to wider imperial considerations and offers of compensation. Owing to Craig's ill-health, Andrews,
supported by senior officials from the Ministries of Finance, Agriculture and Commerce, had undertaken the negotiations in Britain; but in
the middle of March, Craig took over and preferred to act without
officials, presumably so that he could have the freest possible hand.

On 18 March, in response to a long letter from the imperial Prime
Minister,[44] Craig had a private interview with Chamberlain. During this
meeting he promised to support any agreement, provided adequate
compensation was offered to Northern Ireland.[45] The following day he
repeated his willingness to co-operate during a meeting between Northern
Ireland and imperial ministers, the former, at Craig's insistence, un-
accompanied by officials, the latter well flanked with officials from the
Treasury and Dominions Office. What is more, in doing so Craig completely disregarded what had been agreed at an earlier briefing session.
It had been only with the greatest of difficulty that his colleagues and
officials had persuaded him to attend a briefing session prior to the
ministerial meeting, but they might just as well not have bothered. During the briefing session Craig had confirmed Brooke's view that the
Northern Ireland cabinet could not for one moment accept the agreement and that, if it did so, it would be thrown out. Nevertheless, during
the ministers' meeting Craig accepted the agreement in principle, offered
to have a commendatory resolution passed by the Northern parliament,
diverted the conversation to financial assistance for Northern Ireland,
and left it to Andrews to criticise the agreement. Hoare had previously
told Spender and Andrews that as he had resigned once on principle, he
did not intend to do so again but would take any steps short of that in
support of Northern Ireland's resistance to the proposed agreement.
Now he found that there was no resistance to support, since Andrews
and Brooke were so dumbfounded at Craig's *volte-face* that they did
not like to refute their Prime Minister openly.[46]

The fight was not yet over, however. After the meeting on 19 March
Andrews again considered resignation but was persuaded to stay on by
Spender who felt that 'in regard to Éire the damage was beyond repair
& that the best course open to him was to do what he could for Ulster'.[47]
Although he did not resign, Andrews continued to criticise the proposed
commercial agreement. Once again, Chamberlain appealed directly to
'My dear James'. On 8 April he supplemented an official request by
Hoare that Northern Ireland ministers should cross to London for con-
sultations with a 'personal appeal to you to implement what you said to
me when you came over last time, namely that you meant to help and

not to hinder'. The matter was urgent, he stressed, since Northern Ireland's difficulties were delaying a settlement with Éire just at a time when

> in my anxieties over the international situation it has become almost essential for me to show some evidence that the policy of peace by negotiation can be successful. I have good hopes that I shall be able to bring forward an Anglo-Italian agreement as evidence of this, but if I can accompany that with an Anglo-Irish agreement it would greatly add to the impression made upon the world. And it is very necessary that an impression of solidarity here should be made, and not least in Berlin.[48]

This appeal again brought Craig to London to meet imperial ministers on the evening of 11 April. He was determined to settle quickly. He did not attend, as had been arranged, a preliminary meeting at the Constitutional Club, and, while accompanied by Andrews and Milne Barbour, he did not take any officials with him, although the imperial ministers were again well flanked with experts.[49] During the meeting, Hoare reported, Craig 'had taken a broad view and had shown himself reluctant to upset the prospect of agreement', intimating that 'if he could be given a case that was defensible in his Parliament, he would accept it'.[50] The imperial ministers did agree to pay most, but not all, of the price demanded for Northern Ireland's acquiescence. A proposal for a substantial grant for industrial development was not accepted, but the other requests were, more or less, met, probably because, as the Chancellor told the cabinet, they 'would not involve a great deal of money'.[51] Thus Northern Ireland was given vague promises of increased defence expenditure; agricultural subsidies were, on certain conditions, to be borne henceforth as a matter of principle on the English Ministry of Agriculture's vote; the imperial government would assist Northern Ireland in meeting any future budget deficit; and as long as the trade agreement was in operation Northern Ireland was guaranteed payments under the Unemployment Reinsurance Agreement, even though the £1m limit might be exceeded.[52]

Craig's personal initiative meant not only that Northern Ireland's real or imagined economic interests were subordinated to wider imperial considerations but also that Northern Ireland was handicapped in making out the best possible case for compensation from Britain. For instance, had Ministry of Commerce officials been allowed to argue the case, the request for an industrial development grant might not have been so readily and contemptuously dismissed as 'nonsensical' by Treasury officials and the Chancellor.[53] The episode thus provided an insight into the nature of political leadership and Craig's ascendancy in Northern Ireland. Above all, however, the Anglo-Éire negotiations of 1938 not only illustrated Northern Ireland's powerlessness to control its economic life and the subordination of Northern Ireland to imperial interests, but also further limited Northern Ireland's freedom of action. The failure to secure substantial commercial concessions, and the consequent need to claim financial and other concessions from the imperial government, further accentuated Northern Ireland's dependence on Britain.

2

The need to work within the framework of the 1920 act was the most obvious obstacle to the development of a regional economic policy. Less immediately obvious but even more overwhelming obstacles were Northern Ireland's economic structure and natural economic circumstances. In its attempts to assist existing industries and attract new industries, the government was often reduced to a position of resigned helplessness. And when it did act, it frequently found its range of options limited and its policies foundering.

It was true that existing industries did receive some benefit from the existence of a regional administration responsive to local needs. Most obviously, Belfast's shipyards were assisted by the government's loans guarantee policy. The original Loans Guarantee Act was passed in December 1922 in the hope that the facilitation of cheap loans would stimulate economic activity and reduce unemployment, particularly in the shipyards. The government did not itself lend money or subsidise the shipyards; instead, it guaranteed and negotiated loans made by banks and large insurance companies for capital projects undertaken in the North by private firms such as shipping lines or public bodies. The idea did not originate in Northern Ireland but derived from the British Trades Facilities Act of 1921, which had proved of little assistance to Northern Ireland concerns.[54] The initiative for copying imperial legislation lay between Viscount Pirrie, the head of Harland & Wolff (who was given the opportunity to vet the ministerial speech introducing the first bill), and the Ministry of Finance, where it was regarded as a much cheaper and less demoralising way of relieving unemployment than either unemployment benefit or relief works.[55]

Although the first act had been intended as a temporary and modest measure, adapting the 'much more pretentious'[56] Trades Facilities Act, the Loans Guarantee Acts became an important part of the government's unemployment programme and its distinctive contribution towards the maintenance of the shipbuilding industry, on whose behalf most guarantees were given.[57] The guaranteeing of loans became such a keystone of unemployment policy that, despite persistent criticism from British shipbuilding interests,[58] Northern Ireland continued the policy after its abandonment in Britain. In his 1926 budget speech Churchill, then imperial Chancellor of the Exchequer, had announced that trade facilities would be withdrawn as from 31 March 1927, and thus for several years government assistance was denied in Britain to shipowners and builders.[59] This change in policy momentarily nonplussed the Northern Ireland Ministry of Finance, always anxious to keep in step financially with Britain, but Pollock eventually recommended that the policy should be continued in the North.[60] Conditions in Northern Ireland were so different from those in Britain that the latter's reasons for abandoning trades facilities did not apply with the same force in Northern Ireland. The primary British objection to the loans – that they were seriously interfering with the government's conversion plans – applied also to Northern Ireland, as the guaranteed loans tapped sources to which both governments normally looked for funds for their own purposes. The secondary objection did not apply. In Britain shipowners had complained that the construction of additional cargo ships at a time of diminishing world trade was further depreciating freight, but in Northern Ireland the shipbuilder's view predominated. Pollock was therefore inclined to accept any weakening of the province's credit on account of loans guarantees as a 'further tax necessitated by the unemployment situation'. This decision to continue trades facilities when they had been abandoned in Britain was, Pollock told the House nine years later, 'a matter of life and death for our shipyards', but 'at that critical time, in face of objections from cross-Channel interests, our Government boldly and courageously faced the risks'.[61]

It was not only on general lines of policy that the Northern Ireland shipbuilding industry benefited from the existence of a regional administration in close touch with local needs. It also benefited in matters of detail and speed of response. Guarantees were given on less onerous terms than in Britain in that Northern Ireland shipbuilders were able to use cheaper, foreign steel, whereas the London trades facilities committee had placed an absolute embargo on it. The result was that Belfast shipbuilders were sometimes able to undercut their British competitors, enabling, for example, Workman, Clark & Co. to obtain in 1926 an order for a large passenger ship worth £750,000 and likely to employ 1,100 men.[62] Moreover, when the success of this tender was jeopardised by uncertainty as to the yard's future, the difficulty was overcome by Pollock's readiness, in Craig's absence, to commit the government to further guarantees demanded by the shipping company.[63] In fact, the government took risks and gave additional guarantees for shipbuilding that it was unwilling to do for other industries, occasionally overriding the recommendations of the advisory committee of three experienced businessmen set up to advise on the administration of the acts. In the 1920s it was caution that led the cabinet to decline the committee's recommendation to back hotel-building,[64] but in the 1930s Craig and

Pollock twice gave guarantees to shipping companies against the committee's advice.[65]

The relative success of its loans guarantee policy in assisting shipbuilding simply served to throw into unflattering relief the government's inability to aid other industries in any significant way. The government felt unable to save the linen industry from the consequences of small-scale production. Although the Ministry of Commerce did provide a forum for the industry to discuss price-cutting,[66] the government was unwilling to take the initiative on the central problem of rationalisation. Indeed, it was positively discouraged from doing so by Craig who, although recognising the industry's need to 'speedily secure the advice of an expert with a view to the co-ordination of the whole trade', reckoned that his government should 'let the matter rest until the individuals interested see this for themselves'.[67] This unwillingness to accept responsibility reflected not only the government's general *laissez-faire* attitude but also the dilemma posed by rationalisation. As Andrews was constantly pointing out, amalgamation 'will not help the unemployment position as it would probably be on the basis of the stopping and scrapping of some firms altogether'.[68]

Even when the government was willing and even anxious to act, it found itself hamstrung by economic realities and Northern Ireland's position as part of a larger economic complex. Thus foundered its efforts to solve Northern Ireland's transport problem and provide a co-ordinated and economic system of road and rail transport.

The crux of the problem was the impending bankruptcy and divided ownership and control of Northern Ireland's railway network. Of the nine systems existing in 1934, no fewer than six operated partly in Northern Ireland and partly in the Free State, while another belonged to one of the major British companies. Moreover, all the companies were in financial difficulties in the inter-war years. While costs had increased, receipts were falling, largely because of the rapid growth of road transport, which provided effective competition, especially in the carriage of goods.[69]

Some elements in Northern Ireland thought that the railways had only themselves to blame for their plight. The railway companies had a poor public image in the North, especially among the farming community, which remembered the days of strict regulations and which blamed falling profit margins in the inter-war years on rising railway charges.[70] While there was little sympathy for the state of the railway companies among key sections of society, the government could look upon their deteriorating financial position only with concern. It was not just that the companies constituted an active and prestigious lobby, numbering ministers among their directors and using the Home Affairs Minister's firm of solicitors for some of their legal work. More important was the real contribution that the railways made to the economic life of Northern Ireland. Any closure would mean both unemployment among a labour force which numbered some 6,500 in the 1920s and 5,000 by the late 1930s, and the dislocation of the transport system in both the long and short terms. Too much money had been invested in the railways, and the progressive transfer of traffic, both passenger and goods, from rail to road was not to be lightly contemplated, since road transport had been developing anarchically and often uneconomically.[71]

There was, too, room for optimism. The successful challenge of motor transport had created similar problems throughout Europe, but it was hoped that in such a small area as Northern Ireland the problem would be more susceptible to solution. From the first the government had been convinced that some amalgamation of railway enterprises was essential to their economic survival, and by the mid-1930s it had become equally convinced that the co-ordination and rationalisation of road and rail transport were essential to the country's economic well-being. Yet its efforts to develop a transport policy met with little success. The attitude and position of the railway companies at first forced the government to adopt what it vainly hoped would be the very short-term expedient of giving subsidies to light railways, and then thwarted its plans for reorganisation and co-ordination.

The first problem was brought about by the plight of the London-derry and Lough Swilly Railway Co., a light railway linking North Donegal with the port of Londonderry. Most of its track was in the Free State, but its headquarters and terminus was in Londonderry city, where its principal directors, described as 'large and important rate-payers', lived and voted. It was feared that its closure, which was threatened from 1924 onwards, would affect both Free State and Northern Ireland interests, disrupting transport in Donegal, cutting the county off from its customary port, and causing unemployment in Londonderry both directly through the loss of railway jobs and indirectly by reducing the city's and port's trade with their hinterland.[72]

Although North and South would be affected by the closure of the railway, from the perspective of regional railway policies the situations of the Northern Ireland and Free State governments differed significantly. The main lines of Free State railway policy had been determined by 1924, when all but cross-border railways had been amalgamated as the Great Southern Railways Co. The Londonderry and Lough Swilly Railway was the only non-amalgamated company seeking financial assistance, and the Free State government was the virtual owner of four-fifths of the company's total route mileage. It was therefore comparatively easy for the Free State government to make a grant from 1924 onwards.[73] In Northern Ireland, by contrast, a railway policy had yet to be hammered out. The government's attitude was largely determined by the majority report of the railways commission of 1922, which had recommended the continued private management of railways but with considerable reorganisation and amalgamation.[74] The railways were unenthusiastic about amalgamation and advocated instead the close regulation of motor transport, and since the government was not inclined to take compulsory powers, the question remained in a state of limbo. Moreover, the government was opposed in general to subsidising private enterprise and was in particular disinclined to subsidise local-interest light railways on the grounds that they should be treated not individually but as part of the more general problem of railway development and reorganisation.[75] Nevertheless, the railway policy of the Free State almost obliged the Northern government to advance subsidies to the Londonderry and Lough Swilly Railway; and, once the initial grant had been made in 1925, continued Free State subsidies and Craig's susceptibility to local deputations ensured that a temporary and emergency measure became a permanent grant.[76]

This process was most clearly in evidence in the early 1930s, when there were sound arguments for discontinuing the grant. Studies by the Northern Ministry of Commerce and the Southern Department of Industry and Commerce had demonstrated that the railway could be allowed to close without serious consequences for the trade and port of Londonderry, which could be adequately served by road transport. In addition, it was considered that further government grants would simply benefit the company's debenture-holders and bankers without prolonging the life of the railway – no small consideration at a time of financial stringency when the Northern government was desperately trying to balance its budget.[77] On 12 March 1931, therefore, Craig declared that any further payment would 'only postpone the evil day and would in effect be a question of throwing good money after bad', and the cabinet agreed that no further grant could be justified.[78] Such cold calculation was no match for the political pressure brought to bear by interested parties playing off the two Irish governments. After the Free State government had decided to continue its grant provided the Northern government matched it pound for pound, a deputation from the Londonderry Harbour Board and Chamber of Commerce waited on Craig and Milne Barbour on 25 March, pointing out the Free State's readiness to give a subsidy and emphasising that Londonderry had 'paid heavily for its loyalty, having trade lost through the partition of the country'.[79] Craig and Milne Barbour gave way, agreeing to renew the grant for 1931 and 1932, but only on condition that the request 'represents absolute finality and that no further request for assistance will be made'. The cabinet endorsed this about-face on the following day,[80] and therefore in 1933 no provision was made in the estimates for a further grant. The inevitable deputations descended on Belfast. Fortified by the advice of officials of the Ministries of Finance and Commerce, Craig withstood the first deputation – from the railway company – on 19 May 1933, but he could not resist the cajoling of a second deputation seven days later. The second deputation came from Londonderry Corporation and Harbour Board and plaintively asked: 'Is Londonderry worth to the Empire assistance to the extent of £4,500?'[81] Craig capitulated. He at first agreed to give half the amount requested provided the Corporation and Harbour Commissioners did the same, but when these two bodies refused to co-operate, an irritated Spender recorded in his diary that the Prime Minister had 'decided to give way and to make a further grant of £4,500 per annum for which, of course, no provision has been made in the Estimates'.[82]

In the 1920s its own reluctance to formulate a railways policy had helped to force the government into granting subsidies. Yet in the 1930s, when it showed some determination to establish an efficient and co-ordinated system of public transport, the government found its scope for long-term and comprehensive planning strictly limited. In 1934 the continued decline of the railways and pressure from the companies and trades unions forced the government to take the first of a series of fruitless steps in an effort to secure an efficient and integrated transport system. At the beginning of January 1934 a deputation from the railway companies and relevant trades unions waited upon the Prime Minister and Ministers of Home Affairs and Commerce and expressed their concern at the continued deteriorating position of Northern Ireland's railways. Craig gave no hint as to the government's likely course of action, but at its next meeting the cabinet decided to accept Craig's recommendation that it should seek the advice of 'an expert dissociated from either Railway or Road transport interests'.[83] Accordingly, Sir Felix Pole, former chairman of the London Transport Board, was invited to formulate a policy which would be fair to the interests concerned and yet ensure an efficient transport system. Appointed in January 1934, Pole completed his report in the following June, having taken evidence from users as well as road and rail transport interests. The most obvious course, the establishment of a single transport board to meet the unanswerable case for co-ordination of road and rail services, was rejected by Pole because six of the railways concerned operated partly in the Free State and a seventh was British-owned. The compromise solution was to set up a public utility company to run road transport and a joint committee representing the new Road Transport Board and the railway companies to co-ordinate services, this essential process to be encouraged, it was hoped, by the pooling of receipts.[84] The major recommendations were incorporated by an enthusiastic government into a Road and Railway Transport Bill, which was introduced into the Commons on 18 April 1935, and which aroused considerable interest both inside and outside Northern Ireland as an honest attempt to grapple with a difficult and widespread problem.[85]

The bill quickly became law, but equally quickly it became obvious that it provided no solution to Northern Ireland's transport problem. It proved costly to buy out existing road transport undertakings and to operate the new board; and although there were some instances of co-ordination between the new board and the railway companies, there was little mutual confidence, each side being jealous of the other's contributions to or drawings from the receipts pool. The government's response was to fortify itself against the resultant outcry by arranging a series of committees and inquiries: a technical committee of experts headed by a prominent London accountant, Sir William McClintock; a public inquiry headed by the Recorder of Belfast, Judge H. M. Thomson;[86] and a joint select committee of the two Houses of Parliament to consider the other two reports.[87] The McClintock committee called for bold and urgent action to assist public rail services at the expense of public road services; but the joint select committee, which set about its work with the same lack of courage and foresight that characterised the activities of parliament as a whole,[88] gave priority to road transport and advocated only piecemeal change.

From this conflicting counsel, the government, largely because of Craig, preferred the tenor of expert advice and decided to hand control of public transport to the railways. They had been largely responsible for the many failures of the 1935 act, which, although creating a 'semipublic utility . . . for the purpose of sheltering various vested interests',[89] had not gone far enough for the railway companies, who wanted to become the sole proprietors of public transport in their respective areas. This suggestion had been emphatically rejected by Pole and Bates, who argued that road transport would thus be worked as a mere adjunct to the railways, whereas its true function was much wider.[90] Nevertheless, by July 1939 the railway companies had, at least in principle, won their case. Craig's response to the imperial Treasury's demand and his own government's banker's advice to halt the mounting debts of the Road Transport Board[91] was to offer the railway companies a monopoly of public transport. He told his colleagues at a cabinet meeting on 18 July 1939 that

> Their transport policy should be based on the long view and not with an eye to any possible agitation which would be raised. He considered that there would inevitably be criticism on whatever decision was reached by the Government and he thought that the principles of a sound economic scheme should now be settled. . . . Public transport, both passenger and freight, should be placed in the hands of

the Railways, with proper safeguards. . . . Such a scheme appealed to him as he felt that the Railways were the most experienced body to deal with all classes of traffic: it would prevent dual control; would not involve nationalisation; and should in his opinion secure a substantial reduction in overhead expenditure. He felt that the Government would receive the support of the Railways, rather than their obstruction, if such a course were followed.[92]

Despite the continued reservations of the Minister and Ministry of Home Affairs and the knowledge that the decision would be unpopular, especially among farmers, the cabinet adopted Craig's plan. But, as with most decisions in Northern Ireland, the boldness of the initiative soon disappeared. Negotiations dragged on for over a year and were finally shelved in October 1940,[93] ostensibly owing to war conditions but largely because the cabinet, which discussed the question at almost every meeting between November 1939 and October 1940, was unwilling to make a final decision on terms. Torn between the conflicting demands of the railways and the farmers, the government was reduced to a state of indecision and inaction.

3

The government's efforts to attract new industries were as circumscribed and as unsuccessful as it efforts to assist old ones. With the decline of, and high unemployment in, the old staple industries, the need to broaden Northern Ireland's industrial base was obvious to all, and the government accepted some responsibility for attracting new industries. The trouble was that the obstacles were as obvious as the need, as the government soon discovered when it tried to assist the development of a coal industry. Northern Ireland's natural disadvantages overcame both the enterprise of its leading coal merchant and the enthusiasm of the Ministry of Commerce.

Northern Ireland would have derived at least two advantages from the development of a coal industry. Employment would have been created, and costs of production, hitherto inflated by high fuel costs, would have been reduced to the benefit of both existing industries and the new industries which Northern Ireland hoped to attract. At the beginning of the 1920s such a goal as self-sufficiency in coal did not seem impossible. From time to time over the previous two centuries coal had been worked in outcrops or shallow mines in three coalfields (two in Co. Tyrone and one in Co. Antrim), but no serious attempt had been made to prove the extent and quality of the deposits until 1922–23, when a shaft sunk at Coalisland, close to the southwestern corner of Lough Neagh, disclosed the existence of twelve seams of coal of good steam and household variety.[94] Sir Samuel Kelly,

Northern Ireland's leading coal merchant, owner of a small mine in Cumberland, and former gun-runner, therefore invested some £200,000 in trying to create a mining centre at Coalisland, and he was watched with eager anticipation by the Ministry of Commerce. It reckoned in April 1923 that

> If the coal is found in the quantities anticipated by the experts engaged by him there is no doubt that the whole economic situation in Ulster will be changed, and from being a country necessarily importing all her raw material she will become self-contained in that respect, will be the home of many new industries, and will be in a position to give employment on a very large scale.[95]

The Ministry of Commerce wanted a close and active involvement in mining development and advocated the establishment of a mining authority, but such intimacy was distasteful to some ministers and, more importantly, to Kelly, who preferred government financial aid without government control.[96] The government therefore confined itself to providing a satisfactory legislative framework for mining activities[97] and offering financial inducements to encourage Kelly's Coalisland enterprise. The latter consisted at first of grants or the underwriting of a cheap loan for the building of workers' houses,[98] but it eventually included a direct subsidy for the mine as well.

When in August 1925 the imperial government decided to give the British coal industry a subvention in aid of wages to postpone a national coal strike, Kelly demanded similar treatment. Otherwise he threatened his mine would close.[99] The Ministry of Finance stressed the difficulties of giving such a subsidy in view of the different conditions prevailing in Northern Ireland, but, agreeing with Andrews that the closure of the mine would be 'disastrous', the cabinet decided on 28 October 1926 to give Kelly a subvention on British lines.[100] Two months later the cabinet was somewhat shaken by the size of the subsidies payable to Coalisland (22s 11.1d per ton compared with an average of 2s 1.11d in Britain), but decided to persevere. It was, Londonderry argued, a case of 'development rather than production', while Craig 'did not want it suggested that the owners had to close down the mine owing to lack of support'.[101]

It was fortunate that the cabinet made this decision, because the figures produced to determine the amount of subsidy payable underlined the difficulties of exploiting what natural resources Northern Ireland possessed.[102] Quite simply, coal could not be economically mined on any scale, for costs were three times higher than in Britain (at one time an average of 67s 0.73d per ton of commercially disposable coal compared with 18s 0.58d in Britain). Despite high subsidies, coal could be mined only at a considerable loss, which exceeded that sustained by any operative British mine. Even with the subvention, the mine's accounts could not be made to balance, and with its withdrawal the mine closed in April 1927. There was too much water, and the seams were too soft, of too high an inclination, and too broken with faults to allow the coal to be won without expensive timbering.[103] This was, indeed, the story of coal-mining in Northern Ireland. The development commission may well have been right in estimating that the three coal-bearing areas of Northern Ireland contained coal to the value of £100 million. The difficulty was that economically exploitable seams were soon exhausted, and Northern Ireland had to endure the disadvantages of continued reliance upon the import of such a basic raw material.

Northern Ireland's natural disadvantages also largely explained the failure of the new-industries legislation of the 1930s to broaden the North's industrial base. The New Industries (Development) Acts of 1932 and July and December 1937 offered increasingly comprehensive incentives to new and, later, to existing industries,[104] but they achieved little. The only large industry attracted to Northern Ireland in the inter-war years was an aircraft factory, Short & Harland, established in 1937. Although it was given a site grant under the 1932 act, it is probable that the factory would have been established regardless of the £2,709 received annually from the government. The other industries established under the 1932 act may have extended the range of goods produced, but they consisted of only a few small firms offering limited employment.[105] More firms were given aid under the later acts, but although the Ministry of Commerce claimed in 1939 to find comfort in the fact that their output covered a wide range of goods (including various types of clothing and other textile products, foodstuffs, furniture and furnishings), they provided fewer jobs, and those for women rather than for men.*[106] In July 1939 the Ministry of Commerce boasted that its new-industries legislation would eventually help in creating some 12,500 jobs, but even this modest expectation was not realised. Employment in such firms reached a peak of 7,292 in 1949.[107] Neither in the short term nor in the long term did the new-industries legislation do much to broaden Northern Ireland's industrial basis or alleviate unemployment.

*Under the 1932 act grants were given to eight companies, one of which quickly closed down, so that by May 1939 only seven companies, in receipt of site grants totalling £2,878, were operating under the act, providing 6,552 jobs, mainly for men (6,273 at Short & Harland, 8 at an insecticide firm, 13 at a fruit-spraying machine factory, 47 at a jute factory, 14 at a chromium-plating works, 132 at a firm making ties, and 65 at a woollen spinning mill). By the middle of 1939 20 firms were operating under the 1937 acts, providing work for 1,235, and a further 22 firms had been granted aid but had not begun operations. When all 42 firms were in operation it was hoped that a further 4,815 jobs would be provided.

In part, the government was to blame. Policy was ill-considered and poorly executed. The initial legislation was adopted not as a result of careful consideration. Rather, it was sprung on ministers and their departments by Craig, who on 21 October 1931, during the imperial election campaign, in order to rebut charges of apathy in face of rising unemployment, announced that the government would offer rent-free sites to industrialists wishing to establish new industries. It was then left to the departments to divine what Craig really had in mind and to hammer out the details;[108] and cabinet discussions of the consequent measure centred not around how far the provision of free sites would really attract new industries, but around how important it was that the government should avoid 'becoming owners of the land and should be careful they were not ultimately left with sites which would become a charge on the Exchequer'.[109] Moreover, when it soon became clear that the 1932 act was not attracting new industries (enabling one Independent Unionist to inquire in December 1933 'whether if the Government set up a few new chip shops they would not give more employment'),[110] the government let it run its full five years before it considered further action. When the act finally expired, the Ministry of Commerce opposed the introduction of another general measure. Instead, it recommended that there should be the utmost flexibility in dealing with proposals to establish new industries. Milne Barbour argued that the government should 'merely hold ourselves free to consider on its merits any proposition that may offer itself'. Each case 'should be dealt with according to its particular needs and Parliamentary sanction to whatever assistance is required sought and obtained as occasion demands'.[111]

This idea had much to commend it, since it took advantage of Northern Ireland's possible strengths – speed of decision-making and adaptability. With the government's assured parliamentary majority, inducements could be tailored to meet the needs of individual cases, and this did happen. Nestlés, the large British milk manufacturing concern, was encouraged to set up a factory at Ballymoney in Co. Antrim, not only by the offer of loans under the 1937 acts but also by the readiness of the Ministries of Agriculture and Commerce to commit the government to amending its milk legislation so as to render milk supplied to the new factory eligible for payments from the Milk Fund.[112] Again, to encourage a French firm of silk and artificial silk stocking manufacturers to set up a factory (which, it was forecast, would eventually provide 1,100 jobs), the cabinet decided on 23 March 1939 to waive in this instance recent legislation banning a 6 a.m. start for women workers, so that the firm would be able to introduce the most efficient shift-system. Although during the passage of the 1939 Factory Act M.P.s had been particularly keen to limit women's working hours, the cabinet felt that 'the House would readily endorse the action of the Government when all the facts are explained'.[113]

Despite its obvious advantages, such an open-ended policy as suggested by the Ministry of Commerce did not recommend itself to the cabinet. It was better to be seen to have a policy, whatever its efficacy, than to be accused of having no policy at all. Thus the 1937 legislation contained detailed proposals to bring incentives offered in Northern Ireland into line with those available to new industries in areas of high unemployment, the 'distressed' or 'special' areas, in Britain, after an informal interdepartmental committee on unemployment had investigated the working in Scotland of the Special Areas (Amendment) Act of 1937.[114]

Even within the limits of the measures adopted, it is doubtful whether full benefits were derived from what they had to offer. Publicity, regarded as the key to success, was inefficiently handled, partly because of Craig's insistence on appointing a personal friend and former Commander-in-Chief in Northern Ireland as the country's first Agent-General in Britain,[115] and partly because of fear of arousing the vocal resentment of existing voluntary bodies interested in industrial development.[116] More vitally, the policies were cautiously administered to avoid upsetting existing industries[117] and incurring financial loss. The Ministry of Commerce was prepared to take risks, and so too was the advisory committee of experienced businessmen set up to advise the government on applications for aid; but the Ministry of Finance proved less flexible. Strangely enough, it was not the civil servants but Andrews, by then Minister of Finance, who proved the obstacle to the speedy and adventurous consideration of applications for aid. The guidelines used by the advisory committee in considering the 106 applications submitted to it between 17 December 1937 and 26 July 1939 were exacting,[118] but they were not exacting enough for Andrews, who insisted that his junior minister should personally vet every recommendation for assistance, especially on the part of smaller firms. The result was not only delay but also the rejection of a number of applications by the Ministry of Finance – an outcome which seriously perturbed Spender. Indeed, Andrews's attitude was so destructive of Ministry of Commerce morale and so likely to arouse 'further criticism of Civil Service red tape'[119] that Spender would on occasion have welcomed what he normally condemned – intervention by Craig with his disregard for constitutional and bureaucratic proprieties.[120]

Not that the government was alone in Northern Ireland in having a limited view of policy. It was always under pressure from supporters and opponents to take action, but it received little by way of positive guidance from outside quarters. There was, indeed, a striking contrast between the way economic policy was discussed in Northern Ireland

and in Britain. In Britain economic problems were widely investigated and discussed by universities and private bodies as well as by the government, but in Northern Ireland no such informed public existed from whom the government could seek advice and support. The most widely favoured policy to cure unemployment was a massive programme of public works, but nobody came up with an alternative workable scheme for attracting new industries. Even after the government had extended the scope of the new-industries legislation, it found difficulty in securing the co-operation of Belfast Corporation, which was prepared to remit rates only under the restricted terms of the 1932 act.[121]

Yet, gratifying though it may be to castigate the limitations of politicians and civil servants and the underdeveloped state of economic thought, the fundamental reasons for the failure to attract new industries lay in Northern Ireland's economic and financial position. Northern Ireland was not alone in seeking new industries in the inter-war years, and had to compete on unequal terms with distressed areas in Britain and with the Free State. The North's natural disadvantages – distance from raw materials and markets – were thrown into even greater relief by the inducements offered to new industries in Britain and the Free State. In Britain by 1937 the resources of both the state and a wealthy private donor, Lord Nuffield, were being used to attract new industries to distressed areas there, while the Free State was able to offer industrialists a guaranteed monopoly. Although the Northern government could never match the Free State inducement, it was within its power to outbid the British incentives. Yet Northern Ireland's financial position in the 1930s precluded such an effort, and the Ministry of Finance insisted that financial incentives should not exceed those available in Britain. Thus the two 1937 acts tried only to match the facilities available in special areas in Britain, and in the following year another proposal for flexibility was shot down. In the spring of 1938 W. Robson, the Ministry of Commerce official in charge of industrial development, suggested the establishment of a development fund on the lines of the Nuffield Fund but more flexibly administered. Andrews was unenthusiastic, and the project foundered without ever reaching the cabinet in face of Spender's insistence that any grants would have to be made with the same degree of security as those given from the Nuffield Fund. Otherwise, he stressed, there would be objections from the Treasury.[122]

Even when new industries were attracted, Northern Ireland did not reap the full benefit. Particularly needy areas were neglected. One of the frequent complaints after the Second World War was that the government's industrial policy discriminated against Catholic areas, and certainly in the inter-war years firms established with government assistance were concentrated in and around Belfast.*[123] Such concentration was not any part of the government's policy. It and the new-industries advisory committee did try to encourage the dispersal of industry throughout the province, and their anxiety to do this led them to sanction, much to Labour M.P.s' disgust, the organisation of cottage industries in parts of Co. Fermanagh. The plain truth was that the government had to be grateful for what it could get. The Ministry of Commerce was always at pains to point prospective manufacturers to the north and to the west, but could not persuade them to establish themselves outside the traditional industrial area, even in such a loyal town as Coleraine.[124]

Not only were certain areas neglected, but Northern Ireland's share in whatever prosperity was generated by new industries was limited by the lowness of the income and employment multipliers.[125] Their lowness not only stressed and summarised the relative disadvantages of the Northern Ireland economy; it also emphasised the folly of a scheme of devolution which treated Northern Ireland as a separate area responsible for its own industrial development.

*Of the 27 firms actually operating under the new-industries legislation by the middle of 1939, 15 were situated in Belfast, a further 3 in the industrial complex centring on Belfast, 3 in Londonderry, 2 in Newry, and the remaining 4 in Counties Antrim, Down and Fermanagh.

6

Adaptability: Agriculture

> If a farmer wanted somebody to blow his nose some hon. Member
> would get up and raise the question in this House, and a man would
> be appointed not only to blow the farmer's nose but to wipe it for
> him.[1]

Thus one of the Independent Unionist M.P.s for Belfast summed up the
degree to which the state had become involved in agriculture in Northern
Ireland in the inter-war years. Governments throughout the world were
trying to foster the development of agriculture during that period, and
in the United Kingdom these efforts took the form of research, education, protection, marketing schemes and subsidies. However, the particular type of help given to agriculture in Northern Ireland, the way in
which its particular needs were identified and catered for, does provide
a cogent argument in favour of the devolution of government. Yet the
degree of initiative displayed by the Ministry of Agriculture in shaping
and sustaining policy does raise the question of whether such responsiveness could have been achieved simply by administrative rather than by
parliamentary devolution.

1

The creation of a new region with its own Ministry of Agriculture did
provide the opportunity to develop policies suited to Northern Ireland's needs. The new department was not an inexperienced one, as
many of its senior officials were drawn from the old Irish Department
of Agriculture and Technical Instruction; and with the existence of a
regional parliament, more parliamentary time was available for the
consideration of the detailed problems of agriculture in the six counties. Yet, although the need for a distinctive agricultural policy was
clear, the obstacles to its development were considerable.

The most obvious obstacles were the limitations imposed upon the
powers of the government and parliament by the 1920 act. Although
the act was amended to allow the regulation of agricultural exports to

other parts of the British Isles,[2] Northern Ireland never had the power
to control imports. The result was that more radical schemes to help
agriculture had to await the change in imperial fiscal policy which
occurred in the early 1930s.

Just as real as legal limitations, and sometimes more daunting, were
the obstacles within Northern Ireland itself to the development of a
distinctive agricultural policy. The biggest of these obstacles lay in the
nature of the agricultural problem. The small farmer's intense conservatism and suspicion of government intervention threatened at one
time to reduce the Ministry of Agriculture to impotence,[3] and when it
did act the ministry was in danger of being hoisted on the government's
own Unionist petard. Often the farmers' cry was for proceeding 'step-
by-step' with Britain, at least where agricultural policy entailed financial relief and the minimum of state intervention. The Northern Ireland
Ministry of Agriculture, by contrast, insisted that conditions in the
North necessitated a greater degree of state intervention in and control
of agriculture than in the rest of the United Kingdom. Whatever the
social, economic and political benefits, the elimination of landlords and
the predominance of small owner-occupied farms were not, the Permanent Secretary of the ministry once argued, 'without certain distinct
disadvantages'. The agricultural industry did 'not provide leadership
within its ranks to the same extent as in England, where the larger
farmers and those landlords who take an interest in the welfare of their
tenants play a very important part in the development, welfare and
organisation of the industry'.[4] The natural independence and conservatism of Northern Ireland farmers and traders disinclined them to voluntary co-operation, while the small-scale and mixed nature of their
operations meant that they often lacked the ability and information
necessary to devise and maintain, for example, the elaborate marketing
schemes which were essential if Northern Ireland produce was to compete successfully in the British market.

The Ministry of Agriculture had its way as far as marketing schemes
were concerned. Not only did such schemes predate those in the rest of
the United Kingdom, but they were compulsory and necessarily em-
braced the whole of a particular section of agriculture and were supervised closely by the ministry. The British schemes were, in the main,
voluntary, partial and operated by the interested parties themselves.
Whereas the British Agricultural Marketing Acts of 1931 and 1933
emphasised the principle of producer initiative, consent and control,
the 1933 Northern Ireland act vested responsibility for preparing
schemes in the Ministry of Agriculture, which acted virtually as a permanent reorganisation commission and did not, unlike the British measures, provide for a poll of producers.[5] These differences caused some
debate within the cabinet, but Craig supported the Ministry of Agri-

culture. Farmers, he told his ministers on one occasion, 'will gradually have to be taught that they can successfully export their produce only by taking advantage of expert advice'.[6]

Farmers were, however, united and successful in their insistence on keeping in financial step with their British counterparts. Whenever financial relief was afforded to British farmers, there was an immediate demand for equal relief for Northern Ireland farmers. The crucial battle here was fought in 1923, when the imperial government granted rate relief in an attempt to help British farmers in a period of falling prices. An equivalent sum was made available for the relief of Northern Ireland agriculture, and opinion in the government was divided as to how this money could be most usefully spent. Some ministers and officials, particularly those belonging to Finance, Agriculture and Education, favoured its expenditure on research and development, especially since the little relief (mainly between 2s 6d and 7s 6d per farm annually) afforded would, according to Pollock, 'probably cause more disappointment than pleasure'.[7] Craig and Andrews, by contrast, were reluctant to depart from the British example, the latter holding that 'the farmers would expect to get in actual cash the sum which was being given to similar farmers in Great Britain and that there would be violent criticism on their part if they found that they were being treated differently'.[8] Farmers did, indeed, react fiercely when they learned that the government was contemplating using the money on projects other than rate relief, and the government was bombarded with resolutions from the council and branches of the U.F.U.[9] In the circumstances, the government set up a committee under Lord Pirrie to investigate the matter, and the committee quickly and unanimously reported in favour of the relief of rates.[10] The precedent having been established, there was no need for a similar agitation in 1928, when further derating was announced in Britain. The government, without proper consideration of its merits or likely consequences, quickly conceded the point and even derated agricultural land on more generous terms than in Britain.[11]

Finance was a third problem. Northern Ireland's financial resources were limited in the inter-war years. In addition, in an atmosphere in which spending priorities were always closely scrutinised, there was more than a suspicion among urban dwellers that farmers' cries of distress and demands for cash and relief of burdens were exaggerated and unjustified, especially in view of their almost complete immunity from income tax and the increasing amount of rate relief being made available. When Fermanagh farmers in February 1926 cited as evidence of their acute distress the fact that 'little family nest eggs . . . handed down from father to son for generations' had for the first time in many years been withdrawn from local savings banks,[12] the Ministry of Finance predictably retorted that the 'very considerable assistance' hitherto given to farmers had entailed a general burden on the whole body of taxpayers, many of whom in industrial centres have been hit quite as badly as farmers. Manufacturers in Belfast and elsewhere have had to fall back very largely on the accumulations of past years, and Mr Pollock sees nothing extraordinary, therefore, in the fact that the farmers' deposits in local Savings Banks have been reduced.[13]

Given the context of Northern Ireland's financial relations with Britain in the inter-war years, the financial problem was almost insuperable and prevented a comprehensive attack upon some fundamental problems. It was impossible for the government to countenance the abolition or reduction of land-purchase annuities, which gave a net income in the 1930s of over £650,000 a year.[14] The problem of the under-capitalisation of farms was never systematically tackled. And wrangling over finance, not only between the government and local authorities but also among local authorities themselves, prevented an adequate response to the pressing drainage problems presented by the flooding of Loughs Erne and Neagh and the River Bann.[15]

The other obstacles to the development of a regional agricultural policy were not, however, insuperable. In many respects the lack of organisation in the countryside worked in the government's favour, particularly when dealing with a problem affecting only one section of farming, while in such a small area as Northern Ireland it was possible for the Ministry of Agriculture to canvass its ideas widely and intimately before attempting to implement them. Even in such a small area, ignorance, misunderstanding and misrepresentation remained features of agricultural debate, but the government tried to minimise suspicions by exploiting to the full such representative organisations as did exist. On specific questions specialised trade associations were consulted, but in general the ministry relied on its own consultative committee of agriculture for the six counties which it had set up in 1922, the county committees of agriculture which it had inherited from the old Irish department, and the U.F.U. and the U.A.O.S.

The ministry's relationship with the U.A.O.S. was somewhat equivocal, entailing, for example, the withdrawal of a state grant in 1924. Nevertheless, the U.A.O.S. was useful to the government. With its central council and its creamery organisation made up of committees of farmers, the U.A.O.S. was the only organised aspect of the dairy industry, and the only one with a degree of conscious direction, which made the society in the 1920s a staunch advocate of the state regulation of the industry. Whenever possible, therefore, the Ministry of Agriculture did co-operate with the U.A.O.S., consulting it on most agricultural measures.[16] The ministry found the U.F.U. even more useful. Although it represented only a minority of farmers, usually the more substantial, it did have branches throughout the country and was the

only general farmers' organisation. From the start the ministry culti-
vated close relations with the U.F.U., cementing the alliance by persuading the government to give financial assistance to prevent the bankruptcy and failure of the Ulster Farmers' Produce Society, a none-too-
successful enterprise closely associated with the U.F.U. which aimed at
supplying cheap inputs to farmers.[17] This harmonious relationship
lasted until 1938, when there was a change of officers in the union,[18]
but as long as it lasted the government found it particularly useful in
defending, if not formulating, policy. Whenever he was called upon to
defend the Ministry of Agriculture's insistence on compulsion, Craig
almost unfailingly referred to the 'view taken by an old friend of mine,
a good, sound agriculturalist, Mr David Wright, who is vice-president of
the Ulster Farmers' Union . . . that if the organisation and cooperation
of farmers could not be done by voluntary means there must be some
coercion'.[19]

Such consultations were a two-way process and often meant that
measures brought before parliament had been fully agreed upon beforehand between the government and interested parties. The result was
that parliament contributed little to agricultural policy-making, and
during the passage of a bill through parliament the government almost
invariably made only minor concessions, often to reassure farmers'
representatives that the Ministry of Agriculture was not planning to
assume control of the whole industry. Sometimes, however, consultation and reassurance could not alter opinions, and there came a point
where a decision had to be made and the implementation or abandonment of a particular line of policy depended upon the government's
determination, a determination often supplied by such permanent
officials as Scott Robertson. Indeed, Scott Robertson's appointment
as Permanent Secretary in 1932 both introduced a new crusading zeal
into, and stiffened the resolve of, the Ministry of Agriculture – so
much so that he was in danger of alienating the government's supporters.
'I'm afraid', protested the hon. secretary of the U.U.C. in 1937, '[that
Scott Robertson] is making lots of trouble for us & is running his
Minister'.[20]

The price of such determination was to increase tensions within the
Unionist Party. Sometimes expectations were created that the government could not satisfy or satisfy quickly enough, as over the delay,
through overwork, in copying Britain's milk marketing scheme.[21] More
often than not, however, it was the activity rather than the inactivity
of the Ministry of Agriculture that caused increasing alarm. Agricultural
policy, particularly with the growing number of inspectors, did interfere with traditional routines on farms, and it became the most persistent source of criticism of the government. The Ministry of Agriculture's insistence upon compulsion created considerable resentment

among farmers who liked to contrast what they regarded as the 'departmental dictatorship' exercised in Northern Ireland with the respect
shown for producers' rights in Britain;[22] and Unionists, Nationalists and
Independents were never quite sure whether what they were condemning was Nazism or socialism.[23] It was on matters of agricultural policy
that Unionist backbenchers most frequently divided against the government;[24] and it was agricultural policy that led to particularly acrimonious disputes between the government and farmers, culminating in the
dissolution of the Pigs Marketing Board in February 1939 and the
resignation of first the U.A.O.S. representatives on the Butter and
Cream Board and then the entire board in 1938–39.[25]

It may not be without significance that the two inter-war Ministers
of Agriculture, Archdale (1921–33) and Brooke (1933–41), became
notorious for their anti-Catholic remarks.[26] It may be simply that they
were both Fermanagh men, but it was also true that assertions of
loyalty were one way of reassuring critics and rallying opinion. Usually
the debate over agricultural policy was conducted in terms of the
benefits or otherwise agriculture would derive from the particular
aspect of policy over which there was disagreement. Sometimes, however, the debate was conducted among Unionists in terms of 'loyalty',
Unionist critics accusing the government of betraying Unionism and
ministers responding in like terms. Thus the government and particularly
the Ministry of Agriculture were roundly condemned in 1935 for allowing a Cork firm, rather than the U.A.O.S., to establish a creamery at
Newry. There were sound economic reasons for giving preference to the
Cork firm.[27] Nevertheless, when justifying the decision in public to a
Unionist meeting in Co. Down, Brooke could not resist answering his
critics in traditional terms. The head of the Cork firm, he said, was a
staunch loyalist and a Freemason, otherwise the application to establish
a creamery in Newry would have been refused. The speech thus gave
the *Irish Press* good copy for an editorial on the government's attitude
towards the Catholic and nationalist minority.[28]

All policy in Northern Ireland could eventually be brought back to
this fundamental issue, but the tensions created by the development of
a regional agricultural policy were more than offset by its benefits.
Agriculture in Northern Ireland did have distinctive problems which
merited special treatment. There were, it is true, obstacles to the development of a distinctive policy, but there also existed a determination on the part of the government, especially among officials of the
Ministry of Agriculture, to increase agricultural prosperity by taking
advantage of, and where necessary extending, its devolved powers to
devise measures suited to conditions in Northern Ireland. On the one
hand, schemes were adopted in Northern Ireland which had no parallels
in the rest of the United Kingdom. On the other hand, measures apply-

ing to the United Kingdom as a whole were adapted to suit the requirements of Northern Ireland farming.

2

In the 1920s it was difficult for agricultural policy in Northern Ireland to be other than different from British policy. With the dismantling of wartime controls, the imperial government had reverted to its traditional posture of minimal interference with agriculture. A generous subsidy to develop the sugar beet industry was untypical, and the state's role was limited to helping farmers help themselves by the development of research, the provision of credit facilities and rate relief, and the encouragement of voluntary marketing schemes.[29] In Northern Ireland, however, the Ministry of Agriculture was more interventionist and exploited its devolved powers to develop a policy of agricultural modernisation which differed significantly from the *laissez-faire* policy continued in Britain.

That the ministry intended to adopt a distinctive regional policy was evident from its first major measure – the 1922 Live Stock Breeding Act. Designed to improve the standard of breeding in the North's most prestigious agricultural pursuit, the act was a prompt response to a long-felt need which the Westminster parliament had not been able to satisfy under the Union. Since 1907 Irish agricultural opinion had been pressing for legislation to outlaw the 'scrub bull', but although time had been found to pass a Horse Breeding Act in 1918, a matter of concern to particular classes throughout the United Kingdom, Archdale told the Northern Ireland Commons, 'the difficulty of getting an Irish act pure and simple through the House of Commons was too much'.[30] The Live Stock Breeding Act, which preceded similar legislation in Britain and the Free State by nine and three years respectively, was thus framed in immediate response to regional opinion and conditions. What is more, experts agree that the act, the administration of which was sensitive to highly localised needs and susceptibilities,[31] did lead to 'a marked improvement in the general quality of the cattle'.[32]

The distinctive contribution of the Ministry of Agriculture to the modernisation of agriculture lay in the compulsory marketing scheme, designed to improve both production and marketing. The 1924 Eggs Marketing Act did, as Archdale proudly told the House,[33] break new ground in the United Kingdom. The scheme, to ensure that only fresh, clean and graded eggs were offered for sale in Britain, was carefully framed to surmount the limitations imposed by the 1920 act. Administratively the simplest course would have been the regulation of only the 200 exporters of eggs, but since at that time the 1920 act forbade the making of laws in respect of trade out of Northern Ireland, the ministry had to undertake the more complicated but nevertheless manageable operation of regulating the activities of all the North's 2,000 egg dealers.[34] Indeed, throughout the eggs marketing scheme avoided reliance upon Westminster's powers and the straining of Northern Ireland's financial resources. It relied for its effect neither upon import control nor upon subsidy, but upon regulation, to which end considerable powers were conferred on the Ministry of Agriculture to ensure proper testing, grading, packaging and inspection. It was the success of such regulation in improving the egg trade that emboldened the Ministry of Agriculture to press in 1926 for a limited extension of Northern Ireland's powers.[35]

Although the ministry normally initiated marketing schemes, it preferred to proceed by consultation with interested parties. Thus the original Eggs Marketing Act, and subsequent alterations in 1926, 1928, 1931 and 1936, were all preceded by widespread consultation and presented to parliament as agreed measures. Parliament was thus left with virtually no role in the formulation of agricultural policy. It was true that members on all sides of the House had little positive to offer. Rather, they were concerned to limit schemes which meant more ministry intervention and more inspectors, but even then they could achieve nothing negative. The most that critics of eggs marketing legislation could achieve was the postponement by one week of the 1936 bill.[36] In agriculture as in other matters, the opinions of outside parties were of more concern to the government than those of parliament, as M.P.s found out when they attended a meeting called by the Ministry of Agriculture to discuss criticisms of the 1926 Eggs Marketing Bill.

> I was invited to a conference a few days ago [related one rural M.P.]. I understood it was merely a conference among what I might call agricultural members, those who were naturally interested in egg production, but to my astonishment when I went into the room I found there were egg buyers, egg shippers, egg collectors, egg inspectors, egg eaters, and egg producers — I do not mean hens.[37]

Although the Ministry of Agriculture preferred to proceed by consultation and consent, it was prepared to do without the latter in order to preserve its marketing schemes. The initiative for the 1930 Fruit Marketing Bill came from Portadown Chamber of Commerce, in the heart of Northern Ireland's small apple-growing belt,[38] but its implementation and retention, in face of fierce opposition from fruit-growers, was due entirely to the determination or obstinacy of the Ministry of Agriculture.

The only apparent obstacle to a fruit marketing scheme had been doubt as to whether Northern Ireland possessed the necessary powers. It was more than possible that the prescription of trade designation marks would be *ultra vires,* as coming under the heading 'merchandise marks', which were specifically excepted in clause 4 of the 1920 act. However, consultations with the Home Office and English Ministry of Agriculture eventually persuaded the former to make no objection to the final terms of the bill, which sought to improve both the home and export apple trades.[39] The ministry and the government as a whole were thus taken aback when a virulent campaign against the bill was launched by the newly formed Ulster Fruit-Growers' Defence Association (U.F.G.D.A.).[40] Since the prime mover was a speculator in apples and an agent for an insecticide earlier proved useless by ministry tests, Ministry of Agriculture officials dismissed the agitation as factious and self-interested.[41] Factious or not, the agitation gained considerable sympathy among M.P.s, not only those accustomed to denounce measures as 'Socialistic and coercive',[42] but also normally amenable M.P.s from the apple-growing area who thought the government should 'go slowly in this matter. . . . Seeing the amount of public opinion against this Bill . . . it is a case of legislation being rather too far in advance'.[43] In return for a favourable second reading in October 1930, Craig therefore promised to postpone the bill pending further consultation.[44]

The postponement left the Ministry of Agriculture the more determined to get its bill. In the winter of 1930–31 it launched a propaganda campaign, which included Craig's meeting on 30 January 1931 a deputation of reasonably sympathetic fruit-growers, to whom he promised that the ministry would 'go gently', and the foundation of a new organisation in support of regulation – the Ulster Fruit-Growers' Marketing Association (U.F.G.M.A.).[45] Indeed, the ministry took such heart from its campaign that it proposed to make the original measure more stringent as regards the home market.[46]

The cabinet was less concerned with the technical efficiency of the measure than with its general acceptability. In particular, there was concern lest any change in the original bill could be represented as a breach of the 'agreement' reached by Craig with fruit-growers at the end of January. When, on 26 February 1931, the cabinet considered at some length the proposed amendments, Craig said that

> He would not like to make any alterations to the Bill without again consulting the members of the Deputation. To do so, he felt, would look like breaking faith with them. In any case in view of the agitation which had taken place . . . it would be much wiser for the Minister to arrange for one of the Members who had already identified himself with the matter to move the amendments on the Committee stage of the Bill when the Government would readily accept them.[47]

This course was adopted. In a forceful speech Archdale reintroduced the bill in March 1931 in substantially the same form as before,[48] and its smooth passage was ensured by some horsetrading behind the scenes by Ministry of Agriculture officials with interested M.P.s.[49]

The passage of the act did not end controversy, as apple-growers and traders liked to blame all their troubles in the 1930s on the government and its regulations laying down minimum standards for exports. Thus to the continued criticism of the U.F.G.D.A. was gradually added the increasing discontent of former supporters of regulation, including members of the U.F.G.M.A. Discontent reached its peak in 1937, when urgent pleas were sent to Craig seeking the repeal of the Fruit Marketing Act and, if necessary, its substitution by a voluntary system on the lines of the English National Mark scheme. When this 'injustice' is removed, the secretary of the U.F.G.M.A. assured Craig in June 1937, 'you can still depend on the fruit growers of Armagh as your faithful followers, as they have been in the past'.[50]

The Ministry of Agriculture remained impervious to such implied and open threats, despite the qualms of the Unionist leadership. The ministry had confidence in its legislation, and exports of apples had improved sufficiently over the poor years of the 1920s to enable Brooke to tell the Commons in June 1937 that 'The much maligned Fruit Act has, as it was intended, borne fruit in abundance'.[51] Moreover, senior ministry officials, especially the Permanent Secretary, Scott Robertson, had little respect for either the intelligence or reasoning of their fruit-growing critics. One of the most vocal complainants, a staunch Unionist said to represent the bitter state of feeling among government supporters in Co. Armagh, was dismissed by Scott Robertson as 'a very decent man. Hot-headed, an intense individualist who would object to any interference with personal liberty including the law against murder if it was a new venture'.[52] Ministry officials also rejected the reasoning of such critics. Instead, they argued that if growers could not dispose of their poorer-quality apples at home, there was little chance of selling them in Britain, that the adoption of the English National Mark criteria would involve stricter grading and control, and that the only way to maintain Northern Ireland's trade was to insist on high standards.[53]

3

Until 1932 Northern Ireland's agricultural policy had to be developed within a very limited framework. In the 1930s, however, a fundamental change in imperial policy opened up the possibility of more far-reaching measures, when the imperial government abandoned its *laissez-faire* attitude in an effort to prevent British agriculture from being overwhelmed by depression. By providing stable prices and a stable market, the new agricultural policy sought to protect British agriculture against the influx of low-priced imports which supplied as much as 60 per cent of the United Kingdom's food requirements, and to stimulate the revival of British farming under conditions which would ensure its permanent survival.

The methods adopted were protection by either tariffs or import quotas; subsidies, either directly from the government or indirectly from the consumer by means of levies; and the organised marketing of home production. The last method was the most characteristic and important form of government assistance to farmers in the 1930s, as statutory marketing schemes were set up under the Agricultural Marketing Acts of 1931 and 1933 and protected by voluntary or compulsory import quotas. The wisdom of the whole new agricultural policy, as well as of its component parts, was open to debate, especially when temporary expedients became permanent and pricing policies could be described as the 'economics of Bedlam'.[54] Nevertheless, the one certainty was that, despite their unceasing complaints about government miserliness, farmers at the time derived considerable benefit from policies which increased the cost of state assistance to agriculture from £45m in 1934 to £100m by 1939.[55]

The government of Northern Ireland's response to this new direction in agricultural policy was governed by two principles: agriculture in Northern Ireland was entitled to the same assistance as agriculture in Britain; and British practices should be modified to suit local conditions. These principles did not imply passivity or a simple reaction to British policy, but also involved efforts to persuade the English Ministry of Agriculture to adopt policies particularly helpful to Northern Ireland interests. The implementation of these principles was far from straightforward, especially since financial difficulties in the 1930s made Northern Ireland reliant upon British subventions to finance agricultural policy. The voting of money to Northern Ireland was irksome not only to those in Britain who found Ulster Unionism ideologically unacceptable, but also to British farmers, who frequently regarded Northern Ireland farmers not as fellow-citizens in the United Kingdom but as unwelcome competitors in the British market. A regional agricultural policy in the 1930s therefore involved much bargaining both within and without Northern Ireland and a series of compromises, often entailing the application of policies unsuited to local conditions, in all of which permanent officials rather than elected representatives played the key role.

Some of the problems confronting Northern Ireland were highlighted by the very first measure which the imperial government undertook to help a particular section of agriculture. The object of the Wheat Quota Bill, introduced in the imperial parliament in the spring of 1932, was not to reorganise and stimulate the production of wheat but to give a subvention to a relatively small but vocal and powerful group of farmers in eastern England.[56] Since the subsidy was to be financed by a processing tax on every sack of flour milled in or imported into the United Kingdom, it was essential that, although agriculture was a transferred service, the measure should apply to the whole of the United Kingdom. Otherwise Northern Ireland might become a wheat haven.

The difficulty was that the bill was of little benefit to agriculture in Northern Ireland, where little wheat was grown and the potential for increase was limited by climate and soil. In fact, it could only impose burdens on Northern Ireland citizens to the tune of some £200,000 a year. Although it would also impose similar burdens in Britain, the difference was that a sector of English agriculture would benefit from guaranteed wheat prices, whereas the direct benefit to Northern Ireland agriculture would be minimal.[57] Nevertheless, the government agreed to Northern Ireland's inclusion in the scheme, and was duly castigated in parliament for allowing the imperial government to throw 'completely . . . overboard the interests of the farmers of the Six Counties'.[58] This charge was ill-founded. In agreeing to Northern Ireland's inclusion, the government was fully alive to both the economic and political implications of the bill. It had been fully consulted beforehand by the English Ministry of Agriculture, Scott Robertson, then an Assistant Secretary in the Northern Ireland ministry, taking the leading role in the negotiations.[59] By stressing the serious political difficulties which would arise from Northern Ireland's inclusion in the wheat scheme, the regional government hoped to obtain from the English ministry a declaration in favour of a livestock policy which would be of benefit to Northern Ireland farmers. The Northern Ireland Ministry of Agriculture's view was that in the long run an acknowledged sacrifice on the Wheat Quota Bill would be a small price to pay for the goodwill and indebtedness of the English ministry in other directions.

This calculation proved correct, for it eventually resulted in a situation whereby Northern Ireland was relieved of much of the cost of agricultural subsidies. The first fruits of this policy of Northern Ireland manfully playing up to its role as a full partner in the United Kingdom occurred in 1934, when the imperial Treasury provided a grant for the Northern Ireland milk marketing scheme.

A milk marketing scheme had been introduced in Britain late in 1933 and modified the following year to enable the milk industry to withstand the effects of foreign competition in the form of such milk products as milk powder and condensed milk, which by 1933 had helped drive the price of butter below the pre-war level.[60] Since a full-blown protectionist policy was precluded for a few years by the Ottawa agreements, the modified scheme tried, in the meantime, to stabilise and support prices by a government subsidy. The British scheme was unsuitable for and did not apply to Northern Ireland, where there immediately sprang up a vocal demand, spearheaded by the U.F.U., for a comparable scheme to protect milk producers and the creameries.[61] Not to have secured a remunerative price for manufacturing milk (which comprised the bulk of milk production in Northern Ireland) would have had serious repercussions on the whole of agriculture, since the rearing of calves, pigs and poultry were all, to a greater or lesser degree, dependent on the maintenance of the dairy herds.[62]

Despite the need, finance proved a serious obstacle to the framing of a satisfactory milk marketing scheme in Northern Ireland. Unless state aid, equivalent to that given to the British scheme, was made available, farmers would receive considerably less for their milk than farmers not only in the rest of the United Kingdom but also in the Free State (4½d a gallon as against 6d in the Free State and 11d or 1s in Britain).[63] In the 1920s such expenditure would have been offset as equivalent expenditure against the imperial contribution, but since in the early 1930s there was only a nominal contribution, the government had to seek direct financial assistance from the imperial Treasury. Moreover, a settlement of this question became a matter of some political urgency to the government, for Pollock's budget, due on 16 May 1934, not only did not follow Britain in restoring some of the economy cuts made in 1931, but also imposed an education rate. An announcement of imperial financial assistance for the Northern Ireland milk scheme would, Spender urged a senior Treasury official, alleviate the gloom of the budget speech.[64]

The way in which the question of imperial aid for the milk marketing scheme was resolved provided a telling example of the key role played by permanent officials in determining issues between the two governments. On 13 March 1934 the Northern Ireland Cabinet Secretary, at Scott Robertson's prompting, put to the Home Office the case for a special money grant. The case was, quite simply, that it would be improper for Northern Ireland to assume financial responsibility for a price support policy which was, after all, a transitional stage in the conduct of an imperial policy over which Northern Ireland had no control.[65] The English Ministry of Agriculture was reluctant to concede Northern Ireland's claim by right, but after the ubiquitous Scott Robertson had done some sterling work on the imperial Market Supply Committee, the claim eventually led at the beginning of May 1934 to discussions between Treasury officials and Pollock and his officials. The latter emphasised both the state of the creameries and their importance to Northern Ireland and made much play of the fact that while Northern Ireland paid some £200,000 per annum for the wheat levy, it got nothing in return. By strange coincidence, £200,000 was the sum needed to put Northern Ireland's milk marketing scheme on the same financial basis as the British scheme. Impressed by these arguments, Treasury officials eventually agreed to tack onto the British Milk Marketing Amending Bill a clause enabling a grant to be made to Northern Ireland for its creameries.[66] The amount agreed upon was £200,000, but there remained some doubt as to whether this should be £200,000 per annum until the British scheme lapsed, or £200,000 for the two years that the British scheme was in existence. In view of the impending budget, Northern Ireland ministers wanted a quick settlement. Accordingly, negotiations, undertaken by Scott Robertson and Captain C. H. Petherick (a Principal in the Ministry of Finance) with Waley and Hopkins of the Treasury, resulted in a compromise on 15 May 1934, giving Northern Ireland £200,000 for the first year but leaving the future to be settled in later discussions. As Petherick reported to Spender, 'Waley stated that he would have to approach the Chancellor if we pressed for a definite commitment over two years at the rate of £200,000 per annum, and that this would mean delay'.[67] Pollock was therefore able to conclude his budget speech the following day by triumphantly announcing the grant.[68] The grant, he later told M.P.s, showed

the fairness of the British Government, because undoubtedly they imposed a tax on Ulster equally with the rest of the Kingdom in regard to the subsidy on wheat. Inversely, therefore, when it goes in the opposite direction they include Ulster in the benefits the milk industry are intended to get in Great Britain.[69]

Pollock was too generous in his tribute. The extent of imperial aid to Northern Ireland agriculture depended upon the extent to which British interests were affected. Where it suited British interests, Northern Ireland was automatically included in British schemes, but otherwise, as continued haggling over the exact terms of the milk grant indicated,[70] concessions were hard won. Nor did the agreement reached between the imperial and Northern Ireland governments during the Anglo-Éire negotiations in 1938 alter the situation. Agricultural subsidies in Northern Ireland were to be borne on the English ministry's vote only where 'circumstances are such as to justify corresponding subsidies' there. This qualification not only meant that there was a year's discussion and delay before Northern Ireland copied the 1938 British Bacon Industry Act introducing price guarantees for bacon pig producers; it also meant that the terms of the 1939 Northern Ireland Bacon Industry Act were not wholly suited to conditions there.[71] As with the Wheat Quota Act, however, the argument was that sacrifices had to be made to maintain the principle of equal treatment and thus ensure ultimately greater benefits.[72]

It was, then, an important part of the Northern Ireland government's role to see that agriculture did not suffer from the existence of a separate regional administration. Much time and energy was spent trying to achieve equality of benefits, and it was largely, but not always, successful. Northern Ireland benefited from inclusion in the subsidy schemes for beef, oats, barley, lime and slag, and land reclamation. Yet it suffered a net loss on the wheat scheme, a total loss on the sugar beet subsidy, had eventually to bear part of the state contribution towards financing the milk scheme, and not only experienced a year's delay in formulating a scheme of price insurance for pig producers but also had to accept financial responsibility for a scheme not wholly suited to regional conditions.

4

Such disadvantages were more than offset by the advantages Northern Ireland agriculture derived in the 1930s from the existence of an active and responsive regional Ministry of Agriculture. These advantages derived from the power to adapt agricultural reforms to meet local conditions. In the first place, as the acceptance and amendment of the controversial Wheat Quota Bill showed, specific Northern Ireland interests could be pressed and safeguarded in measures passed by the Westminster parliament and applied to the United Kingdom as a whole. Not only did the government of Northern Ireland take the opportunity of the bill to press the case for a United Kingdom policy on livestock and livestock products, but it also gave Northern Ireland interests ready access to imperial departments and an influence upon Westminster legislation, thus ensuring that milling and baking interests would not be unduly jeopardised by an increase in the price of flour.[73] In the second place, it enabled specific marketing schemes to be tailored to suit local requirements and susceptibilities. The most obvious difference between British and Northern Ireland schemes was the degree of influence exercised by the respective Ministries of Agriculture, for in Northern Ireland the ministry not only framed schemes but also retained a greater control over them. However, the crucial differences related to the detailed operation of the schemes, as was amply demonstrated by the pigs and milk marketing schemes, introduced in 1933 and 1934 respectively.

The reorganisation of the pig and bacon industry was the first major agricultural reorganisation undertaken by the imperial government. The object was to enable and encourage United Kingdom farmers to take advantage of the large home market which existed for pig products but of which 85 per cent was supplied by foreign and dominion countries, Denmark in particular. Price guarantees had to wait until 1938, and the initial scheme, approved by producers and curers and operating from 15 September 1933, relied on the quota system. This system restricted the quantity of bacon and ham marketed in the United Kingdom, gave home producers first claim on the home market, limited the import of pig products, and required two newly formed boards, the Pigs Marketing Board and the Bacon Marketing Board, representative of producers and curers respectively, to organise the production of the domestic quota and determine the price of bacon pigs.[74]

A reorganisation of the pig industry had long been urged by the Ministry of Agriculture and certain farmers in Northern Ireland on account of its actual and potential importance to agriculture there. Pig production was eminently suited to the small-farm economy, since it needed little capital and gave both a high return per acre and a quick turnover. Indeed, the pig was a most convenient 'medium for marketing surplus products such as potatoes and by-products such as separated milk'.[75] Nevertheless, the full exploitation of the pig had been restricted by violent fluctuations in dead pig prices, which in the early 1930s ranged between 120s and 38s per cwt.[76] Under such conditions it was almost impossible to develop the industry satisfactorily in a country such as Northern Ireland where the farmers' financial resources were limited. Not surprisingly, therefore, the reorganisation of the United Kingdom pig industry was welcomed in the North as promising higher and more stable prices.

Because of the different circumstances obtaining there, the British scheme did not apply to Northern Ireland. Instead, Northern Ireland was left to devise its own scheme. Certainly conditions in the North did merit a separate scheme. Most obviously, one of the key provisions of the British scheme – the forward contract – was both unnecessary in and inappropriate to Northern Ireland. Whereas in Britain the fresh pork market offered producers a clear alternative to the bacon market, in Northern Ireland the market for fresh pork was negligible, and pig producers were accustomed to send the bulk of their output to curers. In addition, the contract system would have been largely unworkable in Northern Ireland, where the average number of pigs per farm was less than three, and where the very mention of contracts seems to have put the fear of the lawyer, if not the Lord, into Northern Ireland farmers.[77] Moreover, the state of the pig industry in Northern Ireland required special and sympathetic attention if farmers were to be able to take full advantage of the gap left by the exclusion of imports. The traditional marketing system, whereby pigs were home-killed and then sold as dead meat in the local pork market, needed revision, since it was uneconomic and militated against quality control.[78] Curing needed to be made more efficient to enable the pig producer to receive a higher percentage of the bacon price.[79] Above all, there was some doubt as to whether Northern Ireland was producing the right sort of pig for the new dawn.

Pigs in Northern Ireland had long been used mainly in the roll bacon and ham trade. While the reputation of the large 16–26 lb Belfast or Ulster hams was unchallenged, the market for roll bacon – boned but not skinned – was restricted. It found a ready market at a high price in the north of England and in the south and south-west of Scotland, but there were doubts about the extent to which it could profit from the exclusion of imported bacon. Whereas the traditional market was being impoverished by industrial depression, the wealthier market in the south of England, left exposed by import limitation, had developed a taste for the lean 'Wiltshire' side of bacon, a Danish speciality. Some producers and curers reckoned that such consumers would thus be forced to buy roll bacon, the production of which could then be expanded, but the Ministry of Agriculture thought that the industry should try to fill the gap by supplying lean bacon. Such a change involved, however, a drastic reorganisation of the bacon industry. Whereas the existing cure, which processed dead, dressed pigs, did not require extensive premises and equipment, the Wiltshire cure, which processed live pigs, involved expensive capital outlays. Moreover, the pig produced by farmers would have to be altered. It was not just the fact that pigs fattened to a heavy dead weight to produce the required ham weights resulted in the production of very fat bacon unsuitable for the Wiltshire cure; but the breed itself was wrong. The traditional breed, the Large Ulster White, was docile, prolific and capable of giving a quick return, while its thin skin and light hair made it particularly suitable for the roll bacon trade. The trouble was that most of these qualities were the very reverse of what was required for the Wiltshire trade, which needed a lean animal which travelled well, such as the Large White York, which was less highly regarded in the North than the traditional breed.[80]

The Northern Ireland pig and bacon marketing schemes had, therefore, to be designed to raise standards and diversify the industry without deterring farmers from expanding pig production. In general outline the Northern Ireland scheme, drawn up by the Ministry of Agriculture under the 1933 Agricultural Marketing Act, resembled the British scheme.[81] Two marketing boards, the Pigs Marketing Board and the Bacon Marketing Board, were established to organise the Northern Ireland share of the United Kingdom market, but there the similarities ended. The Ministry of Agriculture had more control over the scheme than its British opposite numbers, and that power increased with the lapsing of the bacon scheme and the formation in 1935 of the Pig Industry Council.[82] Secondly, conditions were less stringent than those of the British scheme. Forward contracts, although encouraged, were not made compulsory, and the introduction of a grading system was delayed for a year after the operation of a similar system in Britain to enable the ministry to overcome what Brooke described as 'amazing and regrettable' misapprehensions.[83] Finally, conscious efforts were made to encourage the production of Wiltshire bacon. Higher prices were offered for suitable pigs, and a system of licensing new curing factories was used to limit the expansion of the roll bacon trade and encourage the establishment of Wiltshire factories.[84]

This policy of encouraging the Wiltshire trade aroused considerable controversy. This was particularly true when prices fell in 1937;[85] when, much to Craig's perturbation, the refusal to license a new roll bacon factory in Limavady was denounced by the chairman of the Urban District Council as 'Socialism and rank injustice';[86] and when the establishment of large-scale Wiltshire factories gave rise to fears that monopolies would be established to the disadvantage of producers used to the wide range of choice offered by the multiplicity of roll bacon curers.[87] Nevertheless, analyses of prices showed that consumers were willing to pay high prices for the more limited amount of Danish bacon available.[88] Thus confirmed in its contention that the roll bacon trade could be expanded only by selling at substantially lower prices, the Ministry of Agriculture stood firm and fortified the cabinet to withstand criticism.[89] The result was that by 1939 four Wiltshire factories, capable of processing 450,000 pigs annually, had been established in strategic parts of the province.

Sensitivity to local needs and susceptibilities did pay off. A specially tailored scheme did encourage the doubling of the pig population within two years. Admittedly, this rapid expansion created problems, outstripping the requirements of local curers and threatening price stability. But the scheme was flexible enough to cope with such problems. The Pigs Marketing Board took over the trade in live pigs, sending some to Wiltshire curers and shipping the rest to Britain.[90] Although this trade could have been handled more efficiently and less corruptly, farmers throughout the province – not, as previously, only those on the main shipping routes to Britain – were able to participate, and all producers did receive a return on their pigs, which became the most important single item in the agricultural economy, representing 9.5 per cent of the value of agricultural output in the 1920s and 27 per cent by the later 1930s.[91] Moreover, it had become a more soundly based industry. Admittedly, Scott Robertson's ambition to have 'all our pigs . . . cured here'[92] was not achieved by the outbreak of the Second World War, but the introduction of grading and the Wiltshire cure were important for the future and also enabled farmers at the time to take advantage of the different markets available in Britain.

It was mainly the producer who profited from the development of a regional pigs policy, but, as the case of milk marketing showed, the consumer could benefit as well from the existence of a regional agricultural policy. The nub of the main British milk marketing schemes was the 'pool' price, whereby the liquid milk producer and consumer in effect subsidised the producer of manufacturing milk.[93] This was possible in Britain, where liquid milk accounted for 70 per cent of milk production, but not in Northern Ireland, where only 30 per cent of milk went onto the liquid market and the liquid trade was thus in no position to support manufacturing milk on the same scale as in Britain. Moreover, the pool scheme would have jeopardised the supply of liquid milk. Under the scheme there would have been nothing to prevent milk hitherto sent for manufacturing being switched at the height of summer production to the liquid milk market, thereby endangering the financial position of the genuine liquid milk producer, who had to maintain supplies throughout the year, especially in the expensive winter months. With a depressed summer price, Brooke told the House in 1934, the genuine liquid milk producer 'would not have sufficient reserves to feed his cows in such a manner that they would keep up a sufficient supply of milk in the winter'.[94]

Northern Ireland was, therefore, obliged to adopt in the 1934 Milk and Milk Products Act a different scheme, which out of preference was more far-reaching than the British.[95] Whereas the British milk marketing scheme was operated largely, some said solely, in the interests of the producers, the Northern Ireland scheme did not merely devise alternative methods of price support but also tried to cater for the wider interests of the community. By stringent regulations, by differential levies, and by bounties, the government of Northern Ireland sought to protect consumer interests, improve standards of milk production, and raise the consumption of milk from its generally acknowledged 'lamentably low'[96] level. Indeed, the difference in emphasis between the British and Northern Ireland schemes was summed up in the composition of the respective boards. The main British scheme, set up under the Agricultural Marketing Acts, was administered by the English Milk Marketing Board controlled by producers.[97] The Northern Ireland scheme, by contrast, was established by statute and administered by a Joint Milk Council representing producers, distributors, consumers and the Ministry of Agriculture, and possessing the power to fix the retail price as well as the price paid to producers. Otherwise, Brooke explained to the House, 'It would be possible for the producer to cover, perhaps, disorganised distribution by placing the full financial burden on the consumer'.[98]

Not only was the Northern Ireland milk marketing scheme well suited to local conditions, but it was also generally recognised to be much superior to the British schemes.[99] Certainly the price of liquid milk was lower and its quality higher in Northern Ireland than in Britain, and the Northern Ireland scheme did at least present the impression of orderly marketing. In milk production and marketing, at least, Northern Ireland went not step-by-step with Britain but rather strode on ahead. In 1936 the minimum retail price of milk in England and Wales was 3d per pint compared with 2d in Belfast and 1½d in country districts. Thus, when asked by a Nationalist M.P. if he would follow step-by-step with Britain, where a subsidy of £50,000 had recently been announced to provide milk at 2d a pint to unemployed families in distressed areas, Brooke took great pleasure in replying:

> No, we have gone further. We have reduced the price of milk to everybody in Northern Ireland. Milk can be obtained cheaper here than it can be by those living in distressed areas in England under special schemes. . . . The hon. and learned Gentleman asked me if we would keep step by step with England. We have gone further. We supply cheaper milk to everybody.[100]

Such successful policies as the milk and other marketing schemes provided a vindication of the concept of the devolution of government, but not necessarily of parliamentary devolution. The adaptability that characterised agricultural policy in Northern Ireland between the wars was often achieved despite rather than because of the existence of regional representative institutions. Admittedly, the existence of a regional parliament did enable the adoption of a regional agricultural policy, but in both the conception and implementation of that policy the crucial role was played by officials of the Ministry of Agriculture. First and foremost, therefore, the history of agricultural policy in Northern Ireland provides an overwhelming endorsement of the advantages to be derived from administrative devolution.

Compromise: Social Services

I can only say that we will most carefully and most jealously look into any steps that are taken across the water. . . . It will never be said that the workers in our midst worked under conditions worse than those across the water. My right hon. friend [Andrews, Minister of Labour] has not got full control over that, but where unemployment and benefits are concerned it will be his duty to see, and he will see, that a man is treated as well on this side of the water as he is across the water.[1]

If Craig's pledge of a step-by-step policy, made in the House of Commons on 14 March 1922, is strictly interpreted, it was redeemed. Unemployment benefits always operated on the same basis as in Britain. However, in so far as the step-by-step policy came to be applied to the whole range of social services, it was a failure. Unemployment benefits apart, Northern Ireland lagged behind the rest of the United Kingdom. Pensions and health insurance were not put on the British basis until 1925 and 1930 respectively, while health services and housing in the six counties never caught up in the inter-war years.[2]

This uneven performance in the social services represented a compromise between conflicting ideas and interests and the constraints placed upon Northern Ireland by its peculiar position within the United Kingdom. There was never any attempt to hammer out Northern Ireland's social priorities and a system of social services tailored to meet Northern Ireland's needs and wishes. Rather, social services were developed (or not developed) in a piecemeal fashion and were largely imitative. The impetus normally came from Britain, and the extent to which British examples were followed depended on the relative strengths of the various lobbies, both within and outside the government.

1

The arguments in favour of a step-by-step policy were at first regarded as self-evident. Very little discussion preceded Craig's announcement in

March 1922. Ever since the setting up of the new state there had been an assumption that the people of Northern Ireland should in no way suffer from having a parliament of their own, and it was only gradually that the reasons for a step-by-step policy were articulated as it became necessary to defend the policy against criticisms within Northern Ireland and to justify Northern Ireland's expenditure to the imperial Treasury and the Joint Exchequer Board.

The fundamental argument in support of the step-by-step policy was based on a plea of equity. It was the same argument that was used to justify the claim for a minus imperial contribution. Northern Ireland should not suffer a lower standard of services by having a regional government and parliament that the majority of its inhabitants had not wanted; and since Northern Ireland did remain part of the United Kingdom and paid taxes, most of which were imposed by the imperial parliament, at the same rate as the rest of the United Kingdom, its inhabitants should be entitled to equal benefits.[3] Moreover, as with the case for the reamalgamation of the Unemployment Funds, the economic interdependence of the two areas was held to underline the necessity for equal social standards. Northern Ireland industries, such as shipbuilding, engineering and the making-up trades, were 'part and parcel of industries organised on a United Kingdom basis'; while workers largely belonged to the same trades unions as those in Britain, were employed under the same industrial conditions, and moved regularly between the two areas.[4]

To fail to maintain equal standards would therefore, it was argued, entail both economic and political disadvantages. Skilled workers might emigrate permanently to Britain if standards of benefit were higher there. While it may be difficult to prove or disprove such assertions, some ministers certainly believed that unemployment insurance helped to retain in Northern Ireland reservoirs of labour essential to enable its industries to take advantage of any upswing in the economy. Trying to reassure farmers that the extension of unemployment insurance to agricultural workers would stem rather than encourage the drift from the countryside, Craig told a deputation from the U.F.U. that Harland & Wolff had told him that 'it was owing to the operation of Unemployment Insurance that they had been able to undertake the immense amount of work that they had recently secured and to find the necessary workmen to do it'.[5]

Failure to maintain equal social standards would have political repercussions also. It would alienate the working classes and make the government's position impossible. Trades unions and articulate working men did demand equal standards, and thus Andrews felt that 'The plain truth is that we cannot carry on as a Government here unless our working classes enjoy the same social standards as their brother Trade Unionists in Great Britain'.[6] He blamed Unionist losses in Belfast in the 1925 general election on Northern Ireland's failure in the previous year to follow Britain in abolishing the thrift disqualification clause for old-age pensions.* 'The effect of this action of ours', he told Londonderry in May 1925 when canvassing support for the reamalgamation of the Unemployment Funds and the adoption of a new British pensions scheme, 'would really be infinitesimal compared with what would follow our getting out of step in regard to unemployment insurance or this great new scheme of Mr Churchill's.'[7]

Finally, the step-by-step policy became almost self-perpetuating. To have abandoned the notion of equal social standards would have been financially disastrous. Key arguments in the revision of the unsatisfactory financial basis of the 1920 act had been that expenditure on transferred services, and not the imperial contribution, should be the first charge on Northern Ireland's revenues, and that Northern Ireland should enjoy standards of social services equal to those of Britain. This claim had been successful, and although the Colwyn Award had recognised the possibility of lower standards of services in Northern Ireland, politicians, officials and the general public chose to ignore what could have been an important limitation on Northern Ireland's social expenditure.[8] The claim to equal standards thus became the cornerstone of Northern Ireland's financial relations with Britain, making it essential that Northern Ireland should not appear to lag behind in major ameliorative measures. Otherwise, Craig told his brother in June 1925, rejecting suggestions that Northern Ireland should not follow Britain's example and introduce contributory old-age pensions,

> The screw will be put on and we will be told that of our own initiative we refused to give the same benefits to people living in our area afforded to those on this side of the channel, and that as we had adopted that attitude there was no necessity for our financial affairs to be so adjusted that we could live pari passu with the English and Scotch *in other directions.*[9]

2

An equally convincing case could be and was made against a step-by-step policy. This case was based upon two separate but not unrelated notions: reservations about the concept of a welfare state, and reservations as to the extent to which Northern Ireland should copy Britain's social legislation.

---

*The means test embodied in the 1908 Old Age Pensions Act was said to have discouraged thrift and was so amended in Britain in 1924 that a single person was allowed to have up to £39 in savings (£78 for a married couple) without the pension being affected.

The former and more fundamental objection sprang, to put it uncharitably, from a low level of social awareness and responsibility in Northern Ireland, or, to put it more neutrally, from doubts about the desirability of state action in social and economic matters. Such doubts arose from a dislike of government expenditure, taxation and compulsory contributions, all of which were regarded as essentially unproductive, and from a suspicion that the working classes were being unduly pampered at the expense of other sections of the community. Many in Northern Ireland looked with dismay and resentment at rapidly rising expenditure on such services as state insurance and pensions, £1.5m in 1923 but £5.9m in 1939.[10]

Employers, both industrial and agricultural, were fond of complaining about the burdens imposed by the development of social services. Taxation and contributions, they argued, raised costs of production and made industry and agriculture less competitive and almost unprofitable at a time of increasing foreign competition, lower prices and higher wages — wages, it was often said, artificially inflated by the excessive wages and doles paid out by the government and local authorities. In January 1925 the head of the 'wee yard' protested:

> Not until more factory gates are closed and no money is forthcoming with which to pay rates out of which sheltered men and dole lifters receive their demands, will authorities and men believe that there is a limit to what employers can stand.[11]

Usually such protestors did not bother to work out just how far industry was being unnecessarily disadvantaged by the cost of social services, and it was generally left to the Ministry of Finance to represent and develop the case against the extension of such services. Of course, the ministry had a departmental interest in opposing the extension of services which were always in danger of unbalancing the budget. Yet the depth of the ministry's opposition sprang not merely from budgetary considerations, but rather from a deep-seated belief in the unproductiveness of social expenditure and its harmful effects upon the economy. To Pollock and his officials a substantial reduction in taxation and in the level of state activity was infinitely preferable to handing out doles, increasing state responsibility and imposing additional burdens on industry 'at a moment when foreign competition (of an unfair character) is rendering trade conditions so difficult'.[12]

This recurrent Ministry of Finance theme was best expressed in a long letter sent by Spender to the Cabinet Secretary on 23 January 1931.[13] At a cabinet meeting two days previously Andrews had urged that more should be done to alleviate unemployment in both Britain and Northern Ireland. Pollock had not been present, and Spender as a civil servant had not considered it proper to answer Andrews during the meeting. Nevertheless, his letter, which he asked to be shown to the Prime Minister, made it quite clear that the Ministry of Finance thought that much — indeed, too much — was being done for the working classes. Wholesale prices were below the pre-war level; retail prices had been falling over the previous six years without any corresponding reduction in general wages; workers were generally working shorter hours than in 1913 and 'have not only been relieved of taxation but have acquired many added benefits in the manner of insurance, pensions, education and housing grants'. Taking the position of the workers as a whole, Spender therefore concluded that

> They are far better off now than they were in 1913, when there was not talk of acute distress. We find, for example, that although there is less traffic on the Railways and although the workers have shorter hours, they are nearly getting three times the wages that they had in 1913; i.e., in 1913 £47,000,000; in 1930 £114,000,000.

By contrast, Spender continued, employers were paying in taxation and rates 'perhaps four or five times as much as they were paying in 1913', and industry was further hampered by Unemployment Acts which were 'making it difficult to render labour as flexible as it ought to be at a time when home industries are obviously over-equipped for any possible world market'. No wonder, Spender argued, that United Kingdom industries were finding it difficult to compete in world markets against those countries where taxation was 'so much less than with us and where wages have been drastically reduced'. The only remedy was to return to the good old pre-war days of lower taxation, lower wages and less state responsibility. Commenting upon Andrews's assertion that if unemployment benefits were stopped or substantially reduced, the workers would starve and there would be a revolution, Spender asked rhetorically:

> But surely if we could get back to the 1913 level of wages, hours of work, and retail prices, there would be no starvation and no undue hardship, even though there would certainly have to be a general lowering of the standard of living. This result has already been achieved in Italy without serious distress and with a consequence that Italy is now able to beat us in the industries in which we used to be supreme — shipbuilding, etc. If Mr Andrews' statements were pressed to their logical conclusion, it would almost amount to work or maintenance by the State.

The less fundamental but nevertheless important challenge to the step-by-step policy was the feeling that it was not justified by conditions in Northern Ireland. This argument was almost always put in the most negative sense. There seems to have been only one occasion when it was suggested that Northern Ireland should adopt a different set of priorities in social services expenditure. Opposing the adoption in 1925 of a costly new British contributory pensions scheme, Pollock questioned 'whether the money available could not be utilised to better purpose in child welfare or in schemes which will improve employment'.[14] Sound though this argument was in view of the North's higher rates of unemployment and of infantile and maternal mortality, its use by the Ministry of Finance was somewhat disingenuous in view of that ministry's constant efforts to limit expenditure on such alternative schemes.[15]

Those who argued that Northern Ireland conditions did not merit a step-by-step policy were basically arguing in favour of a generally lower level of services. It was foolish, the financial relations committee concluded, for a small and relatively poor province to try to keep pace with such a wealthy country as Britain, whose yield per head from reserved taxes was more than double that of Northern Ireland.[16] Nor was it sufficient for step-by-steppers to argue that the imperial government should, if necessary, subsidise Northern Ireland services, for disparities in taxable and rateable capacities were matched by other disparities. Lower costs of living or lower levels of earnings might also have merited lower rates of contributions and lower rates of benefits.

It is almost impossible to determine accurately differences between the cost of living in Northern Ireland and Britain in the inter-war years. A Ministry of Labour departmental committee, set up in 1922 to consider this question, concluded that on balance the cost of living was much the same in both areas. Rents and rates were lower in Northern Ireland, but fuel and light were dearer, while there was no great difference in food costs.[17] On the other hand, the U.F.U. argued in 1936, in 'an exporting country like Northern Ireland with a large surplus of farm produce, the cost of living in country districts is much lower than in a country like Gt Britain'.[18] Not only were potatoes, vegetables, meat and milk supposed to be cheaper, but so also were house rents and fuel.

Whatever the relative costs of living in Britain and Northern Ireland, there seems little doubt that the level of wages was lower in the latter area.[19] Prior to 1948 data relating to workers' average earnings, as distinct from minimum wage rates, were not collected in a sufficiently detailed form to enable a valid comparison to be made with earnings in Britain. Nevertheless, Isles and Cuthbert have shown that in the late 1940s the average weekly earnings of employed workers in Northern Ireland were significantly lower than the average for the United Kingdom as a whole. Adult males in Northern Ireland earned between 86.3 and 88.2 per cent of the United Kingdom average for adult males, while Northern Ireland females over eighteen earned between 78.6 and 80.3 per cent of the United Kingdom average for such female workers.

It is more than likely that such differences were even more marked in the inter-war years. All the reasons advanced by Isles and Cuthbert to explain the relative lowness of average earnings after the Second World War operated, perhaps with even more force, before 1939.

Lower levels of earnings, implying as they did lower social standards, might have been grounds for the adoption of lower scales of benefits and contributions in Northern Ireland in respect of the major cash social services. It was not, however, until it was proposed to extend unemployment insurance to agricultural workers in the mid-1930s that this argument was pressed with any vigour – by the U.F.U. supported by the Ministry of Agriculture. There was no dispute that agricultural wages were far below those in Britain, the average ploughman's wage being around 24s 9d in Northern Ireland and 33s 9d in Britain.[20] Thus in some parts of Northern Ireland unemployment benefit would exceed the normal wage, which, according to the Minister of Agriculture, would be contrary to 'a cardinal feature of Unemployment Insurance that the benefits should bear a proper relation to wages so that unemployment would not be made as attractive as employment'.[21] Insisting that lower wages were more than justified by lower living costs, the ministry and the U.F.U. therefore advocated a lower rate of benefit in Northern Ireland with, of course, correspondingly lower contributions. To do otherwise, the farmers argued ingeniously and disingenuously, would be to breach the step-by-step policy, for

> To give the same amount of money in benefit to an unemployed farm worker in N. Ireland as in Gt Britain would . . . not be a step by step policy, but would make the N. Ireland unemployed farm worker very much better off than the unemployed farm worker in Gt Britain.[22]

Finally, it was argued that Northern Ireland was not entitled to claim equal treatment with Britain. The lower proportion of rate-borne public expenditure in Northern Ireland, especially in respect of education and the police, enabled the Ministry of Finance to argue constantly that 'The principles of equal social standards with equal taxation have never held because whatever the social standards may be we have never had equal taxation'.[23] Since the nature of local authority finance was a legacy of the Union, this was not a wholly convincing argument. Nevertheless, given the distribution of powers between the state and local authorities in the United Kingdom, the question as to who should finance what always complicated debates on social policy. Local authorities were either unable or unwilling to undertake costly services, arguing instead that individuals should take care of themselves or that the state should bear the lion's share of the cost of services. For its part, the regional government was always uncomfortably aware that the imperial Treasury had strong views that Northern Ireland local authorities should live up to their responsibilities.

Some local authorities were worse than others, but Belfast was particularly prone to provide minimal services and to throw the blame on the government of Northern Ireland. There was, for instance, always a running battle between the Corporation and the Ministry of Home Affairs on the one hand and the Ministry of Finance on the other over the financing of health services. In 1930 the Ministry of Finance refused to help the Corporation ward off criticism of the city's rising rate of infant and maternal mortality by giving a 50 per cent grant, as was done in Britain, towards the cost of a new mother and child welfare scheme.[24] The claim to equal treatment could not, Pollock impatiently pointed out, be sustained in face of the relief, equal to a 4s 2d rate, which the city received in respect of education and the police.[25] It was the same over mental health services. When in the later summer of 1936 a controversy developed around conditions in the mental hospital run by the Corporation, the latter pressed the Ministry of Home Affairs for increased government aid. The ministry was willing, but was thwarted by the Ministry of Finance raising the spectre of the 'very critical eye' with which the imperial Treasury was examining Northern Ireland's expenditure. 'I am afraid', Spender told the Cabinet Secretary,

> that the Treasury will remember that when they criticised the small contribution of 1/- on the rates which our Government was imposing the arguments which we put forward included the statement that in some ways, e.g. contributions to the Local Authorities for lunatics, our grants were below British standards, so that if we now say that we are going to give British standards in these services our case before the Joint Exchequer Board will be weakened to that extent.[26]

The most bitter, prolonged, and instructive battle between the Corporation and the government occurred over the question of outdoor relief.[27] Section 13 of the Local Government (Ireland) Act, 1898, had empowered Boards of Guardians to grant outdoor relief to able-bodied workers. The Belfast Guardians were willing enough to provide outdoor relief for the disabled and to apply the workhouse test to others, but by the late 1920s they objected to paying outdoor relief to the able-bodied on any scale. In the first place, they refused to subsidise what they regarded as idleness. They reckoned that it was only the idle and improvident who sought outdoor relief, for 'The respectable artizan, when thrown out of regular employment, endeavours to obtain casual work even on farms and considers it an indignity to have to ask for relief'.[28] Oblivious to the effect of chronic unemployment around them, the Guardians singled out for special condemnation the increasing number of applications for aid from young men between twenty and thirty years of age 'who have never worked and who apparently are not anxious to work, but who, nevertheless, have taken on themselves the responsibilities of marriage and families'.[29] Moreover, there was some resentment that 'about 60% of the applicants are Roman Catholics from a particular quarter of the City' who, members of the outdoor relief committee suspected, were encouraged 'to get as much as they can from the rates' while also receiving relief from Catholic charities.[30] Faced with such sloth, fecklessness and iniquity, one Guardian reckoned that the Guardians' duty was to discourage idleness and 'to create a spirit of independence', since 'much of the money of the poor was wasted'. He himself knew 'three betting shops in one street which did a roaring business among the poor'.[31] The only way to encourage such independence was to limit relief, for, the chairman of the outdoor relief committee argued, people 'would make an effort to find work and would be able to work if they found they could not get relief'.[32]

A second justification offered by the Belfast Guardians for limiting outdoor relief was to argue that the relief of the able-bodied poor was the responsibility of the state not local authorities. Section 13 of the 1898 act had been enacted when there had been no state insurance, but the introduction of unemployment insurance and extended benefit had transferred responsibility for the able-bodied poor to the state. Furthermore, the chairman of the outdoor relief committee contended that section 13 had never been intended to cover 'normal' unemployment but had been 'merely brought in to make provision for a state of dire distress, e.g., A Potato Famine might occur'.[33] In vain did ministers point out that the Guardians were 'the one and only body who, under the law, were empowered to deal with destitution as such'[34] and that benefit under the Unemployment Insurance Acts could be granted only to persons who had paid statutory contributions and complied with statutory conditions. The Guardians simply retorted that section 13 should be confined to those, such as domestic servants and farm labourers, who were not insured and had no right to claim unemployment benefit. The Guardians' hope was that with the discontinuation of outdoor relief, 'the taking care of these people, not being their duty, will fall on the shoulders of those who we think are responsible'.[35] Well might Andrews have expostulated to Craig after a particularly acrimonious meeting with the relief committee of the Board of Guardians: 'How they can call themselves the guardians of the poor I do not know as they approach the whole problem from the one viewpoint alone, namely, saving the ratepayers'.[36]

Repeated, acrimonious and, according to Andrews, humiliating, conferences might have been avoided, and the unemployment riots of 1932 averted, had the government suppressed the Belfast Board of Guardians and assumed its powers. The transfer to the government of responsibility for outdoor relief was the real object behind the many demands made upon the government by the Guardians as the price of continuing to operate under section 13 of the 1898 act, but the government was not prepared to make concessions which would too obviously transfer the whole matter to parliament and provide more opportunity for discussion of the government's record on unemployment and distress.[37] Moreover, there was always the imperial government's view of the proper sphere of activities to be considered.[38]

Not all Belfast Guardians were so reluctant to expend ratepayers' money. Nor were Guardians in other areas, such as Newry, as reluctant as those in Belfast to operate section 13 to support the able-bodied poor in times of acute distress.[39] Admittedly, too, the 1934 Unemployment Assistance Act attempted to solve this particular problem by transferring to the state responsibility for the maintenance of most of the able-bodied poor.[40] Nevertheless, while it lasted the question of the application of section 13 of the 1898 act was indicative of two recurrent themes in the debates on social policy in Northern Ireland: a distrust of social services as pauperising the population, and the attempt by local authorities to shift to the state moral and financial responsibility for social services – a strategy often resisted by the Northern government.

3

From this conflict between the impetus provided by the British connection and local ideas of the proper sphere of state responsibility and expenditure there developed in Northern Ireland a distinctive system of social services. It was of a lower standard than would probably have obtained had Northern Ireland been governed in the same way as the rest of the United Kingdom, but probably of a higher standard than if Northern Ireland had been left to itself or become part of an autonomous united Ireland.

Northern Ireland's constitutional, financial and economic links with Britain, together with the existence of a large and reasonably well-organised industrial work-force, created the conditions for a standard of social services equal to those obtaining in Britain, for the step-by-step policy. Not entirely voluntary, it was a policy which produced the curious situation whereby measures denounced as irresponsibly red by Ulster Unionists at Westminster became a respectable blue when they crossed the Irish Sea. On the other hand, contradictory considerations ensured that the step-by-step policy was only partially and not always enthusiastically followed. There was a widespread feeling not only that state aid demoralised the individual and hindered economic development, but also that conditions in Northern Ireland were so different from those in Britain as to merit not so much a different order of priorities but a lower standard of services. Even when it was acknowledged that some problems were beyond the scope of individual or private enterprise, there was often a dispute as to whether the cost of the necessary correctives should be borne primarily by the taxpayer or the ratepayer, a dispute made the more difficult to resolve in view of Northern Ireland's precarious financial position and dependence on the goodwill of the imperial Treasury.

Divisions of opinion in the country at large were reflected among ministers and civil servants. Craig, Andrews and, to a lesser extent, Bates may sometimes have wished that imperial policy on social services was different, but usually agreed upon the desirability of following it. By contrast, Pollock and especially his officials at the Ministry of Finance opposed the tendency to expand the social services and fought rearguard actions to limit the government's financial obligations. No coherent regional policy was thus developed. In respect of the major cash social services, the advocates of step-by-step usually had their way. Major British legislation relating to unemployment benefits and contributory pensions was quickly imitated, and in the budgetary crises of the early 1930s Craig and Andrews quickly scotched the Ministry of Finance's proposals to make economies in these areas.[41] Yet in the less dramatic and less politically sensitive areas of social services the opponents of extension had their way. Thus in 1924, at the Ministry of Finance's insistence, Northern Ireland did not immediately follow Britain in abolishing the thrift disqualification clause for old-age pensions,[42] while there was a long struggle to bring Northern Ireland's system of health insurance into line with Britain's.

The 1911 National Insurance Act, which enabled sick persons to receive through approved societies money payments during illness and medical attention from a panel doctor, had been applied to Ireland in 'a mutilated form'.[43] Irishmen could claim money (sickness benefit) whenever they were certified as too ill to work, but they received no treatment (medical benefit) unless they paid for it themselves or received it under the Poor Law. The exception had been made because of the supposedly superior standard of health enjoyed by agricultural Ireland and because the existence of the Poor Law dispensary system provided, at least in theory, elementary medical services for the poor. In return for this reduced service, Irishmen paid a lower rate of health insurance contributions than did contributors in Britain.

With the foundation of Northern Ireland, trades unionists of all political parties began to press for the introduction of medical benefit.[44] And with good reason. The failure to conform to the British system was held to be at least partly responsible for lower standards of health. Northern Ireland's oft-quoted high rate of infantile and maternal mortality reflected a high general mortality rate compared with the rest of the

United Kingdom.[45] Moreover, while much attention was focused upon the thousands of persons in Northern Ireland who were unemployed because they could not find work, little was heard in public of the 20,000 persons unemployed because they were certified as sick and unable to work. Sickness benefit per head of insured persons was sigficantly higher than in the rest of the United Kingdom: £1 1s 6d in England and Wales, £1 0s 1d in Scotland, but £1 14s in Norther Ireland.[46]

Despite a demonstrable need for reform, the government was deterred by the likely cost and resisted trades unionists' demands.[47] In 1928, however, this internal pressure was supplemented by external pressure. The imperial government was pressing Northern Ireland to come into line with Britain because it wished to ratify on behalf of the United Kingdom as a whole certain international health conventions. More importantly, the approved societies were threatening to treat Northern Ireland differently from the rest of the United Kingdom. Two-thirds of Northern Ireland's insured population were members of United Kingdom societies, which were involved in such heavy deficit expenditure in Northern Ireland that their members there were living on the profits of their British members. The approved societies, therefore, began to consider seeking powers to value Northern Ireland members separately until a system of medical benefit was introduced.[48]

The suggestion of separate valuation was anathema to Andrews. It would have been a vital blow to the step-by-step policy he had so long advocated, and since Northern Ireland was 'too small an Insurance field to stand alone', it would probably have led to a repetition of the anxieties and losses which had arisen over the separation of the Unemployment Funds.[49] He therefore pressed Craig[50], who was immediately convinced of the need for change by the linking of health insurance with the vexed question of unemployment insurance. As ever, though, Craig was fully alive to local political considerations. With an election due by 1930, immediate action was undesirable, for there would be an outcry from the farming community if a further increase in health stamps were suggested. Thus Craig convinced Andrews that the time to introduce medical benefit 'will be immediately *after* our General Election. The effects of any unpopularity would then have worn off before another appeal to the country at the end of four or five years'.[51]

When the government did decide to introduce legislation after the 1929 election, Andrews and his officials conscientiously set about consulting all interested parties — trades unions, dispensary doctors, approved societies and the farmers. It was the farmers who gave most trouble by initially demanding the exclusion of agricultural labourers from any scheme of medical benefit. They objected to increased contributions, which they reckoned would cripple agriculture, and argued that no change was necessary in the countryside, where the dispensary system provided an adequate medical service and 'agricultural labourers are the healthiest members of the community'.[52] So vehement and vocal were the protests of farmers and their sidekicks, the rural local authorities, that Bates suggested that rural areas should be excluded.[53] Andrews would not countenance such exclusion, arguing that it would be administratively unworkable, would not meet the demands of the imperial government and approved societies, and would be unfair to farm labourers, who, popular notions notwithstanding, did not enjoy any better health than industrial workers.[54] Instead of making concessions, Andrews set about winning over the farmers and rural local authorities, offering reasoned replies to resolutions and deputations and tactfully countering various objections. It all took time, but it was time well spent, for, as Andrews told the Commons, 'I have never yet met a farmer who when the whole matter was explained to him and he understood the correct position maintained his objection'.[55]

Andrews was happily patient with outside groups, but he reacted fiercely to criticism from within the government. So important did he regard the introduction of medical benefit that at a cabinet meeting on 8 January 1930, presided over by Pollock, he demanded before proceeding further with the measure, and evidently received, the expressed approval of each member of the cabinet.[56] He was therefore alarmed and angry when at the end of March 1930 the Ministry of Finance seemed intent on delaying, if not sabotaging, his measure. Such intervention was only to be expected. Ever since 1921 Andrews had been at loggerheads with the Ministry of Finance over the cost of social services, and thus in 1928 he had taken the precaution of sending to Pollock copies of his correspondence with Craig on medical benefit.[57] To be informed, however, was not to be reconciled, and it had been the Ministry of Finance's reservations about the financial implications of the measure that had caused the cabinet to set up on 11 July 1929 an interdepartmental committee on the subject.[58] Now, in March 1930, since the scheme would involve a state contribution of some £13,500 a year, and since Northern Ireland was in danger of going into the red, Ministry of Finance officials were anxious to delay the scheme. They therefore, without consulting Andrews, persuaded the Prime Minister and the cabinet secretariat that the full operation of medical benefit should be delayed, and then instructed the Ministry of Labour staff to hang fire.[59] Salt was further rubbed into the wound when Spender wrote to the Ministry of Labour that Pollock was 'willing to *withdraw his opposition* to the Measure provided certain conditions are conformed to'.[60] This was said despite the facts, as Andrews angrily pointed out to Craig, that Pollock had presided over several cabinet meetings which had decided in favour of the measure, and that there had been a definite reference to it in the King's Speech on 11 March 1930.[61] *Amour propre* apart, Andrews had no patience with the demand for delay, arguing that since the approved societies were willing to invest in medical benefits twice as much as the government, their wishes should be met.[62] Furthermore, delay was false economy. The best way to save the Northern Ireland treasury from expense was 'to take every step that is open to us to reduce the existing drain in sickness benefit', as roughly 'out of every 20/- paid in sickness benefits in Northern Ireland, Mr Pollock has to find 3/4d'.[63] Craig and the cabinet were appealed to, but on 7 May they decided to let Pollock and Andrews arrange matters between themselves.[64] The result was a compromise. The date given in the bill for the start of benefit was 5 January 1931, but Andrews assured the House that it was the government's intention to bring the benefit side of the measure into operation on 1 October 1930.[65]

The reasons for its introduction and the wide consultations that preceded it meant that parliament could contribute little when the National Health Insurance Bill was eventually introduced on 13 May 1930 to bring Northern Ireland into line with Britain by providing medical benefit.[66] Nevertheless, the measure did interest M.P.s on all sides and provoked a most pertinent comment from Joseph Connellan, the Nationalist M.P. for South Armagh, who thought it a pity that the measure had been forced on Northern Ireland from outside. While it was 'very good to get a good thing irrespective of where it emanates from', he argued, 'it discloses a weakness somewhere when none of these good things originate among ourselves, and when they all have to be imported'.[67]

4

That it was indeed depressingly difficult for 'good things' to originate in Northern Ireland was underlined by the fate of housing. Lloyd George's slogan of 'homes fit for heroes' had helped to focus attention throughout the United Kingdom on the question of housing. Everywhere had its housing problem, a shortage of adequate houses, and Northern Ireland was no exception. It was true that the full extent of the problem was never appreciated in the inter-war years, since no attempt was made to enumerate dilapidated and overcrowded dwellings, and the scale of the problem remained concealed until in 1944 the first housing survey showed that some 100,000 new dwellings were urgently needed.[68] Nevertheless, there was sufficient evidence — that of the eyes and nose, high rents, and the statistics of the 1926 census — of considerable overcrowding throughout the province.[69] Two classes were particularly affected — the small farmer and the urban and rural working classes — but more attention was directed towards the problems of the latter.

There were three broad avenues of approach to Northern Ireland's housing problem: the construction of houses, rent restriction, and the clearance or improvement of slum areas.[70] Since slum clearance was impracticable without provision for rehousing, and since rent restriction could only be withdrawn when sufficient houses were available to reduce demand, housing policy in Northern Ireland was directed towards the construction of new houses through the Labourers Acts and a series of Housing Acts. The Labourers Acts, a legacy from the Union and continued by the Northern Ireland government except for a break between 1931 and 1935, empowered rural district councils to build with government assistance labourers' cottages,[71] while fourteen Housing Acts between 1923 and 1939, based upon British examples, offered financial incentives to house-builders. The object of these Housing Acts was to increase the housing stock not only in order to relieve the pressure on housing created by the loss of house production during the First World War and by an expanding population, but also in order to meet the higher standards of comfort and amenity beginning to be demanded. The act of 1939, providing for the renovation of existing houses and the large-scale construction of cheap housing by local authorities, never became effective because of the outbreak of the Second World War.[72] Thus the keystone of Northern Ireland housing policy in the inter-war years was the series of thirteen acts between 1923 and 1936 which offered state subsidies to local authorities and private builders and empowered local authorities to supplement the government grants to private builders.

A study of these thirteen Housing Acts provides a precise commentary upon the operations of regional government in Northern Ireland. Firstly, it shows how policies diverged from those pursued by the imperial government and were adopted to suit the ideas and particular circumstances, although not necessarily the long-term needs, of the region. Secondly, it demonstrates the influences on decision-making in Northern Ireland and, in particular, a recurrent difficulty in the operation of devolved government in a small area – the problems created by the overmighty subject in the shape of Belfast Corporation. Such was the influence of Belfast on housing policy that M.P.s from outside the city were led to ask who governed Northern Ireland – parliament or the Corporation.

Northern Ireland's housing policy differed from policies pursued in Britain in at least three important respects. In the first place, it relied almost entirely upon private enterprise. The government hoped to stimulate private enterprise to produce a surplus of houses, thus enabling the law of supply and demand to reduce rents and house prices. This confidence in private enterprise and the inexorability of economic laws was part of the government's general economic philosophy, which in respect of housing was reinforced by the recollection that Belfast's pre-war housing surplus had been achieved solely by the efforts of private builders.[73] Such reliance upon private enterprise harmonised with the intentions of the British housing measure passed by the Conservative government in 1923, the Chamberlain act, which was intended 'to serve only as a temporary stimulant for private house construction'.[74] It differed substantially, however, from the policy of the other major British Housing Act of the early 1920s, the Wheatley act, passed in 1924 during the first brief Labour administration, and promising long-term government support for local authority house-building.[75] This act, the most successful of all the nine major British housing measures passed between 1919 and 1938, was virtually ignored in Northern Ireland. In reviews of housing policy aimed at showing the virtues of private enterprise, members of the government scarcely mentioned it, while Unionist backbenchers, wilfully or otherwise ignorant of its achievements, mentioned it only in terms of the utmost disparagement.[76]

As the success of the Wheatley act and the number of houses built by local authorities in Britain showed,[77] private enterprise was not the only way open to the government of Northern Ireland in its efforts to tackle the housing problem. This was recognised in Northern Ireland. After 1925 Labour and Nationalist M.P.s began to demand that the state should assume complete responsibility for housing.[78] No Unionists were prepared to go that far, but many did come to hope that local authorities would take a more serious interest in house-building, one or two even advocating compulsion.[79]

The government ignored these suggestions and until the late 1930s clung to its belief in the efficacy of private enterprise. The idea of full state responsibility for housing was so anathema to the government that ministers never bothered to make out a case for rejecting the Opposition's suggestions. The participation of local authorities was, however, another matter. The government did hope to interest local authorities in housing, but largely by enabling them to supplement, by means of rate relief or direct subsidy, its own inducements to private building. Even in this limited respect there was no attempt at compulsion, and Bates, whose Ministry of Home Affairs was responsible for housing legislation, was always at pains to stress that provisions affecting local authorities were merely permissive.[80] The nearest approach to forcing local authorities to assist the housing drive came in the form of moral compulsion in the 1933 Housing Act, which made the grant of a government subsidy dependent upon an equivalent grant or rate exemption by local authorities.[81] Otherwise the government expected little from local authorities, and this limited expectation was probably realistic.

From the very start there had been few grounds for expecting whole-hearted co-operation from local authorities, and as the years went by their performance served only to confirm this initial forecast. Despite the favourable terms available under the Labourers Acts, rural district councils did little to improve the countryside's housing stock,[82] and the record of urban authorities was little better. The earliest pre-war Housing Act, passed by the imperial parliament before Northern Ireland was created, had produced few houses[83] and much aggravation. Not only did it involve the new government in a long and unseemly wrangle as Belfast Corporation successfully tried to evade its financial responsibilities;[84] but this early Corporation excursion into the field of municipal housing had been distinguished for a distinct lack of regard for the public good and a decided preoccupation with private interest. The incompetence, graft and corruption exposed by an official inquiry not only revealed how ill-equipped the Corporation was to run the affairs of a modern city, but may also have done much to reinforce existing prejudices against the direct involvement of local authorities in housing schemes.[85]

A second significant difference between British and Northern Ireland policy related to subsidies. Whereas the British subsidies took the form of an annual payment for a period of years, the Northern Ireland subsidy consisted of a lump sum, on the grounds that this represented a greater incentive to the private builders upon whom the government of Northern Ireland placed so much reliance. More vitally, the levels of subsidy differed. It was true that housing subsidies were continued in Northern Ireland five years after they had been abandoned in England and Wales, but subsidies in Northern Ireland were smaller and more frequently changed than in Britain. Subsidies in England and Wales were, under the Chamberlain act, £6 a year for twenty years (representing a capital sum of £75) and, under the Wheatley act, £9 a year for forty years (in capital terms £156). Admittedly, the subsidies were reduced to £4 and £7 10s respectively in 1926, but the Wheatley cut was restored in 1929, when the Chamberlain act was allowed to die.[86] Northern Ireland subsidies never attained such heights and consistency. The initial subsidy of £60 was increased to £80 in 1925 and to £100 in 1927, but reduced to £50 in 1931 and £25 in 1932, and withdrawn completely in 1937.[87] Only the aborted 1939 Housing Act offered generous subsidies, this time to local authorities, comparable to those formerly given in England and Wales under the Wheatley act.

The reason for these fluctuations was the fluctuating state of Northern Ireland's finances. The first Housing Act was introduced in 1923 at a time when Northern Ireland was struggling to find its financial feet and the unrealistic financial basis of the 1920 act was being renegotiated through the Colwyn committee. Caution was thus the keyword. Although Pollock was unable to persuade his colleagues to provide what he considered to be the smallest subsidy acceptable to private builders, namely £50, the figure eventually adopted, £60, was the most pessimistic capitalised equivalent of the Chamberlain subsidy.[88] Despite the continued reservations of the Ministry of Finance,[89] the Colwyn Award did enable and encourage the government to increase the subsidy in the late 1920s, but the virtual disappearance of the imperial contribution by 1930 played into the hands of the Ministry of Finance, at whose behest the subsidy was progressively reduced in the early 1930s.

The Ministry of Finance opposed the housing subsidy on grounds of principle and expense, and the reduction of the subsidy from £100 to £50 in 1930 represented a compromise between Pollock's demand for its abolition and Bates's insistence, supported by Andrews, that the subsidy should continue as long as there was a housing shortage.[90] Further victories for the Ministry of Finance followed in 1932 and 1933 as it tried to curb government expenditure and soften Treasury criticism of the low proportion of public expenditure borne by Northern Ireland's local authorities. When the Housing Act came up for renewal at the beginning of 1932, Pollock demanded not only a reduction of the subsidy to £25 but also that the government subsidy should be conditional upon an equivalent local authority contribution.[91] The latter suggestion had been made by the Ministry of Finance in 1928 but had been rejected by the Ministry of Home Affairs and the cabinet, who felt that it would mean that no houses would be built in the poorer areas.[92] Bates again resisted the proposition and also the proposal to halve the subsidies, but this time Pollock, having appealed beforehand to the Prime Minister, managed on 19 January 1932 to secure a cabinet decision in his favour.[93] Although the subsidy was reduced, the provision making the government grant dependent upon a local authority contribution was 'for some reason' omitted from the 1932 act.[94] Thus, when the act came up for consideration in the summer of 1933 and Bates was pressing for an increased subsidy in view of the small number of houses constructed with the reduced subsidy,[95] the Ministry of Finance returned to the charge. This time it was fortified by the knowledge that housing subsidies had been abandoned in England and Wales, and incensed by the fact that Belfast Corporation had ceased to offer any supplement to the government grant.[96] Pollock and his officials would have liked to have abandoned subsidies altogether, but were reconciled to their continuation by Craig's arguments that they were necessary to save the government's face in respect of house-building and that, anyway, the cost would be insignificant. 'It was apparent from the fact that only 50 houses ranked for subsidy last year', Craig reckoned, 'that the Government was not running any great risk in continuing the subsidy of £25 per house for another year or two'.[97] Nevertheless, Pollock and

Spender successfully insisted that the subsidy should be conditional upon equivalent local authority assistance, being at pains within and without the cabinet to link this question with the wider issue of Northern Ireland's financial relations with Britain.

A third point of divergence lay in the area of controls. Whereas the Wheatley act provided for the construction of houses for rent and rent only and placed an upper limit on rents, the government of Northern Ireland was loath to impose such restrictions. Committed as it was to the view that the law of supply and demand would eventually bring down house prices and rents, it believed that any restriction would be counter-productive, deterring investors and builders from constructing much-needed houses by depriving them of a legitimate profit. As Bates told the Commons in March 1932 when rejecting demands for rent control, 'After all, builders are not philanthropists, and people are not prepared to invest their money in houses which are subject to restricting conditions of this kind'.[98] Only in 1933 was the idea of rent control for subsidy houses incorporated into a Northern Ireland Housing Act. Even then, it was a mild, permissive provision empowering local authorities to impose, when granting their own housing subsidies, rent restrictions for a limited period.[99] It was not until the aborted 1939 Housing Act that the imperative need for rent restriction was statutorily recognised.

A study of the Housing Acts not only illustrates the way in which policy was modified to suit local conditions; it also illustrates the influences upon policy- and decision-making. It underlines the relative unimportance of parliament in framing legislation and the importance of the Ministry of Finance and of vested interests and pressure groups, such as local authorities and especially Belfast Corporation.

Housing was an issue which aroused considerable interest among M.P.s, drawing many of them into debates. It was also an issue which cut across party lines. Nevertheless, the housing debates did highlight many of the limitations of the Northern parliament. Members, whatever their party labels, seemed incapable of taking a broad and substantial view of issues. Their allegiances were first and foremost to their localities. Even under P.R., with its supposed lack of identification between M.P.s and their large constituencies, M.P.s tended to take a special interest in their home areas and in the activity or inactivity of their nearby local authorities. Cahir Healy, the Nationalist M.P. for Fermanagh and Tyrone, was forever bringing to the attention of the House the lack of concern for working-class housing shown by the Unionist-controlled council in his home town of Enniskillen.[100] Other members, who enjoyed more amicable relations with local councils, often acted as their spokesmen. For example, two of the Unionist M.P.s for Co. Armagh made a point in 1928 of reminding the House of the views of the county's urban district councils on the size of houses eligible for subsidy, Shillington singling out Armagh, and Davison Lurgan.[101] This particularism was even more pronounced when members for Belfast intervened in housing debates and turned them into discussions of Belfast's housing problem and the Corporation's policy. So pronounced was this tendency from the very beginning that in 1923 one of the Londonderry members felt constrained to reprove his Belfast colleagues for trying to make Belfast questions the one point of debate. Instead, he hoped that when the House was considering such questions as housing, 'We will not look upon them from the point of view of the Belfast Corporation, that we will drop that and look upon them as they affect the whole Six Counties'.[102] In fact, most members found it difficult to achieve a six-counties view of questions, and the aspirations of most M.P.s were summed up by the remarks made by the Unionist M.P. for North Armagh. Commenting in 1929 on the vexed question of the area of houses eligible for subsidy, he appealed to members 'to try to approach this question not from the point of view of Belfast or the country districts, but from the point of view of what their local knowledge is'.[103]

A second characteristic revealed by Northern Ireland M.P.s during the debates on the Housing Bills was their essential amateurism. They lacked information, and contributions to debates were usually vague. Members of all parties liked to throw out suggestions which they thought it the government's duty to take up. In 1925 Elliott, the most vocal Unionist M.P. for Fermanagh and Tyrone, wanted the qualifying period for subsidy extended in rural areas. Therefore he very prettily asked the government 'to yield to those of us who represent rural areas in this particular respect. I do not want to put down an amendment to what I think is an admirable Bill, but I hope the Government will grant this concession to those of us who reside in rural areas'.[104] The government's opponents shared this diffidence.[105] It was true that procedural rules did limit their effectiveness, but M.P.s did not take advantage of the ample scope left to them to influence housing policy. Between them 10 backbenchers moved only 19 amendments to only 6 of the 13 Housing Bills introduced between 1923 and 1936: 5 Unionists moved 11 of these amendments; 3 Labour members 5; and 2 Nationalists 3. Not even on matters where there was a good deal of unanimity, such as the desirability of using native building materials in the construction of subsidy houses,[106] and, more significantly, the need for rent control (considered necessary by a select committee of the House),[107] were amendments moved by private members. When Unionists did bring themselves to move amendments to Housing Bills, they were reluctant to press them to a division in face of government opposition, particularly if it meant voting with the Opposition, as in 1929 when

Shillington was obliged to vote against two of his own amendments after the government had argued against them and the Opposition had refused him leave to withdraw them.[108] There was an even greater reluctance to accept responsibility for moving the rejection of, and voting against, an entire major government social measure. Although one of the U.U.L.A. M.P.s, McGuffin, 'absolutely' disapproved of the renewal of the housing subsidy in 1924, he told the House during the second-reading debate: 'I will not vote against the passing of this Measure'.[109] Members on the other side were as reluctant to show the courage of their convictions by voting against a major measure. Condemning the 1932 Housing Bill for reducing the subsidy and the area of eligible houses and for omitting rent restriction, O'Neill, the Nationalist M.P. for Mourne, talked himself out of moving its rejection:

> I do not know whether I am doing the right thing in not moving the rejection of this Bill. I would not hesitate to do so, but for the fear that the Government might accept it. . . . On the whole, I believe it is better to pass a Measure of this sort, although it is defective, than not to have houses built at all. Therefore, I do not know whether I am right in refraining from moving the rejection of the Bill. I should regret doing anything that would stop the building of houses.[110]

The parochialism and timid amateurism of most M.P.s helped to explain ministers' attitude towards parliament. It was true that from time to time some ministers did show scant regard for the House, inadequately explaining measures and not answering points raised in debate.[111] It was not, however, true that members had no influence on housing policy. Well-thought-out amendments or suggestions conforming to the main lines of its policy were accepted by the government. Of the nineteen amendments moved by backbenchers, six (one Nationalist and five Unionist) were accepted by the government.[112] In addition, in 1929 concessions were made to the ideas contained in two Unionist amendments which the government felt unable to accept as they stood.[113] Furthermore, on at least one occasion and perhaps two the government itself moved an amendment in deference to views expressed in the House.[114] Finally, in 1936 the government, having been 'deeply impressed by the desires expressed from all parts of the committee', announced at the end of the committee stage that it was prepared to recommend that nothing but British materials should be used in the construction of subsidy houses.[115] All such changes, save the last recommendation, were in line with declared government policy. Of the remaining private members' amendments, five were ruled out of order; one, a Nationalist amendment, was withdrawn since its mover had misunderstood the intention of the clause he was proposing to delete; and five the government declined to accept as being contrary to its policy of encouraging private enterprise to build with the minimum of restriction 'cheap, self-contained, well-built, and healthy' houses.[116]

That the government was not prepared to allow its basic policy to be thwarted by the House was underlined by the repeated discussions of the maximum area of houses eligible for subsidy. Although the maximum size fluctuated between 550 and 950 square feet, the government's preference for smaller, kitchen houses of between 550 and 650 square feet prevailed. It prevailed because the government had a constant aim and precise information, whereas its critics and advocates of larger houses lacked both.

The most vocal critics of the smaller houses were Devlin and the Labour and Independent M.P.s for Belfast. They argued that such cramped and claustrophobic houses would quickly turn into slums and drive fathers to drink and children onto the streets. Yet their repeated condemnations were not accompanied by any calculations, apart from some vague ramblings by Beattie, a Labour M.P., of the likely cost of the larger houses complete with gardens which they considered necessary to produce a happy and contented population.[117] M.P.s from outside Belfast were even less precise. Many argued that larger houses should be permitted in the countryside, because building costs were lower than those in Belfast,[118] but they produced no hard calculations as to costs of land, building materials and labour. Not only did M.P.s and local authorities outside Belfast content themselves with vague assertions, but they were often in danger of forgetting that the object of the Housing Acts was to provide homes for the working classes. It would be 'unwise and extremely unfair', asserted one of the Londonderry M.P.s, to exclude from the benefit of subsidy 'the middle and lower middle classes . . . perhaps, the heaviest taxed in the community considering their means'.[119]

The government was, by contrast, more clear-sighted and better informed. It varied the maximum size to concentrate on the building of cheap working-class housing and to prevent the building of, for example, seaside bungalows as as second homes.[120] Ministers did not claim that such small houses were ideal, and Craig naïvely thought that occupancy would be determined by family size;[121] but they did argue that the smaller houses were comparatively cheap, comfortable and convenient and, above all, a vast improvement on the previous overcrowded dwellings of their inhabitants. They rejected the Opposition's pessimistic picture of an increasingly alienated population having to sleep with their legs hanging out of bedroom windows. Instead, George Boyle Hanna, the Junior Minister of Home Affairs, described a charming scene of a 'clean and tidy' wife and children and a father of three or four who does not want to go out either to a public-house or to a Local Option meeting, he wants his 'Evening Telegraph' – and after having patted the children on the head and said good night to them he sits down in that house which is his own or becoming so more and more every day. . . .[122]

Of course, many of the arguments produced during these discussions were highly subjective, but where they were capable of factual substantiation the government had the edge over its critics, whatever their politics. It had the true measure of local authorities' lack of enthusiasm for house-building,[123] and, more importantly, it was acutely aware of the costs of building and the relationship between size and price and rent, on which matters it consulted building experts and especially Belfast Corporation, who provided the model kitchen house displayed since 1926 in the Commons' smokeroom.[124]

In fact, parliament's opinion counted for little when compared with outside influences. As far as housing was concerned, the most important influence was Belfast Corporation. Belfast and its problems loomed large in the government's thinking on housing policy. Cabinet discussions frequently revolved around the extent of the Corporation's co-operation or non-co-operation; speeches introducing housing measures usually concentrated on the situation in Belfast; and most of the major amendments to the government's housing legislation were introduced to meet the Corporation's requirements.* M.P.s frequently deplored the Corporation's influence on housing policy, and ministers, too, often resented the need to pander to the Corporation's whims. Nevertheless, Belfast's prominent position was a fact of political and social life that had to be lived with. The government had to come to terms with the Corporation and felt that, in turn, any arrangements between them should be automatically endorsed by parliament. Virtually instructing a disgruntled House of Commons, then consisting only of Unionists, to accept in 1924 certain changes in housing legislation to encourage a reluctant Corporation to supplement the government's subsidy, Craig hoped that the proposed amendment would

meet the general wishes of this House, because I always feel that if we can get the Corporation to work hand in hand with us in a great ameliorative Measure like this we are doing infinite good to the people, whereas if there is a division of opinion, even on some financial matter of this kind, it shows that the two great bodies, the Parliament of Northern Ireland and the Corporation of Belfast, are

*Of the 16 amendments made to Housing Bills in their parliamentary progress, 1923–36, 5 were moved to meet the Corporation's views and a further 3 were put forward by a backbencher on its behalf. The Corporation was also instrumental in securing in 1927 a reduction in the maximum size of houses eligible for subsidy.

not able to see eye to eye, which is a great mistake and, unfortunately, a great cause of unpleasantness amongst those who ought to be working harmoniously along the same lines. . . . There is no use going too much into history. After all they are a body that are up against serious problems. They have an intimate knowledge of the difficulties that arise in connection with the erection of working-class houses, and all that we can say as a Government is, 'How can we help them?'[125]

The framing of the 1933 Housing Act underlined the importance of outside influences. It contained two provisions for which members on all sides had been pressing for some time: a measure of rent restriction previously rejected by ministers as interfering with natural economic laws,[126] and low-interest loans for house-building, a demand hitherto almost ignored by ministers who regarded existing arrangements as adequate.[127] The latter proposal was included as a result of the activities of Stewart, who later founded the Progressive Unionist Party. Since the reduced subsidy of 1932 had produced only a handful of houses, Stewart put forward a scheme for a public housing trust financed by cheap government money and had publicised his plan in such a way as to win the support of Belfast Presbyterians just prior to the annual meeting of the General Assembly.[128] It was in order to make some gesture to outmanoeuvre Stewart that the cabinet inserted in the 1933 Housing Bill cheap-money provisions.[129] The measure of rent restriction was introduced in the same bill at the behest of Belfast Corporation in an attempt to reconcile it to the provision making the government subsidy dependent on local authority aid.[130] Mild though the provision for rent restriction was, and unconvinced though the government was about its likely effectiveness,[131] its inclusion in a Housing Bill did represent a significant departure from the government's long-declared policy of minimum interference with private enterprise. Not surprisingly, the Unionist M.P. for St Anne's complained that the way in which the amendment had been brought about was yet another example of the 'want of consideration shown by the Government to Backbenchers'.[132]

5

In the inter-war years, therefore, devolution enabled Northern Ireland to develop a distinctive housing policy, the main lines of which were laid down by the government, sometimes assisted and sometimes hindered by local authorities, particularly Belfast Corporation. It was a policy that represented the minimum government response to the housing problem and was conditioned less by the needs of the housing situation than by the reluctance of public authorities, central and local, to undertake direct responsibility for housing, and, to a lesser extent, by the province's limited financial resources and the need or desire to placate Treasury opinion. It was a sufficient policy to enable the government to stand up and say that it had a housing policy, but it was a far cry from Devlin's plea for 'a comprehensive housing scheme for the purpose of abolishing all slums',[133] an achievement he thought was eminently attainable in such a small area as Northern Ireland, if only the government would take full advantage of the devolved powers it possessed and stopped looking over its shoulder at Great Britain.[134]

Moreover, the policy of subsidising private enterprise with the minimum of restrictions was scarcely a resounding success. The government did like to claim some credit for stimulating house-building and helping to bring down rents. Nearly all the houses built in Northern Ireland between 1923 and 1939 were erected with state aid. Only some 9,000 houses were built without government help, all but sixteen by private enterprise; but 34,312 houses, most of them small houses, were erected under the Housing Acts of 1923–36, 2,166 by local authorities and 32,146 by private persons.[135] In addition, rents did fall. Whereas houses built for letting commanded 15s a week or more during the early 1920s, it was possible to rent a new house in the 1930s for 8s or 10s a week.[136] How far the government and its £2½m of subsidies were responsible for these developments is questionable. It may be that the subsidy was unnecessary and that private enterprise would have concentrated on the smaller house for which there was a clamant demand. It may be that falling house prices and rents owed more to the falling price of building materials than to government policy. It may also be that rents would have fallen sooner had the government imposed rent and price restriction on subsidy houses or insisted on the construction of more council houses, for most of those built by Belfast Corporation under the Northern Ireland Housing Acts were sold or rented singificantly more cheaply than similar houses constructed for profit by private enterprise.[137]

Even if government policy did stimulate house-building and help to reduce rents, it did not go far enough. Even the reduced rents of the 1930s were beyond the reach of many working men with weekly wages of 30s to 35s, and Northern Ireland was left with, to quote the Ministry of Home Affairs, 'the problem of providing accommodation for the poorer classes, mostly residing in houses more or less unfit for habitation'.[138] Moreover, Northern Ireland's housing record compared unfavourably with that of other parts of the United Kingdom, especially England and Wales. It is true that the leading commentator on British social policy between the wars has concluded that 'of all the missed opportunities of the interwar period, perhaps the failures in housing were the most unpardonable',[139] but even with all the missed opportunities, Britain achieved more than Northern Ireland. Proportionately more houses were built in England and Wales than in Northern Ireland, especially by local authorities. Whereas extensive slum-clearance schemes were undertaken in Britain, none was attempted in Northern Ireland. And opinion on housing was much better informed in Britain than in Northern Ireland, which undertook none of the detailed surveys favoured by the Ministry of Health and private organisations in Britain.[140]

This unfavourable comparison with Britain prompts the reflection whether Northern Ireland's housing problem would have been better served without the existence of a devolved government. Certainly direct rule from Westminster would have removed many of the financial constraints the Northern government laboured under. Westminster legislation did require much more of local authorities than did the Northern Ireland Housing Acts, and it may have been that a Westminster government would have been less afraid to compel local authorities to take action. Finally, Northern Ireland would probably have been included in the many surveys which at least served to educate opinion. The impact that such differences of approach would have had upon Northern Ireland's housing problem is incalculable, and the only certain conclusion is that at least Westminster benefited from devolution. It was relieved of the problem of dealing with one of the worst-housed parts of the United Kingdom.

Indeed, in respect of all the social services, only Westminster benefited from devolution – being relieved of direct responsibility for Northern Ireland's social problems. Yet regional responsibility did not mean that Northern Ireland achieved a standard of social services it either wanted or needed. Those who favoured the minimum provision of social services by public authorities found themselves pushed along by the step-by-step policy, while the minority who advocated social reforms found themselves thwarted by local inertia and by the financial constraints imposed by the 1920 act and had to accept a lower standard of services than obtained in Britain. Social services were imitative and their provision piecemeal. Their fate in the inter-war years thus provided yet another illustration of the failure of devolution in Northern Ireland to produce regional policies appropriate to regional requirements or inclinations.

Part Three

8

Confusion: Law and Order

Every person inside our particular boundary may rest assured that there will be nothing meted out to them but the strictest justice.[1]

The question is so big that I have determined to pursue a steady straight course and to pay as little attention as possible to those critics who — though well-meaning — have not yet been trained in a wider outlook.[2]

In these two sentences, the first occurring in the peroration of his first speech to the Northern Ireland House of Commons, the second in a letter in April 1922 stressing the long-term need for conciliation and perseverance with his peace pact with Michael Collins, Craig summed up Northern Ireland's overwhelming need in 1921–22.

The twelve months before the establishment of Northern Ireland had been marked by animosity and violence. The problems created by the I.R.A. revolt against British rule had been complicated in the North by sectarian conflict. The consequence was an almost complete loss of confidence in the forces of law and order. Protestant and loyalist fears and alienation were to some extent assuaged with the formation of the Ulster Special Constabulary, but the formation of this force only enhanced Catholic and nationalist anxieties. One of the most urgent tasks facing the new government was thus the restoration and then the maintenance of law and order. To achieve this it was vitally necessary to establish quickly a system of law enforcement and administration of justice which would have the confidence of all sections of the community. Clear thinking and a clear direction were essential if there was to be any chance of general confidence being restored, but there was little chance of these requirements being met under the system of government obtaining in 1921–22.

In theory, at least, a system of devolved government should have been admirably suited to the task of restoring law and order, as a local administration might have been more readily able and willing to identify and rectify areas of conflict. The advice and existence of a regional administration did result in distinctive action being taken in Northern Ireland — the growth of an armed police reserve and the passage of the Special Powers Act. More frequently, however, the regional government found itself unable to act, and those actions it did take were tinged with partisanship. The main trouble was that Northern Ireland's security problems could not be, and were not, treated in isolation from the larger Irish policy pursued by the imperial government at Westminster. Security policy in Northern Ireland was thus adversely affected first by Westminster's overriding concern to arrive at and maintain a peace with the South and later by the Provisional Government's need to survive in the South. The demands of the larger Irish policy, Northern Ireland's dependence upon British military and financial aid, Craig's prolonged absences in London, the nature of the Ministry of Home Affairs, and the Northern government's need to carry along its own supporters — all these considerations complicated and confused attitudes towards the problem of law and order. In fact, the development of even a consistent, let alone a satisfactory, response to the problems of restoring and maintaining order in Northern Ireland was inhibited by the existence of conflicting authorities and objectives. From this confusion there emerged a system of law enforcement, which, while not despotic or unduly repressive, did not have — and with some justification — the confidence of a significant section of the Northern Ireland community.*

1

The six counties were hardly handed over to the new government in a state of good order. Until the middle of 1920 it had seemed that the North would escape the worst of the Anglo-Irish war, but a series of I.R.A. attacks at the beginning of June ended that immunity.[3] The consequent problem of maintaining law and order was complicated by outbursts of communal violence, particularly in the cities of Belfast and Londonderry, where rival groups of Protestants and Catholics attacked each other, often with fatal results. In some respects violence in the North developed its own momentum, but the close connection between events there and those in the South, and the formers' relationship to the movement for Irish independence, were underlined by the Southern boycott of Belfast goods, at first imposed spontaneously in the summer by some local authorities but later endorsed by Dáil Éireann.

---

*Since the Northern Ireland constabulary records have not yet been released, and are not likely to be released in the foreseeable future, this treatment of law and order is confined to the years 1921–22. This is the only period for which adequate documentation about law enforcement is available in accessible government papers.

Three separate forces were used in an effort to contain violence in the North. The brunt of the work at first fell upon the regular police force, the Royal Irish Constabulary (R.I.C.). It was controlled regionally by a Divisional Commissioner, after November 1920 Lieutenant-Colonel (later Sir) Charles Wickham, and in Belfast by a City Commissioner, since March 1920 J. F. Gelston. Since the R.I.C. was a highly centralised force, the two commissioners were responsible to the Chief of Police in Dublin, Major-General H. H. Tudor, appointed in May 1920 as Police Adviser to the Lord Lieutenant to command both the R.I.C. and the Dublin Metropolitan Police. The second force, the military units stationed in the North, was also controlled from Dublin Castle. There was, of course, a local command structure, Colonel G. Carter-Campbell, the officer in charge of Belfast, being the officer most involved locally for the greater part of 1921, but the local command was closely supervised by General Nevil Macready, since March 1920 Commander-in-Chief of the British army in Ireland and a man with little sympathy for Ulster Unionism. The army was important not only for the personnel and equipment it could provide but also for the power it could exercise under the Restoration of Order in Ireland Act (R.O.I.A.). The wide-ranging but still clumsy R.O.I.A. had come into effect on 9 August 1920 to supersede the more limited Defence of the Realm Act (D.O.R.A.). It provided for courts martial for a wider range of offences than permitted under D.O.R.A. and made it easier for the authorities to impose curfews, restrict traffic and imprison terrorists under suspicion.

The third force was the most controversial. The Ulster Special Constabulary was based upon various local loyalist vigilante groups that had begun to be formed in the summer of 1920 and upon a revived Ulster Volunteer Force (U.V.F.). The U.V.F. had been revived in July 1920 with the tacit approval of the imperial government, but the experiment had not been a success, partly because of Macready's hostile attitude and partly because the work was too arduous for a volunteer force. In October 1920, therefore, after much discussion, it was announced that a Special Constabulary would be recruited, theoretically from among loyalists throughout Ireland but in practice only from among those in the North. Recruiting began the next month for the force which was divided into three classes: 'A', a full-time and paid force; 'B', an occasional force with an allowance; and 'C', an unpaid reserve. Although the new force was placed under the command of the Divisional Commissioner of the R.I.C. in Ulster, Wickham, the structure of the force meant that considerable independence was enjoyed by local commandants. The Special Constabulary was, in effect, the Northern equivalent to the Black and Tans and Auxiliaries which had been used in the South since the previous spring to reinforce the diminishing and demoralised R.I.C., but its formation was bitterly opposed by Dublin Castle, Macready seeing it as the 'raising of Carson's army from the grave'.[4] An almost exclusively Protestant force, it also came to be hated and feared by nationalists and Catholics throughout Ireland, but this may have been as much for its success in combating the I.R.A. as for the excesses that were undoubtedly committed by some of its members.

Although the use of such forces did help to prevent the six counties dissolving into anarchy, the problem of violence remained a serious one. April 1921 was a particularly bad month. In Belfast two auxiliary policemen on leave from Sligo were murdered; two Catholics, said to be members of the I.R.A., were killed in retaliation; and the consequent funeral parties were accompanied by rioting and looting. There was also considerable I.R.A. activity in Counties Armagh and Tyrone and in the southern part of Co. Down, probably due to the operations of flying columns. Telegraph wires were cut, private houses were raided for arms, mails were intercepted, bridges were destroyed and roads trenched, the Belfast boycott was continued largely in the form of the burning of bread vans, and there were fifteen attacks on security forces. The new state was therefore faced with two related problems of law and order: the suppression of violence aimed at its overthrow or immobilisation, and the ending of communal violence. It was unfortunate that the distinction between these two problems was often obscured by the hostile attitude of the Catholic/nationalist minority to the state. the state.

Although the question of law and order was likely to be a pressing one, it was not at first the formal responsibility of the government and parliament of Northern Ireland. Although they had apparently taken over the internal administration of the six counties in June 1921, there was no immediate transfer of services, and they were not responsible for law and order and had no control over any of the Crown forces. They never would, of course, have control over all Crown forces, since the army was intended to remain a reserved service. Nor did they immediately have control over the police, for the 1920 act simply provided that the police forces should be transferred to the Irish parliaments actually took place on 22 November 1921,[5] so that until then the enforcement of law and order in Northern Ireland remained the sole responsibility of Westminster, acting through Dublin Castle. The military stationed in Northern Ireland remained under Macready's command and the police subject to Tudor. In fact, the Lord Mayor of Belfast, as the city's chief magistrate, had more formal authority in matters of law and order than had the government of Northern Ireland. That, at least, was the strictly constitutional position, but people in Northern Ireland, at any rate the Unionists, looked to their locally elected government for leadership. That government acutely felt its impotence, but all it could do was to make representations to the imperial government.[6]

This may have been a legitimate and fruitful function for a regional government, but at the time the imperial authorities were little inclined to accept recommendations from Northern Ireland. The attitude of the imperial authorities to questions of law and order in Northern Ireland was determined by the needs of a larger Irish policy – the need to reach an agreement with the South. On 24 June 1921 Lloyd George had invited de Valera, the President of Dáil Éireann, and Craig to a conference in London. Craig would not take part in any tripartite talks, arguing that Northern Ireland was satisfied with its status and that the dispute lay between the imperial government and Sinn Féin as to what status should be accorded to Southern Ireland. Lloyd George first met de Valera on 14 July, when Celtic pleasantries were exchanged, but it was not until 11 October that negotiations started in earnest between a British delegation headed by Lloyd George and an Irish delegation headed not by de Valera but by Arthur Griffith, the founder of Sinn Féin, and Michael Collins, the organising genius of the I.R.A. The negotiations were tough and arduous, but eventually resulted in agreement on 6 December with the signing of the Anglo-Irish Treaty.[7]

In the meantime the actions of the Crown forces in Ireland were governed by a truce agreed upon on 9 July between representatives of the Crown forces and those of the I.R.A., and becoming operative at noon on 11 July.[8] During the Anglo-Irish war the Crown forces had never been able to develop an effective security policy, partly because of divided control between military and police and partly because of political considerations,[9] but they were even more hamstrung by the truce. Not only did it give official recognition to the I.R.A., establishing liaison officers to sort out details at a local level, but it also emasculated the Crown forces. This emasculation was particularly felt in Northern Ireland, where the whole burden of keeping law and order was thrown upon the civil authority, in this instance the R.I.C.[10]

There the R.I.C. was deprived of the support of the military, who withdrew from peace-keeping activities and ceased to exercise their emergency powers under the R.O.I.A. The regular constabulary was also deprived of the services of the 'B' class of the Special Constabulary, whose activities were to be suspended during the truce. This decision to immobilise the Special Constabulary, taken without prior consultation with the Northern government, was said to be the logical consequence of a determination not to have an armed constabulary on the streets during the truce, except in emergency: it was said that to have asked the Special Constabulary to have gone on duty without arms would have been a breach of a prior agreement that they should never be called out without arms.[11] Nevertheless, the decision aroused considerable resentment among Ulster Unionists. It was regarded by many as the first step in the disbandment of a force known to be unpopular in Dublin and London; and it was also held to weaken law enforcement in Northern Ireland, because many considered that the Special Constabularly, especially the 'B' class, 'have more influence over these young hotheads than either police or military, for they patrol their own districts, & know the boys by name'.[12] Not only did the truce deprive the R.I.C. of the support of the military and Special Constabularly; it also curtailed the freedom of the R.I.C. itself. Although no precautionary measures were to be relaxed, raids and searches were to cease; the police were to be unarmed, except in emergency; and senior officers were 'held responsible that the spirit of these orders is carried out loyally'.[13]

Moreover, the way in which the Anglo-Irish negotiations developed made it unlikely that the imperial authorities would willingly bend the rules to suit Northern Ireland.[14] The question of Northern Ireland loomed large in the discussions. While Sinn Féin was more interested in Irish independence than Irish unity, Northern Ireland's status provided Irish negotiators with a valuable tactical weapon, a good bargaining point. If the British insisted that Ireland remain part of the Empire, Sinn Féin could in return demand an end to partition. If this demand were refused, a break could be staged on Ulster and the imperial government put in an acutely embarrassing position. The imperial government was confident that it could count on public support for a resumption of the war if talks broke down on the issue of Irish allegiance to the Crown and membership of the Empire, but, as Austen Chamberlain, the Conservative leader in the coalition government, explained to his wife, partition 'would be the worst ground to fight on one can imagine'. Northern Ireland was an 'illogical and indefensible' compromise, and 'you could not raise an army in England to fight for *that* as we could for crown and empire'.[15] The belief that Ulster was jeopardising the peace talks generated considerable hostility in Britain towards Ulster Unionists, a hostility which reached its peak in November 1921 and found expression in a fierce press campaign, in which the *Daily Express* in an article headed 'ULSTER WILL BE WRONG' warned that 'Unless the Ulster cabinet abandons its uncompromising attitude it will be guilty of the greatest political crime in history'.[16]

During the first few months of its existence, therefore, security policy in Northern Ireland was entirely subordinated to the needs of the imperial government's larger Irish policy. The unsatisfactory consequences were all too evident in the response to three serious outbreaks of violence in Belfast between July and September 1921. Only with great difficulty did even the semblance of a coherent and consistent policy emerge from repeated discussions between the government of

Northern Ireland and the military and police authorities. During that time the maximum ill-will was generated all round – the Northern government feeling a loss of face, loyalist groups taking the law into their own hands, and the Catholic community preferring to rely on self-protection. In fact, the only gainer was the I.R.A., which was able to reorganise in Belfast, as elsewhere in the North, under the cover of the truce.

The first serious breakdown of law and order occurred less than a month after the opening of the new parliament. This particular round of disorder was sparked off by an I.R.A. attack upon three policemen, one of whom died, on the night of Saturday 9 July in the Falls Road area of Belfast. The following day a battle raged for four or five hours, the casualties being, according to the City Commissioner, fourteen killed and eighty-six wounded. Tension continued throughout the following week, culminating in rioting on 14 July, in which a young girl was killed and many persons, including the U.U.L.A. M.P., William Grant, were wounded.[17] It really had been, as Spender's wife told her relatives in England, 'rather an anxious week in Belfast'.[18]

The disorders could not have come at a worse time. They occurred not only just after the conclusion of the truce but also during the week of the Twelfth of July celebrations, when many businesses were closed, thus throwing large crowds, particularly of youths, on the streets. The banning of these celebrations under such conditions seems not to have been considered. Indeed, to those who knew what the 'Twelfth' meant to the Ulsterman such an interdict seemed impossible:

> It is part of his religion. . . . Witness the story of the stranger who asked an Orangeman, 'What *is* the twelfth anyway?' The Orangeman looked at him in horror and amazement – 'Ye never heard of The twelfth?! Away home, man, and read yer Bible!'[19]

Finally, the resolution of these problems was rendered difficult by a lack of leadership within Northern Ireland. Many influential figures, including the Prime Minister and the Lord Mayor, were away from Belfast, while the remaining ministers and magistrates were either too inexperienced or too unwilling to make decisions. Thus it was that on the afternoon of Sunday 10 July the City Commissioner, Gelston, 'came in despair' to Spender, then Cabinet Secretary, to say that the police were unable to cope alone.[20]

Though willing to act, Spender's range of manoeuvre was limited. Since the control of the military and police lay not with the government of Northern Ireland but with Dublin Castle, all that could be done was to arrange meetings of ministers, police, military and leading citizens[21] and to submit recommendations to Dublin in the hope that they would be acted upon. It turned out to be a vain hope. On 15 July the cabinet called upon Macready as Commander-in-Chief in Ireland to restore all the peace-preservation measures previously in force and to instruct his local commanders to take full advantage of the power given to them under the R.O.I.A.[22] The response was disappointing. One extra battalion was sent to Belfast, and the military was authorised to continue to act in limited support of the police, but the existence of the truce was held to restrict the army's peace-keeping role. Although, as Macready pointed out, the R.O.I.A. was still in force, 'At the same time my instructions [to] Col. Commandant 15th Brigade, are that . . . troops will be guided by the spirit of the agreement entered for the cessation of hostilities'.[23]

The second wave of serious disorders began on 30 August 1921. Gunmen quickly gained control of a large part of the York Street area. Mills and shops were forced to close. Shipyard workers were attacked on their way to the yards, and within twenty-four hours six people had been killed and thirty wounded.[24]

The Northern Ireland government's response was more vigorous and more indignant than in the previous July. Ever since those disorders the government had come under increasing criticism from its Unionist supporters for its inability to stamp out such continued I.R.A. activity in Northern Ireland as drilling, regrouping and enforcing the Belfast boycott. Accordingly, it had sought assurances from the military and police authorities in Belfast and Dublin and from the Chief Secretary that sufficient forces and powers were available to contain any future disorders. Such assurances had been given,[25] and it was thus with anger and a growing sense of frustration that the government demanded strong measures to contain the new outbreak.[26]

It justified these demands by arguing that the whole future of civil government was at stake in Northern Ireland. The current disorders were, according to the Minister of Home Affairs, 'not an ordinary riot, but operations by the I.R.A.'[27] Unionists living in the disturbed area reckoned that the snipers in control there were not local men but 'gunmen and good shots, who had been imported into Belfast for the purpose'. City Commissioner Gelston was less sure that the trouble was being caused by imported gunmen. He was more inclined to think that men from other parts of Belfast with rifles had been concentrated in the disturbed area, since the truce had allowed the rearming and regrouping of the Belfast I.R.A.

In face of such evidence of I.R.A. activity, the Northern government was concerned lest Unionists should take the law into their own hands. 'The public had lost confidence in the authorities,' one Unionist living in the disturbed area told the cabinet, 'and unless something was done within the next two hours he feared that the loyalists would be wiped out.' Protestants and loyalists were not, however, waiting passively to be wiped out, but were taking their own defensive and offensive measures. As Spender wrote, expressing the government's dismay,

> Nothing can be more disastrous to any community than to allow the rank and file to imagine that Civil Authority has broken down. The people cannot understand why, having elected a Parliament, and the Government having been set up, that Government is not functioning. The concessus [*sic*] of opinion is that the Ulster Parliament could act, if they so choose, or could bring sufficient pressure on the Imperial Parliament to restore law and order. Every day that passes makes the position of the Ulster Government more difficult, and increases the difficulties that the Ulster Government will have when they get into the saddle.[28]

Three measures were demanded: a significant display of military force; the calling out of the Special Constabulary; and the full use by the Crown forces of their powers under the R.O.I.A., in particular the powers of isolated search, arrest and internment. The first measure aimed at restoring general public confidence in the government and Crown forces and convincing the public that there was no necessity to resort to measures of self-protection. Such displays had been considered effective on previous occasions. The second measure, the remobilisation of the B Specials, which was supported by neither the City Commissioner nor the Minister of Education, was intended to reinforce the regular police and military and, more importantly, to act as a restraint in the Specials' own localities. The last measure, the use of the R.O.I.A., was intended to take the gunmen out of circulation, since under existing conditions it was impossible to secure evidence for convictions under the ordinary law. According to the City Commissioner, 'The only way to deal with the gunmen, and other suspected individuals, was to arrest and intern them'.[29]

It was easier to state these demands than to secure their execution. The difficulties started with the local military commander in Belfast, Colonel Carter-Campbell, bound as he was not only by ordinary military regulations but also by the 'spirit of the truce'.[30] Both made Carter-Campbell slow to act in support of the civil power. When an outbreak occurred, it was open to the civil authority, the police, to ask for military aid. It was not, however, obligatory for the military to intervene. It was left to the local military commander to decide whether or not the situation warranted military intervention, and what form that intervention should take. Once the military commander decided to draft troops into an area, he at once assumed command of both military and police within that area, control returning to the civil authority on the withdrawal of troops. Such to-ing and fro-ing of responsibility between police and military was not conducive to decisive action, and so it proved in Belfast during the August riots.

Almost immediately after the outbreak of rioting, Commissioner Gelston requisitioned troops, but Carter-Campbell refused to intervene, reckoning that the civil authorities should be able to handle the situation. Even when it became clear that he had underestimated the seriousness of the situation, Carter-Campbell was slow to act. The armoured cars he provided on the afternoon of 30 August proved inadequate, and it was not until about 11 a.m. on the following day that, on Gelston's further urgent representations, troops were supplied, a joint police and military operation planned, and Carter-Campbell agreed to seek reinforcements and permission to use his powers under the R.O.I.A.

Agreement between the local military and police authorities did not remove all the obstacles to the fulfilment of the Northern government's wishes. Even greater obstacles were the military and civil authorities in Dublin who rushed up to Belfast to contradict the advice given locally. Moreover, although aware 'that it was imperative that the disturbances should be quelled at once as there was a possibility of I.R.A. reinforcements being drafted into Belfast from the South',[31] the Dublin authorities could not agree among themselves as to the best way to meet the disorders.

The Commander-in-Chief, Macready, wanted to limit the military's involvement as far as possible. He disagreed with his local commander's recommendations that more reinforcements should be sent into Belfast and that the power of internment under the R.O.I.A. should be used. Instead, Macready reckoned that the Special Constabulary should be relied on to restore law and order – a matter for the civil authority. The representative of the civil authority, A. W. Cope, Assistant Under-Secretary at Dublin Castle, had different ideas. The very last thing he wanted was the calling out of the Specials. To draft them into the disturbed area, he said, 'would be equivalent to putting petrol on the fire'. While agreeing that the B Specials might have a restraining influence in their own areas, he reckoned that their mobilisation 'would lead to lying propaganda' in the Catholic press and 'the Government would be represented as having taken a party side'.[32] Moreover, it was likely that if the Bs were called out, 'the Catholics would have to call out their own men, and this would result in an attack by Catholics on the "B" men in their own areas'. Instead of naked force, Cope recommended diplomacy and the judicious use of internment, glibly arguing that since peace did not prevail in Belfast, the use of the R.O.I.A. and internment could not be a breach of the truce.

Cope's suggestions were based upon a particular view of the disorders, a view at variance with that of the government of Northern Ireland. Consultations with Protestants and Unionists and Catholics and nationalists had convinced him that the current disorders were not political.

He discounted the idea of an I.R.A. attack upon the state, having been assured by his Catholic contacts that there had been no influx of gunmen into Belfast, and having been told that the origin of the trouble had been the throwing of a bomb into a Catholic house from the Protestant end of a mixed street. 'It was not the same situation as in previous disturbances,' he told the Northern cabinet, 'as this was not political, but Catholic versus Protestant.' Both sides seemed to be in a state of insecurity, blaming the military and police authorities for failing to protect them, and both sides were shooting and bombing. What was needed, in Cope's view, was something to break 'the present vicious circle, in which both sides would "stop if the other would"'. Thus he asked to be 'brought into touch with an influential Unionist who would attempt to influence the Unionists who were shooting', recommended an appeal to the people of Belfast to place confidence in the Crown forces, and advocated the internment of both Catholics and Protestants, 'as both sides were shooting' and the 'arrest of Catholics only would undermine the confidence of that side in the Crown forces'.

These discussions were the frankest ever to take place upon the question of security in Northern Ireland, and some gains were made in the development of an efficient security policy. The local military commander, somewhat chastened by the view that a more prompt dispatch of troops might have saved lives, assured the cabinet that he would act more quickly in future and that the delay in the use of troops, which he attributed to a misunderstanding between himself and the City Commissioner, would not recur. He was prepared to keep both fixed military posts and mobile patrols in the affected areas, even though peace had been restored. Finally, although he could get no more troops, he reckoned that he had sufficient forces to meet further trouble, promising that he would if necessary requisition artillery to meet the cabinet's emphasis on the desirability of demonstrations of military force.[33]

Yet this was the extent of progress. Some fundamental problems were not overcome. First of all, the question of divided control between military and police remained. Carter-Campbell hoped to solve this problem by taking over control of the police. He told Macready that Belfast should be considered as a city 'daily in a state of tumult', in which 'Military control should be over existent'.[34] The advantages to be gained from such an arrangement were listed as single control and responsibility, the avoidance of delay or misunderstanding in the requisitioning of troops, and the obviation of the difficulty of defining the area of military control. However, such a streamlining of the control of the Crown forces was unacceptable to the constabulary authorities. They objected to military control of the police, since it implied the use of the police in a military role. Such a role would, it was feared, undermine public confidence in the police, for, Gelston told Wickham, 'If the Police are called on to fire on the civilians it renders their usefulness as a Police and peace Force afterwards nil. They could not move through their localities and carry on their work as police. This was found to be the case after the 1886 riots and subsequently.' Even in the short term, military control would be inefficient and would harm public relations. The use of police to relieve the military would mean the withdrawal of police from other areas, leaving those areas unprotected, and provoking even more complaints from ratepayers and demands for further protection. Moreover, police morale might also be affected. The police were already doing 'extra work daily at present,' Gelston argued, 'and they would, I fear, very much resent if they were called on to do purely military work'.[35] Finally, if it was not intended to use the police for military duties, no advantage would be gained by placing all police districts directly under military officers for duties and operations. As Wickham told Tudor, the Chief of Police in Dublin, 'It is probable that a trained Police Officer will detail Police duties more efficiently and more satisfactorily to the men than a Military officer unacquainted with Police duties and Police routine'.[36] The police authorities' counter-proposal was a simple one – increase the number of troops engaged in Northern Ireland,[37] but, like most simple suggestions, it was, being unacceptable to the army, impracticable.

Not only did the problem of divided control remain unresolved. The question of how far the truce prevented the use of the R.O.I.A. also remained. Cope had disagreed with the military's view that the truce prevented the use of internment, and he had categorically stated that 'The Government would give the police authority to arrest and hold a suspect in custody pending a Government decision. Instructions would be given to this effect in writing to the police authorities'.[38] That was on 31 August, but by 12 September no such written assurance had been received from Dublin Castle.[39]

A third problem left unresolved was the containment of Protestants and loyalists. The calling out of the Special Constabulary might have prevented Protestants from taking the law into their own hands, but since this course was unacceptable to the Dublin authorities, Cope's idea to use informal local influence was developed when Northern Ireland ministers met a deputation on behalf of 250 Protestant ex-servicemen working on Queen's Island.[40] They came to offer their services to the government because, they said, they had no confidence in the police and, more particularly, the young and inexperienced military who seemed incapable of distinguishing between the well-intentioned and evil. Since no attempt had been made to tackle the root of the trouble – imported gunmen – there was a pervading sense of insecurity on the part of inhabitants of certain areas and men travelling daily to their work. 'They had no animus,' said the leader of the deputation, 'towards those of a different religion, but they did wish to secure that they might be allowed to live peaceably and quietly'.[41] Rather than join, as they were being pressed to do, loyalist self-protection societies, they 'came not in a spirit of hostility, but to secure the advice of the Government as to what should be done'.

The Northern Ireland government tried to use this opportunity to discourage the formation of loyalist 'defence' bodies and to channel these energies in a more constructive direction. Craig, the master-mind of the U.V.F. of 1912–14, knew all about the difficulties and dangers of irregular forces and urged that 'Nobody in the present circumstances could undertake the protection of citizens except the State'.[42] To form vigilante groups, he warned the deputation, would only play into the hands of Northern Ireland's enemies. Craig therefore suggested that the deputation should form a 'special Watch Committee, and they might come and tell him what they thought was wrong'. From this suggestion grew a proposal for the selection of certain trustworthy citizens, probably drawn from among the B Specials, to work informally with the police and military in an attempt to control the less ruly elements in the event of future disturbances. The idea was not a new one. Local men of influence had co-operated with the police and military in past disorders,[43] and there were many willing to do so in 1921. The suggestion was not, however, implemented, because of disagreement as to how such peace auxiliaries should be organised. The scheme was acceptable to the military and police authorities only on certain conditions. The conditions were sensible, but the scheme foundered mainly on the insistence that the new organisation should be separate from the B Specials – a provision which, it was feared, would wipe out the older force.*[44] Thus Protestants and loyalists continued to organise privately, and from September onwards there were rumours that the U.V.F. was being revived.[45]

The third series of disorders began on the night of 23 September 1921. Although the initial trouble seemed to have been easily dealt with, during the following week Belfast again suffered the familiar cycle of shootings, bombings, assaults and intimidation, during which Protestants seemed likely to gain the upper hand.[46] On this occasion the authorities acted with something approaching vigour and dispatch and with the minimum of debate. The most significant step was the use of the Special Constabulary in Belfast. On the morning of 26 September a meeting of representatives of the Northern government, Belfast Corporation and the military and police authorities decided to recommend the

---

*The other conditions were that the police should select the personnel, who should be unarmed and should be used only outside curfew hours and in their own areas to control those of their own political and religious views.

remobilisation of the Special Constabulary.[47] This time Dublin Castle, evidently reluctant to increase the number of troops in Belfast, did not disagree but only laid down conditions restricting the use of the B Specials to the protection of Protestant areas and the prevention of outbreaks of rowdy elements on the Protestant side, and stipulating that the patrolling of Catholic areas should continue to be entrusted solely to the military and the regular R.I.C.[48] Unionists were delighted, and on the following day, 27 September, an optimistic Craig wrote to the Chief Secretary, Sir Hamar Greenwood, that 'I am glad to say that the effect was instantaneous; we had a perfectly peaceful night and a sense of safety and security seems to be established'.[49]

Appearances were deceptive. On the evening of 27 September Catholic retaliation was followed by Protestant counter-attacks, and the continued violence paved the way for a military initiative. Four Catholics and four Protestants were arrested under regulation 55 of the R.O.I.A.,[50] and as from midnight on 29–30 September the military assumed control of the police in Belfast, including the Special Constabulary.[51] The constabulary authorities protested against the assumption of military control,[52] but the military initiative seemed to have an effect and the current series of disorders petered out.

During the September disturbances the military and police authorities had taken all the action that had previously been demanded of them. Such action did not, however, restore Unionist confidence in the Crown forces; and three criticisms in particular had the support of Northern Ireland ministers and civil servants.

One source of friction was the tendency of military communiqués to present the disorders as a religious conflict,[53] thus obscuring what Ulster Unionists regarded as their fundamentally political nature and discrediting the government of Northern Ireland.[54] A further ground of complaint was the failure to recruit the remobilised Special Constabulary up to full strength complete with arms. Only in this way, reckoned the Ministry of Home Affairs, could 'the services of well-disposed citizens ... be obtained for assisting the Military and Police authorities'.[55] The third bone of contention was the arrest by the military of four Protestants under the R.O.I.A. Unionists objected to the use of special powers against themselves. They regarded the arrest and detention without trial of loyalists (as the detained Protestants were automatically dubbed) as a ploy to reconcile their opponents to the need for stern measures. Rumours were rife that Dublin Castle had, through Cope, issued to the Crown forces an instruction to the effect that 'If you arrest a Sinn Féin criminal you must arrest a Unionist alongside him'.[56] Accordingly, a vigorous agitation was launched to secure the release of the four – an agitation directed particularly against the Ministry of Home Affairs. Their only crime, said their supporters, was loyalty to Ulster, the King and the constitution.[57]

The agitation met with some sympathy within the ministry. The Permanent Secretary, Watt, argued that the R.O.I.A. had been passed to suppress Sinn Féin and doubted whether

> it was ever contemplated that these extraordinary powers should be used against those who are loyal to the Crown. If any of the latter class should be arrested it is a matter for consideration whether the ordinary Law should not be put into force rather than the extraordinary emergency legislation which was passed to deal with disloyal and disaffected persons.[58]

The Junior Minister of Home Affairs, R. D. Megaw, a barrister, was more cautious. He argued that the military had been quite within its rights in making the arrests, and in view of police reports as to the criminality of one of the arrested loyalists,* he was unwilling to take responsibility for remonstrating with the army.[59] Nevertheless, in view of the agitation, some action was deemed necessary, and so after three weeks the army was asked whether it intended to bring the three more respectable Unionists to trial.

It so happened that the embarrassment of the Ministry of Home Affairs was matched by that of the military. The army did not know what to do with any of the eight arrested men.[60] There seemed insufficient evidence to secure convictions before a military court, and it was deemed impolitic to apply internment orders. So anxious was the local military commander to be shot of the detainees that he suggested that, if he brought them up before the magistrates, 'It might be possible for the Prime Minister of Northern Ireland to suggest to the Magistrates that they should all be dealt with by being "bound over" '.[61] Quite properly, Craig replied that 'he was very anxious not to interfere in any way with the Courts of Justice or with the complete independence of the judicial administration from political control'. Nevertheless, part of the military's proposed solution was adopted. It was deemed expedient to bring the men before the magistrates, for Craig 'felt sure that the Magistrates who had been appointed irrespective of political considerations, would carry out even justice'.[62]

All in all, Unionist distrust of the forces of law and order persisted. The results were seen not only in the local protection societies which operated in parts of Belfast but also in the re-formation in November of the U.V.F., a development which the Northern government only arrested

---

*Known locally as 'Snatch' because as a boy he used to snatch ladies' purses, he had been convicted of larceny, lived off immoral earnings, had married a woman of known immoral character, was active in a gang of roughs creating disorder in the York Street area, and frequented betting houses and every gambling den in his area.

by trying to absorb its potential recruits into an expanded Special Constabulary.[63]

2

The problem of law and order had thus proved intractable and almost self-perpetuating in the first few months after the establishment of Northern Ireland. Not only had the question of law and order been beyond the legal competence of the new regional government and parliament, but the attitude of the competent authorities had been determined by events outside Northern Ireland. It was hoped that the transfer of power in respect of law and order and a settlement between the imperial government and Sinn Féin would both lessen the security problem in Northern Ireland and enable a more prompt yet considered response to such diminished disorder as might arise. The government of Northern Ireland duly took over responsibility for law and order on 22 November 1921, and the Anglo-Irish Treaty was signed on 6 December, but the anticipated transformation did not materialise. The Treaty, particularly by raising doubts about the future of Northern Ireland, intensified and increased the problems of maintaining law and order. And the Northern government found that, although it had the formal responsibility, it scarcely had the resources or the freedom to counter disorder and develop a satisfactory security policy.

Article 12 of the Treaty, proposing a Boundary Commission in the event of Northern Ireland opting out of the Free State, may have been a masterstroke in preventing negotiations breaking down on the Ulster question, but it served only to intensify the problems facing Northern Ireland.[64] It heightened apprehensions among Unionists, particularly those living in border areas, who were alarmed at the possibility of being transferred to the Free State. It also created among nationalists in North and South an expectation that Northern Ireland would soon disappear and a notion that its territory was a legitimate target for seizure. The difficulties created by the Treaty in the North were further accentuated by the split in the South over its terms.[65] The supporters of the Treaty, largely led by Collins, formed a Provisional Government, but the critics, led by de Valera, took up an increasingly hostile stance that culminated in civil war. A developing civil war in the South was fraught with sufficient difficulties for the North, but agreement between the contending factions seemed all the more dangerous. The activities of the I.R.A., which had never ceased to operate in the North, received a new impetus as pro- and anti-Treatyites among its members co-operated in a campaign against the North. The Northern divisions of the I.R.A. were reorganised and supplied with arms by Collins so that they might be equipped to protect Catholics and nationalists and prevent the Northern government from establishing control. In these circumstances the Collins–de Valera electoral pact of 20 May 1922 was regarded by Ulster Unionists as a prelude to a concerted attack. Therefore in 1922 the government of Northern Ireland had to face not only the problem of maintaining law and order within (itself a complicated enough task involving both resistance to subversion and keeping Protestant and Catholic apart) but also the problem of securing a long border line against attacks from without.

The seriousness of this double security problem should not be under-rated.[66] The border was in a constant state of tension which was brought almost to fever pitch by such dramatic incidents as the kidnapping of loyalists and the occupation of Northern Ireland territory. On 8 February 1922 columns of the I.R.A. from Monaghan invaded Tyrone and Fermanagh, seized a large number of well-to-do Unionists, farmers and others, and carried them over the border to be held as hostages for the release of I.R.A. prisoners. Three days later a party of eighteen Special Constables, six of them armed, on their way from the training camp at Newtownards, Co. Down, to Enniskillen in Co. Fermanagh were foolishly sent via the most direct rail route, which ran through Free State territory and involved changing trains at Clones, Co. Monaghan, a few hundred yards from the border. Here they clashed with members of the I.R.A., a clash during which the I.R.A. commander and four Specials were killed. On the arrival of the train with its wrecked and blood-stained compartments at Lisbellaw, Co. Fermanagh, there was a minor riot. At the end of May members of the I.R.A. entered Belleek, a village wholly in Northern Ireland, in Co. Fermanagh, and fired on a party of Special Constabulary in Pettigo, a village divided by the border, being partly in Co. Fermanagh and partly in Co. Donegal. The panic created among loyalists by this incursion was deep and its effects long outlasted the speedy evacuation by the I.R.A. In November 1922 the imperial government's representative in Northern Ireland reported:

> The events of last May have reduced the local Unionists to a state of nerves, comparable only, so far as my experience goes, to the panic among the better class of inhabitants of villages which the Bolsheviks have once held and threaten to revisit.[67]

Internally, there were incidents in most parts of the six counties, but the main trouble-centre was Belfast, where bombing, arson, intimidation, expulsion from home and murder became a part of life as political crime and ordinary crime masquerading under a political guise went unpunished. In Belfast, as elsewhere, the violence and disorder reached its peak in the second and third weeks of May 1922. The I.R.A. certainly seems to have set the pace, not always confining itself, as it supporters suggested, to 'empty warehouses and uninhabited castles, railway stations and government property'.[68] On the weekend of 22 May fourteen murders were perpetrated, and in the following week there were twenty two outbreaks of fire, directed chiefly against Protestant business premises in the Catholic districts. Violence bred violence. On 31 May the shooting of two Special Constables brought a number of Specials in armoured cars into the Catholic streets, which they raked with machine-gun fire. Renewing the attack at night, they broke into houses and set fire to them. In that one night over eighty Catholic families were rendered homeless and eight Catholics were killed.

Nationalists liked to represent violence in Belfast, as elsewhere, as part of a deliberate attempt by official and unofficial loyalist and Protestant forces to exterminate Catholics. Certainly more Catholics were killed than Protestants, but such a simplistic view took little account of I.R.A. activity in the North and the number of Protestant casualties as well. There was some disagreement over casualty figures for the first six months after the Northern government assumed responsibility for law and order; yet even the most pessimistic statistics covering Belfast in the period 6 December 1921 to 31 May 1922 underlined not only the extent but also the impossibility of any glib explanation of the problem facing Northern Ireland in 1922. In that period 236 people were killed and 346 injured. Of those killed, 16 were members of the Crown forces, including 5 Catholics; 73 were Protestants; and 147 were Catholics, many of whom may have been killed by indiscriminate I.R.A. firing in their own areas. Of the wounded, 37 belonged the the Crown forces; 143 were Protestants; and 166 were Catholics.[69]

That the security problem was more serious in 1922 than in 1921 was one difficulty facing the Northern government. The second difficulty was that the government was scarcely master of its own house. Some problems were beyond the control of any government. It is difficult to assess the relationship between social problems and violence, political or otherwise, but Northern Ireland certainly had its share of social problems. In particular, it suffered from a housing shortage and a high rate of unemployment,[70] both of which prevented the government from successfully tackling such problems as the rehousing of people driven from their homes and finding employment for those expelled from their work, let along restoring them to their original homes and occupations.

In addition, the government lacked resources – legal, manpower and financial – to develop independently a response to the security problem it faced, especially since this lack made it dependent upon Britain. Special powers for dealing with disorder derived from the R.O.I.A. and had to be used in conjunction with a reluctant military.[71] Not until April 1922, with the army's encouragement, did the government equip itself with frankly despotic powers, similar to those held by the army under the R.O.I.A., when the controversial Civil Authorities (Special Powers) Act received the royal assent.[72] The regular police force, the

R.I.C., was not only considered demoralised by its experiences in the Anglo-Irish war, but was also in the process of disbandment as part of the British withdrawal from Ireland. Its strength, under 2,400 and almost 400 below establishment at the beginning of the year, consistently dwindled down to its disbandment on 31 May 1922, when it was replaced by the new R.U.C., which was modelled on its predecessor. Although it was intended that the new force should eventually have an establishment of 3,000 men, by the mid-summer only 1,100 had been taken on.[73] In the meantime the Northern government had to rely upon the army or the Special Constabulary. At its peak in the early summer of 1922 the military presence in the six counties numbered sixteen battalions, but many of these consisted of raw recruits, were below strength, and since for different reasons over-reliance upon the military was unacceptable to both the Northern and imperial governments, the troops were usually kept in reserve rather than used actively.[74] The brunt of security work, therefore, rested upon the Special Constabulary, which expanded throughout the first half of the year and to which a new category – the C1 force, in effect a Northern Ireland territorial army – was added. By the mid-summer of 1922, apart from a large but unestimated number of the old class C (a police reserve, mostly of elderly men, used only in a static role close to their homes), the establishment of the Special Constabulary was 42,250 and its strength 32,000 (5,500 class A; 19,000 class B; and 7,500 class C1).[75] The building up and maintenance of such a large force raised Northern Ireland's third limitation – its lack of money. Although strictly a transferred service, the Special Constabulary had to be financed by the imperial government to avoid a large deficit in Northern Ireland's budget, for in 1921–22 the Specials cost £1,500,000 and the estimate for 1922–23 was £2,700,000.[76]

Imperial co-operation was forthcoming, but it could never be relied upon and had to be constantly fought for. The reason for this uncertainty was that imperial policy in Northern Ireland continued to be determined not by the needs of the security problem there but principally by the needs of a larger Irish policy. The imperial government's overriding concern in 1922 was that the Treaty should succeed and should not founder on the Ulster question. It was determined to help supporters of the Treaty establish their authority in the South and to provide them with as little excuse as possible for reneging on the Treaty.[77] This preocupation, therefore, subjected the Northern government to some degree of supervision from the South as well. At the beginning of 1922 the fate of Northern Ireland did not arouse much controversy in the South. The Treaty debates there revolved around Ireland's position in the Commonwealth, and towards the end of January there seemed a prospect of an accommodation between the

198 *The Factory of Grievances*

two Irish governments. However, with the prolongation and deepening of the split over the Treaty in the South, the question of Northern Ireland became an important issue. There was always the temptation to seek unity in directing attention to the North, and, in addition, events in Northern Ireland could be used as a stick with which to beat the pro-Treaty government.[78] Collins, in particular, took an intense personal interest in events in the North, especially the treatment of the minority there. It was, however, an interest determined not by any clear analysis or comprehension of the problems facing the Northern government. Rather, Collins' attitude towards the Northern security problem was subordinated to his task in the South. It also had something of a 'school-boy manner'[79] and was often expressed in hysterical denunciations of the Northern government and strong representations to the imperial government that the extermination of Catholics in Northern Ireland, as he put it, was undermining his position and, therefore, the Treaty in the South.[80]

Since the question of law and order in Northern Ireland often upset the Provisional Government, the imperial government had, therefore, to interest itself in the North, even though the administration of law and order was a transferred service. Yet it never undertook responsibility for developing a satisfactory system of law enforcement. Only Winston Churchill, the Colonial Secretary, and, to a lesser extent, Arthur Balfour, Lord President of the Council, among imperial ministers, and none of the senior imperial officials involved with Irish affairs, understood or tried to understand the problems facing Northern Ireland in 1922. To them the problem of disorder in Northern Ireland was a rather tiresome side-issue which might upset the great work of Irish reconciliation. It was therefore hoped that law and order in Northern Ireland would be established with the minimum of direct British involvement, part of the general policy enshrined in the 1920 act of limiting the imperial commitment in Ireland. The policy therefore involved a refusal to halt the disbandment of the R.I.C.; the very limited use of the military; a substantial grant towards the cost of equipping and maintaining an expanded Special Constabulary; and a constant series of lectures to Craig, often at the Southern government's behest, on the need to put an end to the killing, maiming and expulsion of Northern Catholics. All this was combined with a reluctance to press the Northern government too far lest it resign and once more embroil Westminster directly in Irish affairs.[81]

The interdependence and interreaction of the problem of law and order in the North with the need to safeguard the Treaty settlement was well demonstrated at the end of May and the beginning of June, when the draft Free State constitution was being considered by Westminster. The draft constitution, submitted to the imperial government on 27 May 1922, was considered unsatisfactory, as it failed to give adequate weight to the concepts of Crown and Empire considered so vital in Britain. So gravely did imperial ministers regard the situation that there was talk of a reversion to Crown colony government in the South, and the next few weeks were spent in negotiations with representatives of the Provisional Government in an attempt to alter the constitution to conform with the imperial view of the Treaty.[82] These discussions coincided with the peak of violence in Northern Ireland, so that there was a danger that the Southern Irish leaders would take advantage of events there to break off negotiations.[83]

When Lloyd George and Austen Chamberlain saw Collins and Griffith on 30 May, the Irishmen were 'more anxious about the North-East than anything else'.[84] Talking of the 'extermination of Catholics' there, they argued that since it was paying for the police in Northern Ireland and had handed over law and order to the Northern government, the responsibility rested with the imperial government. This conversation alarmed the majority of imperial ministers, who reckoned that a break on Ulster had to be avoided, since it would render them powerless to enforce the Treaty settlement in the South. Public opinion at home and in the Empire would scarcely rally in support of any action to defend a situation in which, Lloyd George observed, more Catholics than Protestants had been killed, no murderers had been apprehended, and the imperial government had taken no action except to finance the Special Constabulary, the very people the Provisional Government accused of perpetrating crimes against Catholics.[85]

Some imperial response to events in Northern Ireland was therefore considered necessary to 'eliminate the Ulster issue and leave a clean issue of "Republic versus British Empire" '.[86] The Southern Irish leaders had suggested either a judicial inquiry or the imposition of martial law (with the army assuming full control of law and order in the North). The latter course was considered undesirable and impracticable: it would be unacceptable to the Northern government, beyond the capacity of the forces available, and, above all, it would put the imperial government in an embarrassing position, even leading it into direct conflict with the South. Opinion therefore favoured a judicial inquiry. Only Churchill and Balfour opposed what they regarded as a proposal to put Northern Ireland in the dock. The majority of ministers, however, believed that a judicial inquiry would not only relieve the imperial government of responsibility but might also bring a sufficient respite to enable the question of the Free State constitution to be settled. During such an inquiry, perhaps carried out by a Protestant and a Catholic judge, Lloyd George suggested, 'Neither side would care to create evidence against itself, and they might thus be able for a time to stop the outrages and give time for the other issue to develop'.[87]

In the event, no judicial inquiry was held. Craig was summoned to London to discuss with Balfour the imperial cabinet's fears. He defended Northern Ireland and criticised the South's campaign against the North, but he did make what had become almost his ritual acknowledgment of imperial aid to Northern Ireland and did agree to an inquiry, provided it was made to appear as being held at his government's request.[88] His colleagues, however, vehemently opposed the idea, arguing that such an inquiry would undermine the government's authority;[89] and, anyway, the question of the Free State constitution was satisfactorily settled by the middle of June. The only positive result, therefore, from this flurry of activity was a private one-man investigation into the reasons for the breakdown of the peace pact of 30 March.[90] There was also a negative result. As had often been the case in the past, and was to be so in the future, the intermeshing of Northern Ireland affairs with the needs of the Irish settlement meant that Craig was absent from Northern Ireland at critical times. During the discussions on the Free State constitution, when his government was making an all-out effort to stamp out disorder, Craig felt obliged, at the suggestion of Balfour and Churchill,[91] to spend much of the time in London defending Northern Ireland's interests. As he explained to Spender,

> After every conference [of imperial ministers] with the members of the Southern delegation, it is necessary for me to supply a 'corrective', otherwise action on our behalf is delayed. I have been doing this work five times during last week and this with, what I believe to be, good results.[92]

Craig's presence in London may have done Northern Ireland's case a power of good in Britain, but it did mean that his government was deprived of his leadership, support and encouragement at home. He was the one man in Northern Ireland with sufficient authority and vision capable of at least trying to correct the myopia that affected Ulster Unionism, but during his frequent absences security policy was left in the hands of his uncompromising colleagues, whose attitude towards law and order was theoretically stern and impartial but was in practice partisan.

The events at the end of May and the beginning of June typified the complications surrounding the development of security policy in Northern Ireland – too many partially interested parties and insufficient concentration upon what were Northern Ireland's particular needs. The consequence was that in 1922 security policy was distinguished for its confusion and inconsistency.

For example, although much depended on the Special Constabulary, there was confusion about its role. Was it primarily a military force or primarily a police force? Was its main task to defend the border against attack or to help restore order internally? This confusion was summed up in Craig's invitation to Field-Marshal Sir Henry Wilson to advise him on security matters; the subsequent appointment of an English major-general, A. Solly Flood, as military adviser in charge of Northern Ireland's peace-keeping forces; and Flood's endeavours to build up what was in effect a territorial army equipped with planes and tanks, efforts which had to be restrained by Craig and the Colonial and War Offices.[93] Had there been full confidence that the imperial government would defend the border and maintain Northern Ireland's territorial integrity, perhaps this confusion would not have arisen. As it was, the imperial government was sparing in its use of troops, with the result that after the February border raids the government of Northern Ireland had to use, as Craig delicately put it, the 'best members' of the Special Constabulary to guard the frontier, while 'the less excellent parts of the Special force were being used for dealing with the chronic and at the present time acute disturbances in Belfast'.[94]

Similarly, the government was reluctant to take the fullest powers or to take full advantage of the powers it did possess, lest it appear provocative. Controversial though it was,[95] the Special Powers Act did not go as far as the R.O.I.A. A clause in the original draft bill had provided for the establishment of special courts with wide powers to take the place of courts martial, but the provision was dropped after the Attorney-General had opposed it as a reflection on the judiciary and as unnecessary in law-abiding Northern Ireland.[96] The slow processes of ordinary law, the difficulty of obtaining convictions, and the almost impossibility of protecting witnesses, later led the police and military authorities, with some support from the Ministry of Home Affairs, to renew the demand for special courts with wide powers, including the ability to impose the death penalty.[97] The cabinet, however, preferred to stick to the ordinary courts and try to expedite the hearing of cases, because 'the establishment of special Courts would have a bad effect in England where it would not be understood'.[98] The preoccupation not to appear provocative inhibited the government from using its powers to take preventive action. By the middle of April the police authorities were forecasting an I.R.A. onslaught on Northern Ireland sometime in May and wanted to forestall it by interning suspects under the Special Powers Act,[99] but on 19 April the cabinet decided that

> Authority could not be given *now* to intern persons suspected of evil designs, but lists should be prepared and kept up to date, so that arrangements for the internment of those who are citizens of Northern Ireland and possibly for the deportation of those who are not, might take place instantly if the crisis arises.[100]

Only when the crisis did break towards the end of May did the government take full advantage of its special powers, proclaiming illegal certain nationalist organisations, interning suspects and imposing curfews.[101]

Such reluctance to use its powers would have been the more understandable had there been a real determination to pursue a consistent and positive conciliatory policy. There was collectively no such determination, however. Craig and Londonderry were the advocates of conciliation, of enforcing the law with discretion, but their views did not prevail and attempts at conciliation were not persevered with.

The two most dramatic attempts to solve Northern Ireland's security problem by agreement were the Craig—Collins agreement of 24 January 1922 and their peace pact of 30 March. The first agreement was the outcome of a meeting sought by Craig to find out Collins's 'future intentions towards Ulster, and to determine his future policy based on whether Southern Ireland intended to declare Peace or War with Northern Ireland'.[102] The result of a three-hour meeting in London was a promising concordat with harmony as the keynote. The most important gains for Northern Ireland were that Collins implicitly recognised that Northern Ireland had a right to exist and that the Treaty could be amended. Collins made it clear that he wanted 'a real peace', and it seemed as though the boundary question might be settled by mutual agreement between the North and South and the dreaded Boundary Commission superseded. The March peace pact, signed in London by Craig, Collins and Churchill, was more specific. It hoped to cure unrest and disorder in Northern Ireland by creating Catholic confidence in the government and securing Catholic co-operation in the maintenance of law and order, largely through the establishment of two committees – an advisory committee composed of Catholics to assist in the selection of Catholic recruits to the Special Constabulary; and a conciliation committee composed equally of Catholics and Protestants, with an independent chairman and direct access to the heads of government, to hear and investigate complaints as to intimidation, outrage, etc. In return, I.R.A. activity in the six counties would cease, thereupon justifying the optimism of clause 1 of the pact: 'PEACE is today declared'.[103]

It would have been too much to have expected that such agreements could have transformed the security situation in Northern Ireland. Feelings were running too high for that. Whereas Catholics and nationalists thought that Collins had given way too much in January,[104] Unionists reckoned that Craig had been outwitted in March.[105] There was, too, much to criticise in arrangements made by Craig in London with those without full responsibility for Northern Ireland's affairs. Such agreements were largely public relations exercises, and however momentarily they may have relieved the signatories' consciences, they were counter-productive.

On the one hand, such agreements with Collins strengthened the position of the more uncompromising nationalists in Northern Ireland. The dominant nationalist tradition in Northern Ireland was that of the Irish Parliamentary Party, the constitutionalist tradition. There were indications from the last week of March onwards that some such Nationalists would be prepared to recognise and co-operate with the Northern government, and there had been discussions between Craig and certain Belfast Catholics, who reported to the local bishop, as to what the government could do to encourage such recognition. However, they complained unceasingly that their influence was undermined by the virtual recognition of Collins as the leader of the Northern minority. By making representations to the imperial government, and having both it and the Northern government responding, Collins was able to appear to be supervising affairs in the North, thus increasing the influence of the Sinn Féin party there.[106] Moreover, talk about the return of people expelled from the shipyards or their homes, a feature of both agreements, was unrealistic in the economic circumstances of 1922 and merely created expectations that could not be fulfilled and thus provided occasions for future recriminations.[107]

On the other hand, Unionist fears and resentments were increased. Provisions relating to the Special Constabulary, when taken in conjunction with the virulent nationalist propaganda against the force, could hardly be seen as other than an attempt to immobilise it, while the numbering and disarming of police seemed simply to invite identification and assassination.[108] Furthermore, there was considerable resentment at the way in which the imperial and Southern governments seemed intent on blackening Northern Ireland's reputation.[109] Such was the feeling of desertion and isolation among Ulster Unionists that they were little inclined to take a broad view of any question. It became almost impossible to consider rationally, for example, how far complaints against the Special Constabulary were justified and might be remedied.[110] On the contrary, leaders, Craig included, found it constantly necessary to reassure the force by expressing unbounded confidence in it and in all its works.[111]

While miracles could not be expected from conciliation, it might have been expected that the detailed working out of at least some aspects of these agreements could have provided the basis for co-operation between the government and the minority. The potentialities were demonstrated by the way in which Andrews, the Minister of Labour, secured the co-operation of Collins and Catholics in his administration of the unemployment grant provided by the imperial government under clause 9 of the peace pact.[112] His conciliatory and patient approach proved a striking contrast to the way in which questions directly affecting law and order were handled by the responsible ministry, the Ministry of Home Affairs, and the Attorney-General.

It was true that the agreements did have serious implications for the maintenance of law and order, particularly by raising the question of the extent to which the executive should intervene in the due processes of law. It was also true that Collins's forgetfulness[113] and impetuosity[114] hardly facilitated the implementation of the peace pact, and that the police and conciliation committees must have been very difficult to deal with, the former wanting to alter the constabulary's recruiting regulations, the latter demanding judicial functions and a large government grant.[115] Furthermore, there was genuine difference of opinion over the interpretation of clause 10 of the pact, providing for the release of political prisoners. Craig reckoned that it applied only to persons who had committed technical offences owing to their political views, such as a funeral firing party and 'the motor load of Shinnies who turned off the straight path to get drinks at a Pub'.[116] Collins, however, believed that it should apply to all persons who could, however serious their crimes, claim to have been politically motivated, and he thus submitted a list of 169 prisoners for release.[117] Craig was undismayed by the length of the list and was anxious that, in order to fulfil the 'spirit as well as the letter of the agreement', Bates, as Minister of Home Affairs, should get in touch directly with his opposite number in Dublin.[118] The pact was, however, unpopular with the military and police authorities,[119] and ministers and officials connected with law and order showed little imagination or generosity in implementing it. The Junior Minister of Home Affairs, R. D. Megaw, and the Attorney-General, Richard Best, threatened to resign if there was a general amnesty. Bates would not act against their advice and was eventually prepared to release only fifteen of the prisoners on Collins's list.[120] In addition, the ministry's attitude towards the committees was simply obstructive, there being, for instance, some difficulty in convening the first meeting of the conciliation committee, as Bates was unwilling to issue an official notice by the government.[121]

In fact, generally at this time the Ministry of Home Affairs showed a contemptuous rather than an accommodating attitude towards the minority. Although Bates expected, as he told the Cabinet Secretary on 21 April 1922, 'the better R.C. element to break off from S.F.',[122] his ministry not only showed scant courtesy to those Catholics who waited upon it, making them wait for hours on end,[123] but was also responsible for drawing up a bill abolishing P.R. in local elections, thereby removing what nationalists claimed was a valuable minority safeguard.[124] All this was going on when Craig was in London, trying to arrange the financing of the Special Constabulary, instead of supervising the implementation of the peace pact in Belfast. This latter task was left to the Cabinet Secretary, who not only lacked Craig's authority but hardly sympathised with the pact.[125] Nevertheless, he did loyally try to see that the pact was observed in letter and spirit. It was left to Spender to tell the Permanent Secretary of the Ministry of Home Affairs that he must make definite appointments to meet Catholic representatives, as 'naturally such evasion leads to suspicion of the Government'.[126] It was left to Spender eventually to arrange for a notice of the first meeting of the conciliation committee to be sent out 'on unstamped paper without any covering signature'.[127] It was left to Spender to press Bates – without avail – to release some political offenders *'quickly'*.[128]

There was, indeed, a sad contrast between the Prime Minister's good intentions and the hostile spirit in which the Ministry of Home Affairs acted. It was, however, a contrast with aptly captured the confusion surrounding the maintenance of law and order in 1921–22.

9

Discrimination (1): Justice

Out of the confusion surrounding the maintenance of law and order in 1921–22 there emerged a sectarian security policy. Shaped principally by a small group of ministers and officials consistently on the spot and with the most clearly defined views on the administration of justice – the Ministry and Ministers of Home Affairs, the Attorney-General, the police authorities and the Chief Whip – the policy involved the application of a dual standard. The law was rigorously enforced against Catholics and nationalists, but its application to Protestant and Unionist offenders was often tempered by discretion and political considerations. The existence of this dual standard was most clearly evident in repeated arguments in 1922–23 about the treatment of Catholic and nationalist prisoners in Northern Ireland, and in the handling of Protestant terrorists in 1922.

1

In addition to emphasising the importance of clause 10 of the peace pact of March 1922, which provided for the release of political prisoners, both the Provisional Government and Free State governments from time to time sought clemency for Catholic and nationalist prisoners in the North. During his meeting in January 1922 with Craig, Collins had asked for a review of the cases of the so-called Monaghan footballers and the Londonderry murderers.[1] The former had been arrested in Co. Tyrone on their way, so they said, to play in a Gaelic football match, but Unionists claimed that they were really going to rescue the three men sentenced to death for the murder of a prison officer, struck on the head and then poisoned with chloroform, during an attempted break from Londonderry jail.[2]

Similarly, in the following summer the Provisional Government asked the imperial government to secure an end to flogging in the North. Although flogging had been an optional extra under the 1916 Larceny Act, the Special Powers Act had, without any clear idea of its effect, extended its use, and some judges did begin to take advantage of the extended power of flogging.[3] Between 26 April and 17 July 1922 twenty-one prisoners were sentenced not only to long terms of imprisonment but also to lashes of either the cat or birch. Much to the government's relief,[4] the first person sentenced to flogging was a Presbyterian, but of the twenty-one so sentenced only three were Protestants (all Presbyterians), the rest being Catholics. The three Presbyterians and three of the Catholics had been involved in robberies, but the remaining fifteen Catholics had been found in possession of arms and explosives. By the summer the flogging sentences had been carried out on two of the Presbyterians and two of the Catholics, but the Provisional Government sought to secure the remission of the remaining sentences.[5]

Finally, the Provisional Government and then the Free State government asked the imperial government to secure the release of, and later a reduced sentence for, one of its army officers, Captain Thomas Heuston, a Co. Fermanagh man from Newtownbutler and a former member of the I.R.A.[6] Having strayed across the convoluted border on 7 November 1922, he was arrested by a Special Constabulary patrol and recognised as one of the leaders of the attack on the Special Constables at Clones railway station and as having been involved in earlier attacks against Crown forces in the North, not all of which had been amnestied and some of which had been organised in the very district where he was apprehended. Once he was taken in, 'all sorts of local political considerations came in'.[7] He was eventually charged with offences arising out of an ambush of a Special Constabulary patrol at Wattlebridge, Co. Fermanagh, in the previous February and was later sentenced to ten years' penal servitude.

The justification for these pleas for clemency was twofold. Firstly, it was alleged that the arrests were hasty and/or the sentences harsh. Secondly, release or mitigation would help the Southern government to establish itself and also help to improve relations between the different parts of the British Isles. The flogging sentences imposed for purely technical offences such as the possession of arms were, Cosgrave, Collins's successor in the South, told Churchill, 'unnecessarily harsh and savour of political revenge'. To continue this 'very humiliating punishment' would militate against improved relations, while its abandonment would 'most favourably affect opinion in Ireland and would go far to promote more cordial relations between England and Ireland'.[8] On the Heuston case, the precarious position of the Southern government, anxious to maintain friendly relations with the Empire but fighting for its life against Republicans and troubled by its own militarists, was emphasised. After a conversation with Cosgrave in April 1923 the imperial representative in Dublin reported that the Free State premier had stressed that

Heuston's detention was fraught with serious possibilities of danger which might break out at any time without warning and is at the same time a continued source of embarrassment to the F.S. Government, as it causes disaffection in the minds of the Northern section of the Army with whom Heuston is very popular.[9]

Such requests were supported by the imperial governments, coalition or Conservative. Ministers and officials agreed that some sentences were unduly harsh. Flogging sentences, in particular, imposed along with long prison sentences, as happened in Northern Ireland, did appear to be simply vindictive, since they could have no deterrent value. As one official argued, the important consideration was

> not whether the individual concerned is such a beast as to deserve to have his back cut in strips, but whether the fact that he has had a flogging, and that a flogging means getting your back cut in strips, will become notorious among persons likely to commit similar crimes.[10]

Ministers and officials were also concerned to bolster up the pro-Treaty party in the South and were concerned lest such an apparently small case as Heuston's would become 'just one of those unhappy incidents that time and again in Irish history have assumed an importance wholly disproportionate to their intrinsic worth and have produced effects of great political magnitude'.[11] Since law and order was a transferred service, there was a limit as to how far the imperial government could force its views upon the North, but senior imperial officials argued that by largely financing Northern Ireland's police force the imperial government had a right and even a duty to intervene and override if necessary the views of the regional government. It was argued by Lionel Curtis, the Colonial Office Adviser on Irish Affairs, that

> In law the Government of Northern Ireland are exclusively responsible for the infliction of sentences, but according to all constitutional practice, the British Government shares the responsibility so long as parliament is being asked to vote millions for the maintenance of order in Northern Ireland.[12]

The Southern claims for clemency, vigorously backed as they were by the imperial government, also had the sympathy of Craig and Londonderry, when acting as Craig's deputy. They were sensitive to the wider issues of Irish peace and the need to maintain good relations with the imperial authorities. Craig was, for instance, inclined to give way to Churchill's pressure for the remission of flogging sentences. For, he told Blackmore, he had 'a good many favours to secure', including the royal assent for the Local Government Bill, and was thus anxious to 'go as far as possible to meet the wishes of the one man who is helping us'. Moreover, he was reassured by Churchill's assessment that Northern Ireland would find Cosgrave and his government 'more reasonable to deal with than Collins and that anything we could do to meet their reasonable wishes would go a long way to help in the future'.[13] Londonderry, when acting as Prime Minister during Craig's holiday in France at the end of 1922 and the beginning of 1923, was much impressed by the strength if not the fairness of the imperial government's representations in favour of Heuston's release. He reported to Craig that Bonar Law, then Conservative Prime Minister, was 'a little outspoken as regards our selfishness and obstinacy, and how people would eventually resent our attitude and probably oppose us in regard to the Boundary'.[14]

Yet such weight of opinion was disregarded by the majority of Northern Ireland ministers, who argued that the law should take its course without interference from the executive. They refused to agree to the unconditional release of the Monaghan footballers and refused to recommend the commutation of the death sentence on one of the Londonderry murderers, Warder Leonard.[15] In both these instances their advice was overruled by the Lord Lieutenant who, undismayed by the Northern government's threat of resignation, acted on the advice of imperial law officers and ministers and in full awareness that the advice of the Northern government had to be 'modified in the event of my considering the special interests affecting the Empire &c'.[16] This use of the prerogative was greatly resented by Unionists in Northern Ireland. It smacked, they said, of a return to hated Dublin Castle methods and of discrimination against loyalists, for no Protestant prisoners were released.[17] The general feeling of outrage was summed up by the *Northern Whig*'s contention that 'A grave outrage has been committed against the Northern Parliament and against constitutional law — an outrage more suited to Stuart times than our own day'.[18] Moreover, it was plausibly argued that the recrudescence of violence at the end of February 1922 owed much to this concession to nationalist demands. A constitutional crisis was, however, avoided, since Craig felt committed to the abandonment of proceedings against the footballers and thought that the consequences of resignation would be worse than acceptance of the Lord Lieutenant's action.[19] Nevertheless, Craig assured the House that he had told the imperial government that 'if anything of the kind occurs again I will resign at once',[20] and this episode seems to have made both him and the imperial government reluctant to strain his colleagues' patience in the future. For the next two years, despite his own inclinations, Craig relied solely on the advice of the responsible ministers — Bates and Megaw of Home Affairs and Best, the Attorney-General, all advocates of no compromise.[21] It was they who prevented the release of prisoners after the peace pact.[22] It was Megaw who, supported by Bates, successfully argued in favour of the execution of flogging sentences.[23] And it was Best who, sustained by the permanent officials of the Ministry of Home Affairs,[24] persuaded his colleagues that Heuston should not be released, and who, despite a carpeting by the imperial Prime Minister,[25] maintained the opinion that he, as Attorney-General, was 'solely responsible for criminal prosecutions', 'must act on his unfettered judgement without any hint or pressure from the Executive', and could not be 'influenced by motives, however excellent in themselves, which are unconnected with the proper administration of the Law'.[26]

Not until 1924 was the government of Northern Ireland persuaded to take a broader view of questions relating to the administration of justice, and then it was only in response to financial threats, which had been lacking in 1922–23. This change of heart involved the release from internment of, and the lifting of a restriction order on, Cahir Healy, the Sinn Féin M.P. for the Westminster constituency of Fermanagh and Tyrone, interned under the Special Powers Act since May 1922 for being, according to the police, an I.R.A. intelligence officer of advanced views, a registrar of the Sinn Féin courts, and a Sinn Féin organiser in his home district of Enniskillen.[27] Healy was only one of a large number of long-serving internees who had refused to seek release by appearing before a three-man advisory committee appointed in July 1922 to hear representations by and on behalf of internees,* but his case began to achieve prominence after his election to the Westminster parliament in November 1922. When shortly afterwards the question of privilege was raised there, the Speaker ruled that there was no *prima facie* case for raising Healy's detention, which prevented him from having access to his constituents and the House, as a matter of privilege; but Healy's re-election in December 1923 aroused such feeling at Westminster in favour of his release that a worried Baldwin, the outgoing Conservative Prime Minister, twice wrote to Craig asking him 'to forestall the troublesome agitation which I foresee'.[28] Healy was not released. Trouble did arise, for the matter was soon raised and a committee of inquiry threatened when the new Westminster parliament assembled in January 1924 complete with a Labour government. Londonderry and Craig, who was unwell at the time, with Spender's background encouragement, did not now think it worth making a stand on Healy,[29] but Bates and his officials were, on police advice, reluctant to release such a 'cunning and clever organiser'.[30] It was only after continued pressure that the Ministry of Home Affairs agreed to Healy's conditional release.[31] He was released on 11 February 1924, but was later served, as was usual on the release of internees,[32] with a restric-

---

*Between May 1922 and 24 December 1924, when the last of the internees were released, 728 men had been interned at one time or another, the highest number at any one time being 575 in May 1923.

tion order prohibiting him from entering his old sphere of influence in the west of Co. Fermanagh, including his home town of Enniskillen.

As Spender and Londonderry had feared, such an order only created further unfavourable publicity, for on the following day Healy was found in Enniskillen and arrested. Although the Attorney-General decided not to proceed against him, since his presence in Enniskillen could be explained away as arising from Healy's misunderstanding of the terms of the restriction order, and although he was released on 14 February, the order remained in force, thus excluding him from part of his constituency.[33] The farce was only brought to an end by a very firm letter from Ramsay MacDonald, the new Labour Prime Minister, to Craig on the following day.[34] While not doubting Northern Ireland's legal right to restrict the movement of Westminster M.P.s, MacDonald asked Craig to reconsider the restriction order which may upset 'harmonious relations between the Government of Northern Ireland and the Imperial Parliament', broadly hinting that otherwise it might be difficult to pass certain Northern Ireland estimates shortly to be presented to the House. This threat was sufficient to persuade the cabinet to disregard for the first time the advice of the Attorney-General and Minister of Home Affairs on a matter relating to security. When the cabinet considered the letter on 16 February 1924, these two ministers opposed the lifting of the ban as being prejudicial to public order, but they were overruled by the Ministers of Finance, Education and Labour (the Prime Minister and Minister of Agriculture did not attend the meeting), who were concerned that nothing should jeopardise the continuance of imperial financial aid.[35] Pollock summed up the case for lifting the order when he argued that

> We ought to take a very broad view of this matter; that it was exceedingly likely that the Imperial Government would be unable to carry their promises of financial assistance to us if the Imperial House were in an unfriendly mood owing to our action towards one of their members. The Imperial House of Commons was jealous of their rights and privileges and would not, in his opinion, appreciate all the legal niceties of the position. He felt that this was a case in which we should run some risks.*[36]

---

*The only other occasion when finance and justice were directly linked was the release of all nationalist political prisoners in January 1926, arranged between Craig and Baldwin, then imperial Prime Minister, without prior reference to the Northern Ireland cabinet, which simply had to accept it. After the settlement of the border question with the tripartite agreement in December 1925 Craig came to an arrangement with Baldwin about the finance of the Special Constabulary, part of the package being that the imperial government should review the cases of all nationalists convicted during the emergency and that the Northern govern-

2

The persistently uncompromising attitude of the majority of Northern Ireland ministers and senior officials, especially those attached too the Ministry of Home Affairs, did not stem simply from blind reaction. Theirs may have been a narrow view, but it was a considered one. Throughout their attitude was that the law must take its course without interference from the executive. Only that way, it was argued, would police and prison officers have the confidence and determination to carry on their work, and the judiciary and magistracy be encouraged to impose realistic sentences, and only then would there develop among the public a respect for law and order and a spirit of co-operation with the police. That there was an all-too-evident need for such developments in Northern Ireland in the early 1920s was underlined by the murder of Esther McDougall on 25 May 1922 in a street in Belfast. A Catholic, she was a key witness in a Protestant bomb trial in which the jury had disagreed and which was to be re-heard at the next assizes. She had been threatened and had left home for a while, but had returned only to be shot in the head by a revolver fired from among a crowd of about a hundred people who seem to have gathered specially for the purpose of giving cover to the murderer, who was never apprehended.[37] In fact, most murders went unpunished. In May 1922 alone ninety murders were committed in Belfast, and Bates told the House when defending internment: 'Not a man was brought to justice. The people knew who committed those murders, but no one had the courage to come forward and give evidence'.[38]

It was maintained in Northern Ireland that this sorry state of affairs was largely, if not wholly, a legacy of the imperial government's failure over the previous few years to maintain respect for law and order in Ireland. Vacillation and ineptitude, Megaw reckoned, had too long characterised the administration of law in Ireland. Such vigorous statements had been made in parliament that 'we occasionally thought that another Cromwell or another Napoleon had arisen', but a week's vigorous action was soon followed by 'the squeals and whines of rebels, and criminals

---

ment should abide by whatever decision was reached. In the event, the imperial government decided to release all Northern Ireland's thirty-three political prisoners, including Heuston. The Ministry of Home Affairs and the police authorities were unhappy about this mass release and proposed to place restriction orders on the released prisoners. This suggestion proved unacceptable to the imperial government, Baldwin sending Craig a strong telegram of protest, and there was an almost cringing truculence in the letter which Bates had to write to the Home Office on 22 January 1926 withdrawing the proposal and assuring that 'It was out of no vexatious or oppressive reason that it was proposed to place Restriction Orders ... but ...'. we had to consider our responsibilities to the public here.' (P.R.O.N.I., CAB 9G/19/3.)

and their sympathisers'. Then 'a fortnight's lethargy would ensue and the police would not know where they were', after which there would be a demand for conciliation, which simply meant 'the gaol doors thrown open, criminals set free and treated as if they were the saviours of their country, while the men who had done their duty had to seek another country'.[39] Ministers in Northern Ireland were therefore determined not to repeat what they regarded as the imperial government's mistakes. For them a crime was a crime, no matter what the political intentions of its perpetrator, against whom the law should be strictly enforced without the intervention of the executive. As Megaw wrote in August 1922, rejecting the case for the remission of flogging sentences, 'The principles applicable to flogging cases are in general those affecting ordinary administration of law and order. Is the law to be firmly administered, or is its administration to be dependent on agitation or pressure from within or without?'[40]

It was argued, therefore, that when arrests were made and releases were considered desirable, the normal routine of the law should be observed, thereby reinforcing the law and securing nationalist recognition of Northern Ireland's legal system. Thus the government wanted the Monaghan footballers to apply for bail, which would not be opposed,[41] established an advisory committee to which internees could apply for release,[42] and was willing to reduce the charges against, but not release, Heuston prior to a trial.[43] When, too, realistic or even harsh sentences were imposed, ministers thought that they should be carried out. This was the argument used against commuting the death sentence on Warder Leonard in January 1922. Otherwise, the Attorney-General argued, 'it would be very difficult to justify exacting the extreme penalty in future cases of murder', while the Divisional Commissioner of the R.I.C. considered that 'from a discipline point of view it would be advisable if Leonard at any rate were executed' and that the difficulties arising from Leonard's execution would be no greater in the long run than the disorder provoked by showing leniency.[44] To have released prisoners following the Craig—Collins pact in the following March would, Bates argued, have greatly affected the confidence of the regular police 'at a period when their minds are already unsettled by the uncertainty as to their future', of the Special Constabulary, who had made some of the arrests, of the prison warders, 'whose reluctance to enforce prison discipline will be intensified if prisoners are being continuously released', and of Resident Magistrates, 'some of whom do not realise the importance of strictly enforcing the law at the present time, more especially under the Firearms Act'.[45]

It was this last consideration that was uppermost in Megaw's mind when he refused to abandon flogging. His ministry regarded flogging as 'a remarkable deterrent' appealing to the 'imagination in a far more em-

214 The Factory of Grievances

phatic way than the punishment of detention', but had been disappointed

214 *The Factory of Grievances*

phatic way than the punishment of detention', but had been disappointed that it had not been more readily used by the magistracy and judiciary, who still showed an alarming leniency in sentencing. While the government could not force judges and magistrates to impose harsher sentences, it could at least support those who did. Thus, Megaw argued, when judges after full consideration had awarded flogging and had seen no reason to mitigate the sentence after reconsidering the case on petition, 'it would be very dangerous policy to interfere with the sentences', especially since in some cases capital punishment could have been inflicted. Ever anxious that due regard should be shown to the courts, Megaw's heart was further hardened against the remission of flogging sentences by the terms of two petitions which suggested that the judges had been instruments of sectarian passion. It therefore seemed to Megaw that the mitigation of sentences by the government after such attacks would 'be an unwarranted reflection on the impartiality and authority of the Judges'.[46]

The restoration of comparative peace by the summer of 1922 did not alter the attitude of the majority of ministers. The argument was then that whatever success had been achieved had been due to the firm administration of the law, a view not wholly without foundation. The clampdown at the end of May did help transform the situation, as witnessed by the heightened morale and determination of the Crown forces and the tributes to the government from different sections of the community. As Londonderry told Bridgeman, the Home Secretary, in December 1922, reporting the cabinet's refusal to release Heuston,

> Whatever success has been attained by the Government of Northern Ireland in restoring law and order has been attained through the firm, impartial and consistent administration of justice, and were we to countenance the release of Heuston we should establish a precedent which would be fatal to the administration of the law here. His case cannot be treated as an isolated one.[47]

It was all very well for the imperial and Free State governments to seek clemency for the sake of the Free State and of Anglo-Irish relations, but the majority of Northern Ireland ministers did not find these pleas convincing. In the first place, they failed to see how interfering with the course of law in the North could in the long run help the restoration of law and order in the South. On the contrary, the civil war in the South made them even more determined to uphold law in the North, for they reckoned that the best way to help the Southern government was to ensure that law and order were strictly enforced in at least one part of Ireland. 'The authority of the law', Londonderry told Bridgeman, 'is dangerously weakened where those who infringe it are allowed to escape by the irregular action of the Executive'.[48]

In the second place, Northern ministers thought that repeated demands for special consideration for nationalist prisoners took too little account of conditions in Northern Ireland. The imperial and Free State governments seemed to forget that it was not only nationalists who could claim to be political prisoners. If general amnesties were granted to nationalists, it would be difficult not to extend them to loyalists as well, a course which the government thought inadvisable. This consideration had dominated the first-ever cabinet discussions of amnesty — on 31 January 1922, following the first Craig–Collins agreement:

> The Parliamentary Secretary Ministry of Finance (Chief Whip) stated most strongly that any Amnesty shown towards Sinn Féin political prisoners must be extended to all Unionist prisoners who could in any way plead political extenuating circumstances. The Parliamentary Secretary Ministry of Home Affairs was of opinion that it would be extremely inadvisable to release the Unionist looters &c., but the general opinion of the meeting was that it would be very difficult to show any discrimination and the ... (Chief Whip) stated that an Amnesty to one side which did not extend to the other could not be justified to the public and that it would really be better to open the Jails completely if a general Amnesty were given which included Sinn Féin prisoners guilty of the most grave offences.[49]

It was this consideration that led Craig to insist that clause 10 of the peace pact should not apply to those guilty of serious offences. 'It must not be forgotten', he wrote to Collins on 15 April 1922, 'that there are many prisoners other than those of the Roman Catholic Faith who have been convicted of similar crimes and the efforts of our Government to restore law and order would be gravely handicapped if all those dangerous characters were released'.[50] Moreover, while in a large country such as England in the 1920s it may have been possible to have exercised executive discretion without undue publicity, this was hardly possible in Northern Ireland. As Bates told Craig when asked at the end of January 1923 to review Heuston's admittedly harsh sentence, 'very great difficulties' might arise if Heuston were 'amnestied', for 'Ulster was in a different position from Great Britain, inasmuch as in a comparatively small community such as Northern Ireland every action of the Government was scrutinised by the whole of the population'.[51]

3

This strict view of the enforcement of law and order had much to recommend it, and it would have had much more to recommend it had it been consistently carried through. Too often, however, it was applied only to Catholic and nationalist offenders. Once Protestant lawbreakers were apprehended, and there was sufficient evidence to secure a conviction in the ordinary courts, the law did take its full course. The trouble was that prompt steps were not always taken to apprehend Protestant offenders. Fear of alienating Protestant opinion sometimes deterred those responsible for the maintenance of law and order from making or carrying out decisions that were known to be just and proper, as was indicated by the special treatment accorded to the Ulster Protestant Association (U.P.A.). The unwillingness of the Ministry of Home Affairs and the police authorities to take vigorous action against this Protestant terrorist group certainly conformed to Watt's assertion the previous year that exceptional legislation should apply only to 'disloyal and disaffected persons', not to those 'loyal to the Crown'.[52]

Originally a respectable Protestant defence association formed in Belfast in the autumn of 1920, the U.P.A. had become by 1922 an efficiently organised gang 'of the lowest and least desirable of the Protestant hooligan element', dedicated to the extermination of Catholics by any and every means.[53] Based upon a public house in East Belfast, it had about fifty hardcore and about a hundred floating members. Subscriptions were forcibly invited, a solicitor retained, and witnesses intimidated; and strict discipline was encouraged by the simple but titillating expedient of stretching offenders against the club's rules naked across a specially constructed flogging-horse and lashing them with a cat-o'-nine-tails. The police had long known about the gang's activities, but had lacked definite information until March 1922, when a member of the association gave the Ministry of Home Affairs details about the location of arms and ammunition. The police took immediate action, but secured a conviction in only one of the two cases that arose from the raids. The chairman of the club was sentenced to eleven months' hard labour under the Firearms Act, but three other men, whose houses gave access to a yard containing a U.P.A. arms dump, were acquitted by a jury.

The renewed I.R.A. onslaught in May put the authorities in a quandary. Police efforts to contain previous disturbances had been hampered by having to 'cope simultaneously with the warring factions. . . . They were quite unable to rely on the restraint of one party while they dealt with the other'.[54] It seems that some members of the U.P.A. may have been among the first internees,[55] but, perhaps through the agency of Dixon, the Chief Whip, who sat for East Belfast, an attempt was made at the beginning of June 1922 to tame these toughs by enrolling them in the Special Constabulary and enlisting their aid in the work of the newly established secret service. One member of the U.P.A., who was later interned, told the internment advisory committee the following November that

I was recommended for the secret service. . . . I was present when some of the looters were brought up at the Club. We handed them over to the police. We used to try them and if they were found guilty they were handed over to the police.[56]

Solly Flood reckoned that this policy was a great success in securing the co-operation of 'Loyal associations which had until then been inclined to take the law into their own hands',[57] but the policy of recruiting extreme gangs was symptomatic of what Spender complained was a widely held view at the Ministry of Home Affairs—'that the law does not matter when dealing with suspected treasonable criminals'.[58]

This attempt to tame the U.P.A. was unsuccessful. Its members were back on the streets of Belfast by the end of August 1922. On 30 August, Blackmore, the Assistant Cabinet Secretary, had written happily to Craig that 'Last week was the first for months that I was able to forward a "Nil" murder return to the Colonial Office'.[59] Next day, however, he had to report the murder in the Crumlin Road Picture House of a sixty-three-year-old Catholic attendant and a fourteen-year-old Protestant boy, as well as a bomb explosion in a Catholic area, which wounded seven children and one adult.[60] It was suspected that the attacks had been carried out by the U.P.A., probably in an attempt to halt a proposed reduction in the Special Constabulary. The matter was evidently left to Dixon, who later reported to Spender that 'he had settled the U.P.A. and prevented them from becoming a very grave danger'.[61] Despite Dixon's assurances, the U.P.A.'s attacks continued, and thus on 18 September a conference at the Ministry of Home Affairs decided on resolute action.[62] A certain area of East Belfast was to be searched thoroughly in the following three weeks, during which stringent curfew regulations were to be enforced and probably a register of all inhabitants compiled; and Bates promised to intern Protestants suspected of being involved in these disorders. 'Very great protest' was expected, especially as the operation would involve the closure of shops on one side of a street earlier than those on the other side and the searching and therefore delaying of workers going to and from work. Nevertheless, Bates was prepared to risk complaints and was duly commended to Craig by a normally critical Spender for showing 'considerable courage in the steps which he is prepared to enforce'.[63]

Such drastic steps, especially internment under the Special Powers Act, were considered necessary because it was impossible to obtain convictions in the ordinary courts. 'Nobody would come forward and testify against the gunmen,' later reported District Inspector Spears, the R.U.C.'s specialist on the activities of the U.P.A. 'Men and women were robbed and fired at, and when confronted with the men who had undoubtedly committed the crime, either would not identify them or did so in such a hesitating manner as to be little better than useless.' Even when evidence of identification was obtained, the U.P.A. 'made it their business to force other witnesses to attend to prove an alibi'.[64]

Despite the need, drastic action was not taken. It was not taken for fear of alienating Protestant opinion. 'The searching of Protestant quarters', Solly Flood told Watt on 28 September, 'has always been a delicate undertaking necessitating special arrangements and selected Personnel to carry it out'; and, he continued, to take 'any drastic action in loyal areas for the sake of punishing a few rogues might incite an outbreak of outrages on a large scale'.[65] Such forbearance simply provided further opportunities for the U.P.A. gunmen.[66] Their last murder was committed on 5 October 1922 with the shooting of a Catholic woman on the Newtownards Road, but their subsequent lack of success was not for want of trying. After the last murder, the sixth of the series, Spears obtained authority to arrest and intern two of the U.P.A. leaders, but they were held only for a month and then deported to England on condition that they stayed away for two years. The government's reluctance to use the full rigours of the Special Powers Act against loyalists meant that the police had to rely mainly upon harassment and isolated searches, which may have shaken the U.P.A. but did not stop their bombings and shootings. On 5 November Spears obtained permission to arrest and intern four more of the leading lights, but for the rest he had to rely upon catching U.P.A. members with bombs and guns in their hands so that they could be charged under the Firearms Acts, and upon sniffing out and confiscating their arms. His diligence did succeed in breaking up the U.P.A. by the end of November 1922, but there is no denying that this could have been achieved earlier and lives saved had the government been willing to use its powers as fully against loyalists as it was against nationalists.

4

These early years were crucial to the subsequent history not only of the administration of justice but also of the whole province. It was in these years that the pattern of law enforcement was established in Northern Ireland. Born of a compromise between regional and imperial considerations, it was a distinctive system which, with the wide powers conferred upon the regional civil authority which also controlled an armed regular police force and an armed part-time force, had no counterpart in the rest of the United Kingdom. The system was also characterised by the precedence given to the narrowest police and legal considerations. In fact, police matters generally took priority in the Ministry of Home Affairs, despite that ministry's wide range of functions, as was seen by the way in which the Permanent Secretary and his deputy almost resigned (submitting their resignations but later withdrawing them) after the minister had sided with the police over the handling of an ammunition contract in 1924.[67] Any mitigation of the narrow view of law and justice was achieved only on the rare occasions when the imperial government linked its requests for the exercise of leniency and imagination with the question of financial aid. Even this potentially broadening influence was removed after the border agreement of December 1925, when the imperial government ceased to concern itself officially with the administration of justice in Northern Ireland.

It was narrow police considerations that led to the retention of the Special Powers Act. Despite nationalist allegations of despotism, the powers were sparingly used. If most Unionists had had their way, Gaelic Sunday sports would have been banned under the act, but, declining a demand that he should use his special powers to ban a Gaelic football match due to be played near Lurgan on Easter Sunday 1923, Bates told the Commons:

> Personally, I think . . . that it is a very objectionable thing to have football matches played on Sunday, but that is not the point that arises here. The question is whether there will be a breach of the peace, and I am advised that there will not. I must rely on the Police officers in the neighbourhood, who are most efficient.[68]

The police and Ministry of Home Affairs did not enjoy using the powers available under the act, but they did feel more comfortable with them. Their convenience overrode broader political considerations – at least where the minority was concerned. After Nationalists had taken their seats in parliament in 1925 the annual renewal of the Special Powers Act had become an unedifying occasion for mutual recrimination.[69] The reaction of the Ministry of Home Affairs and police authorities was not to recommend that the act should lapse, but that to avoid this annual wrangle it should be made permanent. The compromise adopted by the cabinet in 1928 was to renew the act for five years until 1933, when, perhaps understandably in view of the tension caused by de Valera's return to power in the South, it was made permanent.[70]

What rendered this apparently strict attitude inimical to long-term stability in Northern Ireland was the fact that it was one-sided. Whereas in the case of Catholics and nationalists the law was rigorously enforced and the government made full use of its powers where necessary, in the case of Protestants and Unionists political considerations were allowed to operate and ministers were willing to use powers of discretion in the interests of public relations. Thus at the behest of the Minister of Home Affairs, the Attorney-General and Crown Solicitor had a word with magistrates trying the cases of Protestants who had attacked Catholic processions on their way to the International Eucharistic Congress in Dublin in 1932. Bail was in most cases preferable to prison sentences because, Bates told Craig,

I do not want when the New Parliament House is opened, or when . . . we are engaged in very violent disturbances in connection with the Free State, to have the Government handicapped by having 70 or 80 young fellows in gaol.[71]

In sum, devolution produced in Northern Ireland a system of law enforcement which not only differed significantly from that obtaining in the rest of the United Kingdom, but which also discriminated in favour of the majority section of the community.

10

Discrimination (2): Representation

Two topics recur time and again in a cabinet file entitled 'Alleged Disability of Roman Catholics in Northern Ireland'.[1] These topics are education and representation. Typical of the charges of discrimination made against the government on these questions was an article on 'The Catholics of Northern Ireland', which appeared in 1932 in *The Tablet*, the English Catholic weekly, and which criticised the 'intolerable conditions' under which Catholics laboured in Northern Ireland for the sake of their faith in an atmosphere of 'privileged Protestantism'.[2] The author, 'An Englishman', marked out for special condemnation 'a bogus suffrage' which converted Catholic majorities into minorities in local representation and limited Catholic parliamentary representation, and also the 1930 Education Act which, by sanctioning simple Bible teaching in state schools, a formula 'completely antagonistic to the fundamentals of Catholicism', confirmed Catholic exclusion from the state system and placed 'the full burden of education on the private purses of Catholics, who at the same time are paying through their rates and taxes to provide fully subsidised schools for Protestants'.

The government of Northern Ireland had to spend no little time in trying to refute such allegations. Sometimes the task was made easier by the 'literally amazing'[3] inaccuracies of some of the charges. It was not true, for example, that the full burden of Catholic education fell upon the private purses of Catholics, since the state paid the salaries of all teachers in elementary schools, such salaries accounting for 93 per cent of total state expenditure on elementary education, and also after 1930 offered grants towards the purchase of sites and equipment to voluntary schools. It was also possible to retort that if the minority had suffered from the redrawing of local electoral areas, 'they have only themselves to blame' for boycotting the commission charged with defining the new areas.[4] Moreover, many of the criticisms of educational policy and administration could be explained in terms of Northern Ireland's financial difficulties and the slow pace of the administrative machinery which combined a central and full-time ministry with popular and part-time regional education committees.[5]

Nevertheless, since one of the main problems facing the government of Northern Ireland was the hostility of the Catholic and nationalist minority, there was much that was questionable in the policies pursued in respect of education and representation. What was needed was a sustained and imaginative attempt to win over the minority and to assuage their suspicions and fears. Whether or not such an effort would have succeeded it is impossible to say, but what is certain is that no such attempt was made. Instead, policies were adopted which confirmed and even heightened nationalist and Catholic hostility. An avowedly non-sectarian education system was gradually compromised so that it, in effect, endowed Protestantism, while with the abolition of P.R. the systems of both local and parliamentary representation were altered in such a way as to benefit the Unionist Party at the expense of all other parties. What is more, the imperial government, despite its reservations about the wisdom of such policies, did not prevent their implementation. The development of policies relating to education and representation thus underlined two recurrent themes of the process of government in Northern Ireland. On the one hand, it underlined the partisan and short-sighted nature of government there, as the Unionist administration was unable to rise above party considerations. Craig's government was neither vindictive nor deliberately oppressive, and it was often well-intentioned, but it was too responsive to the claims of its supporters and thus unable to correct the imbalance in the state created by the minority's opting out. On the other hand, the development of policies relating to education and representation underlined the unwillingness or inability of the sovereign power, Westminster, to correct the consequences of local myopia.

1

P.R. had been introduced into local and parliamentary elections in Ireland as a safeguard for minorities by the 1919 Local Government (Ireland) Act and the 1920 Government of Ireland Act respectively. In both instances the safeguard had been intended primarily for the protection of minorities in the South of Ireland rather than those within the North. In 1919 partition had not been decided upon, and during the discussions of the 1920 bill little thought had been given to safeguards for the nationalist minority in the North, which, it was thought, would be large enough to look after itself.[6] Nevertheless, the existence of P.R. did come to be regarded as a safeguard for Northern minorities.

The main advantage to be derived from P.R. is that it can allow for the representation of a wider range of interests than the X-voting system. Under an X-voting system the party with the most votes in a ward or constituency takes all the seats, the result being that the larger parties are frequently over-represented and the smaller ones all but annihilated. The system of P.R. adopted for both local and parliamentary elections in Ireland was the single transferable vote in multi-member constituencies, to enable different points of view to be proportionately represented.[7] As the P.R. Society of Ireland explained in 1920, P.R. is 'a system of voting by which every group of citizens can obtain their proportionate share of representation on elected bodies. It means that no group can be excluded if they have had sufficient courage and public spirit to nominate candidates, and to fight.'[8] In other words, under P.R. more votes are (if properly cast) effective than under the X-system. In an X-vote election only the votes cast for the winning party are effective in helping to elect a member or councillor. By contrast, the P.R. system of election has been likened to a 'spectroscope, whose prisms break up the compound beam of light cast upon it, analyse it to its component parts, and reflect, in the Result-Sheets, a spectrum comprising every element in its own place, and in its own relative strength'.[9]

Only one set of local elections (in 1920) and two general elections (in 1921 and 1925) were held under P.R. in Northern Ireland, but the results bore out its supposed theoretical advantages by broadening the field of political representation and debate there. Representation was given to minorities in accordance with their electoral strength without doing injustice to majorities. In Belfast the over-representation of Unionists, which had been traditional under the X-system of voting in both local and parliamentary elections, was dramatically ended. The Corporation had usually consisted of 52 Unionists and 8 Nationalists, but after the 1920 local elections it comprised only 35 official Unionists but also 2 Independent Unionists, 13 Labour supporters, and 10 assorted nationalists.[10] Admittedly, by winning 15 of the city's 16 seats the Unionists held on to their near-monopoly of parliamentary representation in the first election to the Northern Ireland parliament,[11] but the 1925 general election showed how P.R. could help diversify the city's representation.[12] Such was the variety of candidates that the electors were able to consider questions other than that of the 'constitution'. The results were almost a precise triumph for proportionality. Nationalists retained their one seat, but official Unionist representation was reduced from 15 to 8 with the loss of 3 seats to Labour and 4 to Independent Unionists. Moreover, the order of election suggested that the electorate seemed to prefer the newcomers even to those official Unionists who were returned. The new men topped the poll in three of the four constituencies and came second in two, whereas such leading Unionists as Bates and Pollock found themselves failing to achieve a quota of first preferences and slipping in the order of election.*

Outside Belfast, too, the effect of P.R. was to broaden the scope of political representation. In contested urban elections outside Belfast in 1920 a close correlation between votes cast and seats won facilitated the return of Labour candidates for the first time, as at Bangor and Lisburn, and enabled Labour to gain control of Lurgan.[13] Outside the industrial complex surrounding Belfast, where no new groups offered themselves for election, the effect of P.R. was to alter the balance between the two major political groups – Unionists and anti-partitionists. In some local government districts, by overriding the uneven distribution of population characteristic of the pre-1920 electoral areas, P.R. and its larger constituencies caused some dramatic upsets, giving anti-partitionists a clear majority in three such traditionally hotly contested authorities as the Fermanagh and Tyrone County Councils and Londonderry Corporation.[14] In parliamentary elections outside Belfast the existence of large, county-sized constituencies did ensure the representation of available opinion in accordance with electoral strength. In the 1921 and 1925 general elections outside Belfast and the university only two candidates not belonging to the major parties contested elections. The Independent Labour candidate was decisively defeated in Co. Down in 1921, but in 1925 the Unbought Tenants' Association's candidate in Co. Antrim was elected, with the help of nationalist votes, in sixth place, thus unseating the Junior Minister of Home Affairs. Otherwise the 32 county seats were divided between Unionists and anti-partitionists: Unionists won 21 in 1921 to the Irish Parliamentary Party's 5 and Sinn Féin's 6, while in 1925 Unionists secured 20 seats to the Nationalists' 9 and the Republicans' 2. Such results were a fair reflection of the voting. In 1921, for instance, Unionists received 62.01 per cent of first preferences and 65.63 per cent of the representation, while anti-partitionists with 37.65 per cent of first preferences won 34.37 per cent of the representation. Just how sensitive P.R. was to the existence of minority opinion was underlined by the results in Co. Antrim. There the sizeable nationalist vote, some 16 per cent of the electorate, was so distributed that under the old method of voting nationalists had been unable to return a single representative to parlia-

*The 1925 general election in Belfast was not a complete triumph for proportionality, since nationalists were under-represented, partly because of the split between old and new nationalists (which helped to explain why the surplus votes of one brand of nationalists were just as likely to be transferred to Labour as to other anti-partition candidates), and partly because the city's constituencies were too small to give adequate representation to a minority whose votes were largely concentrated in one constituency, West Belfast. Anti-partitionists thus never won the number of seats which their total first preferences, equivalent to four first preference quotas, merited.

ment. Under P.R., however, they were able to secure the return of a Nationalist as one of the county's seven M.P.s.*[15]

Even the most cursory examination of the results of the 1920 local elections and the 1921 and 1925 general elections thus bears out the contention of its proponents that P.R. does justice to minorities without doing violence to majorities. Nevertheless, P.R. was abolished in local elections by the Local Government Act of 1922 and in parliamentary elections by the House of Commons (Method of Voting and Redistribution of Seats) Act of 1929. By these two acts Northern Ireland reverted to the X-method of voting with newly created single-member electoral areas and constituencies for elections to local authorities and to the Northern Ireland parliament.

2

The abolition of P.R., the reversion to the X-system of voting and the creation of new electoral areas had three related effects upon politics in Northern Ireland. In the first place, Unionist representation upon elective public boards was increased at the expense of all other parties and groups. In Belfast official Unionist representation in the Northern Ireland parliament increased from eight in 1925 to eleven in 1929 at the expense of Labour and Independent Unionists. It was true that Nationalists did win a second Belfast seat in 1929, but this gain was offset by losses elsewhere. In the counties Nationalists lost two seats in parliament, no longer returning a member for Co. Antrim and returning only one, instead of two, of the members for Co. Armagh. Moreover, although Catholics and nationalists were a majority of the population in Co. Fermanagh, they could win only one of the three seats allotted to the county in the 1929 redistribution. Thus, whereas under P.R. nationalists had secured some 33 per cent of the parliamentary representation outside Belfast and the university, after 1929 they secured at most 28.1 per cent.[16] On balance, then, nationalists lost one member through the abolition of P.R. in parliamentary elections. Unionist repre-

*While it is proper to judge the results of P.R. by comparing the number of votes cast with the number of candidates returned, in Northern Ireland another standard of comparison was also used, especially by nationalist and Unionist politicians, who liked to relate representation to the religious composition of constituencies and electoral areas. Labour objected to this practice, arguing that religious and political affiliations were not necessarily interchangeable, especially in Belfast. Outside Belfast, however, there was a very close correlation between parliamentary representation and the relative sizes of the Protestant and Catholic populations. Comprising roughly one-third of the population, Catholics felt entitled to 16 or even 17 of the 48 non-university seats and to 11 of the 32 seats outside Belfast and the university. The former figure they never achieved, but they achieved the latter in both the P.R. general elections.

sentation on and control of local bodies was also increased by the abolition of P.R. in local elections. After the 1920 P.R. local elections Nationalists, Sinn Féin and Labour controlled 24 (32 per cent) of the 75 local public bodies in Northern Ireland: 1 county borough, 1 town council, 7 urban district councils, 2 county councils and 12 rural district councils. By 1927 Nationalists and Labour controlled only 12 (16 per cent) of local councils – 1 town council, 7 urban district councils and 4 rural district councils.[17] The most spectacular losses occurred in the west – Fermanagh and Tyrone County Councils and Londonderry Corporation – and the extent of the changes may be judged from the transformation of representation on Fermanagh's public bodies. Under P.R. nationalists had returned 63 members to the Unionists' 57, that is, they had 52.5 per cent of the representation on all local bodies. After its abolition nationalist representation fell to 43, while the number of Unionist representatives increased to 74. In other words, after the abolition of P.R. in local elections Fermanagh's Catholics, who comprised 56 per cent of the county's population, obtained only 36.75 per cent of the representation on public bodies.[18] In the east of the province changes were less dramatic but nevertheless marked, as in Belfast, where official Unionist representation on the Corporation increased from 35 in 1920 to 43 in 1923.[19]

Changes in the character of local representation cannot be attributed entirely to changes in the method of voting and in local electoral areas. In many places nationalists boycotted local elections in the 1920s[20] and Labour did not contest seats, particularly outside Belfast, with the same enthusiasm as in 1920.[21] The reasons for the nationalist boycott were often confused, but in an area where electoral arithmetic had been reduced to a fine art and electoral strengths were widely known a sense of futility may have deterred anti-Unionist candidatures. Certainly the anticipated consequences of the new electoral areas for the Omagh Rural District Council, the only electoral areas for which detailed figures of the religious composition appear to be available, did not encourage nationalist participation. Catholics and nationalists had a majority of 8,179 in the population of the rural district and an electoral majority of 5,381; yet the new electoral areas were so drawn as to give Protestants and Unionists a majority in 21 of the 39 areas.[22]

Secondly, the abolition of P.R. and associated changes helped to fossilise and stereotype political attitudes and alliances in Northern Ireland. Considering the depth of feeling on the 'constitutional question' and the Northern Ireland attachment to the churches, it would be naïve to suggest that P.R. by itself could have revolutionised politics in Northern Ireland. For instance, the Independent Unionists all had sound Protestant credentials and the most successful of them were uncompromising Orangemen. Nevertheless, the existence of P.R. and of multi-member constituencies did help, during their brief lifetime, to broaden the area of political debate and more readily enabled a variety of opinions to be represented in the House. Not only were the two major parties represented but also Labour and an assortment of Independents especially interested in either social and economic questions or farmers' interests or the problems of ex-servicemen.[23] The return to the X-system of voting significantly reduced the range of representation. Labour's representation was reduced, and members especially interested in the problems of farmers and ex-servicemen were eliminated.[24] Representation on local councils became similarly less varied, for the general effect of the abolition of P.R. in local elections was to enhance the dominance of the majority party. Whereas under P.R. Omagh Urban District Council had consisted of 10 Nationalists, 7 Unionists, 2 Labour and 2 Independents, an uncontested election in 1923 resulted in the return of 13 Nationalists and 8 Unionists.[25]

P.R. and multi-member constituencies at least gave the opportunity for finding common ground on other than traditional issues, but their abolition tightened up party lines, as was evident in the electoral relations between Nationalists and Labour in Belfast. During the 1925 parliament Nationalists and Labour had worked closely together and Devlin had even advocated an alliance between them. Under P.R. the tensions between the two parties had been obscured, one Labour M.P. being elected in 1925 on Devlin's surplus, but under the X-system it became obvious that Nationalists and Labour would be competitors for the same Catholic votes. Thus in the contest for the new Falls division of Belfast in the 1929 general election, Billy McMullen, the Protestant and outgoing Labour M.P. for West Belfast, the man who got in on Devlin's surplus in 1925, was on this occasion defeated in 'a dirty fight' by combination of Catholic clergy and laymen.[26]

Moreover, not only did the abolition of P.R. and the return to single-member constituencies sharpen party divisions on traditional sectarian lines; they also tended to insulate members from changes of opinion. This characteristic of the X-voting system, which can lead to a cynical disregard for the democratic process,[27] was the more pronounced in Northern Ireland owing to the large number of uncontested seats. In 1921 no seats were uncontested and in 1925 only 23.1 per cent of returns were unopposed, but with the return to carefully mapped-out single-member constituencies, the percentage of uncontested seats rose rapidly: 42.3 in 1929, 63.5 in 1933, 40.4 in 1938. Although in 1938 one Labour candidate was returned unopposed, it was normally Unionists and Nationalists who enjoyed uncontested elections, usually 6 Nationalists and between 10 and 27 Unionists.[28] It was the same with local elections. Most seats were uncontested.[29] Indeed, by the 1930s local elections aroused so little interest in Belfast that the press first ceased to report speeches in municipal campaigns and later even declined to comment on them editorially.

In the third place, the reputation of the state suffered in the eyes of minority groups as a result of the abolition of P.R. and its associated changes. P.R. did come to be regarded as a safeguard for minorities in Northern Ireland – 'an eminently fair system of representation', according to a manifesto signed in 1928 by 14 M.P.s (9 Nationalists, 3 Labour, 1 Independent Unionist and 1 Independent).[30] Their resentment at what they regarded as attempts to perpetuate the Unionist ascendancy was summed up by the nationalist *Irish News* when reporting and commenting on the 1922 Local Government Bill. 'MUZZLING MINORITIES,' said one headline, while a leader nine days later wryly remarked that the Belfast parliament had made the six counties 'electorally safe for Ascendancy' and kept democracy 'at a respectfully remote distance'.[31]

Nationalists argued that the abolition of P.R. in local elections in 1922 violated the Anglo-Irish Treaty, since, they contended, it was designed to prejudice the work of the Boundary Commission.[32] The abolition of P.R. in parliamentary elections and the redrawing of constituencies in 1929 were considered to be both actual and moral violations of the 1920 act. While reluctantly admitting that the government had the legal right to abolish P.R. under clause 14 of the act, the Opposition – Labour, Nationalist and Independent – argued that the way in which the new constituencies were constituted contravened subsection 5 of clause 14, which required that due regard should be had to population in the redefinition of constituency boundaries, and section 5 of the act, which forbade religious discrimination.[33] Moreover, the Opposition held that the government was morally wrong to abolish P.R. without the consent of the minority and thus appealed to Craig to maintain the safeguard as long as the minority so desired.[34]

This plea went unheeded, thus confirming nationalists in their belief that ever since the establishment of Northern Ireland the Unionist government had been 'trying to crush the Roman Catholics in Northern Ireland, and to deprive them of their rights'.[35] Indeed, with the abolition of P.R. in parliamentary elections, some Nationalist and Labour M.P.s began to wonder whether it was worth while treading a constitutional path.[36]

What is more, it was a legitimate grievance. Despite the exaggerated rhetoric employed by critics of the Northern government, despite the nationalists' responsibility for their own plight by boycotting the state in the early years, and despite its strict legality, it is difficult to deny that the abolition of P.R. was a major act of misgovernment. One of the most urgent problems facing the government of Northern Ireland was the hostility of the nationalist and Catholic minority. The abolition of P.R. and the redrawing of electoral areas simply served to confirm suspicions and to create a real grievance. The very abolition of P.R., which had been significant both as an actual safeguard and as a symbol of respect for minority views, constituted a grievance, but the grievance was made the more real by the way in which the boundaries of electoral areas were so drawn as to maximise Unionist strength at the expense of others. It was true that no voting system whatsoever would have produced a nationalist majority in the Northern parliament, and it was also true that nationalists and Catholics were, in strict constitutional terms, never unrepresented in parliament, since it was, as that indefatigable Unionist Mrs Dehra Chichester (later Mrs Parker) insisted,[37] an M.P.'s duty to represent the views of all his or her constituents. Nevertheless, the fact remained that there were many issues in Northern Ireland on which nationalists and Catholics were unlikely to place much confidence in Protestant or Unionist M.P.s. Objecting to Co. Antrim's loss of its Nationalist M.P. on the abolition of P.R., Devlin argued that if any group needed a representative of its own it was the nationalist and Catholic community of Co. Antrim,

> with educational interests involved where they have all the county boards against them.... There they need a Member to whom they can speak, because if they are dealing with matters germane either to religion or charity they want to go to a man of their own class, of their own persuasion, of their own feeling, who is instinct with that feeling.[38]

Even more vital, perhaps, than the loss of parliamentary representation was the loss of control of some local councils, for these were fonts of patronage. It was not true that all local authorities appointed only their co-religionists or fellow party members to paid posts, or nominated only them to other bodies, such as regional education committees, or allocated houses only to them, but it was a general tendency, particularly in Belfast and the west.[39]

3

The whole controversy over representation raised the whole question of the nature of government in Northern Ireland — its partisanship and short-sightedness. Quite simply, P.R. was abolished and electoral boundaries redrawn in the interests of Unionism and the Unionist Party, with scant regard for, or recognition of, the special interests and views of other sections of the community.

Most Ulster Unionists had long been opposed to P.R. Admittedly, some leading members of the party were active members of the P.R. Society of Ireland, Milne Barbour being at one time a vice-president of the society and president of its Ulster Extension Committee.[40] Moreover, some Unionists with special interests to consider thought that they could gain from P.R. One or two Unionists in the western counties considered that certain forms of P.R. might be beneficial to the Unionist minority there,[41] while working-class Unionists believed that, in Belfast at any rate, P.R. would help to broaden the social basis of the party's representation.[42] Nevertheless, the weight of opinion in the Unionist Party had long been against P.R. Craig had condemned it in 1909 when giving evidence on behalf of the Ulster Unionist Party to a commission on electoral reform.[43] In 1919 Ulster Unionist M.P.s at Westminster had fought a vain battle against its introduction into Irish local elections.[44] And Ulster Unionists had agreed to its inclusion for Irish parliamentary elections only after the urgent representations of the imperial government that such a provision was necessary in the interests of an Irish settlement.[45] The arguments put forward by Ulster Unionists against P.R. were those generally used by its opponents. P.R. was said to be expensive, to make for instability in government, to be unfair to both electors and candidates, and much eloquence was spent in citing different authorities and the experiences of different countries to underline the dangers of P.R.[46]

Northern Ireland's limited experience of P.R. did not bear out the criticisms advanced. Admittedly, the cost of P.R. elections was greater than those under the X-voting system,* but the more fundamental objections proved false in practice. P.R. did not prevent the formation of workable administrations in either of Northern Ireland's two principal elective assemblies. Nor did large parliamentary constituencies or local government electoral areas create insuperable problems of mutual ignorance and lack of identification between candidates and representatives and electors. Whatever problems may have arisen from the existence of large electoral areas could have been overcome by a reduction in their size, but, on the whole, the problems presented by large constituencies or electoral areas were exaggerated in Northern Ireland. Parties did adapt by selecting candidates from different parts of a constituency. Conscientious M.P.s did find ways of communicating with and representing the views of their constituents, and, if the boasts of some M.P.s were to be believed, in such a small community as Northern Ireland elector satisfaction might have been enhanced by the choice of M.P.s available to them. Nor was it true that party machines and richer candidates were better equipped than independent and poorer candidates to fight P.R. elections, for at the 1925 general election Labour and Independent Unionists sometimes topped the polls. Finally, P.R. did not prove to be beyond the comprehension of simple Ulster folk. There was

---

*The 1920 local elections in Belfast cost roughly £4,000 compared with £1,200 a year under the old system.

no gainsaying the fact that under P.R. the calculation of results was a tedious and long-winded process, not readily comprehended. Nevertheless, Northern Ireland electors seemed quite capable of operating the system of voting, as was underlined by the satisfactory outcome of a particularly complicated contest in the Falls ward in the 1920 Belfast Corporation elections.[47]

The case against P.R. in Northern Ireland was, therefore, far from conclusive, but this did not matter, for Ulster Unionists did not bother to evaluate their objections carefully. They were not interested in representative opinion or in questions of minority rights, and felt that local authorities and parliament could well function without other parties. William Grant, the U.U.L.A. M.P., who could always be relied upon to state baldly his party's views, told Opposition M.P.s in 1927:

> I was one of those . . . who never cared whether there was any Opposition in the House or not. I am glad to see them here, but if they went out of the House to-day I would have no regrets. I would not care if they never came back again.[48]

The government did not wholly share this dismissive attitude. Force of circumstance, if not a spirit of generosity, made ministers aware of the need to reconcile the nationalist minority to the new state or, at least, to avoid giving the outside world the impression that it was actively discriminating against the minority. Such an awareness did encourage the government to moderate some of the more extreme demands of its supporters on matters relating to parliamentary and local government representation, but it did not enable the government to place wider considerations of state above party interests. In the last analysis, the government always bowed to party pressure and considerations.

4

The initiative for the abolition of P.R. in local government elections in September 1922 came from rank-and-file Unionists, especially those in the west. There had been no mention of P.R. in the King's Speech in March 1922, and there is no evidence that the matter had been considered by the cabinet. In fact, the Ministry of Home Affairs had enough on its hands without being involved in such a major change. The question was raised, however, on the opening of parliament by various backbenchers. Coote, one of the M.P.s for Fermanagh and Tyrone, thought it 'a very grave omission', and other members echoed Coote's concern in private conversations with the Minister of Home Affairs.[49] Craig's disingenuous reply to Coote that he was awaiting the views of municipal authorities with whom he was personally in touch[50] was evidently taken as an invitation to express opinions. An agitation soon snowballed, and the government was bombarded with demands from Unionist constituency organisations to do something to restore Unionists to their natural position in the local government order.[51] Many suggestions were made, including the raising of the local government franchise, but the main demand was for the abolition of P.R. and the redrawing of local government electoral areas. The motives behind the demand were quite simple. Unionists believed that such changes would increase their representation at the expense of all other parties, especially the Nationalist and Sinn Féin parties.

All local Unionists demanded a return to the old method of voting, but there was some difference of opinion as to what the electoral areas should be. Unionists in urban areas in the east, such as Belfast, thought that the mere reversion to the pre-1919 method of voting and electoral districts would be both justified and sufficient to increase Unionist representation.[52] A demand for change was even more urgently expressed in those areas where Unionists had actually lost control of local councils, but in such areas the call for the abolition of P.R. was coupled with a demand not for a return to the pre-1919 electoral areas, but for a complete revision of local government areas to iron out the inequalities that had existed under the old system and had led to the alleged under-representation of Unionists.[53]

Ulster Unionists believed that they had an incontestable case for demanding a system of local representation which would increase their representation. They argued that since they paid most of the rates, they should have most of the representation, even where they were in a numerical minority. Resentment at not having a controlling voice in local expenditure, when they contributed the greater portion of the rates, was increased by the performance of some nationalist-controlled councils. Not only had twenty-one such bodies been suppressed for refusing to recognise the government of Northern Ireland, but some, particularly, it was alleged, Tyrone County Council,[54] had shown a marked degree of incompetence. Even where nationalist-controlled councils had managed their affairs efficiently, Unionists found irksome the consequences of being in a minority. Mrs Chichester on one occasion spoke feelingly of 'the insults which we had to endure in the past, and the tyranny with which they ground the minority under their heel', reminding M.P.s that

> I come from an area where . . . 247 labourers' cottages were built, and of these only 47 were given to Unionists. . . . We have had to sit there and listen to our King being insulted, to our Government being derided. We have been told that killing was no murder unless committed by the foreign invader.[55]

Such memories rankled, and Unionists were slow to forget, let alone

forgive, such recalcitrant councils and councillors who had 'defied the
law . . . defied the Government, and . . . let the interests of the ratepayers go by default'.*[56]

The Minister of Home Affairs, Bates, readily responded to party
pressure for the abolition of P.R. Although Craig told the Commons
and imperial ministers and officials that no fewer than fifty-nine local
authorities had pressed the government to abolish P.R. in local elections,[57] it was pressure from M.P.s and party organisations that in the
first instance caused the Ministry of Home Affairs to take action. Only
after the ministry had determined to legislate was it decided to obtain
the views of local authorities.[58] Immediately following Coote's speech
and informal approaches in the House, Bates got his officials to work
on the subject,[59] and their sole concern was how to give effect to the
views of the Unionist rank and file agitating for change. There was no
consideration of the wider implications of the abolition of P.R. either
in the cabinet, where the proposal was hardly discussed, or in the Ministry of Home Affairs.[60] In particular, there was no consideration of the
implications of the measure for minorities. Only when Michael Collins
tried to persuade the imperial government to withhold the royal assent
from the bill[61] did it dawn upon ministers that there was more to P.R.
than the satisfaction of Unionist demands for its abolition. Even then,
realisation was tinged with disbelief, Craig arguing that P.R. had proved
'utterly useless' in securing the representation of minorities and asserting that Catholics would be better off under the 'old system'.[62]

In some respects this short-sightedness was understandable. Not only
was the government fighting for its life at this time, and ministers and
officials absorbed in setting up their departments, but also, with the
suspension of nationalist-controlled local councils and the nationalist
boycott of parliament, there were no properly constituted channels of
communication to force the government to consider, as a matter of
course, minority viewpoints. In other respects, however, the failure to
consider the implications of the measure for the minority was simply
inept. At the same time as the Local Government Bill was being drafted
and was going through parliament Craig was trying to persuade certain
Catholics to participate fully in the state and reject the leadership and
protection of Collins, who since the Treaty had tried to act as the
guardian of minority interests in Northern Ireland.[63] Expectations that
they would do so had increased so much by the early summer that on
14 June 1922, between the first and second readings of the Local

*These and similar remarks were occasioned by a government proposal, aban-
doned because of strong Unionist criticism that it was rewarding disloyalty and
sacrificing the loyal to the disloyal, to reinstate in October 1922 suspended councils in rural areas if sufficient numbers of recalcitrant councillors were ready to
discharge their duties according to the law.

Government Bill, Spender reported to Craig that he had a long conversation on the previous day with R. A. Burke, a wealthy shipbroker and one of the government's Catholic contacts:

> He is very anxious about a rumour that you are proposing to have another conference with Mr Griffith or Mr Collins, which he says would be fatal to all the steps towards peace which have been taken by Catholics during the last weeks. . . . He told me that Collins was losing ground daily in Northern Ireland, and only retained any influence owing to the fact that he appeared to be recognised by the British Government as the Catholic spokesman in Ulster. This recognition was warmly resented by the vast majority of Roman Catholics who were now exceedingly anxious to become Loyal Citizens of the Northern Government.[64]

How many Catholics subscribed to Burke's views may be debatable, but what is certain is that Spender believed what Burke said and that both he and Craig hoped and believed that Burke's views were representative. Yet the government failed to relate this seemingly encouraging attempt to win over Catholics to the decision to abolish P.R. in local government elections. This failure did give Collins and his successors in the South a further opportunity to assert themselves in Northern Ireland's affairs by demanding that the imperial government withhold the royal assent. The whole episode was thus very revealing of the limited horizons of the government of Northern Ireland and of Craig's unfortunate tendency to keep, in the words of the Colonial Office Adviser on Irish Affairs, 'several water-tight compartments in his mind'.[65]

Whereas the initiative for the abolition of P.R. in local elections stemmed from the rank and file of the Unionist Party, responsibility for the decision to abolish P.R. in parliamentary elections was explicitly assumed by Craig, whose interest in this question was markedly greater and more consistent than his interest in most other issues.

The government's original intention had been to abolish P.R. in time for a general election in the spring of 1925.[66] Schemes of redistribution were well advanced by the summer of 1924,[67] but in the following winter the government decided to hold fire for fear of prejudicing Northern Ireland's case before the Boundary Commission, then about to start work.[68] Thus it was that Northern Ireland's second general election was held under P.R., and it was not until 25 February 1929, three months before the third general election, that the House of Commons (Method of Voting and Redistribution of Seats) Bill was introduced into the Commons. The short time between the introduction of the bill and the general election was in line with the British practice of usually following measures of parliamentary reform with an almost immediate general election, but it also suited the government's con-

venience. To have introduced the bill any earlier would have exposed
the government, so said the Chief Whip, to 'an uncomfortable time for
the rest of the Session, as of course the Nationalist and Labour people
will bitterly oppose it'.[69]

The expectation of bitter opposition did not deter Craig from abolishing an electoral system which did not give what he wanted. Craig
wanted two things from an electoral system. First of all, he wanted a
strong government, a government with a 'strong solid majority' rather
than one dependent upon 'the whim of two or three Independents who
do not care which way they give their vote'. Secondly, he wanted what
he saw as the fundamental issue of Northern Ireland politics – Unionism
versus nationalism – laid clearly before the electors. According to Craig,
'the real question' at 'the bottom of the hearts of every person in Ulster'
was 'whether we are going to remain part and parcel of Great Britain
and the Empire or whether on the other hand we are going to sub-
merge ourselves in a Dublin Parliament'. The only sure way to achieve
these two related ends, Craig believed, was by the encouragement of
a stable two-party system in which Unionists and Nationalists, the 'two
active, alert, vigorous parties in Ulster', opposed each other in a straight
fight. General elections would then become what Craig thought they
should be: 'a referendum on the question which of two Governments
shall be returned to power'.[70]

Such stability and clarity was held to be impossible under P.R.,
which submerged and clouded the real issue of Northern Ireland politics. Voters' mistakes in listing preferences on their ballot papers and
the tendency of P.R. to encourage the proliferation of candidates could
produce, as in Italy, an unstable combination in parliament, with politicians having to 'bargain here and bargain there' for majorities. They
could also lead to a situation where Ulster 'may one day wake up to
find itself in the perilous position from our point of view of being submerged in a Dublin Parliament'. By contrast, a return to the admirable
British system of X-voting would produce, Craig reckoned, both clarity
and stability, for it would ensure that before an election a candidate
would declare 'not the fad that for the moment he might possibly be
going in for' but party allegiance.

Although the accompanying redistribution did slightly reduce
Nationalist representation in parliament, the abolition of P.R. was not
aimed primarily against the Nationalists. Rather it sought to reduce, if
not eliminate, the representation of parties or groups outside the two
major parties. Unionists had never had any time for the 'socialism' of
the Labour Party and its equivocal attitude on the border, but even
more obnoxious to official Unionists were the Independent Unionists,
who, while claiming to be 'loyal', nevertheless voted with Nationalists
and Labour against the government. However much Independent

Unionists might protest their loyalty to Unionism and to Protestantism, their voting record on other matters laid them open to repeated attacks from official Unionists. Answering Independent Unionists' complaints about Craig's public denunciations of them, the Attorney-General asked:

> What do they expect? Are they not in opposition. . . . They cannot have it both ways. They cannot expect to be flattered by the Government, and deferred to on every occasion, and at the same time walk through the Lobby in every division and vote against the Government. . . . It is not good enough for them simply to say but we are Unionists when they do not support the Government.[71]

The decision to abolish P.R. in parliamentary elections was thus understandable in party terms, but it was a short-sighted policy aiming to create stability by stereotyping politics and political opinion. As over the 1922 Local Government Act, the government never thought out all the possible consequences of abolition. And this time, with Nationalist and Labour representatives in parliament making clear their attachment to P.R., there was less excuse. Craig felt able, however, to ignore the Opposition's objections, partly because he thought that P.R. did 'not help to secure in any way the rights of a minority',[72] and partly because he convinced himself that his bill abolishing P.R. and redistributing seats was an eminently fair one, 'without the slightest hint of partiality in a single line of it'.[73] It was, however, largely his preoccupation with the interests of a narrow Unionism that prevented his government from appreciating the state of mind of its major opponents and imaginatively trying to win them over to a full acceptance of Northern Ireland. Craig never fully thought out the implications of the abolition of P.R. in parliamentary elections, because what he wanted first and foremost

> to get in this House, and what I believe we will get very much better in this House under the old-fashioned plain and simple system, are men who are for the Union on the one hand or who are against it and want to go into a Dublin Parliament on the other.[74]

5

What made the abolition of P.R. so controversial was the consequent redrawing of electoral areas. The need to redraw local government and parliamentary electoral areas put the government in a difficult position, exposing it to charges of gerrymandering from both opponents and supporters. In an effort to avoid foundering on these two rocks, the government's attitude to redistribution was governed by two considerations. As with all governments controlling redistribution, it hoped to ensure that the results were favourable to its own party, but this hope was tempered by an anxiety that the results should be capable of defence if not to nationalists then at least to the outside world. In pursuing these ends, the government managed to do the right thing at the wrong time.

The rearrangement of local government areas was undertaken after attempts at widespread consultation. It was felt possible to revert largely to the pre-1919 areas for urban districts, but not for rural districts. A return to the pre-1919 boundaries was considered undesirable not only because of the Unionist desire to increase their representation, but also because of the glaring anomalies which had existed under the old system. Rural electoral districts had been based upon the Poor Law unions drawn up in the 1840s, and the system had been rendered almost farcical by population changes which had resulted throughout the six counties in gross inequalities between areas.[75] Such discrepancies really did necessitate, as the Junior Minister of Home Affairs told the Commons in October 1922, 'very sweeping changes in the redistribution' of rural districts.[76] The basis chosen for redistribution was laid down in section 7 and the schedules of the 1922 Local Government Act. Re-enacting, in effect, parts of previous imperial legislation, the act gave the Ministry of Home Affairs power to divide counties and apportion rural districts with due regard primarily to 'the equality of the population of every division', but also to valuation and other characteristics. The provision relating to valuation had not been included in the original terms of the bill, but had been added during the committee stage, probably in response to fierce Unionist agitation on the point, so that 'the wealth of the community may be regarded to some extent, not necessarily to a large extent, but at least to some extent by being taken into calculation in the distributing or readjusting of the boundaries of the various constituencies'.[77] The addition proved a useful tool in helping to arrange schemes to the Unionists' advantage.

After some hesitation the government decided not to alter rural electoral districts on its own initiative.[78] County council electoral areas and electoral areas in non-controversial rural districts were decided upon in consultation with the appropriate local authorities, but a commission, under Judge John Leech, the Deputy Recorder of Belfast, was appointed to hold inquiries in those areas where redistribution was likely to be a controversial party issue. A series of public inquiries, to which ratepayers were invited to submit suggestions, was held at the beginning of 1923. The object was to arrive at equitable schemes of representation, largely on a population basis, but 'taking into consideration, to some extent the question of valuation where they could not equalise the population'.[79] The hope was that the government would not be accused of bias and dictatorship. The Ministry of Home Affairs, Judge Leech said at Lisnaskea, had not prepared any scheme, but had simply invited all parties interested, who might care to do so to send in a scheme of representation, so that everybody would be on an equal footing, and that there could be no suggestion that the Government had prepared a scheme with the intention of forcing it upon the people.[80]

In principle it was a good idea, but inappropriate at a time when nationalists were persisting in an attitude of non-co-operation with the government. As on other matters, nationalists largely boycotted the proceedings of the Leech commission, partly because they inaccurately complained of short notice,[81] partly because they mistakenly dismissed the commission as 'a pure farce with the sole object of giving some semblance of public approval to an already cut-and-dried arrangement',[82] but mainly because they feared jeopardising their claims for transfer to the South under the Boundary Commission.[83]

Thus it was that in all but five instances only Unionists were represented at Leech's inquiries, and in only two instances, at Irvinestown and Ballycastle, did nationalists co-operate fully and help shape the new electoral arrangements.* At Irvinestown the only scheme presented to Leech had been drawn up by a committee on which both nationalists and Unionists had been represented,[84] while at Ballycastle the nationalist case for equal representation carried the day in a scheme jointly submitted by Unionists and nationalists.[85] Such agreement between the parties and such nationalist co-operation was the exception, not the rule. Usually only a handful of Unionists attended the inquiries; only one scheme, well worked out in advance and complete with maps and schedules, was submitted; and there were amicable discussions between Leech and the Unionist representatives, the former commending the latter for their industry and the latter thanking the judge for his kind consideration, all to the accompaniment from without of nationalist denunciations of gerrymandering. The Unionist proposals, long pondered in most places by staunch party workers who revelled in the detail of election management, were carefully calculated to maximise Unionist representation and to produce majorities on local councils. They were, in the main, accepted by Leech with only minor al-

---

*A nationalist delegation attended the Dungannon inquiry but offered no comment on the scheme submitted by Unionists and generally took no part in the proceedings. At Omagh the Rural District Council's solicitor intervened only to condemn the proceedings and withdrew after his call for an adjournment had been rejected as mere obstructionism. At Downpatrick a scheme was submitted by two nationalist ratepayers, but they withdrew from the inquiry when Leech ruled, in commenting on the Unionist scheme, that suggestions need not be confined to changes within existing union boundaries but could recommend the transfer of districts from one union to another.

terations which were readily agreed to by the Unionist representatives. At Enniskillen, where only Unionists were represented, so many changes were suggested by the commissioner that the Ministry of Home Affairs later felt able to say that 'The scheme as originally submitted was practically reconstructed and the populations of the divisions brought into much closer harmony'.[86] This was, however, an exception. Leech usually accepted the sweeping changes proposed by Unionists because he was anxious to rectify the glaring anomalies and injustices that had existed in the old areas, and because, with the nationalists refusing to submit evidence, he was probably in no position to grasp all the implications of the Unionist schemes.

Since Leech's recommendations were subsequently endorsed by the Minister of Home Affairs, the reorganisation of local electoral areas in controversial districts was virtually dictated by local Unionists. This fact did give rise to considerable criticism both inside and outside Northern Ireland, but the government felt able to present a plausible case against the charges of gerrymandering. After all, nationalists had had an opportunity, of which they failed to take advantage, to present schemes of their own, and, as Leech said at Lisnaskea, it was people's own fault it they did not present schemes.[87] Moreover, the Ministry of Home Affairs felt inclined to regard nationalist non-participation (other than at Irvinestown and Ballycastle) as a sign of the justice of the schemes put forward and eventually endorsed by the minister. As a Ministry of Home Affairs memorandum, prepared in November 1934 to answer charges of gerrymandering, put it,

> There is, therefore, only one conclusion which can be arrived at, and that is that wherever the Nationalists were satisfied that they had a good case for representation they came forward and obtained it, but wherever they were satisfied that they had no case they did not put forward any scheme or any proposals. It would appear, therefore, that in areas such at Lisnaskea, Cookstown and Magherafelt where there were at one time Nationalist majorities, these were obtained because of the anomalies which allowed in some instances 600 people to have the same representation as 3,100, and in others where 2,158 obtained the same representation as 105.[88]

The procedure adopted in determining the redistribution of parliamentary seats was quite different, but equally well-intentioned. The government itself, and Craig in particular,[89] took full responsibility for producing a scheme which, like many of the government's actions, betrayed a lack of imagination and a deep conservatism. It aimed at complying with the 1920 act by maintaining the number of seats and by redistributing them 'with due regard . . . to the population of the constituencies other than university constituencies'. It tried to cause the minimum amount of disturbance to existing electoral areas and administrative boundaries and to produce accessible constituencies. Above all, the government hoped, as Craig told the Commons in March 1929, to 'secure to this House when it meets again after the next election that it will be composed as nearly as possible of the balance of power which exists today'.[90] This was not, of course, wholly true, since Craig hoped to eliminate the small parties and independents, but it was true as far as the balance between Unionists and Nationalists was concerned. Throughout the drafting of redistribution care was taken not to diminish Nationalist representation unduly.

Yet, however well-intentioned, this way of achieving redistribution was open to serious criticism, most obviously because of the failure to consult the Opposition. When in the early 1920s the minority was not co-operating, the government had decided upon consultation, but in 1929, when Nationalists were participating in politics, the government took full responsibility for deciding upon the new parliamentary areas. It acted on its own initiative in the redrawing of electoral areas and presented its conclusions in various schedules attached to the House of Commons (Method of Voting and Redistribution of Seats) Bill. The only opportunity Opposition members had of commenting on the proposed new constituencies was during the passage of the bill through parliament. When introducing the measure Craig said that he would accept 'any reasonable Amendment. . . . Anything I consider reasonable will be accepted'.[91] In the event he considered none of the Opposition suggestions reasonable and refused all requests for informal consultations. Thus it was that the government's redistribution proposals passed into law unmodified.

This procedure, this lack of consultation, was at the very least impolitic, especially as it created a false impression. Since it was known that local Unionists had long been hatching up redistribution schemes, and since Unionists did have easy access to the government, it was all too easy to represent the government as merely implementing the wishes of its most uncompromising supporters. Contrary to Opposition claims, however, parliamentary redistribution was in fact a distinctive measure produced by the government. Had redistribution been dictated by local Unionist agents, nationalist representation would have been reduced by at least half. Schemes pressed upon the government by local Unionist associations had no other basis than the maximisation of Unionist representation. That suggested by Co. Down Unionists aimed at securing for themselves 7 of the county's 8 seats, instead of the 6 seats which they had won in the 1921 and 1925 elections,[92] while Londonderry Unionists put forward a proposal which would have given them all 5 instead of just 3 of the city's and county's seats, and which would have 'put an end to Nationalist aggression for all time'.[93] (The keystone of this latter scheme was the swamping of the nationalist majority in the city by creating a new two-member constituency combining London-derry with the Protestant towns of Limavady, Coleraine and Portstewart on the model of some Scottish constituencies.) Such proposals the government found both objectionable and indefensible, and it there-fore went to some trouble to dissuade local Unionists from pressing on with them. The only instances where local Unionist opinion may have been decisive in determining constituency boundaries were in Ferman-agh[94] and Belfast, and in the latter case this was largely through the influence of the Chief Whip, whose particular preserve Belfast was con-sidered to be.[95] Even here, however, the government rejected the strong case made out by the U.U.L.A. for two-member constituencies in the city so that richer candidates could subsidise the return of Unionist Labour candidates. The whole justification for the abolition of P.R. was the desirability of a reversion to single-member and accessible constitu-encies, an argument which had been used to defeat the proposals pressed upon the government by Londonderry and Down Unionists. To have permitted double-member constituencies in Belfast would have resurrected the whole controversy.[96]

The impression of partisan government was reinforced by the results of redistribution. The Parliamentary Draftsman reckoned that the new seats had been so arranged as to maintain Catholic/nationalist represen-tation at 12, giving nationalists the same number of seats as they had obtained in the P.R. elections of 1921 and 1925.[97] He calculated that nationalists were likely to win the same number of seats in Counties Down (2), Londonderry (2) and Tyrone and Fermanagh (4). Although their representation was likely to be reduced from 2 to 1 in Co. Armagh, and although the one Nationalist member for Co. Antrim would cer-tainly disappear, these losses would, he thought, bc offset by an in-crease in Nationalist representation in Belfast from 1 to 3. The results of the 1929 general election bore out the general accuracy of this forecast, except that Nationalists won only two seats in Belfast, thus reducing their overall representation to 11, a result which contrasted markedly with the figure of 16 or 17 members which all admitted nationalists should theoretically have returned.

The difficulties of devising a scheme to maintain the balance of par-ties in parliament and to give local communities due representation should not be underrated. The religious denominations were distributed unevenly throughout the province. The 38,619 Catholics of Antrim (some 20 per cent of the county's population) were scattered through-out the county; the 49,990 Armagh Catholics and the 32,455 Ferman-agh Catholics were largely concentrated in particular parts of their counties; and the 95,682 Belfast Catholics (some 23 per cent of the city's population) were similarly concentrated, this time in particular parts of the West parliamentary division.[98] Moreover, the task of surmounting these difficulties was increased by the government's respect for existing boundaries, a conservatism most evident in the desire to give Counties Fermanagh and Tyrone separate representation. Under P.R. Fermanagh and Tyrone had formed one constituency, and there was a case, admitted by the government, for keeping them together after the abolition of P.R. Their combined populations would have enabled eight constituencies to have been devised so as to spread the population more evenly than was actually done in the bill, which gave Fermanagh three seats with an average population of 20,000 and Tyrone five seats with an average population of 26,000. The government preferred, however, to separate the counties, since, Craig told the Commons, each county had its own separate set of officers,[99] and

> The Fermanagh men like to have Fermanagh to themselves, and the Tyrone men like to have Tyrone as a county by itself. . . . Counties in Ulster like to be counties. . . . It is a little bit un-Ulster about people talking about representing Tyrone and Fermanagh.[100]

The redrawing of constituency boundaries was thus bound to present problems, and it was in solving these problems that the government's good intentions faltered. Areas of doubt were always resolved in favour of the Unionist Party.[101] Given the government's limited brief, it is difficult to find fault with the redistribution in Counties Down and Tyrone and most of Co. Londonderry, but elsewhere questions were resolved so as to maximise Unionist representation. Points were stretched where Unionist interests were involved, but not where nationalist interests were at stake. The government readily tolerated inequalities in Belfast, where Unionist constituencies with populations of 18–20,000 contrasted with a nationalist constituency of over 30,000; but Craig dismissed as 'an abortion' and 'outrageously a case of gerrymandering'[102] a Nationalist proposal to carve out a constituency in Co. Antrim, smaller than the others proposed for the county, to enable nationalists to continue to return a representative there. There was also a contrast between the government's treatment of the small Unionist majority in Co. Armagh and its attitude towards an almost equivalent nationalist majority in Co. Fermanagh. The 55.6 per cent Protestant population of Co. Armagh was given 75 per cent of the county's representation, while the 56 per cent Catholic population of Co. Fermanagh was allotted only 33 per cent of the county's seats.

Such decisions could be justified in terms other than of the interests of the Unionist Party. The Catholic and nationalist population of Belfast was heavily concentrated in a small central area, and suburban constituencies had to be so drawn as to allow for the expansion of population. In the three disputed counties, too, the idiosyncratic distribution of the Catholic population provided at least a plausible justification of the government's scheme of redistribution. It was otherwise with the city of Londonderry. There the government's actions were determined solely by the interests of the Unionist Party. The government's manipulation of the city's representation, both local and parliamentary, underlined the partisan nature of the government's attitude to questions of representation and its constant attempts to maximise Unionist representation in as plausible a manner as possible.

6

The electoral fate of Londonderry city, the 'Maiden City', was always of intense and symbolic interest to Unionists and nationalists in Northern Ireland. Much time and energy had long been spent by both sides in devising stratagems to control the city's representation, but with the setting up of the Unionist government in Northern Ireland the advantage lay with the Unionists. They now had the power to neutralise, if they wished, the nationalist majority in the city. In the 1929 parliamentary redistribution the government felt unable to accept the extreme proposals put forward by the Londonderry Unionists for preventing the city from falling into nationalist hands, but it did try to meet its supporters' claims by contravening its own rule that redistribution should conform to existing administrative divisions. The problem was that the city had a majority of 2,000 nationalists on the parliamentary register, and the calamity of nationalist domination of the city was avoided by combining the city with parts of the surrounding countryside, thus creating two constituencies: the city as a safe Unionist seat, and the Foyle division as a safe nationalist seat.[103]

Even more telling was the rearrangement of local government boundaries in 1936. Under P.R. nationalists had controlled the Corporation, 6,868 nationalist electors returning 21 councillors and 6,340 Unionists returning 19. The abolition of P.R. and the reversion to the pre-1919 wards handed back control to the Unionists. Unionist control was at first assisted by a nationalist boycott, but its main basis was the way in which the city was divided into five wards. Three of the wards had a Unionist majority, and the other two nationalist majorities, the nationalist wards being significantly larger than the Unionist.[104] By the 1930s, with nationalists resuming an interest in local affairs, Unionists began to feel insecure. Their majorities were substantial in two wards, but not in North ward, where it was feared that nationalists would soon be able to reverse the Unionist majority. Moreover, Londonderry Unionists were experiencing difficulty in getting suitable people returned to the Corporation, a result of a lack of interest in local politics not peculiar to Londonderry.[105] The city's leading Unionists, therefore, promoted in

1936 a scheme for the alteration of wards and a reduction in the size of the Corporation.

The aim to make the Corporation safe for Unionists had the sympathy of the government. Bates had told Craig in July 1934 that

> Unless something is done now, it is only a matter of time until Derry passes into the hands of the Nationalist and Sinn Féin parties for all time. On the other hand, if proper steps are taken now, I believe Derry can be saved for years to come.[106]

As far as Bates and his ministry were concerned, it was the way things were done that mattered. It was essential that all due proprieties should be observed. Bates had warned Omagh Unionists, when they had been pressing in 1934 for a reorganisation of their urban electoral areas, that any suggestion of 'indecent gerrymandering' had to be avoided, and he also advised his Londonderry friends that undue publicity would 'only add to the difficulties which I must always have in dealing with the alteration of wards where the two parties are closely affected'.[107]

Londonderry Unionists did not, however, see the need for such caution.[108] They produced an outlandish scheme which they expected the government – their government – to implement. They proposed to reduce the total membership of the Corporation from 40 to 24 and to arrange the wards so as to secure the return of 16 Unionists and 8 nationalists. They were somewhat taken aback when the Ministry of Home Affairs insisted that there should be a public inquiry, but they refused to take it seriously and did not bother to present a proper case when the inquiry met between 7 and 9 October 1936. Their scheme was dictated solely by the desire to secure for themselves as large a majority as possible, and in defining ward boundaries it made no attempt to balance considerations of population and valuation. In terms of population and local government electors, the ratio of nationalists to Unionists was 3 to 2 and 4 to 3 respectively, but as regards valuation, although no exact figures seem to be available, it was taken as agreed that Unionists had a majority of 2 to 1. By taking into account only valuation in order to justify a Unionist majority on the council of 2 to 1, the scheme completely ignored the prime determinant of electoral areas – population. Moreover, the case was carelessly presented. Maps were wrong and had to be altered. Such figures as were given were completely upset by well-informed nationalist cross-examination and had to be altered. None of the prime movers of the scheme came forward to give evidence. Such persons as did give evidence had clearly not taken the trouble to familiarise themselves with the details of the scheme, not one of the witnesses having been round the proposed boundary lines, which were particularly devious between the suggested North and South wards. The inspector conducting the inquiry had no alternative but to recommend the rejection of the scheme.

The rejection and the attendant publicity put the Ministry of Home Affairs in an embarrassing position. Even some Unionists were disgusted at such a 'shameless & obvious gerrymander'.[109] Yet key Londonderry Unionists were furious at being let down, as they thought, by the ministry, which accepted the inspector's report and which, in any case, considered the Unionist scheme indefensible. According to the ministry, the scheme had 'no merit' and, if approved, would have faced the minister with 'a great deal of criticism to which no possible answer, even of a plausible character, could be found'.[110] For its part, the ministry was anxious to satisfy the Londonderry Unionists, but felt that their mishandling of the inquiry had 'left us in a position of the maximum difficulty in trying to meet their views'.[111] Throughout the discussions between ministry officials and Londonderry Unionists there was never any question that the government should not assist the latter. The whole issue was how to do so without incurring undue odium 'with opinion outside Derry'.[112] The Ministry of Home Affairs therefore produced and implemented a scheme which gave Londonderry Unionists the substance of what they wanted and was yet capable of defence.

The ministry's scheme reduced the number of councillors to 20 and secured for Unionists a majority of 4 on this smaller council by carefully arranging the electorate into three wards, into one of which the majority of nationalist electors were placed.[113] Two wards contained safe Unionist majorities. The old Waterside ward, which was retained, though with its representation reduced from 8 to 4, contained 2,339 Unionists and 1,443 nationalists, while the newly reconstituted North ward with 8 representatives included 3,515 Unionist electors and 2,021 nationalist electors. By contrast, the South ward, the largest of the three, contained an overwhelming nationalist majority with 6,227 nationalist and 1,590 Unionist voters. Therefore 9,961 nationalist electors returned 8 councillors, while 7,444 Unionist voters returned 12. Despite these discrepancies, the Ministry of Home Affairs thought the scheme capable of an adequate defence. In the first place, unlike the original scheme, it took into account population as well as valuation. In the second place, the boundaries had some clear rationale. The retention of the old and small Waterside ward with its Unionist majority could be justified by virtue of 'its geographical position and its particular character', while the line dividing the North and South wards followed, in accordance with accepted practice, the 'existing statutory line fixed by Act of Parliament for the parliamentary constituencies'.

The ministry's scheme, contained in an order in December 1936,[114] did arouse considerable hostility. Opponents of the Northern government and some of its friends were incensed or distressed by an obvious attempt to prolong the Unionist hegemony in the city. Critics pretended to see it as just another attempt to crush the minority. 'The worst outrage perpetrated since Partition', said the priest-chairman of a Londonderry nationalist protest rally;[115] and one nationalist writer reckoned that it degraded 'a representative system to the level of dishonest farce. Viewed from the standpoint of democratic method there has thus been a scandalous and open violation of essential principle'.[116] For their part, Londonderry Unionists felt utterly let down by the government, especially the Minister and Ministry of Home Affairs. They reckoned that 'The Unionist majority will be so small that the present dangerous situation will be worsened rather than improved',[117] and that 'The Majority will be too small to carry on with any sense of security for any length of time — unless another bite comes off the cherry'.[118] The cabinet, however, stood firmly in support of the ministry's scheme. Only Charlemont, the Minister of Education, saw fit to question its wisdom, and he was put firmly in his place by Craig, who said that 'he was confident that the proposed scheme was in the interests of the Province, and he was prepared to defend it'.[119] On the other hand, the ire and resentment of the Londonderry activists were somewhat assuaged by Craig's visit to the city at the end of the month[120] and by his private assurance that further action would be possible if the ministry's scheme 'does not realise our hopes'. 'You may rest assured', he wrote to the city's M.P., 'that all of us have the one aim in view, and that is to maintain the integrity of the Maiden City'.[121]

Such concern to 'maintain the integrity of the Maiden City' was symptomatic of a siege mentality which affected Ulster Unionism in the inter-war years and which demanded, especially in the border areas, the utmost security from systems of parliamentary and local representation. Members of the government shared this sense of combined insecurity and aggression, with the result that the natural desire of any government to safeguard its majority was heightened in Northern Ireland by the belief that the only way to maintain partition and the state was to sustain the largest possible Unionist majorities on local councils and in the Northern Ireland parliament. Moreover, representation on those bodies was one of the few areas in which the regional government could take decisive action to meet the wishes of its supporters. Ministers thus felt the need to, and readily responded to demands to, make public bodies safe for Unionism. It was true that the government moderated the more extreme demands of its supporters and always tried to present a plausible explanation of any changes in electoral qualifications, electoral areas and methods of voting. Yet the fact remains that, in the last analysis, the power of the state was consciously and consistently used in the interests of the Unionist Party. Indeed, given the circumstances surrounding the establishment of Northern Ireland, discrimination was an almost inevitable consequence of parliamentary devolution there.

11

Discrimination (3): Education

Whereas changes made in the systems of local and parliamentary representation had been designed to make public bodies safe for Unionism, modifications made to the education laws in 1925 and 1930 were intended to make state schools safe for Protestantism. The way in which the religious complexion of Northern Ireland's educational policy was modified in response to agitation fomented by the Protestant clergy has been admirably chronicled in Professor D. H. Akenson's *Education and Emnity: The Control of Schooling in Northern Ireland, 1920–50*.[1] It is true that the recently released cabinet papers show that Westminster took more interest in the amending acts and that the government's capitulation in 1929–30 was more complete than Professor Akenson allows. It is also true that the Protestant clergy would not have succeeded had they not won the support of the Orange Order. Nevertheless, such considerations serve to reinforce Professor Akenson's view that the campaign to amend the 1923 Education Act revealed the political strength and sophistication of many of the Protestant clergy. Northern Protestants had long denounced the Catholic 'priest in politics', but, as Professor Akenson has remarked, 'No band of Catholic priests in the former united Ireland had engaged in politics with the energy and the efficacy of the Protestant clerics who led the United Education Committee of the Protestant Churches'.[2]

1

The 1923 Education Act, the Londonderry act, sought to transform education in Northern Ireland by establishing a non-sectarian system combining efficiency with local popular control. The newly established Ministry of Education took over all the functions associated with the three hitherto self-enclosed systems of national education, intermediate education and technical education which had existed under the Union.[3] The measure of local responsibility was achieved through two county borough education committees and a series of regional education committees, the latter being appointed by the county councils acting as local education authorities. Such changes in administration had long been desired by Unionists in the North of Ireland, where the previous systems had, with the conspicuous exception of technical education, not only failed to produce an adequate supply of satisfactory schools but also had confined effective control of schools to the clergy of all denominations. This had been especially true of the primary schools, the vast bulk of Irish schools. The primary school system, the so-called 'national system', had been financed largely by the state in conjunction with the churches and had been in theory non-denominational. In practice, control of all but a few schools was vested in the parish clergy, who functioned at school managers, so that the schools were *de facto* denominational institutions.

To encourage the popular control of schools and the transfer of voluntary schools to local education authorities, three classes of schools were established, each with a greater or lesser degree of state and local aid and control. The first category consisted of 'provided' schools and 'transferred' schools, the former being schools built by the newly established local education authorities, the latter being schools transferred to civic management by their former managers. In transferred and provided schools the teachers' salaries were paid by the Ministry of Education, and all heating, cleaning, maintenance and capital expansion items were covered by a combination of central and local government funds. Both transferred and provided schools, which became called public elementary schools, were completely under the control of local school management committees which were in turn subordinate to regional education committees or to the county borough education committees. The second category of schools were those whose managers accepted the establishment of a special management committee, four of whose members were nominated by the manager or trustees, and two by the regional education committee. These schools, which became known as the 'four-and-two' schools, received complete payment of teachers' salaries, one-half of all heating, lighting, cleaning and equipment, repair and general upkeep expenses from the local rates, plus a discretionary capital expenditure grant from the local authority. Such schools were also eligible for a capital grant from the Ministry of Education, awarded at the ministry's discretion. The third category of schools were those whose managers chose to remain completely independent of local control. They continued, as under the national system, to receive full payment of teachers' salaries from central funds, but no money whatsoever for capital expenditure. Usually they did receive from the local rates one-half of the cost of heating, lighting and cleaning.

Although the act dealt with all aspects of education other than higher education, it was mainly intended to improve facilities for elementary education, and the success or otherwise of the attempt to establish popular control depended largely upon the vexed question of religious instruction in publicly maintained schools. The original intention of the national system to establish non-sectarian schools had soon been compromised by pressure from the major religious denominations, and by the middle of the nineteenth century the state was subsidising a system of denominational education. Although their religious tenets may have differed, and despite their detestation of each other, the educational principles of the Protestant and Catholic clergy were remarkably similar on key issues. Both believed that children should be taught by teachers of their own denomination, that children should attend school with their co-religionists, and that religious instruction should be woven into the school curriculum. They had bent the national system to suit their ideas and, not surprisingly, hoped to preserve their position in Northern Ireland's educational system.[4]

From the start the Catholics threw away any chance they might have had of influencing state education in Northern Ireland. The Catholic clergy were opposed to any alteration in the national system and had successfully resisted attempts made since the turn of the century to establish both a unified ministry and popular control of education. As a meeting of Catholic clerical school managers warned in Dublin in October 1921,

> In view of pending changes in Irish education, we wish to reassert the great fundamental principle that the only satisfactory system of education for Catholics is one wherein Catholic children are taught in Catholic schools by Catholic teachers under Catholic auspices.[5]

Moreover, they were opposed to partition. The hierarchy therefore refused to nominate representatives to the committee of inquiry, the Lynn committee, appointed in September 1921, which presented the most detailed articulation of the reform ideas that had been discussed by educationalists in Ulster since the end of the First World War.[6] As a result, the committee contained only one Catholic, a very senior and experienced official of the Ministry of Education who came from a substantial Southern family and who, as one education journal noted, 'does not belong to Ulster and whom the Roman Catholics of Ulster would not regard as representing them'.[7] Furthermore, the tone of the refusal was such as to offend the very sensitive Minister of Education and to do little to endear him to Catholic claims, for Cardinal Logue, the Catholic Primate, alleged that the committee would be used 'as a foundation and pretext' for an attack against 'our Catholic schools'.[8] This negative response, which Londonderry saw as a 'direct challenge'[9] to the government, was continued in the following year when about a third of all Catholic elementary schools and a considerable number of secondary schools refused to recognise the authority of the Northern Ministry of Education.[10] By taking this political stand against the recognition of the ministry – and hence against the recognition of the Northern Ireland government – the Catholic school managers placed themselves in a dangerous position. Their political activities made it very difficult in the future to defend their religious and educational interests.

The Lynn committee was thus dominated by Protestants. Although it claimed to have kept in mind Catholic interests, its educational assumptions were inevitably framed according to Protestant educational assumptions. This was most evident in the section relating to religious education in public elementary schools. Although the committee's one page of discussion of religious education was 'ambiguous and thoroughly confusing',[11] the subsequent demands of the Protestant denominations which had been involved in shaping this recommendation indicated that what was wanted was compulsory Bible teaching, which would have meant the effective endowment of Protestantism by the state.

Londonderry, however, refused to accept the Lynn committee's recommendations on religious instruction in public elementary education. The furthest that he went in his original bill was to permit denominational instruction outside the hours of compulsory school attendance by such clergymen or other persons approved by those parents desiring religious instruction for their children. Londonderry did believe that education should be both literary and moral, but he was determined that his act should be non-denominational. 'In some vague and undefined way he was an ecumenist' and opposed to the segregation of children according to religious faith; he even spoke optimistically of schools where children of different faiths might study and play together. His bill, he believed, provided opportunities but not compulsion for denominational education. Furthermore, it was not within the competence of the parliament of Northern Ireland to establish a denominational system of education. Under section 5 of the 1920 act it was *ultra vires* to 'make a law so as either directly or indirectly to establish or endow any religion' or to establish religious tests for teachers maintained out of public funds. Any law contravening this section would have been null and void, while an additional constitutional argument for refraining from making any positive provision for denominational instruction in state schools derived from article 16 of the Anglo-Irish Treaty, which had received the force of law in the Irish Free State (Agreement) Act of December 1922 and which forbade religious discrimination and the endowment of any religion.[12]

The original bill was thus religiously neutral. When the cabinet had been putting the final touches at the end of February 1923, Craig had asked Londonderry 'whether any particular denomination could . . .

with justice assert that it had been penalised'. Although it was thought that the withdrawal, for reasons of economy and principle, of the building grants previously given to voluntary schools would be urged by the Catholics as unfair treatment, it was considered that no discrimination was involved since the ban applied to the other denominations as well. The cabinet was therefore satisfied that 'The proposals of the Bill are impartial in their dealings with the denominations'.[13]

Such fine impartiality was completely unacceptable to the Protestant clergy.[14] Londonderry's refusal to countenance denominationalism meant that the religious provisions of his bill engendered a great deal of bitterness in Northern Ireland as the Protestant authorities spent the years 1923–29 fighting for the inclusion of the Lynn committee's partisan stipulations into the North's educational code. The Protestant churches wanted it clearly spelled out in a statute that religious teaching would be provided in all primary schools under the control of local authorities and that teachers should be permitted to give religious instruction, and many leaders wanted religious teaching to be given during compulsory hours. Moreover, there was dissatisfaction with the method of appointing teachers. Londonderry, in the hope of undermining localism, had given the power of appointing teachers in transferred and provided schools to the regional education committees rather than to the school management committees. Not only were the Protestant clergy, who as managers exercised considerable patronage, reluctant to see their influence reduced, but they were concerned about the possibility that in certain areas the regional committees would be under Catholic control and that Catholics might be appointed to teach in Protestant schools. Since it was the schoolteacher rather than the Protestant clergyman who bore the brunt of religious teaching, the Protestant clergy wanted to ensure that only Protestant teachers would teach in Protestant schools. Such were 'the very grave apprehensions' in the border districts at the prospect of Catholic-dominated regional education committees that the Church of Ireland Archbishop of Armagh suggested to Craig that it would 'be a very wise policy' to 'legislate for Belfast & let the country districts alone for the present'.[15] In fact, the Protestant clergy's demands can be summed up in the phrases 'Bible teaching in schools' and 'Protestant teachers for Protestant pupils'. Should the government not accede to these demands, then Protestant schools would not be transferred.

Initially the government held its ground, particularly during the bill's passage through parliament. In 1923 pressure in the form of public resolutions and private letters and deputations received some support in the cabinet, particularly from Craig and Andrews, but it was largely resisted by Londonderry.*[16] He refused to compromise the formal non-

*It was not wholly resisted, because, following consultations between mem-

sectarian nature of his measure, repeatedly arguing that the alterations proposed by the Protestant agitators were contrary to the general principle of a 'Secular education bill and of doubtful legal validity' as contravening the 1920 act. Moreover, as a politician, too, he felt able to resist the pressure because he 'did not consider that the agitation on this question was really of a serious character, but thought it was largely manufactured by certain interested ecclesiastics'.[17] And in 1923, at any rate, Londonderry was right. The agitation had no widespread support, as was seen by the House of Commons' rejection of the clergy's claim for local (i.e. denominational) control of teaching appointments. It would, argued one of the members for Londonderry, 'cut clean across one of the cardinal and fundamental points in the Bill . . . democratic control', while one of the members for Down reckoned that it 'would without doubt create religious cleavage. It would introduce sectarianism and denominationalism, two things that we are particularly anxious to avoid here in the North of Ireland'.[18]

Yet by 1930 the demands of the Protestant clergy had been realised. An amending act and administrative adjustments in 1925 and a further amending act in 1930 secured compulsory Bible teaching, local control of appointments, and an enhanced role for the clergy in public elementary education. The reason for this change was that the Protestant clergy were able to demonstrate that they had widespread lay support by winning over the Orange Order, and were able to bring such increased support to bear more strategically upon the government.

2

The spearhead of this more effective campaign was the United Education Committee of the Protestant Churches, formed in December 1924 among Protestant school managers by the convenors of education of the three major Protestant denominations – the Rev. William Corkey for the Presbyterians, the Rev. James Quinn for the Church of Ireland, and the Rev. William H. Smyth for the Methodists.[19] Disregarding the views of moderate churchmen such as the Church of Ireland Archbishop of Armagh, who thought that Protestants had secured practically all that they desired, the new trinity launched a virulent campaign against Londonderry and his act, for which they sought the co-operation of the

bers of the government and leaders of the Protestant churches at the beginning of May 1923, Londonderry did agree to make some concessions. The provision dealing with denominational instruction was redrafted to place more emphasis on the education authorities' duty to afford facilities for, but not themselves provide, religious instruction. In addition, he promised that in approving any appointment of teachers the Ministry of Education would take into account the representations of the locality concerned. In effect, some informal religious test would be applied.

Orange Order and Unionist politicians. On 27 February 1925 the United Education Committee met with leaders of the Belfast County Grand Orange Lodge and prominent Unionist politicians, and together they decided to hold a six-counties educational conference early in March to pressurise the government into amending the Education Act.

The preparations for the meeting were most thorough. The United Education Committee printed and distributed a leaflet which bore in large red type the old rallying-cry of 'PROTESTANTS AWAKE' and which asserted that by forbidding education authorities to provide religious instruction and appointing committees to apply religious tests, the 'secularist' Education Act opened the door 'for a Bolshevist or an Atheist or a Roman Catholic to become a teacher in a Protestant school'.[20] The actual meeting, held on 5 March in the assembly hall of the Presbyterian Church, was an impressive demonstration of Protestant unity. It was chaired by the Moderator of the Presbyterian Church; the platform was thronged with leading clergymen; and, most importantly, Sir Joseph Davison, the Grand Master of the County Grand Orange Lodge of Belfast, who claimed to represent 20,000 Belfast Orangemen and had considerable influence among Orangemen throughout the province, was in the forefront. A campaign fund was begun with a goal of £20,000, and by the end of the meeting it was obvious that the Protestant clergymen 'had been able to garner a great deal of lay support and that they now had the financial resources to bring massive pressure to bear on M.P.s and parliamentary candidates'.[21]

Such a demonstration of strength dramatically altered the government's attitude towards amending the act. Hitherto Londonderry's view that the agitation was both unrepresentative and unnecessary had prevailed,[22] but the 5 March demonstration quickly altered Craig's attitude to amendment. On the following day he invited the leaders of the agitation to a meeting at Stormont to resolve what he told Londonderry was a 'critical' situation.[23] A critical situation had developed because this increased Protestant pressure had come at a 'nodal moment'[24] in Northern Ireland politics, when the Boundary Commission was about to start work and Craig was planning a general election to underline to the imperial and Free State governments that 'not an inch' of Northern Ireland territory would be surrendered. The clerical–Orange agitation, therefore, threatened to destroy Craig's hopes of presenting a united front to the London and Dublin governments.

At the Stormont conference the government was represented by Craig, Best, the Attorney-General, and Dixon, the Chief Whip.[25] Londonderry, who had left for England three days earlier, was unable to cross back to attend the meeting since he was confined to bed with flu. Craig kept him informed of his intentions by telegram, and Londonderry remained sceptical that any genuine compromise was possible. Nevertheless, after 'a full and frank' discussion between the government and the clergymen, an agreement was reached whereby the government promised to introduce an amending bill. The bill was speedily sent through all its stages to receive the royal assent on the day parliament was prorogued for the general election.[26] It was a very short bill, adding the appointment of teachers to the list of topics upon which the school management committees of transferred and provided schools might advise the regional education committee, 'if the education authority so desired'; deleting the provision prohibiting local education authorities from providing religious instruction; and repealing the proviso which forbade the education authorities to take cognisance of a candidate's religion in appointments to teaching posts.[27] Although a short bill, it was a timely one, because it got the government over the immediate worry of facing a well-orchestrated Protestant opposition during the election.

Although the amending act enabled the government to go to the country unencumbered by the education question, it did not solve the difficulties. Differences of interpretation soon arose. Londonderry thought that the new act changed nothing, since although restrictions had been removed from the 1923 act, the powers of the regional education committees, in respect of both the provision of denominational education and the appointment of teachers, still remained restricted by those parts of the 1920 act forbidding direct or indirect religious endowment and the application of religious tests. However, the Protestant leaders were under the impression that the amending act had given them all that they desired.[28] They said that they had left the Stormont conference 'completely convinced that they could do everything they wanted by means of the amending bill and that if they could not and we knew they could not . . . the government had been guilty of deceiving the people of Ulster'.[29] The reason for such a misunderstanding was probably due to Craig's handling of the conference. In such conferences Craig was ever anxious to minimise differences between various groups and even more anxious to divert hostility from his government. In meeting the Protestant leaders in Londonderry's absence, Craig therefore gave the impression that the government was in entire sympathy with the agitators' aims but was hamstrung by the constituent act of 1920, over which it had no control. He probably hoped that by offering to remove the restrictions contained in the Northern Ireland Education Act, he could divest his government of any responsibility for the Protestant grievances and divert attention, as on the question of land purchase, from his government to the imperial government. Professor Akenson's suggestion that Craig 'had gained the electoral silence of the Protestant agitators and the continued allegiance of his Minister of Education by promising them both what they wanted'[30] is not wholly true, but it was certainly true, as Craig later told a complaining Londonderry, that the Stormont conference gave 'us breathing space'.[31]

The illusion of agreement was shattered on 24 April when the United Education Committee asked the Ministry of Education if it was prepared to approve the insertion of two conditions in the deeds of transfer of former voluntary schools. These conditions were, firstly, that religious instruction should be given by the teaching staff on a programme approved by the persons or body transferring the school, and, secondly, that if someone religiously offensive to the transferring body was appointed as a teacher, the transferors should have the right to resume control of the school. The ministry replied that under the Government of Ireland Act neither condition would be legal.[32]

The agitation was therefore resumed, once again with the support of the Orange Order. Once again, it assumed threatening proportions as the Twelfth of July demonstrations approached and meetings of local lodges, attended by members of the government, began to prepare hostile resolutions on the education question.[33] Londonderry's colleagues were much concerned lest the dispute remained unsettled by the Twelfth. Many of them sympathised with the aims of the Protestant agitation and felt particularly uncomfortable when, attending church on Sundays, they had to listen to clerical denunciations of the government and its Education Act. As Andrews reported to Craig on 17 June 1925,

> I take it that we are all agreed in desiring that Bible instruction should be given in the schools by teachers acceptable to the parents. . . . Personally I think a settlement is possible, but, on the other hand, if it is not arrived at I very much fear that Elliott, Crawford and many others of our followers will not support us when Parliament meets again, and that the agitation will go on in the meantime amongst Protestants of all denominations. Already the Protestant pulpits are being used for defending what is called 'Protestant rights'. I had myself to listen to two lengthy harangues on the subject on Sunday last in Little's church at Castlereagh. The Orange order are working in co-operation with the churches, and I am afraid that the position will be difficult on the 12th July unless something is done.[34]

Craig and the cabinet secretariat, which was in close touch with the Orange leadership,[35] shared Andrews's concern. On 13 June, Craig had told Londonderry to be firm and 'confidently rely upon me to shoulder with you every responsibility';[36] but by 18 June, after urgent representations from the cabinet secretariat,[37] he was pressing his minister to take the initiative by calling a meeting of the Primate of the Church of Ireland, the Moderator of the Presbyterian General Assembly and the leaders of the United Education Committee 'if possible . . . prior to the 12th July, so that if a final settlement is reached an announcement can be made that will satisfy the Orange Body and therefore prevent any adverse speeches at the various gatherings'.[38]

Londonderry was not immune to such pressures, and there followed a series of negotiations between him and the Protestant leaders which resulted by 25 June in a climbdown by the Minister of Education. In future, local education authorities were to be empowered to require that a programme of simple Bible instruction be given in provided or transferred schools in the period set aside on the timetable for religious instruction. This simple Bible instruction was not to include denominational or catechetical points. In other words, it was tacitly understood that simple Bible teaching was to be Protestant in nature but not distinctive of any Protestant denomination. Secondly, teachers were to be compelled to give such simple Bible instruction as part of their required educational duties. The terms of the settlement, which also included safeguards for religious liberty, were enacted through ministry regulations rather than by a further act of parliament.[39]

As Professor Akenson has argued, this new arrangement did involve an endowment of the Protestant faith.[40] Teachers (whose salaries were paid by the state) could be required to give in schools (whose expenses were met by the state and local authorities) a form of religious instruction which was acceptable to Protestants but not to Catholics. The settlement was therefore contrary to the 1920 act, and Londonderry was at first unhappy with his handling of the whole question. Nevertheless, he soon felt able to justify his bowing to 'the shouting and the threats'[41] of his critics. Not only had representatives of the teachers' unions at a 'very pleasant interview' accepted the need for compulsion,[42] but Londonderry also derived some satisfaction from implementing 'what appears to be the united desire of the people of the Province'.[43] The intervention of the Orange Order had demonstrated that substantial lay support had developed for the clerical agitation since 1923.

3

This was the same sort of argument that enabled Londonderry's successor, Charlemont, to give way to renewed clerical—Orange agitation in 1929. The clerics on their own could not persuade the government to amend further the Education Act and got only sympathy from Charlemont, but once they had established that they had extensive lay support in the shape of the Orange Order, the concessions soon followed.

Agitation for the further amendment of the Education Act got under way in the middle of 1928. It had been occasioned by the refusal in the spring of that year of the Armagh Regional Education Committee to insert in the deeds of the schools it accepted for transfer a clause requiring daily religious instruction, despite stiff warnings from the Ministry of Education that this refusal was jeopardising the truce of 1925. The agitation was formed between March and June 1928, when each of the presbyteries of the Presbyterian Church, at the instigation, it appears, of Corkey, passed a resolution pressing for further amendment of the Education Act, and when Corkey led the General Assembly in framing resolutions demanding further changes. Apart from a general and absurd feeling that the primary education system was giving preferential treatment to Catholics, the campaign emphasised three specific points. In the first place, a guarantee was demanded that in Protestant schools which were transferred to county borough or regional education committees, the committees could not abandon Bible instruction at some date in the future. Secondly, further safeguards were demanded to ensure that only Protestant teachers would be appointed to Protestant schools by ensuring that the views of modified local management committees should prevail. Thirdly, it was demanded that ministers of religion should be regularly appointed to sit on regional education committees and upon school management committees – though sometimes this demand was wrapped up in terms to make it more acceptable to laymen.[44] Provision for the representation of the clergy upon education committees had been included in an early draft of the 1923 bill, but had been dropped for fear of arousing lay hostility. Clergymen had thus had to fight for election or co-option along with the laity, with the result that, according to Corkey, one of the most 'disquieting features' of the 1923 act was that 'representatives of the Protestant Churches have been unceremoniously ousted from almost all the Regional Committees'.[45]

At first Charlemont was not inclined to make any concessions. Such concessions would, he thought, do little to speed up the transfer of schools and were unnecessary to protect the cause of Protestantism in transferred schools, which was safe enough even in Armagh. Moreover, he was opposed to the *ex officio* representation on education committees of clergymen, who were, after all, only experts on the Bible. 'I do not see why', Charlemont told Craig, 'an exhaustive knowledge of the Apocalypse should necessarily qualify any man to decide the amount of money to be expended on lavatory accommodation in any given Primary School!' Although he recognised that the clergy's claim for representation on school management committees might have some substance, he argued that the regional committees were chiefly committees of ways and means, and 'If we have the Churches represented *officially* on these bodies, we shall have sectarianism in its worst form brought in.' In any case, nomination was anti-democratic, since the clergy could always serve on the committees by ordinary elective and co-optive processes 'if the populace are really behind' the agitation. Finally, in the interests of justice, the government would have to nominate Catholic clergymen as well. 'How', Charlemont asked Craig, 'would Corkey & Quinn like that?'[46]

However strongly he and his officials may have held these views, Charlemont was too much of a political realist to close his options. Perhaps mindful of Londonderry's fate, he decided to take a sympathetic attitude and told Craig that in a proposed reply to the United Education Committee's demands for amendments 'I have not banged and bolted the door against possible amendment in the future, so that if you and the Cabinet *do* feel that anything of the kind is advisable, the Government will not be exhibiting a *complete* volte-face!'[47] In the event, Charlemont decided, despite ill-health, to talk to Corkey and Quinn personally rather than to write, and in a not unfriendly interview he told them to get up a deputation in the autumn to find out how much lay support they had.[48] What Charlemont regarded as sufficient lay support was made clear in a letter to Craig the following January:

> So long as I only had the reps. of the Churches to deal with I thought a sympathetic attitude was all that was required, as I had no reason to think that they had any large body of public opinion behind them, but if the Grand Orange Lodge is also with them on this question it will make a certain amount of difference.[49]

It turned out that the United Education Committee did indeed have the support of the Orange Order. On 21 February 1929 Craig and Charlemont received a joint delegation from the Committee and representatives of the Grand Orange Lodge of Ireland, during which Craig argued that the best method of procedure would be for the Committee to appoint a small subcommittee to negotiate an agreed settlement with the Ministry of Education, which could then form the basis of legislation. The ministry took its time in replying to the proposals submitted by the subcommittee, since it wanted to consult other interested parties, such as its own advisory council and the regional education committees. During the delay the clergy became impatient and threatened to make the amendment of the Education Act an issue in the forthcoming general election on the cry 'Protestantism in danger'. This impatience and threat to split the forces of Unionism in the election due in May caused a rift between the clergy and some Orangemen who began to suspect that their allies simply wanted to revert to the old system of clerical management and to make the maximum amount of trouble for the government.[50] Professor Akenson makes much of this rift to suggest that whereas the clergy wanted both assurances of the continuation of Bible instruction in transferred primary schools and the appointment of clergymen to education committees, the Orange Order would have been content with only the former; and that therefore the government decided to split its critics by conceding the former but not the latter in April 1929. Further, Professor Akenson suggests that the government's decision to include clerical nomination in the 1930 Education Bill, a decision which he argues was made after the 1929 general election, was 'a boon granted to supplicants, not a prize won by conquerors'. According to Professor Akenson, 'The government shrewdly played upon the Orange—clerical divisions, and satisfied the Orangemen's demands. When the clergy saw this happening they quickly joined the government's claque with the hope (correctly as it turned out) that the government would be generous to those who had supported it'.[51]

Plausible though this interpretation may have been on the basis of the evidence then available to Professor Akenson, it cannot withstand critical examination in the light of the Northern Ireland cabinet papers. These papers make it clear that the Orange Order fully supported the clergy's demand for clerical representation on regional education committees and that the government made this concession well before the election and with the election in mind. It was true that on 23 April 1929 the government met an Orange deputation with whom an agreement was reached, but it was also true that this deputation prepared the way for a clerical deputation on the following day, and that agreement was reached between the government and the two deputations on a whole series of matters recorded in a memorandum drawn up by the Cabinet Secretary on 30 April 1929. This memorandum on 'the extent to which the Minister of Education is prepared to meet the case for amendment of the Act, as communicated to the Committees representing the Orange Order and the Protestant Churches in the interviews on 23rd and 24th April respectively'[52] divided the concessions into three sections. Section 1, 'For the Safeguarding of Protestantism', included the provisions that borough and regional education committees were 'to be bound by statute to provide simple Bible instruction in transferred and provided schools'.* Section 2, 'For the maintenance of the interests of the Churches in education', provided 'for the presence on each Borough and Regional Committee of a nominated element representative of the transferors of the schools, such element to be approximately one-quarter of the Committee', and also made concessions about the composition and powers of school management committees, including the stipulation that the composition of such committees was 'to be stereotyped after the manner suggested in the Memorandum submitted by the joint Committee'. After the meeting on 23 April the Orange Order had expressed its satisfaction with the government's proposals, but no such statement was issued by the United Committee on the following day, since the Ministry of Education refused to give way on one point considered vital by the clergymen, namely, the influence of school management committees on teaching appointments.

*It also included a proposal for 'bus-ing', for regional education committees were 'to be bound to provide transport for Protestant children to a Protestant school where no such school is accessible to the children in the ordinary way'.

The Protestant clergy had demanded that regional education committees, when making an appointment to a vacancy in a transferred or provided school, should be bound by statute to select one teacher out of a short list selected by the school management committee. Charlemont was apparently willing to give way,[53] but Wyse, the Permanent Secretary, resisted the proposal. Although in practice teachers were almost without exception appointed in this manner, the ministry thought that to compel regional education committees by statute to confine themselves to the recommendations of the local school management committees 'would arouse opposition, both from the teachers and from the Regional Committees, owing to fear lest this should tend to re-introduce parochial influences'.[54] The Ministry's refusal to concede this point during the meeting on 24 April sparked off further correspondence, in which the United Education Committee invoked the aid of Davison, the Orange leader, who duly obliged by asking Craig: 'Could anything be done . . . so that they can assure their friends that all difficulties are at an end?'[55] Davison suggested that assurances of sympathetic consideration would suffice. Craig's reply was conciliatory,[56] and within the few days he made two speeches (at Holywood and the Reform Club) which reassured Protestant leaders and drew from Quinn a fulsome letter of praise.[57] Well might Charlemont have wryly commented: 'I do think that if he gives you these bouquets he might give me a *buttonhole* at least'.[58]

The government's surrender to the clerical–Orange agitation was therefore complete. A realisation of this fact makes much more sense of the Protestant clergy's decision to stop fighting the government in May 1929 than does Professor Akenson's interpretation of the episode, which attributes too much subtlety to Craig and his colleagues. Corkey's version was right.[59] The Protestant clergymen stopped fighting because they had won. The pledge to appoint clergymen to education committees was given, as were pledges to implement all the agitators' demands, *before* the election and with the full support of the Orange Order. The absence of references to clerical nomination in the government's election manifesto and in ministers' speeches, which so struck Professor Akenson, is to be explained by the need not to aggravate needlessly the resentment of teachers' organisations and the education committees, whose views had been overruled.

In fact, the question of the nomination of the clergy to regional and county borough education committees underlined the importance of the clerical–Orange agitation in determining policy and the relative unimportance of the teachers' unions and the education committees. Immediate political and electoral considerations, rather than broader educational or political concerns, determined the issue. The non-religious bodies involved in primary education did not think that the act was in need of amendment and resented the clergy's agitation as a reflection upon them. While teachers and education committees alike did not object to Bible instruction being made compulsory, they strenuously objected to any enhanced role being given to the clergy, which they thought subversive of both local democratic control and efficiency, clergymen being 'notoriously unbusinesslike'.[60] Moreover, Protestant teachers, in particular, wanted no return to what they regarded as the humiliating conditions of clerical control of appointments.[61]

Such representations may have made Ministry of Education officials hesitate about conceding to the clerical—Orange demands, but the superior political clout of the clergy and their Orange allies convinced the politicians of the wisdom of capitulation. Craig had told a deputation from the Association of Northern Ireland Education Committees on 5 April that nothing should be done 'for political expediency which they thought was wrong and against the best interests of the education of their children', that no amendment of the Education Act should be rushed into without careful consideration, and that 'The more one heard, the better the existing Act appeared to be working and the more one was convinced that the difficulties were not so much advanced by sincere educationists as by carping critics'.[62] These were fine words, but within a month, and with a general election looming large, the government had decided that it was politically safer to promise to amend the Education Act in line with all the clerical—Orange demands.

The concessions were embodied in a bill, which was first drafted in November 1929 but which did not receive its first reading until the following April. It was a controversial measure, one of whose 'legitimate objects', so Craig said, was 'to make the provided and transferred schools safe for Protestant children'.[63] It met with continued opposition from teachers' unions and from regional education committees. Indeed, Charlemont felt 'rather surprised and disappointed at the obvious inability of the Grand Orange Lodge' to render the latter 'more reasonable'.[64] Most importantly, it met with an increasingly vocal attack from the Catholic hierarchy, Catholic organisations and Nationalist M.P.s, who demanded similar concessions to Catholics.

The government's attempt to satisfy the Protestant conscience brought about Catholic intervention into Northern Ireland educational politics for the first time.[65] Catholic schools, along with all other voluntary schools, had suffered at least a theoretical loss from the implementation of the 1923 act, which had withdrawn the government grants of two-thirds of the total cost of buildings and equipment available under the Union. However, the government's attempt to persuade Protestants to transfer their schools provided Catholics with an opportunity for demanding an equivalent concession to the Catholic conscience in the shape of government grants toward voluntary schools on the same basis as had been available under the national system. The government could not afford to ignore this agitation, especially since Catholics and nationalists threatened to challenge the validity of the bill before the Judicial Committee of the Privy Council – an action which would have constituted a real threat to the success of the government's compact with the United Education Committee and Orange Order, in view of Westminster's doubts about the validity of the measure.[66]

At first the government felt unable to agree to building grants, which, it thought, cut across one of the central principles of the 1923 act, namely, popular control in return for public money.[67] It therefore looked for alternative ways of satisfying the Catholic demands. It considered making loans, which proved unacceptable to Catholics; it considered modifying the powers of four-and-two committees to allow church control over non-secular matters, which would have proved irksome to the regional education committees already smarting under the concessions made to the Protestant clergy.[68] Eventually it was decided that the easiest thing would be to give government grants direct to voluntary schools, although not at the rate Catholics had originally demanded, but on the same terms as were available to schools run by four-and-two committees.[69] Thus, in addition to conceding all the demands of the Protestant agitators, the 1930 Education Act also made a concession to Catholic opinion by offering 50 per cent grants for the building expenses of privately managed schools. The grant applied to all voluntary schools in accordance with a cabinet decision that no amendment to the bill would be accepted 'which involves any concession that does not apply equally to both sections of the community'.[70]

4

The 1930 Education Act, which remained unchanged until after the Second World War, did solve one of the government's problems. It put an end to that clerical–Orange agitation which had so harried ministers in the 1920s and threatened the government before two general elections. It did little, however, to speed up the transfer of Protestant schools.[71] Moreover, in attempting to solve one problem, it created another, since Catholics were dissatisfied with the concessions made to them in the act.

There will always be room for disagreement as to how far the Northern Ireland education system, as modified by the 1925 and 1930 education acts and the June 1925 concordat, constituted a legitimate Catholic grievance.[72] Had the clergy been willing to share control with the laity and bend the law a little, they could have worked the system to their own advantage. Moreover, Catholics, along with other denominations running voluntary schools, did reap some direct benefit from the 1930 act in the shape of government grants to cover one-half of the cost of building and equipping new voluntary schools and one-half of the cost of altering, enlarging and equipping existing institutions.[73] These terms, hitherto confined to four-and-two schools, were less generous than those available in the Free State but more favourable than those obtained by voluntary, particularly Catholic, schools elsewhere in the United Kingdom (until 1936) and in the world.

Nevertheless, the fact remained that by the 1930s the education system was discriminating in favour of Protestantism. Although the 1930 act was a carefully drafted measure, which studiously strove to be religiously neutral, its provisions, taken in conjunction with some of those of the 1925 act, boiled down to the effective endowment of Protestantism.[74] In the first place, the appointment clauses of the two measures meant that Protestant interests were able to ensure that only Protestant teachers were appointed to transferred or provided schools. While the 1925 act had removed the prohibition on inquiring into the religious background of applicants for teaching posts, the 1930 act provided that appointments were to be made by the regional committees from among a list of three nominated by local management committees, which were to draw at least half their members from the transferors of those schools taken over by the regional committees and from among those persons who were formerly managers of any elementary school which had been superseded by a provided school. Although the act did not mention the clergy directly, the intention of these parts of the 1930 act was to allow the Protestant clergy, who had previously been prominent in managing schools, to maintain a share in the control of the local elementary schools, even though those schools were ostensibly under local civic control. Secondly, the 1930 act required that in each provided or transferred school it was the duty of the regional or county borough education authorities to provide Bible instruction should the parents of not less than ten children demand such instruction. Bible instruction was to be given under the rules of the 1925 act, which meant that teachers were required to give undenominational Bible instruction but that the children were not compelled to attend against the wishes of their parents. Hence Professor Akenson's conclusion that 'The 1930 Education Act made normative practices which had been only permissive under the 1925 act'.[75]

The actual definition of Bible instruction was given in subsection 5 of clause 4 of the 1930 act:

> For the purpose of this section the expression 'Bible instruction' means instruction based upon the Holy Scriptures according to some authoritative version or versions thereof, but excluding instruction as to any tenet which is distinctive of any particular religious denomination.

Since Bible instruction was to be undenominational, and since it could be based upon any version of the Bible acceptable to any denomination, the government felt able to argue that these clauses were not discriminatory and should not prove an obstacle to the transfer of Catholic schools. Craig put this argument reasonably succinctly in the Commons on 9 April 1930. Bible instruction, he said,

> need not involve the reading of the actual text of the Bible, if this be thought undesirable by the Roman Catholic clergy; it is to be instruction 'based on the Holy Scriptures' for which 'some authoritative version', for example, the Douai version or other version acceptable to Roman Catholic theologians, may be used, and so long as it does not include any tenets which are distinctive of Roman Catholicity as distinguished from other Christian religious denominations, it may be a programme of teaching which includes the great and simple truths of our common Christianity. . . . It need have no odour or taint of Protestant Bible teaching to which Catholics seem to object so strenuously.[76]

Plausible though it appeared, this line of defence missed the whole nature of the Catholic case, namely, that the reading of any version of the Bible without denominational comment was unacceptable to them. Simple Bible teaching was, said Daniel Mageean, the Catholic Bishop of Down and Connor, 'based upon the fundamental principle of Protestantism, the interpretation of sacred Scriptures by private judgement'.[77] Few Unionists seemed able to grasp the importance of the distinction: in the debates on the 1930 bill only the Independent Unionist M.P. for Queen's University, R. N. McNeill, appreciated the fundamental nature of the difference between the Protestant and Catholic attitudes to the Bible.[78] Whereas for Protestants the Bible was the basis of their faith, for Catholics it was only one source. 'It is but a dead letter,' said James McCarroll, the Nationalist M.P. for the Foyle division of Londonderry, 'calling for a divine interpreter. There are the traditions of the [early] Church. . . . There is also the tradition of the Church which is not human opinion but the divine teaching of an infallible apostolate established by Christ Himself'.[79]

The 1930 act was thus not equitable in its treatment of the two major religious groups. Under it, two school systems operated, the clientele of one being Protestant, of the other either Protestant or Catholic. In the transferred and provided schools, which were attended almost exclusively by Protestant children, all capital and daily operating expenses were paid out of central and local government funds, whereas the voluntary schools, Catholic and Protestant alike, received most but not all of their funds from public sources, making up the difference themselves. Had the option of operating transferred and provided schools been open equally to both religious faiths, there would have been nothing inequitable about such an arrangement; but the option was not so open. Catholic schools did not have the opportunity of becoming transferred institutions if Catholics were to adhere strictly to the letter of the law. In effect, the 1930 act 'redefined the religious nature of the transferred and provided schools so as to preclude any Catholic school manager who had a strict sense of the law from transferring his school'.[80] That the parents of ten children should compel teachers in transferred or provided schools to give simple Bible instruction was tantamount to a requirement that simple Bible instruction had to be given in all transferred and provided schools.

Education policy drew from Catholics and nationalists some of their most extravagant denunciations of the government of Northern Ireland and its Protestant supporters. The treatment of Catholic schools was worse than Hitler's treatment of the Jews, declared the Nationalist leader in 1934, when condemning the amalgamation of boys' with girls' schools;[81] and three years earlier Cardinal Archbishop MacRory of Armagh had declared that the Protestant Church in Ireland 'is not even a part of the Church of Christ'.[82] The outlandishness of such outbursts should not obscure the fact that at least the 1930 Education Act constituted a genuine Catholic grievance which was summed up in a statement made on 5 May 1932 by Bishop Mageean.[83] This 'unjust and partisan' act, he declared, which had been passed 'at the dictation of the Orange lodges', closed the door of transferred and provided schools to every Catholic child, who thereby, unlike his Protestant counterpart, had to be educated at great expense to the 'poorest section of the community' in schools receiving only half their building and running costs from the state. Such differential treatment, continued the bishop,

> is against all principles of justice and equity. . . . We form a large portion of the population, and have more children attending primary elementary schools than any other religious denomination. We ask for no privilege, but we claim equality of treatment with our fellow citizens, and we demand our rights.

12

Acquiescence:
Westminster and the Minority Problem

The amendment of the 1923 Education Act and the abolition of P.R. illustrate not only the myopia of government in Northern Ireland but also the imperial government's unwillingness or inability to correct this myopia. Although Northern Ireland remained part of the United Kingdom, and although ultimate sovereignty was reserved to Westminster, the tendency was for imperial governments to allow Northern Ireland to manage its own affairs. There may have been pressure here and there, particularly in financial matters, but the preference was to let the Northern Ireland government and parliament have their heads in the administration of transferred services. One of the consequences of such unwillingness to interfere in Northern Ireland's domestic affairs was Westminister's acquiesence in measures exacerbating the minority problem there.

1

Thus it was that the Opposition failed to persuade the Home Secretary, the imperial minister responsible for Northern Ireland, to prevent the abolition of P.R. in parliamentary elections. A deputation from the Northern Ireland Labour Party did wait upon the Conservative Home Secretary, Joynson-Hicks, in December 1928, only to be told that the question was a matter not for him but for the Northern Ireland parliament. As Joynson-Hicks wrote to Craig, informing him of the deputation, 'I don't know whether you would care at any time to discuss the matter with me; of course I am always at your disposal. But beyond that "I know my place", and don't propose to interfere'.[1]

The Home Office had much stronger reservations about the 1925 and 1930 Education Acts, since a good case could be made out that they both did contravene the 1920 act. Nevertheless, on both occasions the Home Office contented itself with expressing its reservations in private to members of the Northern Ireland government. On 13 March 1925, when signifying the royal assent to the 1925 Education Act, Abercorn, the Governor, warned Craig that but for the impending election in Northern Ireland the Home Secretary would have ordered the reservation of the bill to see if it conflicted with the 1920 act.[2] Although the royal assent was given, the Home Secretary still retained the liberty to determine its validity by reference to the Judicial Committee of the Privy Council, and the same tactic was adopted over the later measure.

After the first draft of the 1930 Education Bill had been seen by Home Office officials, members of the Northern Ireland administration were summoned to the Home Office in London, where, on 26 November 1929, the Minister of Education, his Permanent Secretary and the Parliamentary Draftsman discussed its implications with officials of the Home Office and the English Board of Education.[3] After referring to the difficulty the Home Office had felt in allowing the royal assent to the 1925 act, the Permanent Secretary, Sir John Anderson, expressed his reservations about the current proposals. While admitting that the carefully worded draft 'did not, at any rate, flagrantly conflict with the Government of Ireland Act', he considered that the proposal to make simple Bible teaching obligatory 'would certainly be regarded by Roman Catholics as unacceptable and constituting a preference in violation of section 5' of the 1920 act. After Charlemont and Wyse, his Permanent Secretary, had tried, not too successfully, to show that 'the proposed Bible teaching being confined to portions of Christian teaching common to all Christian denominations should not be regarded as constituting a preference in favour of any one of them', Anderson announced the decision of the Home Office to do nothing at present but to keep its options open for the future:

> Frankly, he would prefer that the matter were not raised. The Government, however, would not recommend that the Royal Assent should be withheld, nor that the Bill should be referred to the Judicial Committee of the Privy Council under the Government of Ireland Act, 1920. If, after the Bill has become law, substantial representations were received against it from responsible parties in Northern Ireland they would refer the question to the Judicial Committee.

2

This Home Office diffidence, typical of the approach of imperial ministers – even Labour ministers – and officials to Northern Ireland affairs, was not surprising in view of the failure of the one and only attempt in the inter-war years by an imperial government to thwart a piece of controversial legislation – the 1922 Local Government Bill. The incident highlighted the problem of a central government supervising the affairs of a regional government, where the governing party had a built-in majority. If matters were pressed to the point of resignation, and the resigning government returned, as was inevitable in Northern Ireland, in the ensuing general election, the central government would be faced with either a humiliating climbdown or the prospect of resuming direct responsibility for the government of the region. And this was the very thing which the 1920 act had been intended to avoid in Ireland.

The Local Government Bill abolishing P.R. in local elections completed its unopposed parliamentary progress on 5 July 1922. The royal assent was not, however, announced until over two months later, on 11 September. The delay was the result of the efforts of the Provisional Government of the twenty-six counties to prevent the bill from becoming law. On 28 June, Collins had initiated a campaign to persuade the imperial government, Lloyd George's coalition, to withhold the royal assent, and this pressure was continued by Cosgrave after Collins's death and was supported by the imperial busybody in Dublin, Cope. The Provisional Government alleged that, by wiping out all effective nationalist and Catholic local representation, the Local Government Bill not only discriminated against the Northern minority, but also jeopardised the whole Irish peace settlement. In fact, according to Cope, members of the Provisional Government reckoned that they 'would not have been so ready to accept Partition as a possibility if they had known that the Northern Government were going to adopt a policy of deliberately weakening the position of the Nationalist minority in the Six Counties'.[4]

At first Collins stressed the injustice done to Catholics and nationalists,[5] but later the Local Government Bill was linked with the Boundary Commission and thus regarded as a violation of the Treaty. 'Do you not see,' Collins asked Churchill on 9 August 1922, 'or have His Majesty's advisers not disclosed, the true meaning of all this?' Not merely was the bill intended 'to oust the Catholic and Nationalist people of the Six Counties from their rightful share in local administration', but it was 'beyond all question, intended to paint the Counties of Tyrone and Fermanagh with a deep Orange tint in anticipation of . . . the Boundary Commission, and so, try to defraud these people of the benefits of the Treaty'.[6] This argument loomed large in discussions, for the Provisional Government considered that the basis of the Treaty had been an understanding between Britain and the South to work towards a united Ireland. Thus, Cope reported, the imperial government should veto the Local Government Bill, which, by differentiating between the electoral systems of North and South, 'is to work away from a policy of reunion and so intensify the separatist tendency in the North'.[7]

Indeed, according to the Provisional Government, the Local Government Bill was likely to jeopardise the whole peace of Ireland. It both increased the difficulty of securing acceptance of the Treaty in the

South and made difficult the maintenance of friendly relations with the North.[8] Belfast politics did react upon Southern politics, so that (as Cope told Curtis, the Colonial Office Adviser on Irish Affairs) the Southern government could not afford 'to be faced with the constant criticism that they are aiding and abetting the people who are oppressing their compatriots in the North'.[9] Moreover, the treatment of the Northern minority did have implications for the Southern minority. Not only did it make difficult the implementation of the pledges Griffith had given to the Southern Unionists to secure their acceptance of the Treaty. It also created the danger of demands for reprisals against the Southern Unionists, which, in turn, might render the imperial parliament hostile to the Irish settlement and precipitate a confrontation between Dublin and Westminister.[10]

The Provisional Government's case against the Local Government Bill put the Colonial Office, the ministry responsible for Irish affairs, in a quandary. On the whole Churchill, the Colonial Secretary, and his officials were sympathetic. The latter were anxious to 'sow and cultivate the seeds of conciliation' between North and South, hoping to render a Boundary Commission unnecessary by persuading Irishmen to 'agree together upon a modus vivendi which will do away with boundaries except for purely local affairs'.[11] Above all, they were desperately anxious that the South should loyally adhere to the Treaty and thus remain truly within the Empire. The only way to ensure that the South would not try to stretch the Treaty to the point of complete separation was, Cope urged, for the imperial government to set an example and to be seen to be observing both the letter and spirit of the Treaty.[12] Thus by raising in an acute form the whole question of the Boundary Commission and the Treaty, the Local Government Bill was regarded as a 'noxious plant in the garden' of conciliation. It was, Churchill agreed with Cosgrave, 'most unfortunate and ill-timed'.[13] Moreover, perhaps some feeling against the Northern government was created by a breakdown in communications which meant that the imperial authorities became aware of the bill only at a very late stage.[14] Even Craig had to admit that such a breakdown of communications might have created a 'false impression . . . that owing to the nature of the Bill we attempted to be secretive or to hustle Churchill or His Excellency in any way'.[15]

It was, however, one thing to be sympathetic towards the Provisional Government's claims, and another thing to act upon them. Responsive though it was to suggestion that the Local Government Bill was endangering the whole peace settlement, the Colonial Office had to consider two obstacles to withholding the royal assent: the constitutional position, and the attitude of the government of Northern Ireland.

There was considerable doubt about the propriety of withholding the royal assent from a measure which fell within the competence of the Northern parliament. At first glance it was clearly within the powers of the Northern parliament to abolish P.R. in local elections. Matters relating to local government were not among the excepted or reserved services listed in the 1920 act, while the only limitation on the power of the Northern parliament to deal with electoral matters related to parliamentary elections. Control over local government and all that that entailed was thus provided for in clause 4 of the act, which transferred to Northern Ireland all powers not explicitly excepted or reserved in clauses 4, 5 and 6. Moreover, paragraph 3 of the summary of the main provisions of the act indicated that the Northern parliament could make new laws in respect of local government and local authorities. The Provisional Government argued, however, that the motives behind and the consequences of the abolition of P.R. made the Local Government Bill a matter of more than local significance. Collins told Churchill that 'This is not a domestic matter, but a matter affecting the Treaty and the Irish Free State . . . an attempt to defeat the obligations of His Majesty's Government contained in the Treaty'.[16]

Collins's suggestion provoked a discussion of the exact status enjoyed by Northern Ireland. The touchstone was whether or not Northern Ireland was a dominion. With its limited powers and its continued representation at Westminister, Northern Ireland clearly did not enjoy dominion status as compared with Canada, Australia or even the Free State. But, according to Sir Francis Greer, the Parliamentary Draftsman in the Irish Office, the legislative powers of the Northern parliament, where not expressly excluded from its jurisdiction, were 'equal to those of a Dominion Parliament' and 'in each case the same constitutional issues are involved in the reservation of Bills'. The withholding of the royal assent from a dominion bill would have created a constitutional crisis and was thus not to be undertaken lightly. It had to be judged against very strict criteria. Greer therefore dismissed as 'very farfetched' the Provisional Government's claim that the Local Government Bill affected the Boundary Commission and thus impaired the rights of the Free State under the Treaty. Greer argued that no boundary question could arise under the Treaty unless an address opting out of the Free State was presented by both Houses of the Northern parliament. The Local Government Bill did not affect the constitution of the Northern parliament or the minority's right to representation in it. It dealt solely with elections to and representation on local authorities which had no voice in the question of opting out or in the determination of the boundary. The contention that the bill infringed the Treaty 'could not be pressed further than this, that the possible effect of the Bill will be to convert a Catholic majority into a Protestant majority in the county council [sic] of Tyrone and Fermanagh, and possibly on some district councils in these counties'. If the boundary was 'to be settled according to a plebiscite of county councils there might be something in the point, but this is not the case'. It would therefore, concluded Greer, be straining constitutional rights 'pretty far' to reverse the bill on such grounds. The only justifiable grounds for reserving it was 'the hope or expectation that it might lead to some settlement'.[17]

The hope that the abandonment of the Local Government Bill might facilitate a settlement was, in fact, the justification used for delaying the royal assent. In a memorandum dated 24 July 1922 a group of senior legal officers, including Greer, had earlier given their legal opinion and argued that the bill was not a matter of purely local concern.[18] The crux of the argument was that dominion conditions were not comparable with conditions then prevailing in Northern Ireland. It was argued that during the critical period of transition the re-establishment of law and order in Northern Ireland was a matter 'not of merely local but of Imperial concern', on which account the imperial parliament had voted large sums for services for which, in normal circumstances, Northern Ireland would be solely responsible. The British taxpayers and the government which represented them were thus 'directly interested in preventing measures which would imperil the prospects of peace being passed into law'. The Local Government Bill was one such disruptive measure, since P.R. had been introduced to secure the protection of minorities and 'At the present moment the security of minorities is a vital question, and hopes of any lasting peace depend to a large extent upon the minority being brought to recognise the Northern Parliament and Government as their Parliament and Government.' As 'rightly or wrongly' the Local Government Bill was regarded as an abrogation of the rights of the Northern minority, its enactment 'would intensify suspicion and distrust and be a fatal obstacle to conciliatory efforts on the above lines'. Since, therefore, the Local Government Bill affected imperial interests both in Northern Ireland and elsewhere, it was, the lawyers concluded, a 'proper subject for the exercise of the power of reservation'. The royal assent was thus initially withheld from the bill.[19]

Such fine arguments ignored the second, and the real, obstacle to the vetoing of the bill – the attitude of the government of Northern Ireland. The withholding of the royal assent angered ministers. The memory of the Lord Lieutenant's overriding earlier in the year the recommendations of the Northern Ireland cabinet, by granting an amnesty to nationalist prisoners and commuting certain death sentences, still rankled. Thus Bates and Megaw, whose Ministry of Home Affairs was responsible for both law and order and the bill, were particularly incensed at what they saw as yet another instance of the 'intolerable' treatment meted out to the Northern government by the Lord Lieutenant who heeded the advice of imperial ministers and officials instead of that given by his duly appointed ministers in Northern Ireland. Megaw held that, while 'strictly legal', the Lord Lieutenant's action in withholding the assent was 'entirely unconstitutional' and urged that unless the assent was given, 'our Government must necessarily lose all confidence and authority'. Unless the Lord Lieutenant withdrew his opposition on 'such a vital issue', Megaw concluded, 'I do not see how our Government can continue in Office'.[20] The majority of ministers and senior officials shared Megaw's view and wanted to precipitate a showdown with the imperial government. After a conversation with Andrews, Bates, Megaw, Queckett (the Parliamentary Draftsman) and others, Spender reported to Craig that there was unanimous agreement that the government 'would be well advised to challenge the Imperial Government at once by resigning and forcing an election'. Such a challenge would do much to clear the air of the suspicion and mistrust then characterising Northern Ireland's relations with the imperial government, for

> No election cry could be more popular in Northern Ireland than that the Imperial Government was challenging our direct rights and preventing us from applying the Oath of Allegiance. Not only would this course be exceedingly popular in Northern Ireland but I fancy it would bring home to the people in England more than any other method of propaganda the fact that the present Government is not playing the game with us. Should you not be successful in getting the total Constabulary charges paid for by the Imperial Government I think that this challenge might be the best way of bringing matters to a head. The colonies too would certainly support us on this issue; at any rate their governments and even the Free State might find difficulty in supporting the action of the L[ord] L[ieutenant]![21]

Craig sympathised with his ministers' feelings. Like them, he was much exercised with the principle of withholding the royal assent from a bill which, he said, dealt with purely local affairs, was certified by the Attorney-General to be within the terms of the 1920 act, and had been approved by 'an overwhelming majority of the people in Northern Ireland'.[22] He had no time for the suggestion that the Local Government Bill infringed the rights of the Irish Free State. Although an earlier intimation of the importance which the imperial government attached to the bill's not becoming law might have secured its withdrawal, by July, Craig argued, it had proceeded too far to be abandoned.[23] Should the assent be withheld, then his government would have no alternative but to resign. 'No Government could carry on in Northern Ireland', he told the Permanent Secretary of the Colonial Office, 'if it knew that the powers of the Parliament ... were to be abrogated'.[24] There can be little doubt that Craig and his ministers would have resigned, as they so decided on 27 July. 'To allow this precedent to be created would', the cabinet agreed, 'warrant the interference by the Imperial Government in almost every Act introduced in Northern Ireland'.[25] It was also true, however, that Craig believed that the imperial government would back down rather than run 'the risk of complete disorganisation in Ulster at the moment'.[26]

Disorganisation there would have been, and a first-rate constitutional crisis, had Craig's government resigned. Imperial ministers quailed before the prospect of Craig's resignation over the Local Government Bill. It was not so much the prospect that the dominions might resent this imperial intrusion into local affairs that concerned them, but its effect in Northern Ireland. Resignation would mean a general election, which, in view of the built-in Unionist majority in Northern Ireland and the widespread Unionist dislike of P.R., would endorse Craig's action. Since there would be no alternative to the Craig administration, the imperial government would be faced with an impasse.[27] It would either have to climb down or take on responsibility for governing the province.

A constitutional crisis of these dimensions was, however, averted by the conciliatory attitude adopted by Craig. He was unwilling to force a showdown with the imperial government and thus played for time. His immediate motive for doing so was his anxiety to obtain extensive financial support for the Special Constabulary. At the time when his ministers were hoping for a confrontation, Craig was in England discussing with Churchill, and Sir Robert Horne, the Chancellor of the Exchequer, the future financing of the Special Constabulary, and he did not want this question linked with that of the Local Government Bill. He hoped to get the financial question settled before pressing the latter matter, as Churchill might use the former issue as a lever to get his own way on the question of the royal assent. When he met Churchill on 18 July to discuss finance, Craig therefore thought 'it wise not to press the matter too far' and agreed with Churchill on a procedure which would 'allow sufficient time to elapse for the Chancellor of the Exchequer to deal with the financial question purely on its merits'.[28] Moreover, Craig was, in general, anxious to work harmoniously with the imperial government. He preferred matters to be settled quietly and amicably between the different parts of the United Kingdom. He told Churchill on 27 July that

> He was anxious, in this, as in all other business which he had to
> conduct with H.M.G., that no issue should arise publicly upon which
> it could be urged by those with whom he had to work in the North,
> that either he had scored a personal success over H.M.G. or, alter-
> natively, he had given way weakly to H.M.G.[29]

Thus Craig tried, with a fair degree of success, to damp down all public reference to the question of the withholding of the royal assent among his ministers and the Northern Ireland press.

Craig would not budge on the main question and stood by the Local Government Bill, but throughout he maintained a conciliatory attitude. He willingly discussed at length the implications of the bill with Churchill and his officials, and took in good part their little lectures about the need to take a broad view of affairs and the importance of winning over the Northern minority. In particular, he made two concessions which enabled the potential crisis to be averted and allowed the imperial government to retreat while offering a concession to the Provisional Government.

In the first place, he consented to a delay in the royal assent until 31 August, agreeing with the Colonial Office that the delay should be explained by 'the circumstance that the Lord Lieutenant had by some accident not been able to study the Bill until it had been finally presented to him for his immediate assent'.[30] This period of delay enabled the Colonial Office to try to assuage the Provisional Government's suspicions by playing down the likely loss of nationalist representation and assuring it of the purity of the Northern government's motives. It also enabled Churchill to offer little homilies. In his letter to Collins on 31 July, Churchill thought that the general constitutional issue would be of interest to the Free State, since, although Northern Ireland was not a dominion, the vetoing of the Local Government Bill could create 'a precedent limiting for the future the powers of Dominion Parliaments'. Churchill also felt 'bound to observe that the continuing refusal of the Catholic minority in the North to recognise the Northern Government robs of much of their substance and possible validity the arguments urged in your letter'.[31] Such delay and such arguments did not reconcile the Provisional Government to the bill, even when Collins was succeeded by the more conciliatory Cosgrave. His communications lacked the passion and invective of Collins's denunciations of the Northern government, but Cosgrave did insist that the Local Government Bill was a matter which concerned not merely Northern Ireland but also the Free State and, through the Treaty, Great Britain, since it was 'calculated to anticipate in the most deliberate way the decision of the Boundary question, one of the most serious issues in Ireland, and so to prejudice in the gravest manner the whole Treaty position'.[32] Cosgrave therefore urged that the royal assent should be withheld until the Boundary Commission had reported.

While not necessarily accepting the Provisional Government's interpretation of the constitutional position, the Colonial Office and the British signatories to the Treaty would have liked to have acceded to this request. At the end of August and the beginning of September, therefore, considerable pressure was put upon Craig not to insist upon the royal assent, to which end he and his ministers were invited to attend a meeting of the imperial cabinet.[33] Craig and his colleagues remained firm, and Craig replied that while he would gladly attend a cabinet meeting, he would not bring along any of his ministers, because, he told Churchill,

> We unanimously decided at our last meeting that it would be impossible to carry on if legislation passed by the Commons and Senate, admittedly within the powers conferred by the Government of Ireland Act, 1920, were to be vetoed by the Lord Lieutenant on behalf of His Majesty at the request of another Government holding different views in Southern Ireland.[34]

Craig 'phlegmatically' resisted all blandishments, but he did, however, agree to consider a suggestion put forward by Colonial Office officials to postpone local elections, which, they thought, by leaving things as they were until the Boundary Commission had done its work, was 'the most hopeful compromise'.[35] The result was that Craig made his second concession and on 9 September wrote to Churchill that his government would as soon as convenient introduce a bill 'either to postpone Elections for County Councils and Rural District Councils . . . for one year, or to have such Elections held under the system of Proportional Representation now prevailing'.*[36] In return for this promise, the government of Northern Ireland received its reward in the form of a telegram on the same day authorising the royal assent to the Local Government Bill.[37]

The episode was an instructive one. It starkly revealed the limits of central control, even when the regional administration was a friendly one anxious to maintain the unity of the state. The imperial government could do little to supervise the conduct of government in Northern Ireland. This incapacity was partly self-induced, arising from an unwillingness to become once more directly involved in Irish affairs and from a respect for the sovereignty of parliaments. But it was also, and very largely, based upon an appreciation of political realities. The plain fact was that there was no alternative government to call upon in Northern Ireland should the Unionists resign in protest against the exercise of Westminster's sovereignty.

---

*The former course was adopted in the Local Authorities (Elections and Constitution) Bill, introduced on 11 October 1922, and postponing rural elections from June 1923 until May or June 1924. The concession was, however, in vain, since, owing to the delay in setting up the Boundary Commission, the postponed elections were held before the commission even began its work.

Conclusion:
The Northern Ireland Problem
and Devolution

The time-span of this book has been deliberately restricted to the period 1921–39 and the treatment detailed, because it is the first account of the processes of government in Northern Ireland in this formative period to be based upon the solid documentary evidence of a working archive. Nevertheless, it can make a contribution to the wider and not unrelated debates on Northern Ireland and on devolution.

Interpretations of the Northern Ireland problem have been so varied that one writer has recently been able to divide them into no fewer than eleven broad categories.[1] One feature that most of these explanations of the present conflict in Northern Ireland have in common is a historical dimension, some going back to the seventeenth century, others concentrating on the more recent history of Ireland. While recognising the importance of events from the plantations onwards, this present study favours a shorter historical perspective, for in a very definite sense the history of the current Northern Ireland problem does date from the setting up of a separate government and parliament in 1921.

The tensions within the Ulster Unionist movement had been masked during the single-minded fight against Home Rule. After the establishment of the regional government, divisions and tensions within the movement not only came once more to the fore but were increased by the Unionist government's need to govern – and to govern, moreover, with limited powers. Both government action and inaction created frustration and potential revolt within the Unionist Party. In turn, the government tried to maintain its position and the loyalty of its supporters by developing an informal style of administration inimical to long-term and overall planning, by handing out doles, and by actively discriminating in favour of Protestants and Unionists on such sensitive issues as education, representation and, to a lesser extent, law and order. The new government inherited a divided and disadvantaged society. It did little to relieve the disadvantages, but helped to confirm and deepen the divisions, thus establishing a pattern of government and politics which eventually ended in violence.

Such a view of government in Northern Ireland means that the present study also lends support to those approaches to the Northern Ireland problem which either emphasise the importance or explain the significance of divisions within the Unionist Party. Thus recent sophisticated Marxist analyses have abandoned a crude two-class model and have instead tried to unravel the divergent economic interests of different groups within the working class and the bourgeoisie.[2] Such an emphasis on intra-Protestant divisions does much to explain both why no Protestant leader has been able to deliver the support of his community for a settlement and why, as a consequence, the present crisis is proving so intractable. It may be, too, that the existence of divisions within the Protestant community helps to explain the peculiar irrationality and intensity of conflict in Northern Ireland. The pity is that the social/psychological approach has been little used in conflict studies there. What limited studies have been carried out show that Protestants feel more embittered than Catholics, when objectively the reverse should be the case.[3] Such findings are likely to be explained only by the application of social/psychological theory to the workings of the Protestant community. As Dr Whyte has remarked, 'It is because Protestant distrusts Protestant, not just because Protestant distrusts Catholic, that the Ulster conflict is so intense'.[4]

This study of Northern Ireland's experience of devolved government in the inter-war years can also contribute to the current debate on devolution in the United Kingdom. In the first place, it provides a cogent argument in favour of administrative devolution. The positive benefits Northern Ireland derived from the existence of a regional government were due largely to the activities of civil servants, especially those attached to the Ministry of Agriculture. In the second place, it does offer, as Dr Boyce has argued,[5] a cautionary tale to advocates of parliamentary devolution. Undoubtedly the main original aim of the imperial government was achieved, at least for fifty years, as the storm-centre of Irish politics moved away from Westminster. In addition, parliamentary devolution entailed a degree of accessibility and responsiveness in government that had been impossible under the Union. The trouble was that these benefits, such as they were, were purchased at a price – the triumph of parochialism and partisanship.

It could be objected that such parochialism and partisanship were the result of particular circumstances in Northern Ireland. Northern Ireland's experience of regional government has been, in some respects, unique. The new regional government was set up in peculiar circumstances, with Westminster insisting that a part of the United Kingdom should accept a form of government which it did not want and which, in the event, applied only to the six counties. Moreover, the new government had to operate in the inauspicious conditions of an ailing economy, an irridentist Southern neighbour, and a political culture distinguished by an intense localism and sectarianism which required that government decisions should be wrapped up in emotive and divisive language. In Britain high-minded public rhetoric may have been used to dress up ignoble and partisan or simply routine decisions. In Northern Ireland, where there was often a similar gap between private intentions and public rhetoric, the latter often took a base form in order to reconcile the hardline faithful to unpalatable but rational and neutral policy and administrative decisions.

Nevertheless, despite these peculiarities, Norther Ireland's experience of parliamentary devolution in the inter-war years cannot be entirely without relevance to the broader question. Parochialism and amateurism are features of the politics and government of many small states and most local authorities even in highly developed societies, while the tensions between a regional authority and the other tiers of government are an inescapable consequence of any devolved or federal system of government. In these respects, therefore, Northern Ireland's experience in the inter-war years is a poor advertisement for parliamentary devolution and a conclusive argument against the form of devolution adopted in 1920.

It may be that some of the deficiencies of government would have been avoided had greater powers of economic management been bestowed upon the regional government and parliament, and had more attention been paid in 1920 to the appropriateness of the political institutions it was proposed should operate or continue to operate in Northern Ireland. The British version of devolution consisted merely of slipping in a new tier of government between the existing central and local authorities, with inadequate appreciation of the role of the new regional parliament and government. In the debates on federalism in the early twentieth century attention was concentrated almost exclusively upon what should be the proper constitutional relationship between Westminster and any regional government. Little or no thought was given to such important questions as the new authority's relations with existing local authorities and how far it should assume the latters' functions.

What is certain, however, is that devolved government in Northern Ireland proved incapable of reconciling regional development with the essential unity of the United Kingdom. It is true that the formal constitutional relationship established by the 1920 act persisted for half a century. Relations between the Northern Ireland and imperial authorities were fraught with potentially grave and disruptive difficulties. Yet a crisis arising from the different Northern Ireland and imperial perspectives was avoided, partly because of the accommodating attitude adopted by Craig and certain of his ministers and civil servants, and partly because of the imperial government's unwillingness to become directly involved in Northern Ireland affairs. Constitutional unity was not, however, matched by a broader and more fundamental unity – a uniformity of treatment in respect of standards of living and citizens' rights. Services, such as education, housing and maternal and child welfare, were of a lower standard in Northern Ireland than in the rest of the United Kingdom, while the nature of the minority question in Northern Ireland underlined not only the failure of the 1920 settlement to secure equality of justice within the United Kingdom, but also the hollowness of the reservation of sovereign power to the central authority. Westminster may have had the moral and legal responsibility for seeing that justice was done by the Northern Ireland government and parliament, but it did not have the effective political power to enforce it in face of the Unionist government's large built-in majority and the lack of an alternative administration.

It may be that other regions in the United Kingdom would be blessed with two or more parties seriously contending for power, thus facilitating a meaningful dialogue between Westminster and the regions. Equally, however, it may be that regional administrations in other parts of the United Kingdom would be less tolerant than the Unionist administration in Northern Ireland of any limitations on their power. Since the latter is more probable than the former, the experience of devolved government in Northern Ireland in the inter-war years does suggest that nineteenth-century opponents of Irish Home Rule were right after all. Parliamentary devolution cannot be a permanent settlement of the political and constitutional problems of the United Kingdom. There really is no half-way house between union and complete separation.

References

The following abbreviations are used in the references.

AC	Austen Chamberlain papers

P.R.O.	Public Record Office, London
CAB	Cabinet papers
CO	Colonial Office papers
HO	Home Office papers
T	Treasury papers

P.R.O.N.I.	Public Record Office of Northern Ireland
CAB	Cabinet papers
COM	Ministry of Commerce papers
D	Document
FIN	Ministry of Finance papers
HA	Ministry of Home Affairs papers
PM	Prime Minister's papers
T	Transcript

Notes

Introduction
THE TROUBLE WITH PARTITION
(pp. 1–6)
1. Sir Wilfrid Spender, Financial Diary (hereafter cited as Fin. Diary), Nov. 1939–4 May 1940, p. 84, P.R.O.N.I., D715.
2. Parliamentary Debates (Commons), i, 23 Jun. 1921, cols 36–7 (hereafter cited as Parl. Deb. (C)).
3. There is no detailed treatment of the processes of devolved government in Northern Ireland in the inter-war years. N. Mansergh, The Government of Northern Ireland: A Study in Devolution (London 1936) is largely a description of the institutions of government rather than their interaction, but makes some useful comments on the theory and practice of devolution. R.J.Lawrence, The Government of Northern Ireland: Public Finance and Public Services, 1921–1964 (Oxford 1965) provides an introduction to the complexities of Northern Ireland finances and a useful summary of the achievements or otherwise of Northern Ireland's experience of devolved government in the inter-war years. Commentaries by contemporaries or near contemporaries also tend to concentrate on general appraisals rather than processes: D. G. O'Neill (ed.), Devolution of Government: The Experiment in Northern Ireland (London 1953) includes some contributions by civil servants; G. C. Duggan, a former Comptroller and Auditor-General who was a senior Ministry of Finance official in the inter-war years, contributed a series of unflattering articles entitled 'Northern Ireland – Success or Failure?' in the Irish Times, Apr. 1950; and H. Harrison, Ulster and the British Empire, 1939: Help or Hindrance? (London 1939) is an Irish Nationalist's denunciation of partition and devolution as it operated before the Second World War.

Nor is there a satisfactory history of Northern Ireland between 1921 and 1939 – or subsequently. F. S. L. Lyons, Ireland since the Famine (rev. ed., London 1973) provides a scholarly introduction and is more satisfactory though less easy to read than M. Wallace, Northern Ireland: 50 Years of Self-Government (Newton

Abbot 1971). A Unionist viewpoint is presented in two biographies of Craig: St John Ervine, *Craigavon, Ulsterman* (London 1949), the official biography, and H. Shearman, *Not an Inch: A Study of Northern Ireland and Lord Craigavon* (London 1942). A Nationalist leader and M.P., T. J. Campbell, has left a few impressions and anecdotes in his *Fifty Years of Ulster, 1890–1940* (Belfast 1941), while M. Farrell, *Northern Ireland: the Orange State* (London 1976), a tirade against the North written from 'an anti-imperialist and socialist standpoint', does produce in pp. 36–149 some useful information on Labour and nationalist politics between 1921 and 1939.

The best general survey of the problems facing Northern Ireland in the twentieth century is the collection of essays edited by T. Wilson, *Ulster under Home Rule: A Study of the Political and Economic Problems of Northern Ireland* (London 1955), while the North's economic problems are brilliantly highlighted in J. R. Parkinson, 'Is Northern Ireland Viable?', the duplicated typescript of a paper presented at the Older Industrial Areas Conference, Regional Studies Association, 1968.

4. Government of Ireland Act, 1920 (10 & 11 Geo. V, c. 7).
5. On the basis of partition and Ulster Unionism see P. Buckland, *Irish Unionism* 2: *Ulster Unionism and the Origins of Northern Ireland, 1886–1922* (Dublin/New York 1973); P. Gibbon, *The Origins of Ulster Unionism: The Formation of Popular Protestant Politics and Ideology in Nineteenth-Century Ireland* (Manchester 1975); *Report of the Irish Boundary Commission, 1925*, with an introduction by G. J. Hand (Shannon 1969); F. Wright, 'Protestant Ideology and Politics in Ulster', *European Journal of Sociology*, xiv (1973), pp. 213–80.
6. On the evolution and intentions of the 1920 act see D. G. Boyce, 'British Conservative Opinion, the Ulster Question, and the Partition of Ireland, 1912–21', *Irish Historical Studies*, xvii (1970–71), pp. 89–112, and *Englishmen and Irish Troubles: British Public Opinion and the Making of Irish Policy* (London 1972), especially pp. 103–30; R. B. McDowell, *The Irish Convention, 1917–18* (London 1970), pp. 195–210.
7. On the law of the constitution see primarily A. S. Queckett, *The Constitution of Northern Ireland*, Parts I–III (Belfast 1928–46), although H. Calvert, *Constitutional Law in Northern Ireland: A Study in Regional Government* (London/Belfast 1968) is less thorough but more widely available.
8. Lawrence, p. 61.

Chapter 1
THE REGIONAL GOVERNMENT
(pp. 9–35)
1. For the files relating to discussions of the structure and staffing of the government of Northern Ireland see P.R.O.N.I., FIN 18/1/190–2, 237.

2. Clark to Craig, 7 Feb. 1921, and enclosures, *ibid.*, FIN 18/1/190.
3. Duffin forwarded his scheme to Clark on 14 Feb. 1921, *ibid.*, FIN 18/1/192.
4. Clark to Duffin, 15 Feb. 1921, *ibid.*
5. The final scheme was sent by Clark to Craig on 26 May 1921, *ibid.*, FIN 18/1/191.
6. See, e.g., the debate on the motion to accept the report of the select committee on the remuneration of ministers, after which 11 Unionist backbenchers voted against the government, *Parl. Deb. (C)*, i, 1 Dec. 1921, cols 334–92.
7. *Ibid.*, 22 Sep. 1921, col. 145.
8. Cabinet Conclusions (hereafter cited as Cab. Conclusions), 10 Jan. 1924, P.R.O.N.I., CAB 4/98/21.
9. Farrell, p. 68. It contains useful biographical information (pp. 68, 336–49), as does J. F. Harbinson, *The Ulster Unionist Party, 1882–1973: Its Development and Organisation* (Belfast 1973), pp. 181–209.
10. Andrews to Craig, 17 Jun. 1925, P.R.O.N.I., CAB 9D/1/5.
11. See, e.g. below, pp. 132–3; and Archdale's protest to Craig and to Milne Barbour, acting Minister of Finance, 3 Nov. 1930, that agriculture was being starved of funds to finance unproductive social services, *ibid.*, CAB 9A/3/1.
12. See below, Chapter 7.
13. Notes by S. G. Tallents, the Lord Lieutenant's Private Secretary and later Imperial Secretary in Northern Ireland, on his visit to Northern Ireland (see below, p. 200), 21 Jun.–1 Jul. 1922, P.R.O., CO 906/24.
14. See, e.g., Andrews to Craig, 6 Sep. 1923, and Spender to Craig, 6,7,11 Sep. 1923, P.R.O.N.I., PM 9/7,9; C. H. Blackmore, Cabinet Secretary, to Craig, 16 Jun. 1927, *ibid.*, PM 9/17; Pollock to Rev. W. Corkey, 10 Aug. 1934, and to Craig, 16 Aug. 1934, *ibid.*, CAB 9C/47/1.
15. See below, Chapter 4.
16. Dixon to Craig, 20 Jul. 1923, P.R.O.N.I., CAB 9B/33/3; Spender to Craig, 21 Sep. 1923, *ibid.*, PM 9/7.
17. Londonderry to St Loe Strachey, 3 Jan. 1923, House of Lords Record Office, S/9/15/9.
18. Bates to Craig, 17 Aug. 1927, P.R.O.N.I., CAB 9B/45/2.
19. Lady Spender, Diary, 24–26 Jun. 1921, *ibid.*, D1633/2/24.
20. Cab. Conclusions, 25 Feb. 1925, *ibid.*, CAB 4/135/18.
21. See below, Chapter 9.
22. Londonderry to Craig, 23 Jun. 1925, P.R.O.N.I., CAB 9D/1/5.
23. On Londonderry's performance of his duties see D. H. Akenson, *Education and Enmity: The Control of Schooling in Northern Ireland, 1920–50* (Newton Abbot/New York 1973), pp. 40–2.
24. Londonderry to A. Chamberlain, 29 Nov. 1925, Birmingham University Library, AC 24/7/18.
25. Buckland, *Ulster Unionism*, pp. 44–67, 128–9.

26. Fin. Diary, Mar.–Oct. 1938, manuscript memo, 2 Aug. 1938, between pp. 122–3.
27. See below, pp. 70, 202.
28. Sir James O'Grady to Craig, *c.* 6 Jun. 1932, P.R.O.N.I., CAB 9B/201/1.
29. Record of conference of interested parties, 6 Nov. 1931, *ibid.,* CAB 9E/111/1.
30. See, e.g., his refusal to listen to criticisms of Bates's handling of law and order in 1922 (Lady Spender, Diary, 2 Mar. 1922, *ibid.,* D1633/2/26; Tallents to Sir J. Masterton-Smith, Permanent Secretary, Colonial Office, 4 Jul. 1922, P.R.O., CO 906/30).
31. See, e.g., the toleration of anomalies in the administration of the Road Fund, Fin. Diary, 1932–33, p. 25.
32. See, e.g., below, pp. 167–8, 173
33. *Mid-Ulster Mail,* 19 Feb. 1927.
34. G. A. Harris, Permanent Secretary, Ministry of Home Affairs, to Blackmore, 2 Jan. 1928, P.R.O.N.I., CAB 9B/136.
35. Synopsis of tour, Feb. 1927, *ibid.*
36. *Mid-Ulster Mail,* 19 Feb. 1927.
37. See below, pp. 119–21.
38. See below, p. 23.
39. Fin. Diary, 1933–34, 9 Jun. 1933 (no pagination).
40. See below, p. 72.
41. See below, pp. 64–5, 72.
42. Fin. Diary, 1 Jan.–30 Nov. 1934, p. 46; 1 Jan. 1937–2 Mar. 1938, pp. 26, 182–3; Mar.–Oct. 1938, p. 38 (memo on the Anglo-Eire negotiations dated 20 Apr. 1938 and marked: 'The Secretary has directed that this note should not be placed on the file.').
43. *Ibid.,* manuscript note between pp. 122–3.
44. *Ulster Year Book, 1932* (Belfast 1932), p. 257; *Ulster Year Book, 1938* (Belfast 1938), p. 310.
45. On the early recruitment of the civil service see the relevant Ministry of Finance files (P.R.O.N.I., FIN 18/1/237, 270, 272, 595) and the minutes of the Selection Board (*ibid.,* CAB 9A/10).
46. S. Watt, Permanent Secretary, Ministry of Home Affairs, to Spender, 18 Jan. 1924, *ibid.,* CAB 9A/90/1.
47. *Ibid.*
48. According to Spender, such appointments 'have proved a handicap to our Service and now constitute rather a problem' (to Londonderry, 30 May 1938, Fin. Diary, Mar.–Oct. 1938, pp. 77–8). Clark shared this disquiet (to Spender, 6, 14 Jan. 1936, *ibid.,* Sep. 1935–Mar. 1936, pp. 191–4).
49. R. E. Thornley, chairman of the Selection Board, to Spender, 18 Jan. 1924, P.R.O.N.I., CAB 9A/90/1.
50. Watt to Spender, 21 Jan. 1924, *ibid.*
51. F. C. Moore to St Loe Strachey, 2 Aug. 1922, House of Lords Record Office, S/21/4/9.

52. Watt to Spender, 18 Jan. 1924, P.R.O.N.I., CAB 9A/90/1.
53. *Ibid.*, CAB 9A/90/2; Fin. Diary, 15 Feb.–16 May 1943, pp. 120–1, 151, 166.
54. Spender to Blackmore, 8 Nov. 1934, P.R.O.N.I., CAB 9A/90/1; Fin. Diary, Sep. 1935–Mar. 1936, p. 95.
55. Note on the religious composition of the R.U.C., 8 Jul. 1936, and C. Wickham, Inspector-General of the force, to Watt, 6 Mar. 1924, P.R.O.N.I., CAB 9A/90/1,2.
56. Fin. Diary, Sep. 1935–Mar. 1936, p. 95.
57. Note on general matters arising out of the 1920 act for Clark's interview with Craig, 6 Apr. 1921, P.R.O.N.I., FIN 18/1/237.
58. Cab. Conclusions, 4 Aug. 1921, *ibid.*, CAB 4/12/6.
59. Thornley to Spender, 18 Jan. 1924, *ibid.*, CAB 9A/90/1.
60. *Ulster Year Book, 1932*, pp. 256–7; Cab. Conclusions and supporting papers, 25 Feb., 29 Jul., 1 Dec. 1926, P.R.O.N.I., CAB 4/162/43, 4/173/31, 4/182/25,26.
61. *Interim Report of the Departmental Committee of Inquiry on Police Organisation in Northern Ireland*, 1922, Cmd 1, p. 5.
62. *Ibid.*, pp. 5, 9, 10; *Parl. Deb. (C)*, ii, 5 Apr. 1922, cols 361, 366–7.
63. Wickham to Watt, 6 Mar. 1924, P.R.O.N.I., CAB 9A/90/1.
64. Watt to Spender, 18 Jan. 1924, *ibid.*
65. Bates to Blackmore, 14 Aug. 1934, and Blackmore to Bates, 17 Aug. 1934, *ibid.*
66. Spender to Sir R. Lynn, 23 Dec. 1935, Fin. Diary, Sep. 1935–Mar. 1936, p. 127.
67. Spender to R. Gransden, Assistant Cabinet Secretary, 28 Sep. 1940, P.R.O.N.I., CAB 9A/90/2; Fin. Diary, 6 May–12 Oct. 1940, p. 189. The Orange Order wished to be consulted before a successor was appointed. Although Andrews, then Minister of Finance, said that the appointment would be made independently of the Order, he felt that he had at least to listen to what the Orangemen had to say. Spender protested that 'If we were to countenance any pressure of this kind it would undermine the confidence of the whole Civil Service.' Spender recorded in his diary that 'If the Minister asked me to attend the meeting I would certainly express very strong views on the subject and shall inform them that I gave up my career in the British Army because of my fear that if Home Rule were introduced in Ireland Tammany methods, of which this would be a typical example, might spread to the United Kingdom.' (*Ibid.*, pp. 193–4.)
68. Wickham to Watt, 6 Mar. 1924, P.R.O.N.I., CAB 9A/90/1.
69. Spender to Watt, 24 Mar. 1924, *ibid.*
70. Spender to Blackmore, 8 Nov. 1934, *ibid.*
71. See below, Chapter 6.
72. Lady Spender (his wife), Diary, 5 Feb., 26 Mar., 4 Aug. 1921, P.R.O.N.I., D1633/2/24.
73. See below, p. 127.
74. Spender to S. D. Waley, Principal Assistant Secretary at the Treasury, 12 Jan. 1939, P.R.O. T 160/1138/15586/1.

75. Andrews to Craig, 27 July 1928, P.R.O.N.I., PM 9/21.
76. Lady Spender, Diary, 29 Jan., 5 Feb., 1 Apr. 1922, *ibid.*, D1633/ 2/26.
77. See below, p. 193.
78. See especially the internal minutes and correspondence for 1924– 25 in the Ministry of Home Affairs file on the proclamation of bank holidays, 1924–33, P.R.O.N.I., HA 8/266.
79. See below, Chapter 11.
80. *Parliamentary Debates (Senate),* xviii, 5 Mar. 1936, cols 99–103 (hereafter cited as *Parl. Deb. (S)).* The book in question was D. C. Somervell, *Bell's Modern School Histories,* Vol. III: *1832–1931* (London 1932).
81. Notes on conference at Treasury, 8 May 1933, Fin. Diary, 1933–34.
82. *Ibid.,* 1 Jan.–30 Nov. 1934, p. 237.
83. Mansergh, pp. 125–68; P. F. Magill, 'The Senate in Northern Ireland, 1921–62' (Ph.D. thesis, Queen's University, Belfast, 1965).
84. *Parl. Deb. (C),* xiv, 11 May 1932, col. 1339.
85. *Ibid.,* xxi, 26 Apr. 1938, cols 719, 720.
86. Mansergh, p. 161.
87. See below, Chapter 11.
88. See below, pp. 137–9.
89. Cab. Conclusions, 19 Aug. 1929, P.R.O.N.I., CAB 4/236/19.
90. Cab. Conclusions, 2 Oct. 1930, *ibid.*, CAB 4/269/18.
91. Cab. Conclusions, 11 Oct. 1938, *ibid.*, CAB 4/402/24; file on marketing system and tolls, *ibid.*, CAB 9B/204.
92. *Parl. Deb. (C),* iv, 14 May 1924, cols 892–3; Cab. Conclusions, 19 May 1924, P.R.O.N.I., CAB 4/115/12.
93. Fin. Diary, 1933–34, 10–17 Oct. 1933; *Parl. Deb. (C),* xv, 17 Oct. 1933, cols 2330–44.
94. *Ibid.,* xix, 9–11 Mar. 1937, cols 177–514; Fin. Diary, 1 Jan. 1937–2 Mar. 1938, pp. 50, 67–8.
95. S. Elliott, *Northern Ireland Parliamentary Election Results, 1921–1972* (Chichester 1973), p. 96, and 'The Electoral System in Northern Ireland since 1920' (Ph.D. thesis, Queen's University, Belfast, 1971), especially pp. 153–76, 211, 285–304, 347–61, 448–52, 481–502.
96. Political Science Department, Queen's University, Belfast, unpublished survey of 'Intra-Unionist Disputes in the Northern Ireland House of Commons, 1921–72', pp. 1–3. I am most grateful to Dr John Whyte for allowing me to consult the results of this research carried out in 1972 and 1973 by undergraduates taking the special subject in 'The Government of Ireland'.
97. Harbinson, *Ulster Unionist Party,* pp. 21–4, 35–96.
98. See below, pp. 223–8.
99. Elliott, *Election Results,* p. 96; Farrell, pp. 66–7, 69, 98–104, 107–20, 142–6; D. Kennedy, 'Catholics in Northern Ireland, 1926–1939', and J. L. McCracken, 'The Political Scene in Northern Ireland, 1926–1937', *The Years of the Great Test, 1926–39,* ed. F. MacManus (Cork 1967), pp. 138–49, 150–60.

100. Elliott, *Election Results*, p. 96; Farrell, pp. 27, 37, 67, 100, 103–7, 111, 114, 115–16, 119, 125, 131–2, 143, 146; J. F. Harbinson, 'A History of the Northern Ireland Labour Party, 1891–1949' (M.Sc.(Econ.) thesis. Queen's University, Belfast, 1966), especially pp. 38–104, 236–81; A. Mitchell, *Labour in Irish Politics, 1890–1930: The Irish Labour Movement in an Age of Revolution* (Dublin 1974), pp. 18, 20, 73, 124–7, 130–2, 220–2.
101. Elliott, *Election Results*, pp. 96, 99, and 'Electoral System', pp. 48, 162, 291–5, 299, 301, 347, 348, 352–3, 357–9, 478–9, 488–500; Harbinson, *Ulster Unionist Party*, pp. 211–16.
102. *Ibid.*, p. 212.
103. *Ibid.*, pp. 219–22.
104. See below, pp. 235–6.
105. Farrell, pp. 69, 112; Harbinson, *Ulster Unionist Party*, pp. 107–13, 122–8; Mansergh, pp. 163–5.
106. *Parl. Deb. (C)*, xxii, 9 May 1939, col. 1373.
107. *Ibid.*, x, 25 Mar. 1929, col. 1310.
108. *Ibid.*, xviii, 28 Apr. 1936, col. 1122.
109. See below, pp. 168–71.
110. *Parl. Deb (C)*, xviii, 29 Apr. 1936, cols 1123–4.
111. See, e.g., her persuading the Prime Minister to relieve her constituents of drainage charges (Fin. Diary, 1933–34, 24–30 Nov. 1933), and the change wrought by a deputation of local agriculturalists in her attitude to the 1935 Road and Railway Transport Bill *(Parl. Deb. (C)*, xvii, 16, 28 May 1935, cols 1741, 1949, 1951).
112. Buckland, *Ulster Unionism*, pp. 136–43; Harbinson, *Ulster Unionist Party*, pp. 36, 58, 67–9, 70, 139.
113. Farrell, pp. 111–14, 115–16.
114. *Ibid.*, p. 116.
115. Political Science Department, Belfast, 'Intra-Unionist Disputes', p. 2.
116. *Parl. Deb. (C)*, xiv, 8 Mar. 1932, col. 44.
117. See below, p. 219.
118. See below, pp. 103, 262.
119. Elliott, 'Electoral System', pp. 155–7, 158–9, 286–7, 288–9, 308–13, 330–1, 448–52, 457–70, 481, 487–90, 504–5, 507–8; Farrell, pp. 118–20, 144–5.
120. See below, pp. 69–70, 72–3.
121. See below, pp. 170–1.
122. *Parl. Deb. (C)*, ii, 4 Apr. 1922, cols 343–6.
123. Typescript extracts from Lady Craig's Diary, 4 Apr. 1922, P.R.N.O.I., D1415/B/38.

Chapter 2
THE OTHER TIERS OF GOVERNMENT
(pp. 36–50)

1. Elliott, 'Electoral System', p. 371; *Ulster Year Book, 1938*, pp. 121–3, 316–19.

2. *Report of the Committee on the Financial Relations between the State and Local Authorities,* 1931, Cmd 131 (hereafter cited as *Financial Relations Report),* p. 22.
3. *Ibid.,* pp. 37—8.
4. Note on rates position, 11 Mar. 1931, P.R.O.N.I., CAB 9A/3/2.
5. *Ibid.*
6. Elliott, 'Electoral System', p. 435. For illustrations of politics and patronage among local authorities see D. P. Barritt and C. F. Carter, *The Northern Ireland Problem: A Study in Group Relations* (2nd ed., London 1972), pp. 97—100; I. Budge and C. O'Leary, *Belfast: Approach to Crisis: A Study of Belfast Politics, 1603—1970* (London 1973), pp. 14—156; P. Livingstone, *The Fermanagh Story: A Documented History of County Fermanagh from the Earliest Times to the Present Day* (Enniskillen 1969), pp. 267—8, 296—7, 311—15, 322—3, 367—74.
7. *Report of the Departmental Commission on Local Government Administration in Northern Ireland,* 1927, Cmd 73 (hereafter cited as *Local Government Report).*
8. Lawrence, p. 128.
9. The words were used by Alderman J. A. Duff, the Unionist chairman of the finance committee, when dismissing a Labour proposal that the Corporation should continue distress relief schemes without government assistance (*Northern Whig,* 2 Dec. 1933).
10. *Financial Relations Report,* p. 34.
11. Lawrence, p. 148.
12. *Local Government Report.*
13. *Financial Relations Report,* pp. 34, 47—9.
14. Lawrence, p. 61.
15. Fin. Diary, 1932—33, p. 1.
16. *Parl. Deb. (C),* iii, 17 Apr. 1923, cols 342—3, 345—7.
17. See below, pp. 94—5.
18. Elliott, 'Electoral System', pp. 218—25; Farrell, p. 84; the cabinet file on Donaghadee U.D.C., P.R.O.N.I., CAB 9B/161; *Parl. Deb. (C),* xxii, 16 Mar. 1939, cols 642—8.
19. Craig to R. D. Megaw, 5 Jun. 1924, P.R.O.N.I., CAB 9B/45/1.
20. See above, p. 27; and the representations against local government reform made by rural district councils, P.R.O.N.I., CAB 9B/40/2,6, 9B/67/1.
21. Spender to Blackmore, 30 Dec. 1927, *ibid.,* CAB 9B/136.
22. Spender to Blackmore, 1, 6 Apr. 1926, *ibid.,* CAB 9B/45/2. For the details of the scandal see Budge and O'Leary, pp. 145—7.
23. Fin. Diary, 1 Dec. 1934—31 Aug. 1935, pp. 46—7. For details of the inquiry and fraud see *Report of the Inquiry concerning the Architect's Department of Down County Regional Education Committee* (Belfast 1935).
24. Fin. Diary, 1 Dec. 1934—31 Aug. 1935, pp. 46—7.
25. See below, p. 101.
26. Synopsis of tour, 28 Feb. 1927, p. 25, P.R.O.N.I., CAB 9B/136;

Cab. Conclusions, 1 Mar. 1927, *ibid.*, CAB 4/187/36; cabinet file relating to the Bangor and Portstewart harbour schemes, *ibid.*, CAB 9F/89/1; correspondence between Blackmore and Craig, 26, 28 Jul. 1927, *ibid.*, PM 9/17,18.

27. Rev. W. O. Uprichard to Craig, 9 May 1928, *ibid.*, CAB 9F/89/1.
28. Cabinet file on the project, *ibid.*, CAB 9F/28/1; *Parl. Deb. (C)*, iv, 26 Mar. 1924, cols 358–61.
29. *Ibid.*, xiii, 14 May 1931, col. 1662.
30. Elliott, 'Electoral System', pp. 181–90, 191–6, 199–210, 362–9, 901–2; Harbinson, *Ulster Unionist Party*, pp. 97–106.
31. See, e.g., Spender's advice to D. D. Reid, the chairman of the Ulster Unionist Party at Westminster, 6 Feb. 1936, on how Northern Ireland should react to the exclusion of Harland & Wolff from the list of firms asked to tender for the second 'queen', *Queen Elizabeth*, P.R.O.N.I., CAB 9A/61/2.
32. Elliott, 'Electoral System', pp. 181–90, 191–6, 199–210, 362–9, 901–2; Farrell, pp. 99–100, 116, 145; Harbinson, *Ulster Unionist Party*, p. 97.
33. R. P. Pim, Assistant Secretary, Ministry of Home Affairs, to Gransden, 12 Oct. 1937, P.R.O.N.I., CAB 9B/205/1.
34. See below, p. 117.
35. See, e.g., below, pp. 210–11.
36. See below, p. 94.
37. See below, pp. 92, 94.
38. See, e.g., Cab. Conclusions, 1 Nov. 1929, P.R.O.N.I., CAB 4/239/24; Pim to Gransden, 12 Oct. 1937, *ibid.*, CAB 9B/205/1.
39. See, e.g., the account of one of his meetings with Lloyd George in typescript extracts from Lady Craig's Diary, 7 Nov. 1921, *ibid.*, D1415/B/38.
40. Craig to Pollock, 31 May 1926, *ibid.*, PM 9/16.
41. Notes by Clark and Pollock of the latter's interviews with Snowden and Thomas, 12 Apr. 1924, *ibid.*, CAB 4/109/1,2,3.
42. J. S. Gordon, Permanent Secretary, Ministry of Agriculture, to Blackmore, 12 Nov. 1928, *ibid.*, CAB 9E/57/1.
43. See below, pp. 86–7, 90, 95–6.
44. Joint submission to the Joint Exchequer Board by the Treasury and Ministry of Finance on the attribution of new import duties, 5 Jul. 1932, P.R.O.N.I., FIN 26/1/9. The Permanent Secretary of the Ministry of Commerce, W. D. Scott, also stressed the need for maintaining close and harmonious relations with imperial civil servants (to Blackmore, 5 Mar. 1932, *ibid.*, CAB 9F/67/2).
45. J. H. Richardson, *British Economic Foreign Policy* (London 1936), *passim.*
46. See below, pp. 110–16.
47. On these different perspectives see, e.g., Boyce, 'British Conservative Opinion', pp. 103–12; Buckland, *Ulster Unionism*, pp. 149–50; T. Jones, *Whitehall Diary*, Vol. III: *Ireland, 1918–1925*, ed. K. Middlemas (London 1971), pp. 90–2, 104–6, 110–

11, 127–32, 134–7, 146–8, 152–74, 180–3, 186–7, 189–91, 194–8, 202–4, 207–8, 209–12.
48. See below, Chapter 4.
49. Cab. Conclusions, 19 Nov. 1930, P.R.O.N.I., CAB 4/273/32.
50. Cab. Conclusions, 5 May 1924, *ibid.*, CAB 4/112/12.
51. Cab. Conclusions, 30 Mar. 1927, *ibid.*, CAB 4/189/23.
52. See below, pp. 106–7.
53. See below, pp. 77, 139–40.
54. See below, pp. p. 108.
55. See below, pp. 76–7, 101–2, 243–6.
56. See below, Chapter 12.
57. See below, p. 106.
58. See, e.g., Andrews's dismay at a letter sent out on official U.U.C. notepaper on the so-called peaceful Catholic penetration of Northern Ireland, thought by the Chief Whip to be excellent elect electioneering propaganda (Spender to Craig, 6, 11 Sep. 1923, P.R.O.N.I., PM 9/7).
59. See below, pp. 274–5.
60. See below, pp. 261–2, 267.
61. Pollock's memo on the proposed extension of the Loans Guarantee Acts, 9 Sep. 1926, P.R.O.N.I., CAB 4/176/15.
62. See below, Chapter 7.
63. See below, especially pp. 103, 157.
64. See below, p. 273.
65. See below, pp. 210–11.
66. See below, pp. 98–102.

Chapter 3
FURTHER CONSTRAINTS
(pp. 51–77)
1. K. S. Isles and N. Cuthbert, 'Ulster's Economic Structure', *Ulster under Home Rule,* ed. Wilson, p. 91. This and a second essay in the same volume ('Economic Policy') virtually summarise the authors' massive *An Economic Survey of Northern Ireland* (Belfast 1957), which, despite its concentration on the period since the Second World War, remains the only substantial discussion of Northern Ireland's economic and industrial problems and policies in the inter-war years. Agriculture is even less well served by published secondary works, but some useful information is collected in S. Greenlees, 'The Structure and Development of Agriculture in Ulster 1900–1939' (M.Phil. thesis, New University of Ulster, 1976).
2. Based on figures in Isles and Cuthbert, *Economic Survey,* p. 95 n. 1.
3. *Ulster Year Book, 1938,* pp. 162–3.
4. Pollock's memo on Loans Guarantee Acts, 9 Sep. 1926, P.R.O.N.I., CAB 4/176/15; *Parl. Deb. (C),* xvii, 27 Mar. 1935, col. 1084.
5. *Ibid.,* xviii, 5 May 1936, col. 1311.

6. Isles and Cuthbert, *Economic Survey*, p. 53.
7. *Ulster Year Book, 1932*, p. 66.
8. On the challenge faced by United Kingdom agriculture and shipbuilding see, e.g., British Association for the Advancement of Science, *Britain in Depression: A Record of British Industries since 1929* (London 1935), pp. 81–151, 233–58; and for a discussion of some of the problems of Northern Ireland's linen industry see Isles and Cuthbert, *Economic Survey*, pp. 519–62.
9. Unemployment statistics prepared by the Ministry of Labour for a meeting between ministers and a deputation from the County Grand Lodge of Belfast on unemployment, Nov. 1938, P.R.O.N.I., CAB 9C/13/2.
10. *Ibid.;* 'Report of the Committee Appointed [by the trade] to Investigate the Principal Causes of the Depression in the Irish Linen Industry', 31 Aug. 1928, pp. 4–5, *ibid.*, COM 27/1.
11. Unemployment statistics, Nov. 1938, *ibid.*, CAB 9C/13/2; Fin. Diary, Mar.–Oct. 1938, p. 23.
12. Farrell, pp. 121–32, for the best published description of events. Relying on polemical speeches, Mr Farrell underestimates both the concern and impotence of the regional governmnt.
13. Isles and Cuthbert, *Economic Survey*, pp. 115–16.
14. *Parl. Deb. (C)*, xxii, 10 May 1939, col. 1427.
15. Confidential memo on board policy by the secretary of the Pigs Marketing Board, 22 Jun. 1936, pp. 7–13, P.R.O.N.I., CAB 9E/97/1.
16. 'Report of the Committee . . . to Investigate the Principal Causes of Depression in the Irish Linen Industry', 31 Aug. 1928, pp. 15–16, 18A–20, *ibid.*, COM 27/1.
17. Isles and Cuthbert, *Economic Survey*, pp. 45–51, 130–53.
18. *Ibid.*, p. 145.
19. The following comparisons are based largely on material contained in various *Ulster Year Books, 1926–38* and a joint publication by the English Ministry of Agriculture and the Department of Agriculture and Fisheries for Scotland, *A Century of Agricultural Statistics: Great Britain, 1866–1966* (London 1968).
20. D. E. L. Thomas, 'Farm Types and Farm Incomes', *Land Use in Northern Ireland*, ed. L. Symons (London 1963), pp. 162–3.
21. P. J. O'Hara, 'Financial Returns for the Seven Years 1930–1937 on Eleven Farms in Northern Ireland', *Journal of the Ministry of Agriculture, Northern Ireland*, vi (1938), pp. 20–1.
22. *Ibid.*, pp. 13–21; J. Glynne Williams, 'An Economic Survey of Small Holdings in Northern Ireland', *ibid.*, iii (1931), pp. 62–82. The results of these surveys are conveniently summarised in J. Mogey, *Rural Life in Northern Ireland* (London 1947), pp. 21–2, and Greenlees, pp. 430–46.
23. See below, Chapter 6.
24. Record of representative conference on the bacon industry held at Stormont Castle, 21 Mar. 1932, P.R.O.N.I., CAB 9E/97/7.

25. Thomas, p. 163.
26. *Reports of the Agricultural Enquiry Committee*, 1947, Cmd 249, p. 212.
27. Greenlees, pp. 297–311, 334–5.
28. *Ibid.*, pp. 271–2.
29. *Ibid.*, p. 94.
30. *Parl. Deb. (C)*, ii, 25 May 1922, col. 677.
31. *Ibid.*, vii, 12 Oct. 1926, col. 1567.
32. J. Meenan, *The Irish Economy since 1922* (Liverpool 1970), pp. 91–2; *Commission on the Natural and Industrial Resources of Northern Ireland. Report on the Northern Ireland Egg Industry*, 1924, Cmd 27.
33. Isles and Cuthbert, *Economic Survey*, p. 457.
34. *Ibid.*, p. 315.
35. *Ibid.*, p. 334.
36. *Ibid.*, pp. 338–9.
37. Lawrence, p. 61.
38. See below, Chapter 10.
39. See below, pp. 249–50, 261–5.
40. See below, p. 173.
41. See below, Chapter 11.
42. On the role of the Orange Order in politics and society see Buckland, *Ulster Unionism*, pp. 2–5, 6, 9, 18–19, 21, 49, 56, 138; M. W. Dewar, J. Brown and S. E. Long, *Orangeism: A New Historical Appreciation, 1688–1967* (Belfast 1967), *passim;* Gibbon, *passim;* Harbinson, *Ulster Unionist Party*, pp. 86–96; R. Harris, *Prejudice and Tolerance in Ulster: A Study of Neighbours and 'Strangers' in a Border Community* (Manchester 1972), *passim.*
43. Lyons, p. 720.
44. See the protest to Craig by Sir Joseph Davison, Belfast's Grand Master, 11 Jan. 1933, and Craig to Davison, 12 Jan. 1933, P.R.O.N.I., PM 6/22.
45. See the thorough preparations for the meeting between ministers and Belfast Orangemen in November 1938 to discuss unemployment, *ibid.*, CAB 9C/13/2.
46. Lynn to Spender, 30 Dec. 1935, Fin. Diary, Sep. 1935–Mar. 1936, p. 128.
47. Bates to Craig, 23 Oct. 1922, P.R.O.N.I., CAB 9B/18. This file and additional correspondence between the cabinet secretariat, Megaw and Craig at the beginning of September in 1922 and 1923 (*ibid.*, PM 9/2,3) provide a sad commentary on the government's toleration of Protestant extremism and the independence exercised by departmental heads.
48. *Ibid.*; Cab. Conclusions, 16, 29 Feb., 7, 20 Mar. 1924, *ibid.*, CAB 4/100/29, 4/102/14, 4/104/15, 4/106/11.
49. Harbinson, *Ulster Unionist Party*, p. 216.
50. *Ibid.*, pp. 216–19; see below, pp. 258–61.
51. For a list of associations etc. see *Belfast and Ulster Directories.*

On the role and value of the Reform Club see, e.g., Spender to Craig, 31 Aug., 24 Sep. 1923, P.R.O.N.I., PM 9/7.
52. Isles and Cuthbert, *Economic Survey*, p. 211.
53. Harbinson, 'Northern Ireland Labour Party', *passim;* and see, e.g., the resolutions sent by labour organisations to ministers on pensions in 1924 (P.R.O.N.I., CAB 9B/22), on unemployment insurance in 1925 (*ibid.*, CAB 9C/1/2) and on health insurance in 1929 (*ibid.*, CAB 9C/15).
54. For Andrews's view on the futility of this conference see his suggestion in Nov. 1930 (*ibid.*, CAB 9C/13/1) that in his speech at the annual dinner of the Lisburn Chamber of Commerce Craig should reply to the *Northern Whig's* criticisms of the government's unemployment policy and its calls for an unemployment conference.
55. *Ibid.*
56. See above, p. 31, and below, pp. 72, 173; the cabinet secretariat's and Ministry of Home Affairs's dealings with Stewart in Jun. and Jul. 1933, P.R.O.N.I., CAB 9B/89/2; Spender to Blackmore, 14 Nov. 1934, *ibid.*, CAB 9A/61/2.
57. Pollock acted with the Belfast Chamber of Commerce to put pressure on Craig to agree to a city office for the Ministry of Commerce (Blackmore to Craig, 28 Jul., 11, 17 Aug. 1922, *ibid.*, PM 9/3; Cab. Conclusions, 12 Sep. 1922, 27 Apr. 1923, *ibid.*, CAB 4/52/18, 4/79/13).
58. See, e.g., below, pp. 66, 120–1.
59. Typescript extracts from Lady Craig's Diary, 2 Apr. 1922, P.R.O.N.I., D1415/B/38; Craig to Davison, 12 Jan. 1933, *ibid.*, PM 6/22.
60. Andrews to Craig, 2 Feb. 1923, *ibid.*, CAB 9C/4/1.
61. There is no history of the Ulster Farmers' Union, but its views and activities are chronicled in its organ, *Farmers' Journal,* a monthly publication with a circulation of 6,500 in 1934 and 7,200 in 1939.
62. See below, p. 66.
63. Greenlees, pp. 297–311, 334–5.
64. See, e.g., below, p. 132; and protests against black scab regulations, P.R.O.N.I., CAB 9E/41/1.
65. Spender to H. B. Thompson, a native of Newry and Canadian Food Controller in the First World War, 10 Dec. 1924, *ibid.*, CAB 9E/23/1.
66. See below, pp. 138–9.
67. Cab. Conclusions, 19 Nov. 1930, P.R.O.N.I., CAB 4/273/32.
68. *Ibid.*, CAB 9E/97/7.
69. See below, pp. 167, 173.
70. Report of Pollock's and Andrews's meeting with W. Strachan, the managing director of Workman, Clark & Co., 1 Dec. 1930, P.R.O.N.I., CAB 9F/28/1.
71. See the cabinet files on land-purchase annuities, 1932–42, *ibid.*, CAB 9E/117/1,2.

72. See below, pp. 109–10.
73. Copy of Dixon's account, dated 5 Feb. 1925, of the meeting, P.R.O.N.I., CAB 9E/117/2.
74. See below, pp. 134, 138–9.
75. Record of conference of interested parties in the milk dispute held at Stormont Castle, 6 Nov. 1931, P.R.O.N.I., CAB 9E/111/1.
76. Memo by J. F. Gordon, Junior Minister of Labour, on Factory Bill, 21 Mar. 1938, *ibid.*, CAB 4/396/16; Cab. Conclusions, 22 Mar. 1938, *ibid.*, CAB 4/396/19.
77. See the cabinet file on the Markets and Fairs Bill, 1932–38, *ibid.*, CAB 9B/204.
78. See below, pp. 118, 122–3.
79. See below, Chapter 11.
80. See below, p. 132.
81. See below, p. 118.
82. Cab. Conclusions, 2, 23 Mar. 1939, P.R.O.N.I., CAB 4/411/18, 4/413/10.
83. On the Treaty and Boundary Commission and their implications for the border see Boyce, 'British Conservative Opinion', pp. 103–12, and *Englishmen and Irish Troubles*, pp. 142–70, 187–91; *Report of the Irish Boundary Commission, passim;* Jones, pp. 87–192, 235–46.
   For general surveys of Southern politics and Southern attitudes to partition see Lyons, pp. 471–550; J. A. Murphy, *Ireland in the Twentieth Century* (Dublin 1975), pp. 39–98. On the South's uneasy relations with the Empire see D. Harkness, *The Restless Dominion* (London 1969). More partisan surveys from opposite points of view are contained in Earl of Longford and T. P. O'Neill, *Eamon de Valera* (Arrow ed., London 1974), pp. 157–344, and D. O'Sullivan, *The Irish Free State and Its Senate: A Study in Contemporary Politics* (London 1940).
84. *Belfast News-Letter*, 30 Jun. 1922.
85. Murphy, p. 78.
86. O'Sullivan, pp. 291–4.
87. See below, pp. 110–11.
88. O'Sullivan, pp. 491–6; Lyons, pp. 518–22.
89. J. Bowyer Bell, *The Secret Army* (London 1970), pp. 99–167.
90. Andrews to N. Chamberlain, 18 Jan. 1939, P.R.O.N.I., CAB 9B/201/1.
91. Typescript extracts from Lady Craig's Diary, 5 May 1921, *ibid.*, D1415/B/38.
92. See below, pp. 203, 204–5.
93. Londonderry to Craig, 2 Feb. 1933, P.R.O.N.I., CAB 9B/201/1.
94. Pollock to Craig, 16 Jan. 1932, *ibid.*, CAB 9R/57/1.
95. *The Times*, 30 Dec. 1937; Proceedings of the [Imperial] Cabinet Committee on the Irish Situation, 14 Dec. 1937, P.R.O., CAB 27/524; Imperial Cabinet Conclusions, 22 Dec. 1937, *ibid.*, CAB 23/90.

96. Andrews to N. Chamberlain, 18 Jan. 1939, P.R.O.N.I., CAB 9B/201/1.
97. See, e.g., the cabinet files relating to the political situation in the Free State, *ibid.*, CAB 9B/201/1,2.
98. See, e.g., Charlemont to Craig, 19 Jun. 1932, and Bates to Craig, 5 Jul. 1932, *ibid.*, CAB 9B/201/1.
99. Bell, p. 155.
100. *Parl. Deb. (C)*, xvi, 24 Apr. 1934, col. 1095.
101. See, e.g., Harrison, pp. 86–7.
102. Harbinson, *Ulster Unionist Party*, pp. 219–22. Andrews thought a general election unnecessary to prove Northern Ireland's Unionism or to strengthen its position during the Anglo-Éire negotiations, but Spender argued that it would strengthen the government internally (Fin. Diary, 1 Jan. 1937–2 Mar. 1938, pp. 197–8, 207).
103. See below, pp. 203, 234, 322 n. 106.
104. See below, pp. 238–9, 249–50.
105. Farrell, pp. 118–20.
106. *Newry Telegraph*, 19 Jan. 1933.
107. For a full discussion of Southern economic policy see Meenan, *passim*, but for an excellent summary see Lyons, pp. 599–624.
108. *Ibid.*, pp. 511–17, 610-14.
109. See the complaints of Northern Ireland's bakers in 1926, P.R.O.N.I., CAB 9R/57/1.
110. Scott to Blackmore, 6 Jan. 1926, *ibid.*
111. See, e.g., the creameries' complaints and the Northern Ireland government's representations to the imperial government in April and May 1933, *ibid.*, CAB 9R/57/2.
112. See, e.g, Scott to Spender, 6 Nov. 1926, and the complaints of a millers' deputation to the Ministry of Agriculture, 6 Jun. 1933, *ibid.*, CAB 9R/57/1,2.
113. Memo on likely effects on Northern Ireland industry and agriculture of draft trade agreement, 15 Feb. 1938, *ibid.*, CAB 9R/60/1.
114. D. S. Johnson, 'The Economic History of Ireland between the Wars', *Irish Economic and Social History*, i (1974), pp. 51–3.
115. See below, pp. 141–2.
116. Scott to Blackmore, 6 Jan. 1926, P.R.O.N.I., CAB 9R/57/1.
117. Report of representations made to the Ministry of Agriculture by a deputation from the Northern Ireland Maize Millers' Association and Flour Millers, 6 Jun. 1933, *ibid.*, CAB 9R/57/2.
118. M. Scott Moore to Blackmore, 27 Mar. 1926, *ibid.*, CAB 9R/57/1.
119. Andrews to Craig, 24 Jun. 1932, *ibid.*, CAB 9B/201/2.
120. Scott to Blackmore, 31 Mar. 1926, *ibid.*, CAB 9R/57/1.
121. Scott to Spender, 6 Nov. 1926, *ibid.*
122. See below, pp. 110–16.
123. Waley to Sir F. Phillips, Under-Secretary at the Treasury, 21 Mar. 1938, P.R.O., T 160/747/14026/04/01.

Chapter 4
IMPOTENCE (1): FINANCE
(pp. 81–104)

1. Lawrence, pp. 40–4, 190–1; chapters on public finance in the *Ulster Year Books, 1926–38.*
2. *Government of Ireland Bill: Further Memorandum on Financial Provisions,* 1920, U.K. Cmd 707.
3. Pollock's statement, *Parl. Deb. (C),* vi, 7 May 1925, cols 450–1.
4. Quoted in Lawrence, p. 41.
5. *Ibid.,* pp. 42, 190–1.
6. On how such changes diminished Northern Ireland's revenue see, e.g., Pollock's budget statements, *Parl. Deb. (C),* iv, 21 May 1924, cols 1043, 1048; vi, 7 May 1925, cols 455–6.
7. See above, pp. 52–3.
8. For a simplified explanation of the process of the attribution of revenue see, e.g., *Ulster Year Book, 1932,* pp. 203–6; but for a technical exposé see the Ministry of Finance file on the attribution of revenue, 1 Aug. 1922–11 Nov. 1940, P.R.O.N.I., FIN 26/1/9.
9. *Ulster Year Book, 1932,* pp. 205–6.
10. Lawrence, p. 190.
11. *Ibid.,* pp. 40–4, 190–1; chapters on public finance in *Ulster Year Books, 1926–38.*
12. Lawrence, pp. 50–1. See below, Chapter 7, for the step-by-step policy; for the extension of social services in Britain see B. B. Gilbert, *British Social Policy, 1914–1939* (New York 1970).
13. Pollock's description during an interview at the Treasury, 3 Jan. 1934, P.R.O.N.I., CAB 9A/3/5. For the unsuccessful efforts of Pollock and his officials in 1928 to restrain Craig, who wanted the most generous possible scheme of derating, see the cabinet file CAB 9A/95/1. Craig's answers to various objections were that derating 'will help us all enormously' at the next general election, and that 'with regard to the possibility of criticism arising regarding the general financial relations between the two countries . . . I do not think we need attach undue importance to the few isolated cases [of discrepancies] that fall under our notice. We are in no way to blame. The Act of 1920 was pressed upon us . . . by the *British Government,* consequently our withers are quite unwrung!' (5, 13 Sep. 1928).
14. *Financial Relations Report,* pp. 16–18, 95–6; *Ulster Year Book, 1935* (Belfast 1935), p. 244.
15. See below, p. 197.
16. Fin. Diary, 1932–33, pp. 4–5. For an instance of how local authorities intimidated the government and prevented its firm control over public expenditure see the cabinet's decision *not* to issue a circular urging economies in 1931 (Cab. Conclusions, 18 Nov. 1931, and supporting memos, especially Andrews's of 28 Oct. 1931, P.R.O.N.I., CAB 4/293/22,23,25,39).

17. *Parl. Deb. (C)*, xi, 12 Jun. 1929, col. 486.
18. Lawrence, p. 42.
19. *Parl. Deb. (C)*, xv, 23 May 1933, cols 1832, 1845.
20. Andrews's memo, 12 Jan. 1934, criticising Pollock's handling of a meeting at the Treasury on 3 Jan. 1934, P.R.O.N.I., CAB 9A/3/5.
21. For details of these early negotiations see Northern Ireland cabinet archives (*ibid.*, CAB 6/27) and those of the Colonial Office (P.R.O., CO 739/1,14) and Treasury (*ibid.*, T 160/150/5814/1,2, 163/6/G256/049).
22. See Joint Exchequer Board, Minutes of Proceedings, 1921–61, P.R.O.N.I., FIN 26/1/3,4; Northern Ireland cabinet files on the imperial contribution, 1925–33 (*ibid.*, CAB 94/40/1) and the financial position, 1933–37 (*ibid.*, CAB 9A/3/5); Fin. Diary throughout the 1930s; Treasury files on the contribution, 1933–34, P.R.O., T 160/550/6562/021/1,2.
23. Fin. Diary, 1932–33, p. 105.
24. See, e.g., Spender's rebuttal on 3 Oct. 1931 of the Treasury's arguments against Northern Ireland's claim for an increased provisional residuary share, P.R.O.N.I., CAB 9A/40/1; Spender's and a colleague's defence of derating, reserves and sinking funds on 3 Jan. 1934, and of Northern Ireland's estimates on 7 Mar. 1935, *ibid.*, CAB 9A/3/5.
25. See, e.g., comment made by Sir R. Hopkins, Second Secretary at the Treasury, to N. Chamberlain, the Chancellor, 10 May 1933, after a meeting with Pollock, P.R.O., T 160/6562/021/1; record of the meeting at the Treasury on 16 Apr. 1935, P.R.O.N.I., CAB 9A/3/5. See also Pollock's conversations with Spender in April 1932 (Fin. Diary, 1932–33, pp. 8,9,10) for the way in which Pollock's concern for his own and Craig's health made him reluctant to insist upon rigorous economies and stricter Ministry of Finance control over expenditure.
26. See, e.g., the fiasco of a meeting of Craig, Andrews and Pollock with S. Baldwin, the Lord President, and N. Chamberlain, 22 Jan. 1934, when the Northern Ireland ministers came away thinking that the imperial ministers had agreed to help make good the North's impending budget deficit, while the latter believed that Northern Ireland would meet the deficit on its own by drawing on reserves, making economies, and perhaps imposing a levy on the rates. The misunderstanding came to light only accidentally during a telephone conversation on another matter between Spender and Hopkins (P.R.O.N.I., CAB 9A/3/5).
27. See below, pp. 96, 98; and Fin. Diary, 1 Jan. 1937–2 Mar. 1938, pp. 26, 182–3.
28. Lawrence, p. 46; memo on imperial contribution, 2 Apr. 1930, by A. S. Queckett, the Parliamentary Draftsman, P.R.O.N.I., CAB 9A/40/1.
29. The following quotations are taken from Andrews's summary of

the 'Key Arguments for the Northern Ireland Case that the Satisfaction of Our Local Expenditure should be the First Charge
upon Our Revenues', *c.* 9 Apr. 1931 (*ibid.,* CAB 9A/3/5), which
was later used as the basis for submissions to the Treasury regarding a minus contribution.

30. Correspondence relating to the Ministry of Labour, Jul. 1921,
ibid., FIN 18/1/270.
31. Lawrence, pp. 50–2. The anxieties of the government of Northern
Ireland during these negotiations are painfully evident in the relevant cabinet files, P.R.O.N.I., CAB 9C/1/2,6.
32. Memo dated 6 Nov. 1924, *ibid.,* CAB 9C/1/2.
33. See note 20 above.
34. For this line of approach see, e.g., Spender's meeting at and correspondence with the Treasury in 1931, P.R.O.N.I., CAB 9A/40/1;
meetings of Pollock and/or his officials with Treasury officials, 3
Jan., 16 Nov. 1934, 7 Mar., 16 Apr. 1935, *ibid.,* CAB 9A/3/5.
35. The clearest statement of most of Northern Ireland's claims against
the Treasury was made by Spender to Waley, 18 Mar., 11 Apr.
1933, P.R.O., T 160/550/6562/021/1.
36. Cab. Conclusions, 19 Nov. 1930, P.R.O.N.I., CAB 4/273/32.
37. See, e.g., the results of meetings between Northern Ireland and
imperial ministers on 16 May 1933 (P.R.O., T 160/550/6562/
021/1,2) and 22 Jan. 1934 (P.R.O.N.I., CAB 9A/3/5).
38. On Treasury attitudes in the inter-war years see S. Howson,
Domestic Monetary Management in Britain, 1919–38 (Cambridge
1975) and S. Howson and D. Winch, *The Economic Advisory
Council, 1930–39* (Cambridge 1977).
39. Niemeyer to Horne, 24 May 1922, P.R.O., T 163/6/G256/049.
40. Niemeyer to Baldwin, the Chancellor, 20 Nov. 1922, *ibid.,* T
160/150/5814/1.
41. Waley to Phillips, 27 Mar. 1933, *ibid.,* T 160/550/6562/021/1.
42. Hopkins to N. Chamberlain, 10 May 1933, *ibid.*
43. Waley to H. Brittain, a Principal at the Treasury, 10 Mar. 1933,
ibid.
44. See, e.g., Fin. Diary, 1932–33, pp. 104–7; Spender to Waley, 10
May 1933, and Waley to Hopkins, 12 Oct. 1933, P.R.O., T 160/
550/6562/1,2.
45. Hopkins to N. Chamberlain, 16 May 1933, *ibid.,* T 160/550/
6562/021/1.
46. C. L. Mowat, *Britain between the Wars, 1918–1940* (London
1968), pp. 386–406.
47. See, e.g., Snowden, the Chancellor, to Pollock, 23 Feb. 1931, and
Waley to Spender, 15 Oct. 1931, P.R.O.N.I., CAB 9A/40/1; Britain
to Waley, 27 Apr. 1933, P.R.O., T 160/550/6562/021/1.
48. *First* and *Final Reports of the Northern Ireland Special Arbitration Committee,* 1924 and 1925, U.K. Cmd 2072 and 2389; but
for a convenient summary see Lawrence, pp. 43–7.
49. Memo by R. G. Hawtrey, an Assistant Secretary, on the Award,

n.d., and Niemeyer to W. Churchill, the Chancellor, 25 Mar. 1925, P.R.O., T 160/150/5814/2.

50. Quoted in Lawrence, p. 45.

51. Memo by J. I. Cook, a Principal, Ministry of Finance, on the variation of the imperial contribution, 10 Jan. 1931, P.R.O.N.I., CAB 9A/40/1.

52. Pollock to Craig, 8 Dec. 1933, reporting a recent meeting with Hopkins at the Treasury, *ibid.*, CAB 9A/3/5.

53. Waley to Phillips, 27 Mar. 1933, P.R.O., T 160/550/6562/021/1. On the extent to which the Treasury's attitude towards the Free State's financial claims impinged upon its response to Northern Ireland's detailed claims see, e.g., Brittain to Waley, 23 Feb. 1933, and to G. Ismay, another Principal, 20 Mar. 1933, *ibid.*

54. See below, p. 115.

55. Lawrence, p. 52 n. 2; Hopkins's comments during a meeting with Pollock and his officials, 3 Jan. 1934, and N. Chamberlain to Craig, 17 Jan. 1934, P.R.O.N.I., CAB 9A/3/5.

56. Quoted in Lawrence, p. 52 n. 2.

57. *Ibid.*, pp. 51–2.

58. See particularly the meetings between Treasury and Ministry of Finance officials, sometimes with Pollock, 16 Nov. 1934, 7 Mar., 16, 17 Apr. 1935, and Waley to Spender, 7 May 1935, P.R.O.N.I., CAB 9A/3/5.

59. See note 20 above for arrangements for the Special Constabulary and unemployment insurance; see below, p. 202, for the provisions of the peace pact.

60. See below, pp. 115, 142–4.

61. Hopkins to N. Chamberlain, 10 May 1933, P.R.O., T 160/550/6562/021/1.

62. Hopkins to Sir G. Upcott, 1 Aug. 1933, *ibid.*, T 160/550/6562/021/2. As a Treasury official, Upcott had been exacting in his dealings with Northern Ireland in the 1920s.

63. N. Chamberlain's minute, 30 Mar. 1933, *ibid.*, T 160/550/6562/021/1. For his officials' recommendations see Brittain to Waley, 25 Mar. 1933, Waley to Phillips, 27 Mar. 1933, and Hopkins to J. B. D. Fergusson, Chamberlain's Principal Private Secretary, 30 Mar. 1933, *ibid.*

64. Hopkins in his talk with Spender, 3 Jan. 1934, P.R.O.N.I., CAB 9A/3/5.

65. Brittain to Waley, 25 Mar. 1933, P.R.O., T 160/550/6562/021/1.

66. *Ulster Year Book, 1932*, pp. 220–3.

67. See, e.g., Snowden to Pollock, 23 Feb. 1931, P.R.O.N.I., CAB 9A/40/1.

68. Hopkins to N. Chamberlain, 10 May 1933, P.R.O., T 160/550/6562/021/1.

69. On the importance attached by the Treasury to revaluation and a redistribution of the cost of education in Northern Ireland see, e.g., both internal memoranda (such as Brittain's note on formulae

for Northern Ireland's contribution, 15 Mar. 1933, and Hopkins's notes to N. Chamberlain, 10, 16 May 1933, *ibid.*) and the pressure put upon the Northern government in correspondence (such as Snowden to Pollock, 23 Feb. 1931, P.R.O.N.I., CAB 9A/40/1, and Hopkins to Pollock, 17 May 1933, P.R.O., T 160/550/6562/021/2) and in discussions with Northern Ireland ministers and/or officials (such as those on 3 Oct. 1931, 3 Jan. 1934 and 7 Mar. 1935, P.R.O.N.I., CAB 9A/3/5, 9A/40/1).

70. Sir E. Clark, Northern Ireland's representative on the Joint Exchequer Board, to Colwyn, the chairman, 25 Mar. 1927, apologising for losing his temper, P.R.O.N.I., CAB 9A/40/1.

71. First Stormont Castle conference on financial position, 12 Dec. 1933, *ibid.*, CAB 9A/3/5.

72. N. Chamberlain to Pollock, 14 Dec. 1931, *ibid.*, CAB 9A/40/1.

73. Pollock to N. Chamberlain, 7 Jan. 1932, *ibid.*

74. Interview with Sir John Anderson, 24 Jul. 1930, *ibid.*, CAB 9A/3/1.

75. Pollock to Andrews, 1 Aug. 1930, *ibid.*

76. See, e.g., the Treasury meeting, 3 Jan. 1934, *ibid.*, CAB 9A/3/5.

77. Spender to Pollock, 5 Nov. 1934, on the effects of the economic war, *ibid.*

78. Treasury meeting, 3 Jan. 1934, *ibid.*

79. Spender's note of meeting with Pollock and Cook, 3 Jan. 1934, *ibid.*

80. Second Stormont Castle conference on financial position, 15 Dec. 1933, *ibid.*

81. Treasury meeting, 3 Jan. 1934, *ibid.*

82. Spender's note of meeting with Pollock and Cook, 3 Jan. 1934, prior to the meeting with Treasury officials, *ibid.*

83. *Financial Relations Report, passim;* file on financial relations between local authorities and the state, P.R.O.N.I., CAB 9A/76/1; first Stormont Castle conference on financial position, 12 Dec. 1933, and Pollock's comments in Treasury meeting, 3 Jan. 1934, *ibid.*, CAB 9A/3/5.

84. Andrews's memo, 'Summary of the Key Arguments for the Northern Ireland Case that the Satisfaction of Our Local Expenditure should be the First Charge upon Our Revenues', *c.* 9 Apr. 1931, *ibid.*

85. *Financial Relations Report,* pp. 6–7, 58–9; Bates's and Pollock's memos on maternity and child welfare schemes, 11, 14 Mar. 1930, P.R.O.N.I., CAB 4/252/19,20; Spender to Blackmore, 17 Sep. 1936, commenting on Belfast Corporation's request for an increased grant towards the treatment of lunatics, *ibid.*, CAB 9A/3/5.

86. *Parl. Deb. (C),* xiii, 24 Nov. 1931, col. 2320.

87. *Ibid.,* 1 Dec. 1931, col. 2422.

88. *Ibid.,* 1 Dec. 1931, cols 2428–9.

89. On the opposition see the Northern Ireland press generally and

the second- and third-reading debates in the House of Commons, *Parl. Deb. (C),* xiii, 1–2, 17 Dec. 1931, cols 2422–74, 2475–538, 2910–70.

90. Quoted by Henderson, *ibid.,* 2 Dec. 1931, col. 2506.
91. See, e.g., Devlin, *ibid.,* 1, 17 Dec. 1931, cols 2475–87, 2944–53; Healy and Collins, *ibid.,* 2 Dec. 1931, cols 2475–87, 2519–29; Leeke, *ibid.,* 14 Dec. 1931, cols 2779–81.
92. See the voting on the second and third readings and the highest division in committee, *ibid.,* 2, 14, 17 Dec. 1931, cols 2536–8, 2747–8, 2969–70.
93. *Ibid.,* 15 Dec. 1931, cols 2800–2, 2810–11, 2813–14.
94. *Ibid.,* 15 Dec. 1931, col. 2866.
95. On the deal with the Treasury see Hopkins to N. Chamberlain, 17 May 1933, and to Pollock, 17 May 1933, P.R.O., T 160/550/ 6562/021/2. On the reasons for the failure to implement the promise see Spender to Hopkins, 22 May 1933, *ibid.;* Craig's comments during the first Stormont Castle conference on the financial position, 12 Dec. 1933, P.R.O.N.I., CAB 9A/3/5.
96. See, e.g., Hopkins's remarks during his meetings with Pollock and Spender at the Treasury, 3 Jan. 1934, and N. Chamberlain to Craig, 17 Jan. 1934, and to Pollock, 13 Feb. 1934, P.R.O.N.I., CAB 9A/3/5.
97. Cab. Conclusions, 25 Apr., 1 May 1934, *ibid.,* CAB 4/321/37, 4/322/11.
98. *Parl. Deb. (C),* xvi, 16, 17 May 1934, cols 1641–2, 1652, 1759.
99. *Ibid.,* 17 May 1934, cols 1743–4, 1751.
100. *Ibid.,* 17 May 1934, col. 1746.
101. *Ibid.,* 17 May 1934, cols 1750–1.
102. *Ibid.,* 17 May 1934, col. 1751.
103. *Ibid.,* 31 May 1934, col. 2003.
104. See, e.g., the criticisms of Belfast M.P.s on the committee stage of the Finance Bill, *ibid.,* 5 Jun. 1934, cols 2108–10, 2115–20.
105. *Ibid.,* 5 Jun. 1934, cols 2110–11.
106. For convenient summaries of the case see Budge and O'Leary, pp. 152–3, and Calvert, pp. 243–4.
107. These efforts are described in Fin. Diary, 1 Dec. 1934–31 Aug. 1935, pp. 67, 71, 89, 96, 186–7, 198–202, 215, 234; Sep. 1935–Mar. 1936, pp. 39, 65, 173.
108. *Ibid.,* 1 Dec. 1934–31 Aug. 1935, p. 67.
109. *Ibid.,* p. 96.
110. Hopkins to N. Chamberlain, 16 May 1933, P.R.O., T 160/550/ 6562/021/1; Hopkins to Phillips, 8 Feb. 1938, *ibid.,* T 160/1138/ 15586/1. After 1931 it so became the practice of the two treasuries to settle matters between themselves that the Joint Exchequer Board was reduced to registering prior agreements. The board did not even find it necessary to meet between 1935 and 1949, and most matters were dealt with by correspondence (Minutes of Proceedings, 21 Jul. 1927–11 Jul. 1961, P.R.O.N.I., FIN 26/1/4).

111. Lawrence, pp. 114, 117.
112. *Ibid.; Parl. Deb. (C)*, xii, 23 Oct. 1930, col. 2096; xiv, 19 Apr. 1932, col. 746; xvi, 26 Apr., 31 May 1934, cols 1197, 1977; xix, 6 May, 12 Oct. 1937, cols 1301, 1874; xxi, 30 Mar. 1938, col. 1261; xxii, 20 Apr. 1939, col. 1056.
113. Robb's memo, 4 May 1939, P.R.O.N.I., CAB 9D/1/9.
114. Cab. Conclusions, 15 May 1939, *ibid.*, CAB 4/417/15.
115. Mowat, p. 498.
116. Lawrence, p. 191.
117. See below, Chapter 11.
118. Cab. Conclusions, 15 May 1939, P.R.O.N.I., CAB 4/417/15.
119. *Ibid.*, CAB 9D/1/9.

Chapter 5
IMPOTENCE (2): TRADE AND INDUSTRY
(pp. 105–129)
1. Suggestions for Craig's speech to the Lisburn Chamber of Commerce, *c.* 30 Nov. 1930, P.R.O.N.I., CAB 9C/13/1.
2. See below, pp. 136–7.
3. Ministry of Agriculture memo to imperial Home Office, 17 Dec. 1926, and its memo on the proposed Potatoes Marketing Bill, 7 Jun. 1926, P.R.O.N.I., CAB 9E/57/1.
4. See, e.g., report of a meeting of officials in London, 14 Nov. 1927, *ibid.*
5. Anderson to Blackmore, 4 Apr. 1927, *ibid.*
6. Report of meeting between A. B. Babington, Northern Ireland's Attorney-General, and Anderson, 11 Jan. 1928, *ibid.*
7. The original draft applied only to trade with Britain, but, at the government of Northern Ireland's request, was modified to include the Free State to prevent ungraded goods being exported to Britain via the Free State. See the exchange of letters between Blackmore and C. G. Markbrieter, an Assistant Secretary at the Home Office, 3, 4 Apr. 1928, P.R.O., HO 45/13144/520494/6.
8. See below, pp. 137–8.
9. *Parl. Deb. (C)*, xi, 5 Nov. 1929, cols 923–4, 938.
10. See, e.g., complaints about the unpatriotic importation of Russian oats in 1930; *ibid.*, xii, 16, 23, 30 Oct. 1930, cols 1911–13, 2100–1, 2276–7, 2315–18; second- and third-reading debates of the first 1937 New Industries Bill, *ibid.*, xix, 1, 8 Jun. 1937, cols 1348–71, 1518–21.
11. Pollock's address to the U.U.C. summer school at Bangor, 7 Jun. 1928, P.R.O.N.I., CAB 9A/40/1.
12. *Parl. Deb. (C)*, xix, 8 Jun. 1937, col. 1520.
13. *Ibid.*, xxii, 19 Apr. 1939, col. 968.
14. For the details of these applications see the relevant cabinet files, P.R.O.N.I., CAB 9F/67/1,2.
15. *Parl. Deb (C)*, xii, 16 Oct. 1930, cols 1962–3.
16. Andrews to Craig, 27 Jul. 1928, P.R.O.N.I., PM 9/21.

17. Cab. Conclusions, 11 Jul. 1929, *ibid.*, CAB 4/235/29. See also Craig to Andrews, 29 Jul. 1927, *ibid.*, PM 9/18; Craig to Pollock, 4 Jul. 1929, *ibid.*, CAB 9F/67/2.
18. See below, pp. 140–1.
19. See below, p. 141.
20. On the particular difficulties of Northern Ireland millers and bakers see G. Scott Robertson to Markbrieter, 28 Jan. 1932, P.R.O.N.I., CAB 9E/93/1; M. Anderson, secretary of the Belfast Millers' Association, to Baldwin, Conservative leader and Lord President, 8 Feb. 1932, enclosing a petition against the bill, *ibid.*; Scott to Blackmore, 15 Mar. 1932, *ibid.*
21. The following account is based mainly upon two letters from Scott of the Ministry of Commerce to the cabinet secretariat, 15 Mar., 12 Apr. 1932, *ibid.*
22. For a convenient summary of the negotiations and agreement see Murphy, pp. 92–5.
23. Imperial Cabinet Conclusions, 13 Apr. 1938, P.R.O., CAB 23/93.
24. *Ibid.*
25. Hoare's report on a conversation with Andrews, 9 Dec. 1937, *ibid.*, CAB 27/527.
26. Craig to Hoare, 6 Jan. 1938, P.R.O.N.I., CAB 9R/60/1.
27. Imperial Cabinet Conclusions, 22 Dec. 1937, P.R.O., CAB 23/90.
28. Fin. Diary, Mar.–Oct. 1938, manuscript note at front.
29. Imperial Cabinet Conclusions, 2 Mar. 1938, P.R.O., CAB 23/92.
30. Proceedings of the [imperial] Cabinet Committee on the Irish Situation, 1 Mar. 1938, *ibid.*, CAB 27/524.
31. *Ibid.*
32. For the imperial view see the 35th–43rd meetings of the [Imperial] Cabinet Committee on the Irish Situation, 14 Dec. 1937–8 Apr. 1938, *ibid.* For the attitude of the government of Northern Ireland see mainly the cabinet files on the negotiations, P.R.O.N.I., CAB 9R/60/1,2,3,5; Fin. Diary, 1 Jan. 1937–2 Mar. 1938, and Mar.–Oct. 1938, *passim.*
33. Imperial Cabinet Conclusions, 9 Mar. 1938, P.R.O., CAB 23/92.
34. Longford and O'Neill, pp. 321–4.
35. Notes on Northern Ireland exports to Southern Ireland, 5 Mar. 1938, P.R.O.N.I., CAB 9R/60/2. For the Northern Ireland critiques of the draft agreements see two memoranda, 15 Feb. and 25 Mar. 1938, *ibid.*, CAB 9R/60/1,2.
36. 25 Mar. 1938 memo, *ibid.*, CAB 9R/60/2.
37. Craig to N. Chamberlain, 19 Feb. 1938, *ibid.*, CAB 9R/60/1.
38. Note presented to Hoare by Andrews, 16 Feb. 1938, *ibid.*
39. For the Northern Ireland claims see, e.g., Craig to N. Chamberlain, 19 Feb. 1938, and memo on effects of proposed agreement on Northern Ireland industry, 25 Mar. 1938, *ibid.*, CAB 9R/60/1,2; Fin. Diary, Mar.–Oct. 1938, p. 5.
40. *Ibid.*, pp. 4–5.
41. Imperial Cabinet Conclusions, 16 Mar. 1938, P.R.O., CAB 23/93.

42. Sir Warren Fisher's minute, 7 Mar. 1938, *ibid.,* T 160/747/14026/04/1.
43. Proceedings of the [Imperial] Cabinet Committee on the Irish Situation, 10 Mar. 1938, *ibid.,* CAB 27/524.
44. N. Chamberlain to Craig, 17 Mar. 1938, P.R.O.N.I., CAB 9R/60/2.
45. Waley to Phillips, 21 Mar. 1938, P.R.O., T 160/747/14026/04/1.
46. Fin. Diary, Mar.–Oct. 1938, pp. 1–3 and manuscript note at front; instruction to permanent officials, approved by the Prime Minister, 19 Mar. 1938, P.R.O.N.I., CAB 9R/60/2.
47. Fin. Diary, Mar.–Oct. 1938, manuscript note at front.
48. N. Chamberlain to Craig, 8 Apr. 1938, P.R.O.N.I., CAB 9R/60/3.
49. Fin. Diary, Mar.–Oct. 1938, p. 36.
50. Imperial Cabinet Conclusions, 13 Apr. 1938, P.R.O., CAB 23/93.
51. *Ibid.*
52. For the extent of the financial concessions, which differed from those in the published statement *(Parl. Deb. (C),* xxi, 26 Apr. 1938, cols 660–3) by including substantial qualifications about agricultural subsidies, see the agreed note sent to the Joint Exchequer Board in May 1938, P.R.O.N.I., FIN 26/1/36. On the hammering out of the details of the concessions see the Treasury files on Northern Ireland's attitude to the trade agreement, P.R.O., T 160/747/14026/04/1,2; Proceedings of the [Imperial] Cabinet Committee on the Irish Situation, 8 Apr. 1938, *ibid.,* CAB 27/524; Fin. Diary, Mar.–Oct. 1938, pp. 30–9.
53. Waley to Phillips, 24 Mar. 1938, and Simon's note of talk with Craig and Andrews, 11 Apr. 1938, P.R.O., T 160/747/14026/04/1,2.
54. *Parl. Deb. (C),* ii, 12 Dec. 1922, col. 1180.
55. *Ibid.,* 12 Dec. 1922, cols 1178–82; Cab. Conclusions, 14 Mar. 1922, P.R.O.N.I., CAB 4/36/11; notes on the administration of the Loans Guarantee Acts, 1922–33, *ibid.,* CAB 9A/42/1; Ministry of Finance memo, 6 Nov. 1922, and file on Loans Guarantee Bill, *ibid.,* FIN 18/2/570, 606.
56. *Parl. Deb. (C),* ii, 12 Dec. 1922, col. 1178.
57. See, e.g., notes on the administration of the Loans Guarantee Acts, 1922–33, P.R.O.N.I., CAB 9A/42/1.
58. See the cabinet files on shipbuilding questions, 1928–45, *ibid.,* CAB 9A/61/1,2.
59. H. W. Richardson, *Economic Recovery in Britain, 1932–9* (London 1967), pp. 228–9.
60. Pollock's memo on the proposed extension of the Loans Guarantee Acts, 9 Sep. 1926, P.R.O.N.I., CAB 4/176/15.
61. *Parl. Deb. (C),* xvii, 27 Mar. 1935, cols 1084–5.
62. Pollock's memo on the proposed extension of the Loans Guarantee Acts, 9 Sep. 1926, P.R.O.N.I., CAB 4/176/15.
63. Pollock to Craig, 28 May 1926, *ibid.,* PM 9/16.
64. Cab. Conclusions, 25 Nov. 1924, 27 Jan. 1925, 26 Jan. 1927, *ibid.,* CAB 4/131/22, 4/134/28, 4/185/24.

65. Notes on Loans Guarantee Acts, 12 Nov. 1934, 20 Oct. 1936, *ibid.*, CAB 9A/61/2.
66. Blackmore to Craig, 29 Jun. 1926, P.R.O.N.I., PM 9/14. On the problems facing the linen industry see above, pp. 54–5.
67. Craig to Blackmore, 1 Jul. 1926, P.R.O.N.I., PM 9/15.
68. Andrews to Craig, 27 Jul. 1928, *ibid.*, PM 9/21.
69. *Report by Sir Felix Pole on Transport Conditions in Northern Ireland*, 1934, Cmd 160, especially pp. 10–15.
70. See, e.g., *Report of the Departmental Committee on the Transit, Prices and Marketing of Agricultural Produce*, 1927, Cmd 75. For the consequent unsuccessful attempt by the government to persuade the railway and shipping companies to make at least a gesture to farmers see the two files on 'Development of Agriculture', P.R.O.N.I., CAB 9E/23/1,2.
71. *Report by Sir Felix Pole on Transport Conditions*, pp. 20–1, 22; Bates's comments introducing the second reading of the 1935 Road and Railway Transport Bill, *Parl. Deb. (C)*, xvii, 14 May 1935, cols 1591–1600.
72. On the political, economic and financial state of the Londonderry and Lough Swilly Railway see H. S. Robinson, a Londonderry solicitor, to Blackmore, 26 Mar. 1925, and Scott to Spender, 21 Jun. 1925, P.R.O.N.I., CAB 9F/18/1; Interim Report of an Interdepartmental Committee on Transport, 11 Jan. 1928, *ibid.*, CAB 4/203/17.
73. On Free State policy on railways in the inter-war years see Meenan, pp. 158–61; on its attitude towards the Londonderry and Lough Swilly Railway in particular see G. Campbell, Department of Industry and Commerce, to Scott, 13 Apr. 1926, P.R.O.N.I., CAB 9F/18/1.
74. *Report of the Railways Commission in Northern Ireland*, 1922, Cmd 10.
75. Its general reluctance to take responsibility was evident in cabinet discussions and consequent correspondence on the state of the Belfast and Co. Down Railway Co. and on the Ministry of Commerce's request for a decision on the principle of financial assistance and its suggestion that ministers should meet representatives of the railway companies, Cab. Conclusions and supporting papers, 24 Mar., 26 Oct. 1926, P.R.O.N.I., CAB 4/163/22,25, 4/180/18,19,28.
76. File on the railway, *ibid.*, CAB 9F/18/1.
77. Milne Barbour's memo on the railway, 9 Mar. 1931, *ibid.*, CAB 4/278/16; Scott to J. Taylor, a Principal in the Cabinet Office, 15 May 1933, *ibid.*, CAB 9F/18/2; Fin. Diary, 1933–34, 15–22, 26–30 May 1933.
78. Cab. Conclusions, 12 Mar. 1931, *ibid.*, CAB 4/278/18.
79. Report on the deputation, 26 Mar. 1931, *ibid.*, CAB 9F/18/2.
80. Cab. Conclusions, 26 Mar. 1931, *ibid.*, CAB 4/281/10.
81. Records of meetings, *ibid.*, CAB 9F/18/2.

82. Fin. Diary, 1933–34, 26–30 May, 9 Jun. 1933.
83. Cab. Conclusions, 15 Jan. 1934, P.R.O.N.I., CAB 4/318/28.
84. *Report by Sir Felix Pole on Transport Conditions*, pp. 23–32; Cab. Conclusions, 11 Jul. 1934, P.R.O.N.I., CAB 4/327/32.
85. *Parl. Deb. (C)*, xvii, 18 Apr. 1935, col. 1539; *The Times*, 23 Jul. (leader), 8 Sep. (report of presidential address to the Economic and Statistics Section of the British Association) 1934.
86. Cab. Conclusions, 24 Feb., 14, 22 Mar. 1938, P.R.O.N.I., CAB 4/392/17, 4/394/18, 4/396/19; *Reports of the Commissioner holding the Public Inquiry and of the Committee of Inquiry into Public Transport in Northern Ireland*, 1938, Cmd 198.
87. Cab. Conclusions, 6, 13 Dec. 1938, P.R.O.N.I., CAB 4/404/10, 4/406/11; *Report of the Joint Select Committee of Inquiry into Road and Rail Transport*, 1939, H.C. 472.
88. Spender to Waley, 17 May 1939, P.R.O., T 160/1138/15586/1.
89. Midgley's description, *Parl. Deb. (C)*, xvii, 15 May 1935, col. 1640.
90. *Report by Sir Felix Pole on Transport Conditions*, pp. 16, 25; *Parl. Deb. (C)*, xvii, 14 May 1935, cols 1601–2.
91. On this pressure see Cab. Conclusions, 10 Jan. 1939, P.R.O.N.I., CAB 4/408/5; Treasury file, 'Northern Ireland Transport Board. Committee of investigation into the finances of the board', P.R.O., T 160/1138/15586/1.
92. Cab. Conclusions, 18 Jul. 1939, P.R.O.N.I., CAB 4/421/16.
93. Cab. Conclusions, 29 Oct. 1940, *ibid.*, CAB 4/453/6; C. H. Petherick, then an Assistant Secretary at the Ministry of Finance, to A. P. Waterfield, an Assistant Secretary at the Treasury, 31 Oct. 1940, P.R.O., T 160/1138/15586/2. Spender almost resigned over this episode: see his letters to Waley, 27 Sep. 1940, and to Hopkins, 10 Oct. 1940, *ibid.*
94. *Interim Report of the Commission on Natural and Industrial Resources of Northern Ireland*, 1923, Cmd 24.
95. Archdale's memo, *c.* 11 Apr. 1923, P.R.O.N.I., CAB 9F/64/1.
96. Cab. Conclusions, 16 Apr. 1923, 10 Jan. 1924, *ibid.*, CAB 4/77/15, 4/98/21.
97. *Parl. Deb. (C)*, vii, 13 Apr. 1926, cols 433–5.
98. Cab. Conclusions, 16 Apr. 1923, 10 Jan. 1924, P.R.O.N.I., CAB 4/77/15, 4/98/21.
99. Kelly to Craig, 5 Aug. 1925, *ibid.*, CAB 9F/64/1.
100. Cab. Conclusions, 28 Oct. 1925, *ibid.*, CAB 4/153/16.
101. Milne Barbour's memo on the Coalisland wages subvention, *c.* 12 Dec. 1925, *ibid.*, CAB 9F/64/1; Cab. Conclusions, 15 Dec. 1925, *ibid.*, CAB 4/156/19.
102. The following figures are taken from Milne Barbour's two memoranda on the subvention, *c.* 12 Dec. 1925 and 28 May 1926, *ibid.*, CAB 9F/64/1.
103. Report of the mineral resources committee of the Ulster Development Council, 27 Nov. 1938 *ibid.*, COM 20/1/2.
104. Since summaries of the new industries legislation usually ignore

the July 1937 act, a better idea of the changes in the scope of legislation is given by the ministerial speeches introducing second readings or money resolutions, *Parl. Deb. (C)*, xiv, 21 Mar. 1932, col. 445–7; xix, 1 Jun. 1937, cols 1348–53; xx, 25 Nov. 1937, cols 1348–53; xx, 25 Nov. 1937, cols 111–12.

105. Ministry of Commerce file, 'Statistics and Reports relating to New Industries Legislation', P.R.O.N.I., COM 20/2/18.

106. *Ibid.*

107. Isles and Cuthbert, *Economic Survey*, p. 381.

108. See the correspondence between the cabinet secretariat and the Ministries of Finance and Commerce in Oct. and Nov. 1931, P.R.O.N.I., CAB 9F/126/1.

109. Cab. Conclusions, 18 Nov. 1931, *ibid.*, CAB 4/293/39.

110. Henderson, *Parl. Deb. (C)*, xvi, 20 Dec. 1933, col. 133.

111. Milne Barbour to Craig, 13 Nov. 1936, P.R.O.N.I., CAB 9F/126/1.

112. *Parl. Deb. (C)*, xxi, 15, 23 Mar., 4 May 1938, cols 262, 405–6, 409–10, 412–17, 886–99; *Parl. Deb. (S)*, xxi, 15 Jun. 1938, col 276; Greenlees, p. 334.

113. Cab. Conclusions, 23 Mar. 1939, P.R.O.N.I., CAB 4/413/10; memo by J. F. Gordon, Minister of Labour, 22 Mar. 1939, *ibid.*, CAB 4/413/8.

114. Fin. Diary, 1 Jan. 1937–2 Mar. 1938, pp. 152–3; Interim and Final Reports of the Interdepartmental Committee on Unemployment, 19 Oct., 9 Nov. 1937, P.R.O.N.I., CAB 9C/13/2. For British policy towards areas of high unemployment see S. R. Dennison, *The Location of Industry and the Depressed Areas* (London 1939).

115. *Parl. Deb. (C)*, xxi, 5 Oct. 1938, cols 1337, 1339–41, 1344–50, 1353–5, 1357–8, 1359–63, 1365, 1367–70.

116. Fin. Diary, 1 Jan. 1937–2 Mar. 1938, pp. 191, 192; Mar.–Oct. 1938, pp. 82, 102; Nov. 1939–4 May 1940, pp. 2, 23, 50.

117. Cab. Conclusions, 29 Apr. 1937, P.R.O.N.I., CAB 4/377/21.

118. The committee tried to satisfy itself on five main points: that additional employment would be provided; that there was adequate security for any loan; that applicants would put up more capital than the government; that the industry would not compete with existing industries; and that the firm would survive, especially against well-established English competition (thus disqualifying applications from a brick company and a wafer-biscuit manufacturer) (minutes of the meetings of the advisory committee, 17 Dec. 1937–26 Jul. 1939, P.R.O.N.I., COM 17/1).

119. *Ibid.;* Fin. Diary, Mar.–Oct. 1938, pp. 61, 71, 102, 151.

120. *Ibid.*, 1 Jan. 1937–2 Mar. 1938, pp. 50–1, 59–60.

121. *Northern Whig*, 22 Jun. 1939.

122. On these problems see, e.g., Milne Barbour's memo on new-industries legislation, 26 Feb. 1937, P.R.O.N.I., CAB 4/373/10; Fin. Diary, Mar.–Oct. 1938, pp. 29, 58.

123. List compiled from schedules of new industries in P.R.O.N.I., COM 20/2/18.

124. Scott to Gransden, 4 Jan. 1940, *ibid.*, CAB 9F/126/2.
125. See above, pp. 58–9.

Chapter 6
ADAPTABILITY: AGRICULTURE
(pp. 130–149)
1. *Parl. Deb. (C)*, xvi, 6 Jun. 1934, col. 2152. There is a useful outline of the development of agricultural policy in Northern Ireland
   in *Ulster Year Book, 1935*, pp. xiii–xxxi.
2. See above, pp. 106–7.
3. See, e.g., the correspondence in the winter of 1924 between Archdale, Spender and H. B. Thompson, who advocated a radical reform of Northern Ireland agriculture, *ibid.*, CAB 9E/23/1.
4. G. Scott Robertson, *Pig Breeding and Marketing in Northern Ireland* (Belfast 1934; from *The Pig Breeders' Annual, 1933–34*),
   p. 2.
5. For a summary of the British acts see British Association, *Britain
   in Depression*, pp. 84–5; for a summary of the Northern Ireland
   act see *Ulster Year Book, 1935*, p. xx, and the Ministry of Agriculture's memo on the proposed 1933 Marketing Bill, *c.* 28 Apr.
   1933, P.R.O.N.I., CAB 9E/57/2.
6. Cab. Conclusions, 2 May 1933, P.R.O.N.I., CAB 4/311/21.
7. Cab. Conclusions, 13 Jun. 1923, *ibid.*, CAB 4/82/9.
8. *Ibid.*
9. Copies, *ibid.*, CAB 9E/1/1.
10. *Report of the Agricultural Aid Committee*, 1923, Cmd 17.
11. *Financial Relations Report*, p. 46.
12. Sir C. F. Falls, an Enniskillen solicitor and lifelong Unionist activ-
    ist, to Craig, 24 Feb. 1926, reporting the views of the local branch
    of the U.F.U., P.R.O.N.I., CAB 9E/47/1.
13. Spender to Blackmore, 4 Mar. 1926, *ibid.*
14. Note on the cost to Northern Ireland if annuities were halved, 3
    Dec. 1938, *ibid.*, CAB 9E/117/2.
15. See the relevant cabinet files, *ibid.*, CAB 9A/37/1,2,3,6,7,9,10,12.
16. Greenlees, pp. 299, 300–1, 302–3, 305, 307.
17. See the cabinet file on the society, P.R.O.N.I., CAB 9E/43/1.
18. On the deteriorating relationship see the renewed demand for a
    reduction of land-purchase annuities in 1937–38, *ibid.*, CAB 9E/
    117/2.
19. *Parl. Deb. (C)*, xiii, 19 Mar. 1931, col. 494.
20. Wilson Hungerford to Blackmore, 26 Jun. 1937, P.R.O.N.I., CAB
    9E/75/2.
21. Scott Robertson to Blackmore, 14 Nov. 1933, *ibid.*, CAB 9E/122/
    1.
22. U.F.U. resolution condemning 1936 Eggs Marketing Bill, 30 Apr.
    1936, *ibid.*, CAB 9E/14/2.
23. *Parl. Deb. (C)*, xviii, 6, 21 May 1936, cols 1345–6, 1734–6; xxii,
    7, 9 Mar. 1939, cols 316, 445–6.

24. Political Science Department, Belfast, 'Intra-Unionist Disputes', pp. 1–3.
25. Greenlees, pp. 333–4, 398–405; *Parl. Deb. (C)*, xxii, 9, 14, 21, 23 Mar., 25, 27 Apr., 30 May 1939, cols 435–79, 539–44, 660–74, 729–96, 1069–76, 1117–20, 1181–8, 1767–70.
26. Harrison, p. 87.
27. See the cabinet file, 'Newry Central Creamery', P.R.O.N.I., CAB 9E/127.
28. *Irish Press*, 10 May 1935.
29. A. D. Hall, *Reconstruction and Land: An Approach to Farming in the National Interest* (London 1941), especially Chapters 3 and 5.
30. *Parl. Deb. (C)*, ii, 25 May 1922, col. 676. For the provisions of the act and its implementation see Greenlees, pp. 336–40.
31. *Ibid.*, pp. 337–9.
32. A. E. Muskett and J. Morrison, 'Agriculture', *Belfast and its Regional Setting*, ed. E. E. Evans (Belfast 1952), p. 144.
33. *Parl. Deb. (C)*, iv, 7 May 1924, col. 738.
34. Ministry of Agriculture's memo to Home Office, 17 Dec. 1926, P.R.O.N.I., CAB 9E/57/1. On the operation of the eggs marketing scheme see Greenlees, Chapter 15.
35. See above, pp. 106–7.
36. *Parl. Deb. (C)*, xviii, 28 Apr., 6 May 1936, cols 1112–27, 1319–76.
37. *Ibid.*, vii, 3 Nov. 1926, col. 2187.
38. A. Lewis, secretary of Portadown Chamber of Commerce, to J. S. Gordon, 23 Nov. 1927, 13 Feb. 1928, P.R.O.N.I., CAB 9E/75/1.
39. On the constitutional difficulty see the exchange of correspondence and the interviews involving the Parliamentary Draftsman and officials of the cabinet secretariat, the Ministry of Agriculture and the Home Office, Apr.–Jul. 1930, P.R.O.N.I., CAB 9E/75/1. For the terms of the bill see *Parl. Deb. (C)*, xii, 7 Oct. 1930, cols 1692–5.
40. On the progress of the agitation see the cabinet file, 'Fruit Grading and Marketing 1927–31', P.R.O.N.I., CAB 9E/75/1; *Armagh Guardian* for 1930–31.
41. G. F. Fidler, Assistant Secretary, and D. Harkness, Assistant Principal and Archdale's Private Secretary, to Blackmore, 2 Sep. 1930, 14 Jul. 1931, P.R.O.N.I., CAB 9E/75/1.
42. *Parl. Deb. (C)*, xii, 7 Oct. 1930, col. 1698.
43. *Ibid.*, 7 Oct. 1930, col. 1697.
44. *Ibid.*, 7 Oct. 1930, col. 1720.
45. On the campaign see the cabinet file on fruit grading and marketing, 1927–31, P.R.O.N.I., CAB 9E/75/1; *Armagh Guardian*, Dec.–Mar. 1931.
46. J. S. Gordon to Blackmore, 19 Feb. 1931, P.R.O.N.I., CAB 9E/75/1.
47. Cab. Conclusions, 26 Feb. 1931, *ibid.*, CAB 4/277/17.

48. *Parl. Deb. (C)*, xiii, 19 Mar. 1931, cols 453–9.
49. *Ibid.*, 31 Mar., 16 Apr. 1931, cols 643–62, 846–9; J. S. Gordon to Blackmore, 21 Mar. 1931, reporting the results of his discussions with interested M.P.s, P.R.O.N.I., CAB 9E/75/1.
50. T. W. Allen to Craig, 11 Jun. 1937, P.R.O.N.I., CAB 9E/75/2.
51. *Parl. Deb. (C)*, xix, 9 Jun. 1937, col. 1531.
52. Scott Robertson to Blackmore, 9 Jul. 1937, P.R.O.N.I., CAB 9E/75/2.
53. See, e.g., Scott Robertson to Blackmore, 15 Jun. 1937, *ibid.*
54. *The Economist*, 7 Aug. 1937.
55. The most detailed accounts of the change in imperial agricultural policy are the articles on agriculture in the British Association's *Britain in Depression*, pp. 81–151, and *Britain in Recovery* (London 1938), pp. 163–236. There is a useful summary in J. H. Richardson, pp. 160–98, and a brilliantly ironical commentary on the policy of 'growing less' in A. S. J. Baster, *The Little Less: An Essay on the Political Economy of Restrictionism* (London 1947), pp. 36–49.
56. British Association, *Britain in Depression*, pp. 89–95.
57. Scott Robertson's memo on 'The Wheat Quota', 26 Nov. 1931, P.R.O.N.I., CAB 9E/93/1.
58. *Parl. Deb. (C)*, xiv, 8 Mar. 1932, cols 20–1.
59. See the internal memoranda and correspondence between the Minister of Agriculture and officials, 1930–32, but especially in Nov. and Dec. 1931, P.R.O.N.I., CAB 9E/93/1.
60. British Association, *Britain in Depression*, pp. 107–21; J. H. Richardson, pp. 170–3.
61. On the demands of the U.F.U. for a milk marketing scheme see P.R.O.N.I., CAB 9E/122/1.
62. Brooke's memo on the Milk Bill, May 1934, *ibid.*, CAB 9E/122/2.
63. Scott Robertson to Blackmore, 10 Mar. 1934, *ibid.*
64. Spender to Waley, 12 May 1934, *ibid.*
65. 'Report on the Milk and Milk Products Situation. Ulster's Case for Similar Treatment', 13 Mar. 1934, *ibid.*
66. Report of meetings at Treasury, 2–3 May 1934, *ibid.*; E. M. H. Lloyd, secretary of the Market Supply Committee, to Scott Robertson, 28 Apr. 1934, enclosing a copy of a letter to the Home Office and English Ministry of Agriculture, 27 Apr. 1934, *ibid.*
67. Extract of letter from Petherick to Spender, 15 May 1934, *ibid.*
68. *Parl. Deb. (C)*, xvi, 16 May 1934, col. 1644.
69. *Ibid.*, 17 May 1934, col. 1723.
70. See the correspondence between Spender and Treasury officials, 6 Mar. 1935, 8, 11 Feb. 1936, P.R.O.N.I., CAB 9E/122/1.
71. Ministerial answers to parliamentary questions and Brooke's speech on the second reading of the 1939 Bacon Industry Bill (*Parl. Deb. (C)*, xxi, 29 Mar., 4 May 1938, cols 499–500, 874–5; xxii, 9 May 1939, cols 1362–71) accurately reflect the bargaining that went

on between officials during the Anglo-Éire negotiations (P.R.O., T 160/747/1406/04/2) and subsequently (P.R.O.N.I., CAB 9E/97/1,3). On the Northern Ireland bacon industry see below, pp. 145–7.

72. *Parl. Deb. (C)*, xxii, 9 May 1939, col. 1366.
73. See above, pp. 108–10, 140–1.
74. British Association, *Britain in Depression*, pp. 132–3, 134, 136–7, 141–2, and *Britain in Recovery*, pp. 214–18.
75. Scott Robertson, p. 3.
76. On the marketing of pigs see Ministry of Agriculture, *Report on the Marketing of Agricultural Produce* (Belfast 1932), pp. 89–107, 155–9. On the fluctuation in pig prices see especially pp. 100–3, 155–9, and the text of Scott Robertson's radio broadcast, 7 Jun. 1933, P.R.O.N.I., CAB 9E/97/1.
77. *Ulster Year Book, 1935*, pp. xv–xxi; Scott Robertson, p. 2.
78. *Ibid.*, p. 4; Ministry of Agriculture, *Report on the Marketing of Agricultural Produce*, pp. 89–107.
79. See above, p. 53.
80. Scott Robertson, pp. 5–6; Scott Robertson to Blackmore, 16 Nov. 1933, P.R.O.N.I., CAB 9E/97/1.
81. For a brief outline of the scheme see *Ulster Year Book, 1935*, pp. xx–xxiii.
82. Greenlees, pp. 384, 386, 390, 398–405.
83. Brooke's statement to a meeting of M.P.s on quality grading for pig carcases, 13 Mar. 1934, P.R.O.N.I., CAB 9E/97/1. The extent of suspicions of ministry proposals and preference for simple methods was evident in parliamentary debates and questions (see, e.g., *Parl. Deb. (C)*, xvi, 19, 20 Dec. 1933, 6 Mar., 25 Apr., 7 Jun. 1934, cols 72, 130–1, 207–8, 1133–4, 1147, 1167, 1182, 1187, 2192).
84. Greenlees, pp. 391, 393–4, 397–8. On Scott Robertson's insistence upon this Wiltshire policy see his letters to Blackmore, 10, 16 Mar. 1933, and the text of his radio broadcast on the future of pig marketing, 7 Jun. 1933, P.R.O.N.I., CAB 9E/97/1.
85. Greenlees, pp. 395–7.
86. *Belfast News-Letter*, 20 Jun. 1935. For ministerial reaction to this condemnation see the correspondence between Blackmore and Scott Robertson, P.R.O.N.I., CAB 9E/97/1.
87. Brooke's memo on the 'proposal to license a further Wiltshire bacon factory', c. 16 Oct. 1936, *ibid.; Parl. Deb. (C)*, xxii, 7 Mar., 9 May 1939, cols 334, 1383–4.
88. Confidential memo on board policy by the secretary of the Pigs Marketing Board, 22 Jun. 1936, pp. 3–7, P.R.O.N.I., CAB 9E/97/1.
89. See, e.g., Scott Robertson to Gransden, 1 Jul. 1936, enclosing the above memo on board policy, *ibid.*
90. Greenlees, pp. 388–9, 391, 398–405.
91. *Ibid.*, p. 375.

92. Scott Robertson to Blackmore, 16 Nov. 1933, P.R.O.N.I., CAB 9E/97/1.
93. British Association, *Britain in Recovery*, pp. 177–88.
94. *Parl. Deb. (C)*, xvi, 6 Jun. 1934, col. 2127.
95. On the reasons for adopting a different scheme and the provisions of the 1934 Milk and Milk Products Bill see Brooke's second-reading speech, *ibid.*, 6 Jun. 1934, cols 2126–32; Greenlees, pp. 312–23.
96. *Parl. Deb. (C)*, xvi, 6 Jun. 1934, col. 2128.
97. For a sardonic commentary on the performance of the English Milk Marketing Board see Baster, pp. 41–5.
98. *Parl. Deb. (C)*, xvi, 6 Jun. 1934, col. 2130.
99. See, e.g., the agricultural correspondent of the *Glasgow Herald*, 31 Aug. 1935; remarks of Dr Haden Guest, Labour M.P. for North Islington, Imperial *Parl. Deb. (C)*, 5 ser., 328, 28 Oct. 1937, cols 327–30.
100. *Parl. Deb. (C)*, xviii, 5 Mar. 1936, col. 442.

Chapter 7
COMPROMISE: SOCIAL SERVICES
(pp. 150–175)
1. *Parl. Deb. (C)*, ii, 14 Mar. 1922, cols 18–19.
2. For an outline of Northern Ireland's social services see the relevant sections of the *Ulster Year Books, 1926–38;* for an appraisal of such services in the inter-war years see Lawrence, pp. 103–17, 147–52, 158–64.
3. See above, pp. 87–8.
4. See above, pp. 88–9.
5. Note of meeting with deputation from the U.F.U., 20 Feb. 1936, P.R.O.N.I., CAB 9C/38.
6. Andrews to Londonderry, 14 May 1925, *ibid.*, CAB 9C/1/6.
7. *Ibid.*
8. See above, p. 92.
9. Craig to C. C. Craig, 23 Jun. 1925, P.R.O.N.I., CAB 9C/11/1.
10. Lawrence, p. 191.
11. W. Strachan to Petherick, a Principal, Ministry of Finance, 5 Jan. 1925, P.R.O.N.I., CAB 9A/8.
12. Pollock's memo on proposed Contributory Pensions Bill, 3 Sep. 1925, *ibid.*, CAB 9C/11/1.
13. Spender to Blackmore, 23 Jan. 1931, *ibid.*, CAB 4/275/40.
14. Pollock's memo on proposed Contributory Pensions Bill, 3 Sep. 1925, *ibid.*, CAB 9C/11/1.
15. See, e.g., below, p. 157.
16. *Financial Relations Report*, pp. 32, 49, 52.
17. *Interim* and *Final Reports of the Departmental Committee on the Cost of Living*, 1922, Cmd 12, and 1923, Cmd 20.
18. U.F.U. memo on 'the Proposed Bill for Setting up a Scheme of Unemployment Insurance for Agricultural Workers in Northern Ireland', 5 Feb. 1936, P.R.O.N.I., CAB 9C/38.

19. This paragraph is based upon Chapter 13 of Isles and Cuthbert, *Economic Survey.*
20. Brooke's memo on unemployment insurance for agricultural workers, Jan. 1935, P.R.O.N.I., CAB 4/334/14.
21. Cab. Conclusions, 18 Dec. 1935, *ibid.,* CAB 4/350/24.
22. U.F.U. memo, 5 Feb. 1936, *ibid.,* CAB 9C/38.
23. Pollock's memo on old-age pensions, 10 Sep. 1924, *ibid.,* CAB 9B/22.
24. Bates's memo on maternity and child welfare, 11 Mar. 1930, *ibid.,* CAB 4/252/20.
25. Pollock's memo on maternity and child welfare, 14 Mar. 1930, *ibid.,* CAB 4/252/19.
26. Spender to Blackmore, 17 Sep. 1936, *ibid.,* CAB 9A/3/5.
27. The following account (pp. 157–9) is based upon the cabinet files relating to outdoor relief, 1921–39 (*ibid.,* CAB 9B/137/1,2), particularly upon the reports of meetings between ministers and members of the Board of Guardians, 9 Feb., 8 Aug. 1928, 6, 16 Sep. 1932, and extracts from the minutes of a meeting of the Board of Guardians on 31 Jul. 1928.
28. 6 Sep. 1932.
29. *Ibid.*
30. *Ibid.*
31. 8 Aug. 1928.
32. *Ibid.*
33. 31 July 1928.
34. 8 Aug. 1928.
35. 31 Jul. 1928.
36. Andrews to Craig, 9 Aug. 1928, P.R.O.N.I., CAB 9B/137/1.
37. See, e.g., Harris to Bates, 22 Sep. 1932, *ibid.,* CAB 9B/137/2.
38. Pollock to Craig, 3 Oct. 1932, *ibid.,* CAB 9B/137/2.
39. Board of Guardians' minutes, 31 Jul. 1928, and Bates's memo on distress, 8 Jul. 1932, *ibid.,* CAB 9B/137/1,2.
40. *Ulster Year Book, 1938,* pp. 176–8, 210–13.
41. Notes on conversation between Pollock and Craig, 9 Oct. 1930, and Andrews's memo on economies, 18 Nov. 1930, P.R.O.N.I., CAB 9A/3/1; file on estimates for 1931–32, *ibid.,* CAB 9A/3/2; Cab. Conclusions, 25 Mar. 1931, *ibid.,* CAB 4/279/26.
42. Andrews's and Pollock's memos on pensions, Sep. 1924, *ibid.,* CAB 9B/22.
43. *Parl. Deb. (C),* xii, 20 May 1930, col. 1355.
44. See, e.g., *ibid.,* ii, 29 Jun. 1922, cols 898–900.
45. Lawrence, p. 136 and n. 2.
46. *Parl. Deb. (C),* xii, 20 May 1930, cols 1356–8.
47. Andrews to N. Chamberlain, then Minister of Health, 23 Apr. 1928, P.R.O.N.I., CAB 9C/27/1.
48. Lawrence, p. 134.
49. Andrews to N. Chamberlain, 23 Apr. 1928, P.R.O.N.I., CAB 9C/27/1.

50. Andrews to Craig, 11 Jun. 1928, *Ibid.*, CAB 9C/15.
51. Craig to Andrews, 13 Jun. 1928, *ibid.*
52. Resolution of the Antrim branch of the U.F.U., 3 Oct. 1929, *ibid.*
53. Cab. Conclusions, 8 Jan. 1930, *ibid.*, CAB 4/247/31.
54. *Ibid.; Parl. Deb. (C)*, xii, 20 May 1930, cols 1362–3.
55. *Ibid.*, 20 May 1930, col. 1362.
56. Cab. Conclusions, 8 Jan. 1930, P.R.O.N.I., CAB 4/247/31.
57. Andrews to Craig, 15 Jun. 1928, *ibid.*, CAB 9C/15.
58. Cab. Conclusions, 11 Jul. 1929, *ibid.*, CAB 4/235/29.
59. Andrews to Craig, 28 Mar. 1930, *ibid.*, CAB 9C/15.
60. *Ibid.*
61. *Ibid.*
62. Andrews to Craig, 31 Mar. 1930, *ibid.*
63. *Ibid.*
64. Cab. Conclusions, 7 May 1930, *ibid.*, CAB 4/260/18.
65. *Parl. Deb. (C)*, xii, 20 May 1930, col. 1367.
66. See, e.g., Andrews's rejection of the half-hearted efforts of the Labour and U.U.L.A. M.P.s to go beyond the British scheme or to have lower rates of contributions, *ibid.*, 20, 22 May 1930, cols 1361, 1507–9.
67. *Ibid.*, 20 May 1930, col. 1381.
68. *Interim Report of the Planning Advisory Board Committee on Housing in Northern Ireland*, 1944, Cmd 224.
69. For the main housing statistics of the 1926 and 1937 censuses see *Ulster Year Book, 1932*, pp. 151–3, and *Ulster Year Book, 1938*, pp. 193–5.
70. Lawrence, pp. 151–2; *Final Reports of the Departmental Committee on the Increase of Rent and Mortgage Interest (Restrictions) Act, 1920*, 1923, Cmd 22; *Report of the Select Committee on Rents*, 1931, H.C. 249.
71. Lawrence, pp. 148–9.
72. *Ibid.*, p. 150 n. 1.
73. *Parl. Deb. (C)*, iii, 6 Nov. 1923, col. 1749.
74. Gilbert, pp. 198–9.
75. *Ibid.*, p. 199.
76. See, e.g., *Parl. Deb. (C)*, iv, 23 Oct. 1924, col. 1501; vi, 28 May 1925, col. 948; viii, 13 Oct. 1927, cols 2038–9.
77. Gilbert, p. 200.
78. See, e.g., Kyle and Beattie, *Parl. Deb. (C)*, vi, 26, 27 May 1925, cols 849, 865; Devlin, *ibid.*, ix, 30 Oct. 1928, cols 2763–4.
79. *Ibid.*, xiv, 15, 16 Mar. 1932, cols 321, 411; xv, 18 Oct. 1933, cols 2412–13, 2432, 2435.
80. *Ibid.*, iv, 23 Oct. 1924, col. 1498; vi, 26 May 1925, cols 848, 858.
81. See below, pp. 167, 173.
82. Lawrence, pp. 148–9.
83. *Ibid.*, p. 149 n. 4.
84. For a summary of the dispute see Alderman Duff's speech and

Pollock's reply, *Parl. Deb. (C)*, iii, 28 Mar. 1923, cols 306–10; for the settlement see *ibid.*, 7 Nov. 1923, cols 1799–1800.
85. Budge and O'Leary, pp. 145–9, 167 n. 34.
86. Gilbert, pp. 198–200.
87. Lawrence, p. 150.
88. Cab. Conclusions, 13 Jun., 6 Oct. 1923, P.R.O.N.I., CAB 4/82/9, 4/89/11.
89. Pollock to Craig, 7 Jul. 1927, *ibid.*, CAB 9B/89/1.
90. Cab. Conclusions, 4, 19 Nov. 1930, *ibid.*, CAB 4/271/26, 4/273/32.
91. Spender to Harris, 16 Jan. 1932, *ibid.*, CAB 9B/89/2.
92. Pollock's memo on housing subsidies, 26 Sep. 1928, and Harris's memo on Housing Acts, 19 Jun. 1929, *ibid.*, CAB 9B/89/1.
93. Pollock to Craig, 18 Jan. 1932, *ibid.*, CAB 9B/89/2; Cab. Conclusions, 19 Jan. 1932, *ibid.*, CAB 4/297/27.
94. Fin. Diary, 1933–34, 9 Jun. 1933 (account of a cabinet meeting on 7 Jun. 1933).
95. Bates's memo on housing policy, 2 Jun. 1933, P.R.O.N.I., CAB 9B/89/2.
96. Spender to Blackmore, 13 Dec. 1932, and to Taylor, 6 Jun. 1933, and Pollock to Craig, 2 Jun. 1933, *ibid.;* Fin. Diary, 1933–34, 9 Jun. 1933.
97. *Ibid.;* Cab. Conclusions, 7 Jun. 1933, P.R.O.N.I., CAB 4/312/21.
98. *Parl. Deb. (C)*, xiv, 15 Mar. 1932, col. 307.
99. *Ibid.*, xv, 17, 25 Oct. 1932, cols 2347–8, 2534–7.
100. See, e.g., *ibid.*, ix, 7 Nov. 1928, cols 3022–4.
101. *Ibid.*, 30, 31 Oct. 1928, cols 2758–9, 2898–9.
102. *Ibid.*, iii, 7 Nov. 1923, col. 1775.
103. *Ibid.*, xi, 27 Nov. 1929, col. 1605.
104. *Ibid.*, vi, 26 May 1925, col. 853.
105. See, e.g., Kyle's and Beattie's annoyance that the government did not bring forward in committee an amendment conceding a demand, widely expressed during the second reading of the 1928 bill, for larger subsidy houses, *ibid.*, ix, 7 Nov. 1928, cols 3016, 3024–5.
106. First requested, 13 Oct. 1927, *ibid.*, viii, col. 2029.
107. First requested, 27 May 1925, *ibid.*, vi, col. 864; *Report of the Select Committee on Rents*, pp. 21–2.
108. *Parl. Deb. (C)*, xi, 27 Nov. 1929, cols 1579–1608, 1610–11.
109. *Ibid.*, iv, 23 Oct. 1924, col. 1512.
110. *Ibid.*, xiv, 15 Mar. 1932, col. 313.
111. *Ibid.* viii, 13 Oct. 1927, cols 2018–21; x, 9 Apr. 1929, cols 1608–52.
112. *Ibid.*, iii, 14 Nov. 1923, col. 1984; xi, 27 Nov. 1929, cols 1618, 1626–32; xiv, 21 Mar. 1932, col. 430.
113. *Ibid.*, xi, 27 Nov., 3 Dec. 1929, cols 1578–1608, 1610–12, 1742–3.
114. *Ibid.*, vi, 28 May 1925, cols 933–5; xviii, 18 Feb. 1936, cols 158–71.

115. *Ibid.,* 18 Feb. 1936, col. 170.
116. *Ibid.,* vii, 16 Mar. 1926, col. 192.
117. See. e.g., Devlin's remarks on the 1927 bill (*ibid.,* viii, 13 Oct. 1927, cols 2041–6) and the Opposition's comments in the 1928 bill (*ibid.,* ix, 30 Oct., 1, 7, 8 Nov. 1928, cols 2750–4, 2576–8, 2759–60, 2763–6, 2894–8, 2899–901, 3018–21, 3022–7, 3030–1, 3032–43, 3048–52, 3075–86, 3093–104).
118. See, e.g., *ibid.,* xi, 13 Nov. 1929, cols 1201, 1212, 1235.
119. *Ibid.,* v, 28 Mar. 1925, col. 936.
120. See, e.g., Cab. Conclusions and supporting papers, 13 Jul. 1927, 28 Sep. 1928, 11 Jul., 19 Aug., 22 Nov. 1929, 19 Jan. 1932, P.R.O.N.I., CAB 4/194/37, 4/218/20, 4/235/29, 4/236/19, 4/242/18, 4/297/27; *Parl. Deb. (C),* xiv, 15 Mar. 1932, cols 305–11.
121. *Ibid.,* vii, 23 Mar. 1926, cols 305–6.
122. *Ibid.,* ix, 8 Nov. 1928, col. 3090.
123. *Ibid.,* ix, 30 Oct., 7 Nov. 1928, cols 2758, 2898, 3020; xi, 12, 13 Nov. 1929, cols 1146–7, 1210, 1211, 1230–1.
124. *Ibid.,* vii, 16 Mar. 1926, cols 191–2; viii, 13 Oct. 1927, cols 2020–1; xi, 13 Nov. 1929, col. 1228.
125. *Ibid.,* iv, 23 Oct. 1924, col. 1521.
126. See above, p. 168.
127. *Parl. Deb. (C),* viii, 8 Nov. 1927, cols 2642–3; ix, 1 Nov. 1928, col. 2906.
128. On the progress of Stewart's campaign see the cabinet file on housing, Nov. 1930–Oct. 1936, P.R.O.N.I., CAB 9B/89/2; *Belfast News-Letter,* 31 May, 6, 7 Jun. 1933.
129. Cab. Conclusions, 7 Jun. 1933, P.R.O.N.I., CAB 4/312/21; Fin. Diary, 1933–34, 9 Jun. 1933.
130. *Ibid.; Parl. Deb. (C),* xv, 17, 25, 26 Oct. 1933, cols 2348, 2534–49, 2580–2.
131. *Ibid.,* 18 Oct. 1933, col. 2438.
132. *Ibid.,* 18 Oct. 1933, col. 2434.
133. *Ibid.,* viii, 13 Oct. 1927, col. 2042.
134. See, e.g., *ibid.,* 13 Oct. 1927, cols 2042–3; ix, 7 Nov. 1928, cols 3034–8; xi, 13 Nov. 1939, cols 1215–22.
135. Lawrence, pp. 148 n. 1, 149 and ns 4 and 5.
136. *Ibid.,* pp. 150–1.
137. *Parl. Deb. (C),* xiv, 16 Mar. 1932, col. 384.
138. *Report on the Administration of Local Government Services, 1937–38,* 1938, Cmd 200, p. 55.
139. Gilbert, p. 203.
140. On the contrast between Northern Ireland and Britain see *ibid.,* pp. 200–3, and Lawrence, pp. 146–52.

Chapter 8
CONFUSION: LAW AND ORDER
(pp. 179–205)

1. *Parl. Deb. (C),* i, 22 Jun. 1921, col. 36.

2. Craig to St Loe Strachey, 14 Apr. 1922, House of Lords Record Office, S/4/15/6.
3. On the Anglo-Irish war in general see D. Macardle, *The Irish Republic* (Corgi ed., London 1968), pp. 290–435, and C. Townshend, *The British Campaign in Ireland, 1919–21* (Oxford 1975). For its impact upon the North and the police forces there see Buckland, *Ulster Unionism*, pp. 121–3, 159–64, and A. Hezlet, *The 'B' Specials: A History of the Ulster Special Constabulary* (Pan ed., London 1973), pp. 1–47.
4. Quoted in Townshend, p. 124.
5. Hezlet, p. 51. On the provisions of the 1920 bill relating to the control of police see Imperial *Parl. Deb. (C)*, 5 ser., 127, 29 Mar. 1920, col. 931; 129, 2, 3 Jun. 1920, cols 1999–2016, 2099–120.
6. For an attempt to hammer out a workable relationship between the Northern government and the military and police authorities in the transitional period see the notes of Craig's meeting with Sir Hamar Greenwood, the Chief Secretary, and representatives of the military, police and Dublin Castle, 23 Jun. 1921, P.R.O.N.I., CAB 4/4/1.
7. Boyce, *Englishmen and Irish Troubles*, pp. 139–71; Jones, pp. 77–192.
8. Townshend, pp. 196–8.
9. *Ibid., passim.*
10. For the instructions issued to the police in Northern Ireland see the orders issued by the Inspector-General, 9 Jul. 1921, and those issued by Wickham to his county inspectors, 10 Jul. 1921, P.R.O.N.I., CAB 6/27.
11. Spender to S. M. Kennedy of Londonderry, 12 Jul. 1921, *ibid.*
12. Lady Spender, Diary, 18 Jul. 1921, *ibid.*, D1633/2/24.
13. Inspector-General to divisional commissioners, 9 Jul. 1921, *ibid.*, CAB 6/27.
14. Boyce, 'British Conservative Opinion', pp. 103–12.
15. Quoted *ibid.*, p. 104.
16. Quoted *ibid.*, p. 106.
17. Hezlet, p. 49; police reports on the state of order in Belfast, 10–17 Jul. 1921, P.R.O.N.I., FIN 18/1/107.
18. Lady Spender, Diary, 18 Jul. 1921, *ibid.*, D1633/2/24.
19. *Ibid.*, 12 Jul. 1921.
20. *Ibid.*, 11 Jul. 1921.
21. *Ibid.*, 11, 12 Jul. 1921; note of meeting between the government and the military and police authorities, 11 Jul. 1921, P.R.O.N.I., CAB 6/27; conference of ministers, 11 Jul. 1921, *ibid.*, CAB 4/8/1,2.
22. Representative meeting, 15 Jul. 1921, *ibid.*, CAB4/9/1,2; Spender's telegram to Macready, 15 Jul. 1921, *ibid.*, CAB 6/27.
23. Bates to Craig, 16 Jul. 1921, *ibid.*, CAB 6/27.
24. Farrell, pp. 42–3; police reports on occurrences in Belfast, 29 Aug.–3 Sep. 1921, P.R.O.N.I., FIN 18/1/107.

25. See, e.g., Cab. Conclusions, 16, 23 Aug. 1921, *ibid.*, CAB 4/14/23, 4/15/12; memos by Watt, 5, 12 Aug. 1921, *ibid.*, CAB 4/15/1,8; Wickham to Spender (and enclosures), 9 Aug. 1921, *ibid.*, CAB 4/14/6; Spender's report on visit to London on 10 Aug. 1921, 12 Aug. 1921, *ibid.*, CAB 4/14/13; Craig to Greenwood, 24 Aug. 1921, *ibid.*, CAB 6/27.
26. The following seven paragraphs are based largely upon the cabinet secretariat's notes of three cabinet meetings (at 12 noon and 6 p.m. on 31 Aug. 1921 and 11 a.m. on 1 Sep. 1921) and upon a typescript, probably by Spender, headed 'History of Attempts to Get Peace Keeping Forces on Satisfactory Footing', all in P.R.O.N.I., CAB 4/17/1,2,4,10. The first meeting was attended by two local Unionists, one of whom was William Grant, the U.U.L.A. M.P.; the second and third meetings were attended by Cope and Tudor from Dublin Castle; and all meetings were attended by the local police commissioners or their representatives and the local military commander. Macready was consulted over the telephone during the first meeting and then came up to Belfast to consult the local commander.
27. 12 noon, 31 Aug. 1921.
28. 'History of Attempts to Get Peace Keeping Forces on Satisfactory Footing'.
29. *Ibid.*
30. 12 noon, 31 Aug. 1921.
31. 6 p.m., 31 Aug. 1921.
32. 1 Sep. 1921.
33. Cab. Conclusions, 12 Sep. 1921, P.R.O.N.I., CAB 4/19/21.
34. Carter-Campbell to Macready, 2 Sep. 1921, *ibid.*, CAB 6/27.
35. Gelston to Wickham, 29 Sep. 1921, *ibid.*
36. Wickham to Tudor, 30 Sep. 1921, *ibid.*
37. Gelston to Wickham, 29 Sep. 1921, *ibid.*
38. Cab. Conclusions, 6 p.m., 31 Aug. 1921, *ibid.*, CAB 4/17/4.
39. Cab. Conclusions, 12 Sep. 1921, *ibid.*, CAB 4/19/21.
40. The deputation met Bates on 9 Sep. and Craig and others on 12 Sep. For records of the meetings see P.R.O.N.I., CAB 6/27.
41. Record of Bates's meeting with deputation, 9 Sep. 1921, *ibid.*
42. Record of Craig's meeting with deputation, 12 Sep. 1921, *ibid.*
43. Buckland, *Ulster Unionism*, pp. 39–40.
44. Craig to Carter-Campbell, 14 Sep. 1921, P.R.O.N.I., CAB 6/27; Carter-Campbell to Craig, 17 Sep. 1921, *ibid.*, CAB 4/22/22; Cab. Conclusions, 19 Sep. 1921, *ibid.*, CAB 4/22/24.
45. Macready to Craig, 23 Sep. 1921, *ibid.*, CAB 6/27.
46. Farrell, pp. 43–4; police reports on occurrences in Belfast, 24–30 Sep. 1921, P.R.O.N.I., FIN 18/1/107.
47. *Parl. Deb. (C)*, i, 26 Sep. 1921, col. 203.
48. Tudor to Wickham, 26 Sep. 1921, P.R.O.N.I., CAB 6/27.
49. Craig to Greenwood, 27 Sep. 1921, *ibid.*
50. See Ministry of Home Affairs internal memos, 5 Oct. 1921, *ibid.*

51. Carter-Campbell to Gelston, 28 Sep. 1921, *ibid.*
52. See above, pp. 189–90.
53. See, e.g., *Belfast News-Letter*, 27–29 Sep. 1921.
54. Watt to Bates, 29 Sep. 1921, P.R.O.N.I., CAB 6/27.
55. Ministry of Home Affairs minute, 3 Oct. 1921, *ibid.*; Craig to Tudor, 5 Oct. 1921, and Sir. H. Wilson to Craig, 8 Oct. 1921, *ibid.*; Hezlet, p. 51.
56. *Parl. Deb. (C)*, i, 20 Sep. 1921, col. 65.
57. See P.R.O.N.I., CAB 6/27.
58. Watt's memo, 5 Oct. 1921, *ibid.*
59. Megaw's memo, 5 Oct. 1921, *ibid.*
60. Record of conference at Cabin Hill between Craig, Macready and General A. R. Cameron, the new Commanding Officer in Northern Ireland, 20 Oct. 1921, *ibid.*
61. *Ibid.*
62. *Ibid.*
63. Hezlet, pp. 53–6.
64. On the boundary question and its implications for Northern Ireland see Boyce, 'British Conservative Opinion', pp. 103–12, and *Englishmen and Irish Troubles*, pp. 142–70, and appendix 1; Buckland, *Ulster Unionism*, pp. 149–50; Jones, pp. 87–192, 235–46; *Report of the Irish Boundary Commission, passim;* M. Wall, 'Partition: The Ulster Question (1916–26)', *The Irish Struggle 1916–1926*, ed. T. D. Williams (London 1966), pp. 84–93.
65. On reactions to the Treaty and events in the South in 1922 see Macardle, pp. 548–752, and Wall, pp. 87–8.
66. On events in the North in 1922 see Buckland, *Ulster Unionism*, pp. 164–75, and Hezlet, pp. 58–102.
67. Tallents's notes on Belleek and Pettigo, 13 Nov. 1922, P.R.O., CO 739/1.
68. Macardle, p. 663.
69. Hezlet, p. 84. Figures supplied by the Northern Ireland Cabinet Office to the Colonial Office for use by the Foreign Office in the United States (P.R.O., CO 739/14) are 152 killed (23 policemen and soldiers, 49 Protestants, 80 Catholics) and 322 wounded (48 policemen and soldiers, 136 Protestants and 138 Catholics).
70. See above, pp. 52–3, 163.
71. See, e.g., Macready to Cameron, 23 Dec. 1921, and Cameron to Spender, 26 Dec. 1921, P.R.O.N.I., CAB 6/27.
72. See below, p. 201.
73. Craig to Horne, 8 Nov. 1921, P.R.O.N.I., CAB 6/27; Hezlet, pp. 51, 66, 79.
74. See, e.g., Cab. Conclusions, 16 Feb., 14 Mar., 23 May 1922, P.R.O.N.I., CAB 4/33/11, 4/36/11, 4/44/25; Cameron to Craig, 23 May (letter and memo), 2 Jun. 1922, *ibid.*, CAB 6/28; Imperial Cabinet Conclusions, 2 Jun. 1922, P.R.O., CAB 23/30; Hezlet, pp. 64, 88, 90; Jones, pp. 210–12.

75. Hezlet, pp. 82, 88–91.
76. See above, pp. 86, 90. On the financial problems created by the Special Constabulary and for Craig's early determination that the imperial government should bear the cost see, e.g., Craig to Horne, 8 Nov. 1921, P.R.O.N.I., CAB 6/27; Cab. Conclusions, 10 Jan. 1922, *ibid.*, CAB 4/29/15.
77. See, e.g., below, pp. 198–9, 269–75.
78. See, e.g., below, pp. 268–9.
79. L. Curtis, Colonial Office Adviser on Irish Affairs, to Churchill, 26 Apr. 1922, protesting against a threat by the Provisional Government to abrogate a railways agreement with the North unless Craig carried out the strict terms of the peace pact, P.R.O., CO 739/14.
80. See, e.g., the tone of Collins's letters and telegrams to Churchill complaining about the outrages in the North (11 Mar., 20, 21 Apr., 20 Jun. 1922) and about the Special Powers Bill (21 Mar. 1922), *ibid.*
81. On the imperial government's constant dilemma on the North see, e.g., its reaction to the February kidnappings (A. Chamberlain's report of a conversation with Craig, 10 Feb. 1922, Birmingham University Library, AC 5/2/3); the reservations of senior officials about financial aid to the Special Constabulary (T. Jones, Assistant Cabinet Secretary, and L. Curtis, Colonial Office Adviser on Irish Affairs, memo of 18 Mar. 1922, P.R.O., CAB 24/134); and the way in which events in Belfast cropped up in informal conversations between imperial and Southern ministers and officials (Jones, pp. 195–6).
82. *Ibid.*, pp. 202–12.
83. The following account of the imperial government's attitude is based largely upon the records of two imperial cabinet meetings (30 May, 2 Jun. 1922, P.R.O., CAB 23/30), during the first of which Lloyd George and Chamberlain reported on a meeting with Collins and Griffith, and during the second of which Balfour reported on a meeting with Craig.
84. 30 May 1922.
85. *Ibid.*
86. *Ibid.*
87. *Ibid.*
88. 2 Jun. 1922.
89. Cab. Conclusions, 31 May, 19–20 Jun. 1922, P.R.O.N.I., CAB 4/45/16, 4/48/21; Bates to Craig, 15 Jun. 1922, P.R.O., CO 906/29; record of meeting at 10 Downing Street, 16 Jun. 1922, *ibid.*, CO 906/26.
90. Carried out by Tallents, P.R.O., CO 906/23–30.
91. Craig to Blackmore, 5 Jun. 1922, P.R.O.N.I., PM 9/2.
92. Craig to Spender, 9 Jun. 1922, *ibid.*
93. For a brief summary of the Wilson–Flood plans see Hezlet, pp. 66–7, 82, 84–6, 87–8. For the difficulties which these plans

created not only with the imperial government but also within the Northern government and Unionist Party see a series of cabinet files dealing with military and police affairs in 1922, P.R.O.N.I., CAB 6/28–30.

94. Balfour's report on a meeting with Craig, Imperial Cabinet Conclusions, 2 Jun. 1922, P.R.O., CAB 23/30.
95. Buckland, *Ulster Unionism*, pp. 158–9, 165.
96. Cab. Conclusions, 13 Mar. 1922, P.R.O.N.I., CAB 4/35/16.
97. Solly Flood to Bates, 19 May 1922, *ibid.*, CAB 6/28.
98. Cab. Conclusions, 19–20 Jun. 1922, *ibid.*, CAB 4/48/21.
99. Solly Flood's discussion document for cabinet, 18 Apr. 1922, *ibid.*, CAB 4/40/24.
100. Cab. Conclusions, 19 Apr. 1922, *ibid.*, CAB 4/40/45.
101. Cab. Conclusions, 20 May 1922, *ibid.*, CAB 4/43/9.
102. Craig's report of meeting, Cab. Conclusions, 26 Jan. 1922, *ibid.*, CAB 4/30/9.
103. Macardle, pp. 622, 894–6.
104. *Ibid.*, p. 598.
105. *Parl. Deb. (C)*, ii, 4 Apr. 1922, cols 318–46.
106. For the contacts of Craig and the cabinet secretariat with certain Catholics and the latter's complaints about Collins see typescript extracts from Lady Craig's Diary, 20, 25 Mar., 3 Apr., 20 May, 25 Jul. 1922, P.R.O.N.I., D1415/B/38; Lady Spender, Diary, 16 Apr., 10 May 1922, *ibid.*, D1633/2/26; Spender to Craig, 10, 21, 22, 24, 25, 29 Apr., 2, 4 May, 7, 8, 14, 15 Jun., 15, 19, 20, 31 Jul., 1, 2, 3, 5, 11, 14 Aug., 18 Sep. 1922, *ibid.*, PM 9/1,3; Blackmore to Craig, 2, 4 Jun., 31 Aug. 1922, *ibid.;* Craig to Spender, 15 Apr., 10, 16 Jun., 19 Jul., 2, 7 Aug., 19, 21 Sep. 1922, *ibid.*, PM 9/2,4; police reports on the state of the counties, 26 Sep. 1922, *ibid.*, CAB 6/30; and the way in which the views of the government's Catholic contacts were taken seriously over some questions arising from internment, particularly arrangements for saying Mass (correspondence and memoranda, Jun.–Aug. 1922, *ibid.*, CAB 9G/19/2). There is also material in the Colonial Office archives: Craig to Churchill, 21 Sep. 1922, Londonderry to Churchill, 21, 25 Sep. 1922, Londonderry to Curtis, 5 Oct. 1922, and Tallents to Curtis, 3 Nov. 1922, P.R.O., CO 739/1; Tallents's conversations with Catholics in Northern Ireland, 22, 23, 30 Jun., 1 Jul. 1922, and with Craig, 21 Jun. 1922, *ibid.*, CO 906/26; Tallents to Masterton-Smith, 4 Jul. 1922, and his formal report on the operation of the 30 March peace pact, 6 Jul. 1922, *ibid.*, CO 906/30; record of meeting, 2 Jun. 1922, between Churchill, H. A. L. Fisher, the Education Minister, Masterton-Smith, and three Belfast Catholic businessmen (R. A. Burke of Messrs John Burke & Co., shipbrokers; H. Dougal of Messrs A. Dougal & Sons Ltd, general carriers; and W. M. Hughes, baker), *ibid.*, CO 906/25.
107. See, e.g., Craig's comments on Collins's claim that he had done nothing to secure the return of expelled workers after the January

agreement, *Parl. Deb. (C)*, ii, 28 Mar. 1922, cols 223–5.
108. *Ibid.*, 4 Apr. 1922, cols 316–17, 322, 324–5, 327–8, 335, 338, 343–4.
109. Spender to Craig, 14 Jun. 1922, P.R.O.N.I., PM 9/1.
110. These deficiencies were recognised by Spender in his letter to Craig, 7 Jun. 1922, *ibid.*
111. See, e.g., *Parl. Deb. (C)*, ii, 23 May 1922, cols 600, 603, 604–6.
112. Tallents's report on the operation of the peace pact, 6 Jul. 1922, P.R.O., CO 906/30; Spender to Craig, 13 Apr., 4, 6 May 1922, P.R.O.N.I., PM 9/1; Cab. Conclusions, 1 Apr. 1922, *ibid.*, CAB 4/37/13; cabinet file on unemployment relief schemes and grants, *ibid.*, CAB 9C/3.
113. Tallents's report on the operation of the peace pact, 6 Jul. 1922, P.R.O., CO 906/30.
114. Spender to Craig, 24 Apr. 1922, P.R.O.N.I., PM 9/1.
115. Tallents's report on the operation of the peace pact, 6 Jul. 1922, P.R.O., CO 906/30.
116. Craig to Spender, 15 Apr. 1922, P.R.O.N.I., PM 9/2.
117. Tallents's report on the operation of the peace pact, 6 Jul. 1922, P.R.O., CO 906/30.
118. Craig to Spender, 15 Apr. 1922, P.R.O.N.I., PM 9/2.
119. Spender to Craig, 10, 15, 17 Apr. 1922, *ibid.*, PM 9/1; Bates's memo on the release of prisoners, 18 Apr. 1922, *ibid.*, CAB 4/40/21.
120. Cab. Conclusions, 19 Apr., 16 May 1922, *ibid.*, CAB 4/40/45, 4/42/16; Spender to Craig, 13, 17 Apr. 1922, *ibid.*, PM 9/1; Tallents's report on the operation of the peace pact, 6 Jul. 1922, P.R.O., CO 906/30.
121. Spender to Craig, 12 Apr. 1922, P.R.O.N.I., PM 9/1.
122. Spender to Craig, 21 Apr. 1922, *ibid.*
123. Spender to Craig, 24, 29 Apr. 1922, *ibid.* This seems to have been a recurrent problem: see Spender to Craig, 5 Aug. 1922, *ibid.*, PM 9/3.
124. See below, pp. 233–4.
125. Lady Spender, Diary, 1 Apr. 1922, P.R.O.N.I., D1633/2/26.
126. Spender to Craig, 24 Apr. 1922, *ibid.*, PM 9/1.
127. Spender to Craig, 12 Apr. 1922, *ibid.*
128. Spender to Craig, 17 Apr. 1922, *ibid.*

Chapter 9
DISCRIMINATION (1): JUSTICE
(pp. 206–220)
1. Cab. Conclusions, 31 Jan. 1922, P.R.O.N.I., CAB 4/31/11; Hezlet, pp. 56, 59.
2. For the legal complications raised by the use of chloroform in this instance see the papers relating to the case in P.R.O.N.I., CAB 9G/19/1.
3. *Parl. Deb. (C)*, ii, 21, 23 Mar. 1922, cols 90–1, 156–7; Megaw's

memo on flogging cases, 6 Sep. 1922, forwarded to Churchill, P.R.O., CO 739/1.
4. Spender to Craig, 28 Apr. 1922, P.R.O.N.I., PM 9/1.
5. Cosgrave to Churchill, 15 Aug. 1922, P.R.O., CO 739/14.
6. For a convenient summary of the case see a memo by Curtis, 24 Jan. 1923, *ibid.*, CO 739/19.
7. Tallents to Masterton-Smith, 6 Dec. 1922, *ibid.*, CO 739/1.
8. Cosgrave to Churchill, 15 Aug. 1922, *ibid.*, CO 739/14.
9. N. G. Loughnane to Curtis, 17 Apr. 1923, *ibid.*, CO 739/18.
10. G. G. Whiskard, a Home Office Principal on loan to the Irish Office, to Curtis, 15 Sep. 1922, *ibid.*, CO 739/1.
11. W. C. Bridgeman, the Home Secretary, to Londonderry, 20 Dec. 1922, P.R.O.N.I., CAB 9G/19/1.
12. Curtis to Churchill, 15 Sep. 1922, P.R.O., CO 739/1.
13. Craig to Blackmore, 29 Aug. 1922, P.R.O.N.I., PM 9/4.
14. Londonderry to Craig, 31 Dec. 1922, *ibid.*, CAB 9G/19/1.
15. The arguments for and (mainly) against release and reprieve are stated in Cab. Conclusions, 31 Jan., 14 Feb. 1922, *ibid.*, CAB 4/31/11, 4/32/12; Bates's memo on the proposed release of prisoners, 19 Jan. 1922, *ibid.*, CAB 9G/19/1; correspondence between Craig and the Lord Lieutenant, 25, 27, 30 Jan., 6 Feb. 1922, and Spender to the Lord Lieutenant, 6 Feb. 1922, *ibid.*
16. Fitzalan, the Lord Lieutenant, to Craig, 25 Jan. 1922, *ibid.*
17. See, e.g., *Parl. Deb. (C)*, ii, 14 Mar. 1922, cols 23–8, 31–3.
18. *Northern Whig*, 25 Feb. 1922.
19. Cab. Conclusions, 13 Mar. 1922, P.R.O.N.I., CAB 4/35/16; *Parl. Deb. (C)*, ii, 14 Mar. 1922, cols 25–6.
20. *Ibid.*, 13 Mar. 1922, col. 25.
21. Craig to Spender, 15 Apr. 1922, P.R.O.N.I., PM 9/2; Craig to Blackmore, 29 Aug. 1922, *ibid.*, PM 9/4; Spender to Watt, 12 Dec. 1922, *ibid.*, CAB 9G/19/1.
22. See above, p. 204.
23. Megaw's memo on flogging cases, 6 Sep. 1922, and Spender to Curtis, 14 Sep. 1922, P.R.O., CO 739/1; Spender to Craig, 15, 16 Sep. 1922, P.R.O.N.I., PM 9/3.
24. Spender to Watt, 12 Dec. 1922, *ibid.*, CAB 9G/19/1.
25. Londonderry to Craig, 31 Dec. 1922, *ibid.;* Masterton-Smith's memo for Bonar Law, 23 Dec. 1922, P.R.O., CO 739/1.
26. Londonderry to Bridgeman, 22 Dec. 1922, *ibid.;* Cab. Conclusions, 22, 28 Dec. 1922, P.R.O.N.I., CAB 4/63/16, 4/64/1.
27. For a convenient summary of the case see the memo on Healy, dated Feb. 1924, *ibid.*, CAB 9G/19/2.
28. Baldwin to Craig, 14 Jan. 1924, following up an earlier letter of 19 Dec. 1923, *ibid.*, CAB 9B/4.
29. Cab. Conclusions, 25 Jan. 1924, *ibid.*, CAB 4/99/21; Londonderry to Spender, 7, 12 Feb. 1924, and Spender to Londonderry, 11 Feb. 1924, *ibid.*, CAB 9B/4.
30. Watt to Blackmore, who acted as the Prime Minister's Private

Secretary as well as Assistant Cabinet Secretary, 12 Dec. 1923, *ibid.;* Cab. Conclusions, 25 Jan. 1924, *ibid.,* CAB 4/99/21.
31. Watt to Spender, 9 Feb. 1924, *ibid.,* CAB 9B/4.
32. Bates to Craig, 19 Jul. 1923, enclosing a police memo on the advantages of restriction and exclusion orders, 10 Jul. 1923, *ibid.,* CAB 9G/19/2.
33. Spender to Londonderry, 13 Feb. 1924, and to the Speaker of the imperial parliament, 14 Feb. 1924, *ibid.,* CAB 9B/4.
34. MacDonald to Craig, 15 Feb. 1924, *ibid.*
35. Cab. Conclusions, 16 Feb. 1924, *ibid.,* CAB 4/100/29.
36. *Ibid.*
37. See the correspondence between the government and military authorities, and the military reports of the incident, *ibid.,* CAB 6/28.
38. *Parl. Deb. (C),* ii, 12 Oct. 1922, col. 1024.
39. *Ibid.,* 21 Mar. 1922, cols 86–90.
40. Megaw's memo on flogging cases, 6 Sep. 1922, P.R.O., CO 739/1.
41. Cab. Conclusions, 14 Feb. 1922, P.R.O.N.I., CAB 4/32/12; *Parl. Deb. (C),* ii, 14 Mar. 1922, col. 26.
42. Watt to Blackmore as Prime Minister's Private Secretary, 12 Dec. 1923, P.R.O.N.I., CAB ᶜ 4; Bates to Craig, 19 Jul. 1923, *ibid.,* CAB 9G/19/2.
43. Curtis's memo on Heuston's case, 24 Jan. 1923, P.R.O., CO 739/19.
44. Cab. Conclusions, 31 Jan. 1922, P.R.O.N.I., CAB 4/31/11.
45. Bates's memo on prisoners, 18 Apr. 1922, *ibid.,* CAB 4/40/21.
46. Megaw's memo on flogging cases, 6 Sep. 1922, P.R.O., CO 739/1.
47. Londonderry to Bridgeman, 22 Dec. 1922, *ibid.*
48. *Ibid.*
49. Cab. Conclusions, 31 Jan. 1922, P.R.O.N.I., CAB 4/31/11.
50. Craig to Collins, 15 Apr. 1922, quoted in Tallents's report on the operation of the peace pact, 6 Jul. 1922, P.R.O., CO 906/30.
51. Cab. Conclusions, 29 Jan. 1923, P.R.O.N.I., CAB 4/69/19.
52. See above, p. 193.
53. The following account is based upon a remarkable report on the Ulster Protestant Association by District Inspector R. R. Spears, a highly regarded R.U.C. officer, 7 Feb. 1923, P.R.O.N.I., T2258.
54. *Ibid.*
55. *Parl. Deb. (C),* ii, 12 Oct. 1922, cols 1014–15.
56. Copy of statement by John W——n to the internment advisory committee, 30 Nov. 1922, P.R.O.N.I., CAB 9G/19/2.
57. Solly Flood to Watt, 28 Sep. 1922, *ibid.,* CAB 6/30.
58. Spender to Craig, 1 Aug. 1922, *ibid.,* PM 9/3.
59. Blackmore to Craig, 30 Aug. 1922, *ibid.*
60. Blackmore to Craig, 31 Aug. 1922, *ibid.*
61. Spender to Craig, 18 Sep. 1922, *ibid.*
62. *Ibid.*
63. *Ibid.*

64. Spears's report on the U.P.A., 7 Feb. 1923, *ibid.*, T2258.
65. Solly Flood to Watt, 28 Sep. 1922, *ibid.*, CAB 6/30.
66. Spears's report on the U.P.A., 7 Feb. 1923, *ibid.*, T2258.
67. See the cabinet files relating to the Pulverman ammunition contract, 1924–26, and to the question of co-ordination between the Ministry of Home Affairs and the R.U.C., 1925, *ibid.*, CAB 9G/57,58.
68. *Parl. Deb. (C)*, iii, 27 Mar. 1923, col. 273.
69. See the debates on the Expiring Laws Continuance Bills, *ibid.*, vi, 27 Oct. 1925, cols 1514–16; vii, 19, 21 Oct. 1926, cols 1759–62, 1847–56; viii, 11, 12 Oct. 1927, cols 1923–5, 1951–78.
70. See the cabinet file on the Special Powers Act, 1922–33, P.R.O.N.I., CAB 9B/83/1.
71. Bates to Craig, 26 Jul. 1932, *ibid.*, CAB 9B/200.

Chapter 10
DISCRIMINATION (2): REPRESENTATION
(pp. 221–246)
1. P.R.O.N.I., CAB 9B/205/1.
2. *The Tablet*, 15 Oct. 1932.
3. See the government-inspired reply, *ibid.*, 19 Nov. 1932.
4. Memorandum on gerrymandering prepared by the Ministry of Home Affairs, Nov. 1934, P.R.O.N.I., CAB 9B/13/2.
5. See above, pp. 102–3.
6. Elliott, 'Electoral System', pp. 73, 74–84, 115–22.
7. The clearest description of the system is in J. Knight and N. Baxter-Moore, *Northern Ireland: The Elections of the Twenties* (London 1972), pp. 19–21.
8. 'The P.R. "Catechism"', quoted in A. Wilson, *P.R. Urban Elections in Ulster in 1920*, with an introduction by R. A. Newland (London 1972), p. 4.
9. *Ibid.*, p. 49.
10. Elliott, 'Electoral System', pp. 129, 133–5; A. Wilson, pp. 10–51. The Belfast figures are based on those published in the *Northern Whig*, 17–19 Jan. 1920, which differ from those given in Wilson in respect of candidates other than those belonging to the official Unionist and anti-partition parties.
11. Elliott, *Election Results*, pp. 2, 4, 6, 8.
12. *Ibid.*, pp. 3, 5, 7, 9; Knight and Baxter-Moore, p. 14.
13. A. Wilson, pp. 56, 57, 58–9; Elliott, 'Electoral System', p. 131.
14. *Ibid.*, pp. 143–8, 316–17.
15. Figures and calculations derived from Elliott, *Election Results, passim,* and Knight and Baxter-Moore, *passim*.
16. Elliott, 'Electoral System', pp. 250–2, and *Election Results*, pp. 3, 5, 7, 9, 11, 13, 15, 17, 19, 35–86.
17. Elliott, 'Electoral System', p. 320 n. 2.
18. *Parl. Deb. (C)*, x, 7 Mar. 1929, cols 588–9.
19. Elliott, 'Electoral System', pp. 249–52.

20. *Ibid.*, pp. 245–8, 252–3, 264–73.
21. *Ibid.*, pp. 248–9; Harbinson, 'Northern Ireland Labour Party', pp. 43, 55–6.
22. Elliott, 'Electoral System', pp. 281–2. For a discussion of the effects of the abolition of P.R. on local elections and the difficulties of determining precisely such effects see *ibid.*, pp. 274–82.
23. See above, pp. 30–1.
24. Elliott, 'Electoral System', pp. 347–61.
25. *Ibid.*, p. 252 n. 1.
26. Farrell, pp. 103–4, 115–16.
27. Knight and Baxter-Moore, p. 16.
28. Elliott, *Election Results*, p. 98.
29. Budge and O'Leary, pp. 150, 169 n. 61; Elliott, 'Electoral System', pp. 272, 434–5; Mansergh, pp. 139–40.
30. Mansergh, pp. 134–5.
31. *Irish News*, 27 Jun., 6 Jul. 1922.
32. See below, pp. 238, 268–9, 274.
33. See, e.g., *Parl. Deb. (C)*, x, 6, 7 Mar. 1929, cols 543–5, 602–3.
34. See, e.g., *ibid.*, 5, 6 Mar. 1929, cols 446–9, 524.
35. *Ibid.*, 7 Mar. 1929, col. 617.
36. See, e.g., the remarks of Devlin and McMullen, a Labour M.P., *ibid.*, 5, 6 Mar. 1929, cols 450, 558–9.
37. *Ibid.*, 21 Mar. 1929, col. 1160.
38. *Ibid.*, 21 Mar. 1929, col. 1147.
39. See above, p. 38.
40. A. Wilson, p. 63.
41. *Parl. Deb. (C)*, ii, 26 Jun. 1922, cols 840–1; vi, 21 Apr. 1925, cols 148–50; viii, 26 Oct. 1927, col. 2360.
42. Craig to Dixon, 4 Jul. 1924, and Dixon to Craig, 10 Jul. 1924, P.R.O.N.I., CAB 9B/13/1.
43. *Royal Commission on Systems of Election: Minutes of Evidence,* 1910, U.K. Cd 5352, pp. 135–41.
44. Elliott, 'Electoral System', pp. 117–22.
45. *Ibid.*, pp. 78–81.
46. For the clearest statements of the Ulster Unionist case against P.R. see Megaw on local elections (*Parl. Deb. (C)*, ii, 26 Jun. 1922, cols 829–38) and Craig on parliamentary elections (*ibid.*, viii, 25 Oct. 1927, cols 2269–77).
47. A. Wilson, pp. 22–3, 37, 40, 44–5.
48. *Parl. Deb. (C)*, viii, 26 Oct. 1927, col. 2353.
49. *Ibid.*, ii, 15 Mar. 1922, col. 30; Watt to Harris, 16 Mar. 1922, P.R.O.N.I., HA 14/161.
50. *Parl. Deb. (C)*, ii, 15 Mar. 1922, col. 30.
51. See the Ministry of Home Affairs file, P.R.O.N.I., HA 14/161.
52. See, e.g., Alderman Duff's remarks during a special meeting of the Victoria Parliamentary Unionist Association, Belfast, 25 Apr. 1922, *Belfast News-Letter*, 26 Apr. 1922.
53. See, e.g., the resolutions of Unionists from the Omagh rural dis-

trict, 15 Apr. 1922, and of the Londonderry city branch of the U.U.L.A., 26 Apr. 1922, which were forwarded to Craig, P.R.O.N.I., HA 14/161.

54. *Parl. Deb. (C)*, i, 6 Dec. 1921, cols 402–5.
55. *Ibid.*, ii, 17 Oct. 1922, cols 1047–8.
56. *Ibid.*, 17 Oct. 1922, col. 1044.
57. *Ibid.*, 5 Jul. 1922, col. 920; Craig to Masterton-Smith, 22 Jul. 1922, P.R.O., HO 45/13371/463565/1.
58. Megaw to Watt, 2 May 1922, and Harris's memo, c. 10 May 1922, P.R.O.N.I., HA 14/161.
59. Watt to Harris, 16 Mar. 1922, and Megaw's minute, 12 May 1922, *ibid.*
60. For the way the measure was drawn up see the Ministry of Home Affairs file, 'Proportional Representation. Local Government Bills, 1922–27', *ibid.*
61. See below, pp. 268–9.
62. Craig to Masterton-Smith, 22 Jul. 1922, P.R.O., HO 45/13371/463565/1; Craig to Spender, 21 Sep. 1922, P.R.O.N.I., PM 9/4.
63. See above, pp. 194, 197–8, 199, 202, 203, 206–7.
64. Spender to Craig, 14 Jun. 1922, P.R.O.N.I., PM 9/1.
65. Curtis to Churchill, 1 Sep. 1922, reporting a conversation with Craig on 31 Aug. 1922, P.R.O., HO 45/13371/463565/1.
66. Cab. Conclusions, 10 Jan. 1924, P.R.O.N.I., CAB 4/98/21.
67. See especially the cabinet file on redistribution, Apr. 1921–Oct. 1927, *ibid.*, CAB 9B/13/1; and also Cab. Conclusions, 7 Mar., 5 May, 19 Jul. 1924, *ibid.*, CAB 4/104/15, 4/112/12, 4/118/16; Spender to Craig, 10, 12 Jul. 1924, and Craig to Spender, 21 Jun., 14 Jul. 1924, *ibid.*, PM 9/10,11.
68. Notes of meeting at Londonderry House, 30 Sep. 1924, *ibid.*, CAB 4/122/1; Cab. Conclusions, 10 Nov. 1924, *ibid.*, CAB 4/129/20.
69. Dixon to Craig, 19 Sep. 1927, *ibid.*, CAB 9B/13/1.
70. This summary of Craig's views is based largely upon his 1927 Orange Day speech (*Northern Whig*, 13 Jul. 1927) and his contribution to the parliamentary debate on a Labour motion, 25 Oct. 1927, asking for a select committee 'to consider and determine whether the Government have legal authority' to abolish P.R. in parliamentary elections and 'if so, to define the boundaries of the new constituencies' (*Parl. Deb. (C)*, viii, cols 2269–77). The quotations are taken from his parliamentary speech.
71. *Ibid.*, 26 Oct. 1927, col. 2366.
72. *Ibid.*, 25 Oct. 1927, col. 2275.
73. *Ibid.*, x, 5 Mar. 1929, col. 438.
74. *Ibid.*, viii, 25 Oct. 1927, col. 2276.
75. On these anomalies see Megaw's remarks introducing the 1922 Local Authorities (Elections and Constitution) Bill, *ibid.*, ii, 17 Oct. 1922, cols 1040–2.
76. *Ibid.*, 17 Oct. 1922, col. 1042.

77. *Ibid.*, 28 Jun. 1922, cols 880–1.
78. Minute sheet L/1148, P.R.O.N.I., HA 14/161; Cab. Conclusions, 31 Oct. 1922, *ibid.*, CAB 4/57/8.
79. *Derry Journal*, 2 Mar. 1923.
80. *Fermanagh Herald and Monaghan News*, 3 Mar. 1923.
81. See, e.g., *Ulster Herald*, 18 Aug. 1923.
82. *Derry Journal*, 23 Feb. 1923, reporting the views of Fermanagh Unionists.
83. See, e.g., a resolution of the Cookstown Catholic and Nationalist Registration Association, *ibid.*, 7 Feb. 1923; protests to Leech by the solicitor of the nationalist-controlled Omagh Rural District Council, *ibid.*, 23 Feb. 1923.
84. *Fermanagh Herald and Monaghan News*, 3 Mar. 1923.
85. *Ballymena Observer and County Antrim Advertiser*, 16 Mar., 6 Apr. 1923.
86. Ministry of Home Affairs memo on gerrymandering, Nov. 1934, P.R.O.N.I., CAB 9B/13/2.
87. *Fermanagh Herald and Monaghan News*, 3 Mar. 1923.
88. P.R.O.N.I., CAB 9B/13/2.
89. *Parl. Deb. (C)*, x, 26 Feb., 5 Mar. 1929, cols 38, 427.
90. *Ibid.*, 5 Mar. 1929, col. 429.
91. *Ibid.*, 5 Mar. 1929, col. 430.
92. Megaw's comments on redistribution in Co. Down, 20 Aug. 1924, approved by Craig, 21 Aug. 1924, P.R.O.N.I., CAB 9B/13/1.
93. Megaw's notes of meeting with a deputation of city of Londonderry Unionists on 28 Apr. 1924, 2 May 1924, and Spender to H. S. Robinson, 6 May 1924, *ibid.*
94. To judge from the tone of the protests of Tyrone Unionists to Bates and Craig in Mar. 1929, *ibid.*, CAB 9B/13/2.
95. Spender to Craig, 10, 12 Jul. 1924, and Craig to Spender, 14 Jul. 1924, *ibid.*, PM 9/10,11; Megaw's progress report, 11 Jul. 1924, and the correspondence between Craig and Dixon in Jul. 1924, *ibid.*, CAB 9B/13/1.
96. See the correspondence between Craig and Dixon in Jul. 1924, *ibid.*
97. Queckett to Blackmore, 12 Feb. 1929, *ibid.*, CAB 9B/13/2.
98. *Census of Population of Northern Ireland 1926. General Report* (Belfast 1929), p. 57.
99. *Parl. Deb. (C)*, x, 5 Mar. 1929, col. 432.
100. *Ibid.*, 5, 26 Mar. 1929, cols 432, 1450.
101. The best single source for the nature of the new constituencies is the report of the committee and report stages of the Redistribution Bill, *ibid.*, 21, 22, 25, 26, 27 Mar. 1929, cols 1143–1200, 1211–79, 1285–388, 1389–482, 1500–6.
102. *Ibid.*, 25 Mar. 1929, cols 1318, 1324.
103. For Craig's explanation of the division see *ibid.*, 25 Mar. 1929, cols 1287–8.
104. Elliott, 'Electoral System', pp. 391–403, 408–9.

105. *Ibid.*, pp. 403–8; Bates to Craig, 24 Jul. 1934, P.R.O.N.I., CAB 9B/13/2.

106. *Ibid.*

107. *Ibid.* On the rearrangement of the Omagh wards see Elliott, 'Electoral System', pp. 375–82.

108. This account is based largely upon a Ministry of Home Affairs memorandum, undated but *c.* 16 Dec. 1936 (P.R.O.N.I., CAB 9B/13/3), relating the episode and particularly the interviews of a Home Affairs official, probably the Permanent Secretary, W. A. Magill, with Londonderry Unionists. This memo provides a gloss on the accounts of the episode given in the local press, particularly the *Derry Journal*, 7, 9 Oct. 1936, and Elliott, 'Electoral System', pp. 404–33.

109. A. Halliday to the King, 24 Oct. 1936, copy in P.R.O.N.I., CAB 9B/13/3. The head of Sherries College, Londonderry, and a member of the North Ward Unionist Association, Halliday gave evidence against the Unionist scheme at the inquiry. He was described by the police as an atheist, infected with the 'red' virus, well-read and inclined to force his views on others. Nevertheless, Magill reported to Blackmore on 23 Nov. 1936, many local Unionists did quietly share his view that the Unionist scheme was unfair to Catholics and nationalists *(ibid.)*.

110. Ministry of Home Affairs memo, *c.* 16 Dec. 1936, *ibid.*

111. *Ibid.*

112. *Ibid.*

113. *Ibid.* for the quotations, but Elliott, 'Electoral System', pp. 419–23 for the details and an appraisal of the scheme.

114. *Derry Journal*, 23 Dec. 1936.

115. *Ibid.*

116. Harrison, p. 80.

117. E. S. Murphy, Unionist Member for Londonderry city, to Craig, 15 Dec. 1936, P.R.O.N.I., CAB 9B/13/3.

118. Maxwell Moore, an old friend of Craig and long a leading Unionist activist in the city, to Craig, 31 Dec. 1936, *ibid.*

119. Cab. Conclusions, 15 Dec. 1936, *ibid.*, CAB 4/369/41.

120. Moore to Craig, 31 Dec. 1936, *ibid.*, CAB 9B/13/3.

121. Craig to Murphy, 18 Dec. 1936, *ibid.*

Chapter 11
DISCRIMINATION (3): EDUCATION
(pp. 247–265)

1. Akenson, *Education and Enmity*, pp. 39–118.

2. *Ibid.*, p. 88.

3. *Ibid.*, pp. 48–64. For the national system see D. H. Akenson, *The Irish Education Experiment: The National System of Education in the Nineteenth Century* (London/Toronto 1970).

4. For a brief discussion of Protestant and Catholic educational philosophies and further references see Akenson, *Education and*

Enmity, pp. 12–13, 31, 53, 76, 82–3, 105–6, 193–4, 216–17, 230–2, 277–8.
5. Quoted *ibid.*, p. 52.
6. The committee issued an *Interim Report* in 1922 (Cmd 6) and a *Final Report* in the following year (Cmd 15), which are well summarised in Akenson, *Education and Enmity*, pp. 51–8.
7. *Journal of Education and School World*, Nov. 1921, p. 714, quoted in Akenson, *Education and Enmity*, p. 52.
8. Cardinal M. Logue, Catholic Archbishop of Armagh, to Londonderry, 2 Sep. 1921, P.R.O.N.I., CAB 4/18/7.
9. Cab. Conclusions, 9 Sep. 1921, *ibid.*, CAB 4/18/24.
10. Akenson, *Education and Enmity*, pp. 44–5, 46–7.
11. *Ibid.*, p. 56.
12. *Ibid.*, pp. 64–71.
13. Cab. Conclusions, 28 Feb. 1923, P.R.O.N.I., CAB 4/72/16.
14. Akenson, *Education and Enmity*, pp. 66–71.
15. C. F. D'Arcy, Church of Ireland Archbishop of Armagh, to Craig, 24 Apr. 1923, P.R.O.N.I., CAB 9D/1/1.
16. See particularly Cab. Conclusions, 16 Apr., 27 Sep., 2 Oct. 1923, *ibid.*, CAB 4/77/15, 4/86/5, 4/88/6.
17. Cab. Conclusions, 2 Oct. 1923, *ibid.*, CAB 4/88/6.
18. *Parl. Deb. (C)*, iii, 16 May 1923, cols 921, 925. Local authorities shared these views: see Akenson, *Education and Enmity*, pp. 78–9.
19. On the organisaton of the campaign see *ibid.*, pp. 79–83, and W. Corkey's own account, *Episode in the History of Protestant Ulster, 1923–47* (Belfast n.d.).
20. Quoted in Akenson, *Education and Enmity*, p. 82.
21. *Ibid.*, p. 83.
22. See, e.g., the way a private warning by Corkey a fortnight before the demonstration was ignored (Corkey to Craig, 18 Feb. 1925, and Blackmore to Corkey, 20 Feb. 1925, P.R.O.N.I., CAB 9D/1/4).
23. Craig to Londonderry, 6 Mar. 1925, *ibid.*
24. Akenson, *Education and Enmity*, p. 81.
25. Report of meeting at Stormont Castle, 6 Mar. 1925, and exchange of letters and telegrams between Craig and Londonderry, 6–7 Mar. 1925, P.R.O.N.I., CAB 9D/1/4.
26. *Parl. Deb. (C)*, v, 10, 11, 12, 13 Mar. 1925, cols 11, 44, 86–91, 98.
27. Akenson, *Education and Enmity*, p. 84.
28. *Ibid.*, pp. 84–5.
29. Londonderry to Craig, 23 Jun. 1925, reporting an interview with Protestant leaders, P.R.O.N.I., CAB 9D/1/5.
30. Akenson, *Education and Enmity*, p. 85. Government ministers' recollections and records of the Stormont meeting on 6 Mar. 1925 all agree that the limitations imposed by the 1920 act were stressed: see reports in P.R.O.N.I., CAB 9D/1/4,5.

31. Craig to Londonderry, 25 Jun. 1925, *ibid.,* CAB 9D/1/5.
32. Akenson, *Education and Enmity,* p. 86; memo of the United Education Committee and Belfast Orangemen to Craig, 11 May 1925, P.R.O.N.I., CAB 9D/1/5; report of meeting between Protestant leaders and Craig and Londonderry, 14 May 1925, *ibid.;* Londonderry to Craig, 15 May 1925, *ibid.;* report of meeting of legal advisers, 30 May 1925, *ibid.;* Cab Conclusions, 4 Jun. 1925, *ibid.,* CAB 4/145/15.
33. R. Wallace, Grand Master of the Irish Orangemen, to Blackmore, 2 Jun. 1925, *ibid.,* CAB 9D/1/5.
34. Andrews to Craig, 17 Jun. 1925, *ibid.*
35. Spender to Craig, 17, 24, 30 Jun., 3 Jul. 1925, *ibid.,* PM 9/12.
36. Craig to Londonderry, 13 Jun. 1925, *ibid.,* CAB 9D/1/5.
37. Spender to Craig, 10, 17 Jun. 1925, *ibid.,* PM 9/12.
38. Craig to Londonderry, 18 Jun. 1925, *ibid.,* CAB 9D/1/5.
39. Akenson, *Education and Enmity,* pp. 86–7; Londonderry to Craig, 18, 23 Jun. 1925, P.R.O.N.I., CAB 9D/1/5.
40. Akenson, *Education and Enmity,* pp. 86–7.
41. Londonderry to Craig, 23 Jun. 1925, P.R.O.N.I., CAB 9D/1/5.
42. Londonderry to Craig, 25 Jun. 1925, *ibid.*
43. Londonderry to Craig, 23 Jun. 1925, *ibid.*
44. Akenson, *Education and Enmity,* pp. 97–101.
45. Corkey to Craig, 23 Mar. 1928, P.R.O.N.I., CAB 9D/1/6.
46. Charlemont to Craig, 5 Jul. 1928, *ibid.*
47. *Ibid.*
48. Charlemont to Craig, 10 Jul. 1928 (and also 4 Apr. 1928), *ibid.*
49. Charlemont to Craig, 16 Jan. 1929, *ibid.*
50. Akenson, *Education and Enmity,* pp. 101–2; correspondence between Charlemont and Quinn, 19, 20, 21 Mar. 1929, and Charlemont to Craig, 21 Mar. 1929, P.R.O.N.I., CAB 9D/1/6.
51. Akenson, *Education and Enmity,* p. 104.
52. P.R.O.N.I., CAB 9D/1/6.
53. Quinn to Davison, 25 Apr. 1929, *ibid.*
54. Memo on 'the extent to which the Minister of Education is prepared to meet the case for amendment of the Act', 30 Apr. 1929, *ibid.*
55. Davison to Craig, 26 Apr. 1929, *ibid.*
56. Craig to Davison, 29 Apr. 1929, *ibid.*
57. Quinn to Craig, 7 May 1929, *ibid.*
58. Charlemont to Craig, 10 May 1929, *ibid.*
59. Corkey, pp. 81–2.
60. Remarks made during a meeting of a deputation from the Association of Northern Ireland Education Committees with Craig, 5 Apr. 1929, P.R.O.N.I., CAB 9D/1/6.
61. See, e.g., the resolution of the Newtownards branch of the Ulster Teachers' Union, 6 May 1929, *ibid.*
62. Report of interview with deputation, 5 Apr. 1929, *ibid.*
63. *Parl. Deb. (C),* xii, 9 Apr. 1930, col. 725. For the details of the

act see Akenson, *Education and Enmity*, pp. 111–13.
64. Charlemont to Craig, 25 Jun. 1929, P.R.O.N.I., CAB 9D/1/6.
65. Akenson, *Education and Enmity*, pp. 104–11.
66. See below, p. 267.
67. Cab. Conclusions, 1 Nov. 1929, P.R.O.N.I., CAB 4/239/24; Charlemont's memo, 30 Oct. 1929, *ibid.*, CAB 4/239/21.
68. Cab. Conclusions, 29 Apr. 1930, *ibid.*, CAB 4/259/22.
69. Cab. Conclusions, 7 May 1930, *ibid.*, CAB 4/260/18.
70. Cab. Conclusions, 15 Apr. 1930, *ibid.*, CAB 4/258/18.
71. Akenson, *Education and Enmity*, pp. 140–1.
72. This question and the options open to Catholics are discussed *ibid.*, pp. 114–17.
73. *Ibid.*, p. 141.
74. This is amply demonstrated *ibid.*, pp. 111–12, 113–14, 117–18.
75. *Ibid.*, p. 112.
76. *Parl. Deb. (C)*, xii, 9 Apr. 1930, col. 726.
77. Quoted in Akenson, *Education and Enmity*, p. 114.
78. *Parl. Deb. (C)*, xii, 9 Apr. 1930, cols 736–8.
79. *Ibid.*, 9 Apr. 1930, col. 815.
80. Akenson, *Education and Enmity*, p. 113.
81. *Parl. Deb. (C)*, xvi, 13 Nov. 1934, col. 2737.
82. *Irish News*, 18 Dec. 1931.
83. *The Tablet*, 19 Nov. 1932.

Chapter 12
ACQUIESCENCE: WESTMINSTER AND THE MINORITY PROBLEM
(pp. 266–75)
1. Joynson-Hicks to Craig, 14 Dec. 1928, P.R.O.N.I., CAB 9B/38/1. Home Office officials, despite the files on the subject, seemed to know little about the electoral system in Northern Ireland, writing to ask on 19 Feb. 1928 whether P.R. had been abolished in local elections (P.R.O., HO 45/13371/463565/2). They did show some interest in the bill abolishing P.R. in parliamentary elections, but their reservations (about its implications for the electoral register for the imperial parliament, the aptness of its title, and the Northern Ireland parliament's right to repeal two orders-in-council) were dispelled by consultations with the Permanent Secretary of the Ministry of Home Affairs (Harris to Queckett, 4 Mar. 1929, P.R.O.N.I., CAB 9B/38/1).
2. Abercorn to Craig, 13 Mar. 1925, *ibid.*, CAB 9D/1/4.
3. Note of interview at Home Office, 26 Nov. 1929, *ibid.*, CAB 9D/1/8.
4. Cope to Curtis, 31 Aug. 1922, P.R.O., HO 45/13371/463565/1.
5. Collins to Churchill, 28 Jun. 1922, *ibid.*
6. Collins to Churchill, 9 Aug. 1922, *ibid.*
7. Cope to Curtis, 31 Aug. 1922, *ibid.*
8. Cosgrave to Churchill, 8 Sep. 1922, *ibid.*
9. Cope to Curtis, 31 Aug. 1922, *ibid.*

10. *Ibid.*
11. *Ibid.*
12. *Ibid.*
13. Churchill to Cosgrave, 1 Sep. 1922, *ibid.*
14. See the correspondence between Spender and Tallents, 8, 13 Jul. 1922, *ibid.*
15. Craig to Masterton-Smith, 22 Jul. 1922, *ibid.*
16. Collins to Churchill, 8 Aug. 1922, *ibid.*
17. Note by Sir Francis Greer, 11 Aug. 1922, *ibid.*
18. Legal opinion of Sir Frederick Liddell (first Parliamentary Counsel), Sir Francis Greer, Sir John Risley (Colonial Office Legal Adviser) and Sir John Anderson (then Irish Under-Secretary), 24 Jul. 1922, *ibid.*
19. Fitzalan to Craig, 5, 8 Jul. 1922, P.R.O.N.I., CAB 9B/40/1.
20. Megaw's minute, 13 Jul. 1922, *ibid.*
21. Spender to Craig, 13 Jul. 1922, *ibid.*, PM 9/3.
22. Craig to Masterton-Smith, 22 Jul. 1922, P.R.O., HO 45/13371/463565/1.
23. Masterton-Smith's report of conversation between Churchill and Craig on 27 Jul. 1922, 28 Jul. 1922, *ibid.*
24. Craig to Masterton-Smith, 22 Jul. 1922, *ibid.*
25. Cab. Conclusions, 27 Jul. 1922, P.R.O.N.I., CAB 4/50/10.
26. Craig to Spender, 18 Jul. 1922, *ibid.*, PM 9/4.
27. Churchill to Cosgrave, 1 Sep. 1922, and Curtis's report to Churchill, 1 Sep. 1922, of his and Cope's meeting with Craig on 31 Aug. 1922, P.R.O., HO 45/13371/463565/1.
28. Craig to Spender, 18 Jul. 1922, P.R.O.N.I., PM 9/4.
29. Masterton-Smith's report of conversation between Churchill and Craig on 27 Jul. 1922, 28 Jul. 1922, P.R.O., HO 45/13371/463565/1.
30. *Ibid.*
31. Churchill to Collins, 31 Jul. 1922, *ibid.*
32. Cosgrave to Churchill, 30 Aug. 1922, *ibid.*
33. Churchill to Craig, 31 Aug. 1922, *ibid.*
34. Craig to Churchill, 1 Sep. 1922, *ibid.*
35. Curtis's report to Churchill, 1 Sep. 1922, of his and Cope's meeting with Craig on 31 Aug. 1922, *ibid.*
36. Craig to Churchill, 9 Sep. 1922, *ibid.*, HO 45/13371/463565/2.
37. Churchill to Craig, 9 Sep. 1922, *ibid.*, HO 45/13371/463565/1.

Conclusion
THE NORTHERN IRELAND PROBLEM AND DEVOLUTION
(pp. 277–280)
1. J. Whyte, 'Interpretations of the Northern Ireland Problem: An Appraisal', (This as yet unpublished but masterly survey of the current state of research and debate on the causes of conflict in Northern Ireland was prepared for a seminar on interpretations of the problem held in the Institute of Irish Studies, Queen's University, Belfast, 29 Oct. 1977.)

2. See, e.g., P. Bew, 'The Problem of Irish Unionism', *Economy and Society*, vi (1977), pp. 89–109.
3. Whyte, pp. 17–20.
4. *Ibid.*, p. 26.
5. D. G. Boyce, 'Dicey, Kilbrandon and Devolution', *The Political Quarterly*, xlvi (1975), pp. 280–92.

Select Bibliography

(This bibliography is not exhaustive but includes only the published and unpublished material which proved most helpful in the preparation of this book. Works containing useful bibliographies are marked with an asterisk.)

A. PRIMARY SOURCES

I. MANUSCRIPT MATERIALS

1. Birmingham University Library
Austen Chamberlain papers

2. British Library
Arthur James Balfour papers, Add. MSS 49683–49962

3. House of Lords Record Office
Andrew Bonar Law papers
David Lloyd George papers
St Loe Strachey papers

4. Public Record Office
i. Cabinet papers:
Cabinet Conclusions and supporting papers, especially May–June 1922 (CAB 23/30, CAB 24/*passim*) and Dec. 1937–Apr. 1938 (CAB 23/87–93)
Proceedings and memoranda of the Cabinet Committee on the Irish Situation, especially Dec. 1937–Apr. 1938 (CAB 27/524,527)

ii. Departmental papers:
Correspondence relating to the governments of Northern and Southern Ireland, 1922–23 (CO 739/1,14,15,16,17,18,19)
Papers of S. G. Tallents relating to his investigation of conditions in Northern Ireland, Jun.–Jul. 1922 (CO 906/23–30)
Local Government (Northern Ireland) Bills, 1922–28 (HO 45/13371/463565)

Northern Ireland (Miscellaneous Provisions) Act, 1928 (HO 45/13144/
520494)

'Northern Ireland. Interview between the Chancellor of Exchequer &
Sir James Craig on Saturday 6 May 1922. Matters discussed.' (T 163/
6/G256/049)

'Appt of a c/ee to consider whether, in view of ratification of constitution of Irish Free State, any alteration is needed in present scale of
contribution of Northern Ireland to cost of Imperial Services', 1921–
25 (T 160/150/5814)

'Northern Ireland contribution towards the cost of Imperial Services
and provisional residuary share 1933/34' (T 160/550/6562/021)

'UK–Éire draft trade agreement – Attitude of Northern Ireland', 1938
(T 160/747/14026/04)

'Northern Ireland Transport Board. Committee of investigation into the
finances of the board', 1939–40 (T 160/1138/15586)

5. Public Record Office of Northern Ireland

i. Cabinet Conclusions, 1921–40 (CAB 4/1–456)

ii. Cabinet papers relating to

Ministry of Finance:

CAB 9A/3/1	Financial situation, Jan. 1924–Dec. 1930
3/2	Estimates, 1931–32. Departmental savings. Salaries etc.
3/4	Financial situation. Economies, Jun. 1931–Dec. 1933
3/5	Financial position Jan. 1933–Nov. 1937
8	Trade Facilities Act, 1921–26
10	Minutes of Selection Board, Aug. 1921–Aug. 1926
14/1–5	Budget statements, 1924–40
37/1,2,3,6,7,9,10,12	Drainage schemes, 1923–36
40/1	Imperial Contribution, May 1925–May 1933
42/1–3	Finance (Loans and Exchequer Provisions) Bill: loans guarantee facilities: Government Loan Bill: Jun. 1923–1943
61/1,2	Shipbuilding questions, May 1928–Apr. 1945
76/1	Financial relations between local authorities and the state, 1930–32
87/1	Sales tax in Northern Ireland, 1933–34
90/1,2	Employment of Roman Catholics in government service, 1924–45
95/1,2	Local Government (Finance) Bill. Derating, Aug. 1928–Nov. 1934

Ministry of Home Affairs:

CAB 9B/4	Cahir Healy, 1922–24
13/1–3	Redistribution, 1922–1946
18	D.I. J. W. Nixon, 1922–24

22	Old-age pensions, 1924–24
33/3	Ulster Reform Association, 1923
38/1	Proportional Representation, 1927–29
40/1,2	Local Government Bills, 1922–33
45/1	Belfast Corporation housing scheme, 1923–24
45/2	Belfast Corporation housing inquiry, 1925–28
67/1	County council administration, 1926
74/1,2	Roads administration, 1923–47
83/1	Civil Authorities (Special Powers) Act, 1922–33
89/1–3	Housing, Dec. 1921–1948
136	The Prime Minister's tour, 1927–28
137/1,2	Outdoor relief, Feb. 1924–Jul. 1939
161	Donaghadee U.D.C., 1929–36
200	International Eucharistic Congress, Dublin, 1931–32
201/1,2	The political situation etc. in the Irish Free State, 1932–47
204	Marketing system and tolls etc. Markets and Fairs Bill, 1932–38
205/1	Alleged disability of Roman Catholics in Northern Ireland, 1932–Jul. 1961

Ministry of Labour:

CAB 9C/1/1,2	Unemployment Insurance Fund, Dec. 1921–Oct. 1933
1/6	Unemployment Insurance Agreement, Nov. 1923–Feb. 1926
3	Unemployment relief schemes and grants, 1922–24
4/1–13	Commission on natural and industrial resources of Northern Ireland, 1923–45
11/1,2	Widows', orphans' and old-age pensions, 1925–39
13/1–3	Unemployment relief schemes and grants. Proposals to mitigate unemployment, 1923–Mar. 1943
15	Provision of medical benefits to insured persons in Northern Ireland, 1923–31
27/1	National Health Insurance Bill, 1928–38
40	Railway strike, 1933
47/1	Infiltration of Éire workers into Northern Ireland, Apr. 1934–Nov. 1943

Ministry of Education:

CAB 9D/1/1	Education Bill, 1922–Sep. 1923
1/3–6,8,9	Education Act, Sep. 1923–Dec. 1943

Ministry of Agriculture:

CAB 9E/1/1	Agricultural aid committee, 1923
14/1,2	Marketing of Eggs Acts, 1924–Apr. 1938

23/1,2	Development of agriculture in Northern Ireland, 1923–47
41/1	Black scab in potatoes, 1925–29
43/1	Ulster Farmers' Produce Society, 1925–36
47/1	Assistance for farmers by relief from rates, 1923–28
57/1,2	Marketing of agricultural produce, 1926–34
75/1,2	Fruit grading and marketing, 1927–44
93/1	Statutory quota of home-grown wheat to be used by millers in their gristings, 1930–32
97/1,3,6,7	Development of pig industry in Northern Ireland, 1930–44
111/1	Milk dispute, 1931–32
117/1,2	Assistance to farmers. Payment of land annuities, Oct. 1932–1942
122/1,2	Milk and Milk Products Bill, 1932–38
127/1	Newry central creamery, 1935–36

Ministry of Commerce:

CAB 9F/18/1,2	Londonderry and Lough Swilly Railway Co., 1923–34
28/1	Londonderry (Carlisle) bridge, Nov. 1923–Aug. 1932
64/1	Coalisland coalfields, 1923–26
67/1,2	Safeguarding of industries. Linen, 1924–32
89/1	Bangor and Portstewart harbour improvement schemes, 1927–39
126/1,2	Attraction of new industries to Northern Ireland, 1931–May 1945

Military and police:

CAB 6/27–31	Military and police, Jun. 1921–Dec. 1922
CAB 9G/19/1–3	Internees, 1922–45
57	Pulverman ammunition contract, 1924–26
58	Receivership of constabulary forces. Co-ordination between Ministry of Home Affairs and R.U.C., 1925

Civil service:

CAB 9Q/7	Independent inquiry into organisation and conditions of employment of civil service in Northern Ireland, 1925–29

Imperial government:

CAB 9R/57/1,2	Tariffs. Irish Free State, Mar. 1923–33
60/1–5	Anglo-Éire negotiations, Dec. 1937–Dec. 1940

iii. Prime Minister's papers:
Correspondence between Craig and the Cabinet Secretary and ministers

during Craig's absences from Northern Ireland, 1922–Sep. 1930 (PM 9/1–26)
Grand Orange Lodge of Ireland, 1926–42 (PM 6/22)

iv. Departmental papers:
Report of the Committee Appointed to Investigate the Principal Causes of the Depression in the Irish Linen Industry, 31 Aug. 1928 (COM 27/1)
New Industries (Development) Act, 1937. Minutes of the meetings of the advisory committee, 17 Dec. 1937–26 Jul. 1939 (COM 17/1)
Papers relating to the Ulster Development Council, Dec. 1937–Jun. 1939 (COM 20/1/1–4)
Statistics and reports relating to new-industries legislation (COM 20/2/18)
Police reports on the state of order in Belfast, 1 Jan.–30 Sep. 1921 (FIN 18/1/107)
Papers relating to department and staff schemes of the government of Northern Ireland, 1921 (FIN 18/1/190,191,192,237,595)
Copies of correspondence of Ministries of Finance, Home Affairs and Labour, 1921 (FIN 18/1/270–2)
Papers relating to Loans Guarantee Bill, 1922 (FIN 18/2/570,606)
Joint Exchequer Board, Minutes of Proceedings, 2 Dec. 1921–11 Jul. 1961 (FIN 26/1/3,4)
Attribution of revenue, 1 Aug. 1922–11 Nov. 1940 (FIN 26/1/9)
Joint Exchequer Board. 1938 agreement between the United Kingdom and Northern Ireland governments as to financial arrangements (FIN 26/1/36)
Proportional Representation. Local Government Bills, 1922–27 (HA 14/161)
'Bank holidays. Proclamation of. Annually' 1924–33 (HA 8/266)

v. Other papers:
Typescript extracts from Lady Craig's diaries, 1905–40, including some enclosures of original material (D1415/B/38)
Report on the Ulster Protestant Association by D.I. R. R. Spears, 7 Feb. 1923 (T2258)
Lady Spender, Belfast, London and Wales. Personal diary – social, domestic and political. 1914–41 (D1633/2)
Sir Wilfrid B. Spender, Financial Diary, 1931–44 (begun during Northern Ireland's financial crisis at the beginning of the 1930s as a record of financial discussions and warnings but continued as a record of Spender's official life as permanent head of the Ministry of Finance and civil service and as an increasingly critical commentary on the performance of the government of Northern Ireland) (D715)
Local authority records (LA 1–86)

II. PRINTED MATERIALS

1. Official publications
i. *Northern Ireland*
Interim Report of the Departmental Committee of Inquiry on Police Organisation in Northern Ireland, 1922, Cmd 1
Interim Report of the Departmental Committee on the Educational Services in Northern Ireland, 1922, Cmd 6
Report of the Railways Commission in Northern Ireland, 1922, Cmd 10
Interim Report of the Departmental Committee on the Cost of Living, 1922, Cmd 12
Final Report of the Departmental Committee on the Educational Services in Northern Ireland, 1923, Cmd 15
Report of the Agricultural Aid Committee, 1923, Cmd 17
Final Report of the Departmental Committee on the Cost of Living, 1923, Cmd 20
Final Reports of the Departmental Committee on the Increase of Rent and Mortgage Interest (Restrictions) Act, 1920, 1923, Cmd 22
Interim Report of the Commission on Natural and Industrial Resources of Northern Ireland (Lough Neagh coal basin), 1923, Cmd 24
Commission on the Natural and Industrial Resources of Northern Ireland. Report on the Northern Ireland Egg Industry, 1924, Cmd 27
Report of the Departmental Commission on Local Government Administration in Northern Ireland, 1927, Cmd 73
Report of the Departmental Committee on the Transit, Prices and Marketing of Agricultural Produce, 1927, Cmd 75
Report of the Inter-Departmental Committee on Medical Benefit in Northern Ireland, 1930, Cmd 113
Report of the Committee on the Financial Relations between the State and Local Authorities, 1931, Cmd 131
Report by Sir Felix Pole on Transport Conditions in Northern Ireland, 1934, Cmd 160
Reports of the Commissioner holding the Public Inquiry and of the Committee of Inquiry into Public Transport in Northern Ireland, 1938, Cmd 198
Report on the Administration of Local Government Services, 1937–38, 1938, Cmd 200
Interim Report of the Planning Advisory Board Committee on Housing in Northern Ireland, 1944, Cmd 224
Reports of the Agricultural Enquiry Committee, 1947, Cmd 249
Returns of Local Taxation, 1922–39 – published annually as command papers

Report of the Select Committee on Rents, 1931, H.C. 249
Report of the Joint Select Committee of Inquiry into Road and Rail Transport, 1939, H.C. 472
Appropriation Accounts, 1921–39; Estimates for Services, 1921–39; Supplementary Estimates for Services, 1921–39; Finance Accounts,

1921–39 – all published annually or more frequently as House of Commons papers

Journal of the Ministry of Agriculture, Northern Ireland, i–vi (Belfast 1927–38)

Parliamentary Debates (House of Commons and Senate)

Census of Population of Northern Ireland 1926. General Report (Belfast 1929)

Report of the Inquiry into the Housing Schemes of the Belfast Corporation, held by Mr R. D. Megaw, K.C. (Belfast 1926)

Report on the Marketing of Agricultural Produce (Belfast 1932)

Report of the Inquiry concerning the Architect's Department of Down County Regional Education Committee (Belfast 1935)

Ulster Year Books, 1926–38 (Belfast 1926–38)

ii. *United Kingdom*

Royal Commission on Systems of Elections: Minutes of Evidence, 1910, Cd 5352

Government of Ireland Act, 1920 (10 & 11 Geo. V, c. 7)

Outline of Financial Provisions (Government of Ireland Bill) 1920, 1920, Cmd 645

Government of Ireland Bill: Further Memorandum on Financial Provisions, 1920, Cmd 707

First Report of the Northern Ireland Special Arbitration Committee, 1924, Cmd 2072

Final Report of the Northern Ireland Special Arbitration Committee, 1925, Cmd 2389

Parliamentary Debates (House of Commons and House of Lords)

Report of the Irish Boundary Commission, 1925, with an introduction by G. J. Hand (Shannon 1969)

English Ministry of Agriculture and Fisheries and Food and Department of Agriculture and Fisheries for Scotland. *A Century of Agricultural Statistics: Great Britain, 1866–1966* (London 1968)

2. Newspapers and periodicals
Armagh Guardian; Ballymena Observer and County Antrim Advertiser; Belfast News-Letter; Belfast Telegraph; Blackwood's Magazine; Daily Express; Derry Journal; The Economist; Farmers' Journal; Fermanagh Herald and Monaghan News; Glasgow Herald; Irish News; Irish Press; Irish Times; Journal of Education and School World; Mid-Ulster Mail; Newry Telegraph; Nineteenth Century and After; Northern Whig; The Tablet; The Times; Ulster Herald

3. Memoirs, diaries and other contemporary works
Campbell, T. J., *Fifty Years of Ulster, 1890–1940* (Belfast 1941)

Churchill, W. S., *The World Crisis: The Aftermath* (London 1929)

Corkey, W., *Episode in the History of Protestant Ulster, 1923–47* (Belfast n.d.)

D'Arcy, C. F., *The Adventures of a Bishop: A Phase of Irish Life: A*

Personal and Historical Narrative (London 1934)

Dicey, A. V., *England's Case against Home Rule* (3rd ed., London 1887)

Duggan, G. C. ('Periscope'), 'The Last Days of Dublin Castle', *Blackwood's Magazine*, ccxii (1922), pp. 137–90

'Northern Ireland – Success or Failure?', *Irish Times*, Apr. 1950

Harbinson, R., *No Surrender* (London, 1960)

Harrison, H. *Ulster and the British Empire, 1939: Help or Hindrance?* (London 1939)

Jones, T., *Whitehall Diary*, Vol. III: *Ireland, 1918–1925*, ed. K. Middlemas, (London 1971)

Londonderry, Marquess of, 'Public Education in Northern Ireland: The New System', *Nineteenth Century and After*, xcv (1924), pp. 328–34

Macready, F. N. C., *Annals of an Active Life*, 2 vols (London 1924)

National Council for Civil Liberties, *Report of a Commission of Enquiry Appointed to Examine the Purpose and Effect of the Civil Authorities (Special Powers) Acts (Northern Ireland), 1922 & 1933* (London 1936)

North East Boundary Bureau, *The Handbook of the Ulster Question* (Dublin 1923)

O'Hara, P. J., 'Financial Returns for the Seven Years 1930–1937 on Eleven Farms in Northern Ireland', *Journal of the Ministry of Agriculture, Northern Ireland*, vi (1938), pp. 13–21

Scott Robertson, G., *Pig Breeding and Marketing in Northern Ireland* (Belfast 1934; repr. from *The Pig Breeders' Annual, 1933–34*)

Williams, J. Glynne, 'An Economic Survey of Small Holdings in Northern Ireland', *Journal of the Ministry of Agriculture, Northern Ireland*, iii (1931), pp. 62–82.

Wilson, A., *P.R. Urban Elections in Ulster in 1920*, with an introduction by R. A. Newland (London 1972)

Wilson, T. (ed.), *The Political Diaries of C. P. Scott, 1911–1928* (London 1970)

4. Works of reference

Annual Register, 1921–40 (London 1922–41)

County Borough of Belfast, *The Belfast Book: Local Government in the City and County Borough of Belfast* (Belfast 1929)

Belfast and Ulster Directories, 1921–40

The British Imperial Calendar and Civil Service List, 1920–40

Craig, F. W. S., *British Parliamentary Election Statistics, 1918–1970* (Chichester 1970)

Deutsch, R. R., *Northern Ireland, 1921–1974: A Select Bibliography* (New York 1975)

Dictionary of National Biography

Dod's Parliamentary Companion

Elliott, S., *Northern Ireland Parliamentary Election Results, 1921–1972* (Chichester 1973)

Maltby, A., *The Government of Northern Ireland, 1922–72: A Cata-*

logue and *Breviate of Parliamentary Papers* (Dublin 1974)
Thom's Irish Almanac and Official Directory, 1921–40
Who Was Who, 1916–1928 (London 1928); *Who Was Who, 1929–1940* (London 1941); *Who Was Who, 1951–1960* (London 1961)

B. LATER WORKS

1. Published

Akenson, D. H., *The Irish Education Experiment: The National System of Education in the Nineteenth Century* (London/Toronto 1970)
Education and Enmity: The Control of Schooling in Northern Ireland, 1920–1950 (Newton Abbot/New York 1973)

Andrews, S., *Nine Generations: A History of the Andrews Family, Millers of Comber* (Belfast 1958)

Arthur, P., 'Devolution as Administrative Convenience: A Case Study of Northern Ireland', *Parliamentary Affairs*, xxx (1977), pp. 97–106

Barritt, D. P. & Carter, C. F. *The Northern Ireland Problem: A Study in Group Relations* (2nd ed., London, 1972)

Baster, A. S. J., *The Little Less: An Essay on the Political Economy of Restrictionism* (London 1947)

Beckett, J. C., 'Northern Ireland', *Journal of Contemporary History*, vi (1971), pp. 121–34

Beckett, J. C. & Glasscock, R. E. (eds), *Belfast: The Origin and Growth of an Industrial City* (London 1967)

Beckett, J. C. et al., *The Ulster Debate: Report of a Study Group of the Institute for the Study of Conflict* (London 1972)

Bell, J. Bowyer, *The Secret Army* (London 1970)

*Bew, P., 'The Problem of Irish Unionism', *Economy and Society*, vi (1977), pp. 89–109

Boyce, D. G., 'British Conservative Opinion, the Ulster Question, and the Partition of Ireland', *Irish Historical Studies*, xvii (1970–71), pp. 89–112
Englishmen and Irish Troubles: British Public Opinion and the Making of Irish Policy (London 1972)
'Ulster – Some Consequences of Devolution', *Planet*, no. 13, (1972), pp. 3–9
'Dicey, Kilbrandon and Devolution', *The Political Quarterly*, xlvi (1975), pp. 280–92

British Association for the Advancement of Science, *Britain in Depression: A Record of British Industries since 1929* (London 1935)
Britain in Recovery (London 1938)

Buckland, P., *Irish Unionism 2: Ulster Unionism and the Origins of Northern Ireland, 1886–1922* (Dublin/New York 1973)
'The Unity of Ulster Unionism, 1886–1939', *History* lx (1975), pp. 211–23

Budge, I. & O'Leary, C., *Belfast: Approach to Crisis: A Study of Belfast Politics, 1603–1970* (London 1973)

Calvert, H., *Constitutional Law in Northern Ireland: A Study in Regional Government* (London/Belfast 1968)

Callwell, C. E., *Field-Marshal Sir Henry Wilson: His Life and Diaries,* 2 vols (London 1927)

Campbell, J. J., *Catholic Schools: A Survey of a Northern Ireland Problem* (Belfast 1964)

Chubb, B., *The Government and Politics of Ireland* (Stanford/London 1970)

Clark, W., *Guns in Ulster: A History of the B Special Constabulary in Part of Co. Derry* (Belfast 1967)

Coe, W. E., *The Engineering Industry of the North of Ireland* (Newton Abbot 1969)

Crotty, R. D., *Irish Agricultural Production: Its Volume and Structure* (Cork 1966)

Dane, M., *The Fermanagh B Specials* (Enniskillen 1970)

Dennison, S. R., *The Location of Industry and the Depressed Areas* (London 1939)

Dewar, M. W., Brown, J., & Long, S. E. *Orangeism: A New Historical Appreciation, 1688–1967* (Belfast 1967)

Digby, M., *Horace Plunkett: An Anglo-American Irishman* (Oxford 1949)

Edwards, O. Dudley, *The Sins of Our Fathers: Roots of Conflict in Northern Ireland* (Dublin 1970)

Ervine, St John, *Craigavon, Ulsterman* (London 1949)

Evans, E. E. (ed.), *Belfast and its Regional Setting* (Belfast 1952)

*Farrell, M., *Northern Ireland: the Orange State* (London 1976)

Freeman, T. W., *Ireland: A General and Regional Geography* (4th rev. ed., London 1972)

Gallagher, F., *The Indivisible Island: The History of the Partition of Ireland* (London 1957)

Gibbon, P., *The Origins of Ulster Unionism: The Formation of Popular Protestant Politics and Ideology in Nineteenth-Century Ireland* (Manchester 1975)

Gilbert, B. B., *British Social Policy, 1914–1939* (New York 1970)

Gwynn, D., *The History of Partition, 1912–25* (Dublin 1925)
The Irish Free State, 1922–27 (Dublin 1928)

Hall, A. D., *Reconstruction and the Land: An Approach to Farming in the National Interest* (London 1941)

Hancock, K., *Survey of British Commonwealth Affairs,* Vol. I: *Problems of Nationality* (Oxford 1937)

Harbinson, J. F., *The Ulster Unionist Party, 1882–1973: Its Development and Organisation* (Belfast 1973)

Harkness, D., *The Restless Dominion* (London 1969)
'England's Irish Question', *The Politics of Reappraisal,* ed. G. Peele & C. Cook (London 1975), pp. 39–63
History and the Irish (Belfast 1976)

Harris, R., *Prejudice and Tolerance in Ulster: A Study of Neighbours and 'Strangers' in a Border Community* (Manchester 1972)

Heslinga, M. W., *The Irish Border as a Cultural Divide* (Assen 1962)

Hezlet, A. *The 'B' Specials: A History of the Ulster Special Constabulary* (Pan. ed., London 1973)

Howson, S., *Domestic Monetary Management in Britain, 1919–38* (Cambridge 1975)

Howson, S. & Winch, D., *The Economic Advisory Council, 1930–39* (Cambridge 1977)

Isles, K. S. & Cuthbert, N., 'Ulster's Economic Structure' and 'Economic Policy', *Ulster under Home Rule: A Study of the Political and Economic Problems of Northern Ireland,* ed. T. Wilson (London 1955), pp. 91–114, 137–82

An Economic Survey of Northern Ireland (Belfast 1957)

Johnson, D. S., 'The Economic History of Ireland between the Wars', *Irish Economic and Social History,* i (1974), pp. 49–61

Johnston, J., *Irish Agriculture in Transition* (Dublin 1951)

Agricultural Co-operation in Ireland (London 1965)

Jones, E., *A Social Geography of Belfast* (London 1972)

Kee, R., *The Green Flag: A History of Irish Nationalism* (London 1972)

Kennedy, D., 'Catholics in Northern Ireland, 1926–1939', *Years of the Great Test,* ed. MacManus, pp. 138–49

Knight, J. & Baxter-Moore, N., *Northern Ireland: The Elections of the Twenties* (London 1972)

Laver, M., 'Cultural Aspects of Loyalty: On Hirschman and Loyalism in Ulster', *Political Studies,* xxiv (1976), pp. 469–77

Lawrence, R. J., *The Government of Northern Ireland: Public Finance and Public Services, 1921–1964* (Oxford 1965)

Livingstone, P., *The Fermanagh Story: A Documented History of County Fermanagh from the Earliest Times to the Present Day* (Enniskillen 1968)

Longford, Earl of & O'Neill, T. P., *Eamon de Valera* (Arrow ed., London 1974)

*Lyons, F. S. L., *Ireland since the Famine* (rev. ed., London 1973)

Macardle, D., *The Irish Republic* (Corgi ed., London 1968)

McCracken, J. L., *Representative Government in Ireland, 1919–48* (London 1958)

'The Political Scene in Northern Ireland, 1926–1937', *Years of the Test,* ed. MacManus, pp. 150–60

McDowell, R. B., *The Irish Convention, 1917–18* (London 1970)

MacManus, F. (ed.), *The Years of the Great Test, 1926–39* (Cork 1967)

Mansergh, N., *The Government of Northern Ireland: A Study in Devolution* (London 1936)

Meenan, J., *The Irish Economy since 1922* (Liverpool 1970)

Mitchell, A., *Labour in Irish Politics, 1890–1930: The Irish Labour Movement in an Age of Revolution* (Dublin 1974)

Mogey, J., *Rural Life in Northern Ireland* (London 1947)

*Moody, T. W., *The Ulster Question, 1603–1973* (Cork 1974)

Mowat, C. L., *Britain between the Wars, 1918–1940* (London 1968)

Murphy, J. A., *Ireland in the Twentieth Century* (Dublin 1975)

Muskett, A. E. & Morrison, J., 'Agriculture', *Belfast and its Regional Setting,* ed. Evans, pp. 139–48

O'Donovan, J., *The Economic History of Live Stock in Ireland* (Dublin/ Cork 1940)

O'Leary, C., *The Irish Republic and its Experiment with P.R.* (Indiana 1961)

O'Neill, D. G. (ed.), *Devolution of Government: The Experiment in Northern Ireland* (London 1953)

O'Sullivan, D., *The Irish Free State and its Senate: A Study in Contemporary Politics* (London 1940)

Pakenham, F. (*see also* Longford) *Peace by Ordeal: The Negotiation and Signature of the Anglo-Irish Treaty, 1921* (N.E.L. ed., London 1967)

Peele, G. & Cook, C. (eds), *The Politics of Reappraisal, 1918–39* (London 1975)

Queckett, A. S., *The Constitution of Northern Ireland*, Parts I–III (Belfast 1928–46)

Richardson, H. W., *Economic Recovery in Britain, 1932–9* (London 1967)

Richardson, J. H., *British Economic Foreign Policy* (London 1936)

Rose, R., *Governing without Consensus: An Irish Perspective* (London 1971)

Northern Ireland: A Time of Choice (London 1976)

Shearman, H., *Not an Inch: A Study of Northern Ireland and Lord Craigavon* (London 1942)

Symons, L. (ed.), *Land Use in Northern Ireland* (London 1963)

Thomas, D. E. L., 'Farm Types and Farm Incomes', *ibid.*, pp. 162–75

Townshend, C., *The British Campaign in Ireland, 1919–21* (Oxford 1975)

Wall, M., 'Partition: The Ulster Question (1916–26)', *The Irish Struggle*, ed. Williams, pp. 84–93

Wallace, M., *Northern Ireland: 50 Years of Self-Government* (Newton Abbot 1971)

Wheeler-Bennett, J., *John Anderson, Viscount Waverley* (London 1962)

Williams, T.D. (ed.), *The Irish Struggle, 1916–1926* (London 1966)

Wilson, T. (ed.), *Ulster under Home Rule: A Study of the Political and Economic Problems of Northern Ireland* (London 1955)

Wright, F., 'Protestant Ideology and Politics in Ulster', *European Journal of Sociology*, xiv (1973), pp. 213–80

Younger, Calton, *A State of Disunion* (London 1972)

2. Unpublished

Elliott, S., 'The Electoral System in Northern Ireland since 1920' (Ph.D. thesis, Queen's University, Belfast, 1971)

*Greenlees, S., 'The Structure and Development of Agriculture in Ulster 1900–1939' (M.Phil. thesis, New University of Ulster, 1976)

Harbinson, J. F., 'A History of the Northern Ireland Labour Party, 1891–1948' (M.Sc.(Econ.) thesis, Queen's University, Belfast, 1966)

Magill, P. F., 'The Senate in Northern Ireland, 1921–62' (Ph.D. thesis, Queen's University, Belfast, 1965)

Parkinson, J. R., 'Is Northern Ireland Viable?' (Paper presented at the Older Industrial Areas Conference. Regional Studies Association, 62 Chandos Place, London, WC2N 4HH (1968). Duplicated type-script.)

Political Science Department, Queen's University, Belfast, 'Intra-Unionist Disputes in the Northern Ireland House of Commons, 1921–72' (Research carried out in 1972 and 1973 by undergraduates taking the special subject in 'The Government of Ireland')

Whitford, F. J., 'Joseph Devlin, Ulsterman and Irishman' (M.A. thesis (external), London University, 1939)

*Whyte, J., 'Interpretations of the Northern Ireland Problem: An Appraisal' (Paper prepared for a seminar on interpretations of the Northern Ireland problem held at the Institute of Irish Studies, Queen's University, Belfast, 29 Oct. 1977)

Index

Andrews, J. M. & Co. Ltd, 12

Andrews, John Miller (Minister of Labour; Minister of Finance), 11, 12, 16, 64, 97, 153, 154, 272; compassion, 13, 158, 203; at loggerheads with Ministry of Finance, 13, 24–5, 162; accessible to businessmen, 64, 105; conciliatory on labour and trades union questions, 30, 65; opposes Belfast Board of Guardians, 158; responsive to Protestant clergy and Orange Order, 13, 251, 255; and Nationalists, 35; contemplates resignation, 113, 114 financial views, 13, 97; advocates minus contribution, 87–8, 97, and reamalgamation of Unemployment Funds, 88–9; on Britain's financial responsibilities towards N.I., 86, 87–8, 96, 98; and financial negotiations with Treasury, 96, 97; absorbs Treasury notions, 103, 127; advocates step-by-step policy, 132, 150, 151–2, 160, 161, and extension of social services, 13, 88–9; and health insurance, 161–3; and housing, 167; and education, 103, 251, 255; concerned about unemployment, 118; dissatisfied with rejection of linen-safeguarding application, 108, 118; unhelpful role in industrial policy, 124, 127; and law and order, 211; and peace pact, 203; and I.R.A. attacks, 70; seeks assurances from Britain, 71; concerned about South's advantages in negotiations with Britain, 76, 113, 114–15

Anglo-American trade agreement, 1938, 108

Anglo-Eire agreements, 1938, 26, 69, 77, 92, 109, 110–16, 143

Anglo-Irish Treaty, 1921, 5, 45, 70, 71, 73, 110, 183, 184, 194, 197–8, 199, 228, 233, 250, 268, 269, 270, 274

Anglo-Irish war, 70, 180, 182, 183, 197; truce in, 183–4, 186

Anglo-Italian agreement, 1938, 111, 115

Antrim, Co., 2, 30, 32, 57, 123, 126, 129, 224–5, 229, 241, 242

Archdale, Sir Edward Mervyn (Minister of Commerce; Minister of

Agriculture), 11, 12, 21, 135, 211; and agricultural reform, 57–8, 136, 138; divided ministerial loyalties, 10

Armagh city, 69–70, 169

Armagh, Co., 2, 60, 139, 168, 182, 225, 241, 257

Armagh Regional Education Committee, 256

Army, 181, 183, 185–6, 187–8, 189–90, 191–2, 193, 196, 197, 199, 201

Association of Northern Ireland Education Committees, 103, 261

Association of Rural District Councils, 40, 74

Australia, 16

Auxiliaries, 181

Babington, Anthony Brutus (Attorney-General), 219, 236

Bacon industry, 53, 66, 143, 144–7

Bacon Marketing Board, 145, 146

Bakers, 74, 75, 109–10

Baldwin, Stanley, 1st Earl Baldwin of Bewdley, 210, 211–12

Balfour, A. J., 1st Earl Balfour, 198, 199, 200

Ballycastle, 238, 239

Ballymoney, 126

Bangor, 12, 224

Bann, River, 133

Barbour, James Milne (Junior Minister of Finance; Minister of Commerce), 11, 18, 22, 107, 109, 115, 120, 121, 126, 229

Bates, Sir Richard Dawson (Minister of Home Affairs), 10–11, 12, 13 17, 18, 25, 27, 34, 118, 223; timidity, 14, 61, 165; fear of Catholics, 21, 22; fear of Belfast Corporation, 14; and local authorities, 43; and step-by-step policy, 160, 162; and housing, 165, 167, 168; and transport policy, 121, 122, 123; and law and order, 186, 204, 206, 209, 210, 211, 212, 213, 215, 217, 219–20; and peace pact, 204, 205; slack on police discipline, 61; primacy of police functions in ministry, 218–19; and abolition of P.R., 231, 233; and local government redistribution, 244; opposes withholding of royal

91, 106–7, 128, 130, 131–2, 134, 139, 141, 142–3, 147, 153–4, 157, 162, 185, 204–5; *see also respective ministries under* Government, Northern Ireland

Civil Service Commission, 21

Clark, Sir Ernest (Ministry of Finance), 9–10, 19, 21, 24, 41

Clones incident, 195, 207

Clydeside, 89

Coal: in Britain, 53, 108, 124; N.I.'s shortage, 54; attempts to develop industry, 123–5; high costs, 124–5

Coalisland, 123, 124

Coleraine, 129, 241

Coleraine Academical Institution, 12

Collins, J. H. (Nationalist M.P.), 73

Collins, Michael, 16, 35, 68, 72, 93, 179, 183, 194, 195, 198, 199, 202, 203, 204, 207, 209, 215, 234; wants release of N.I. prisoners, 204, 206; opposes 1922 Local Government Bill, 233, 268–9, 270, 274

Colwyn, Frederick Henry, 1st Baron Colwyn, 92

Colwyn Award, 92, 95, 152, 166, 167

Commons, House of, *see* Parliament

Connellan, J. (Nationalist M.P.), 163

Constitutional Club, 115

Cooke-Collis, Sir James (Agent-General), 127

Cookstown, 17, 239

Cooper, J. (Unionist M.P.), 35

Coote, W. (Unionist M.P.), 231

Cope, Sir Alfred William: and Belfast riots, 188–9, 190, 192; and 1922 Local Government Bill, 268–9, 275

Cork, 135

Corkey, Rev. W., 252–3, 257, 258, 260

Cosgrave, W. T., 69, 71, 209; wants release of N.I. prisoners and end of flogging, 207–8; opposes 1922 Local Government Bill, 268–9, 274

Cost of living, 155

Craig, C. C. (James's brother and Unionist M.P.), 152

Craig, Sir James, 1st Viscount Craigavon of Stormont (Prime Minister), 2, 11, 13, 14, 23, 27, 71, 76, 88, 117, 154, 158, 211, 219, 257,

258; character and background, 15–16; initial optimism, 1; naivety, 171; political myopia, 233–4, 236, 240–1; paternal and informal style of leadership, 16–17, 25, 65, 66, 67; tours, 17, 41; easily influenced, 17–18, 27, 120–1, 138; fears criticism, 66, 124, 138, 147, 161; dominance, 16, 65, 108, 114–15, 122–3; courage and strength in early years, 45, 208–9, and restraining influence, 49, 273–4; loses grip, 18, 72, 86, 87, 96, 98, 123; partisan rhetoric, 72; harmful absences from N.I., 180, 185, 200, 204–5, 209; defects of style of leadership, 17–18, 41, 42–3, 67–8, 126, 127, 167, 222, 233

helps shape structure of government, 9–10, 26; loyalty to ministers, 18, 209–10; supports Ministry of Agriculture, 131–2, 134; and civil service, 19, 21, 23; and House of Commons, 34, 35, 172–3, 240; accommodating attitude to local authorities, 39, 41, 42–3, 231; wary of Belfast Corporation, 40, 172–3; concessions to Londonderry Corporation, 42–3, 101, 102, 120–1, 244, 246; hemmed in by extremists, 70; and U.U.L.A., 61, 65; responds to Orange Order, 61, 62–3, 261; Orange Order more important to Craig than teachers' unions or education committees, 261; resists temperance reformers, 63; crushes Progressive Unionists, 65, 72; and U.F.U., 134; and agricultural interests, 66, 138, 139; and nationalists, 34–5, 72, 228, 233–4, 236, 240, 242, 264

Handles relations with Britain, 45, 49, 86, 90, 200, 208, 273, 274–5; wants amicable relations with Britain, 273, 279; imperial interests take precedence, 96, 108, 111; resents Treasury supervision, 95, 100; threatens resignation in face of Westminster's intervention, 209, 272–3, 275; emphasises Union only issue in N.I. politics 19, 72, 236, but capable of contemplating a united Ireland, 16; refuses talks with de Valera in

councillor), 38, 64
Duffin, A., 9–10
Dungannon, 238

The Economist, 140
Economy, 5, 51–9, 74–7, 105–6, 279; interdependence with Britain, 51–2, 59, 88–9, 151; relative disadvantages summed up in lower private civilian income, 58, and low multipliers, 58–9, 129; effects of Free State policy on, 5–6, 73–7, 97, 128; *see also* Agriculture; Industry
Edinburgh, 52
Education, 6, 13, 25, 27, 33–4, 41, 49, 59, 60, 61, 68, 97, 102, 221–2; financing of, 37–8, 94, 95, 98, 99–101, 102–3, 156, 157, 247–9, 262–3; discrimination in system, 256, 263–5, 277; *see also* Acts of parliament (Northern Ireland): Education Acts
Education levy, 41, 50, 98, 99–100
Éire, 5–6; political developments in, 69–70; attitude to border, 69, 71, 279; economic war, *see* Irish Free State; agreements with Britain, 47, 69, 74, 109, 110–16; refuses to make concessions to N.I., 110
Elliott, R. (Unionist M.P.), 169
Elliott, S., 38
Enniskillen, 35, 168,195, 210, 211, 239
Erne, Lough, 133
Eucharistic Congress, 69, 219

Factory legislation, 67–8, 126–7
Fairfield, Baron, *see* Greer, Sir Francis
Falls, Sir Charles, 132
Farmers: numbers and size, 55–6, 145; low income, 56; technical conservatism, 56–7, 66, 131; failure to co-operate, 57, 131; volubility, 33, 64–6, 67, 131–2; want to follow British practices, 131, 132; financial demands, 56, 66, 67, 132; Craig wary of, 66, 138, 161; consulted by G.N.I., 66, 161–2; and markets, 27; and transport question, 118, 122–3; oppose extension of social services, 151, 155, 156, 161–2; *see also* U.A.O.S.; U.F.U.
Farrell, M., 34, 35

Fermanagh, Co., 2, 12, 129, 132, 135, 195, 207, 225, 226, 241, 242, 268, 270
Fermanagh County Council, 12, 224, 226
Fermanagh Pig Breeders' Association, 66
Fianna Fáil, 69, 73
Finance, 6, 46, 117; budgets and estimates, 27, 42, 82, 84, 93; 1920 estimates inaccurate, 82–3, 84. Revenue: transferred, 4, 81; reserved, 3, 4, 82–4, 89–90, 99–101; special, 77, 82, 86, 92, 115, 142–3, 143–4, 203; low yield, 83, 155; G.N.I. little control over, 44, 82. Expenditure: transferred, 84, 86, 153, 197; reserved, 26, 84, 86; imperial contribution, 3, 84, 89, 92, 100, 103, 142; little control over expenditure, 49, 84–6, 122, 131, 152; less rigorous financial control than in Britain, 25, 41, 85; G.N.I.'s orthodox finance, 13, 86, 96–7, 126; disagreements between ministers over, 13, 87
  attempts to balance the budget, 87–90, 91–4, 96, 102; discussions between imperial and N.I. governments, 45, 86–7, 95–6, 97–8; key role of officials, 45–6, 86–7, 90–1; 94, 142–3; imperial government accepts need to help N.I., 90–1; source of disagreement between N.I. and imperial governments, 47, 90, 91, 92–3, 95, 98, 99, 100; open breach avoided, 95–8; minus contribution, 87–8, 92, 96, 97, 115; different financial structure in N.I., 37–8, 89, 94–5, 156, but attempts to achieve uniformity, 98–102; finance inhibits policy-making and planning, 49–50, 100, 102–4, 128, 157, 162, 167–8, 197, 211, 273; *see also* Colwyn Award; Local authorities; Government, imperial: Treasury; Government, N.I.: Ministry of Finance
Fisher, Sir Norman Fenwick Warren, 113
FitzAlan, Viscount, *see* FitzAlan-Howard, Edmund Bernard

Law, A. Bonar, 15, 92, 209, 210
Lawrence, R. J., 6, 59, 81
Leech, Judge J., 237–9
Leonard, Warder, 209, 213
Limavady, 147, 241
Limavady U.D.C., 147
Linen, 1, 12, 52–3, 53–4, 64, 75, 88–9, 118, 151; government and, 48, 68, 108, 118
Lisbellaw, 195
Lisburn, 224
Lisnaskea, 237, 239
Little, Rev., 13, 255
Lloyd George, David, 1st Earl Lloyd George of Dwyfor, 45, 82, 163, 183, 199, 268
Local authorities, 27, 64, 68, 103, 153; structure, 4, 36–7, 39–40; finance, 37–8, 39, 41, 82, 155; derating, 39, 85, 131; limited views of, 4, 38, 133, 157–9, 166; their partisanship, 38, 59, 232; government wary of, 14, 40, 100, 147; Craig encourages, 17, 39, 42–3, 85, 101; disagreements with government, 41–3, 50, 100–1, 102, 128, 157–9; unhelpful distribution of powers between authorities and G.N.I., 3, 4, 36, 39–43, 82, 85, 101–2, 103, 128, 133, 156–9, 173, 279; M.P.s and, 27, 40, 41, 168–9; suspension of, 40, 232
    political complexion of, *see* P.R. *and* Redistribution; and housing, 38, 164, 165–7, 172–5; not bear same burdens as in Britain, 37–8, 94, 156; Treasury critical of, 94, 95, 103–4, 157, 159; attempts to equalise burdens of, 50, 98, 99–100, meet resistance, 41, 98, 101
    Boards of Guardians, 37, 53, 157–9; regional education committees, 37, 39–40, 247–8, 251, 252, 254, 256–7, 258–61, 263; rural district councils, 27, 37, 38, 162, 226, 237–9
Logue, Michael, Cardinal, Roman Catholic Archbishop of Armagh, 249
London, 16, 24, 45, 47, 52, 115, 180, 184, 200, 202, 204
London Transport Board, 121
Londonderry, Marquess of, *see* Vane-

Tempest-Stewart, Charles Stewart Henry
Londonderry city 37, 42–3, 48, 75, 76, 77, 101–2, 109, 119, 120, 121, 129, 180, 241–2
Londonderry Corporation, 37, 42–3, 101–2, 121; political complexion, 224, 226, 243–6; ward structure, 243, 245
Londonderry, Co., 2, 57, 241, 242
Londonderry County Council, 42, 224
Londonderry jail-break, 206, 209
Londonderry Harbour Board, 120, 121
Londonderry and Lough Swilly Railway Co., 18, 119–21
Loughnane, N.G., 207–8
Lurgan, 169, 219, 224
Lynn, Sir Robert John (Unionist M.P.), 20, 61, 138, 233; and committee of inquiry into educational services, 249, 250, 251

McCarroll, J. J. (Nationalist M.P.), 264
McClintock, Sir William, 122
MacDonald, Malcolm, 110–11, 112, 113
MacDonald, (James) Ramsay, 211
McDougall, Esther, 212
McGuffin, S. (U.U.L.A. M.P.), 170
McHugh, J. (Nationalist M.P.), 228
McMullen, W. (Labour M.P.), 227
McNeill, R. N. (Independent Unionist M.P.), 264
Macready, General Sir Nevil, 181, 182, 185–6, 188, 189
MacRory, Joseph, Cardinal, Roman Catholic Archbishop of Armagh, 265
Mageean, Daniel, Roman Catholic Bishop of Down and Connor, 264, 265
Magherafelt, 239
Magill, W. A. (Ministry of Home Affairs), 218, 245
Masterson-Smith, Sir James, 272
Megaw, Robert Dick (Junior Minister of Home Affairs), 27, 40, 224; and law and order, 193, 204, 206, 209, 212–14, 215; and redistribution, 237, 240; opposes withholding of royal assent from 1922 Local Government Bill, 271–2
Methodists, 60, 252, 253, 255

253; divisions among, 31, 41,
278; limited political philosophy,
5, 12–13, 38, 53, 72, 128, 157–8;
sense of insecurity, 70, 71, 72,
179, 186, 195; and 1920 Government of Ireland Act, 2, 82; against
compromise with South, 46–7,
70, 203, and firm on partition,
2, 46–7, 71; jealous of South's
powers, 74, 75–6; suspicious of
Westminster, 99, 184, 192, 209,
but faith in British connection,
95; follow British examples, 95,
131, 159; insensitivity to minority
claims, 20–3, 219, 229, 231,
240–1; hostility to Independents,
235–6

G.N.I. identifies with, 11–13,
15, 25, 41, 77, 255, and discrimin-
ates in favour of, 6, 215–18,
219–20, 222, 233, 239, 242,
244, 245–6, 247, 253–6, 258–64,
277; complaints against government,
2, 42, 99, 100–1, 135, 137–9,
147, 157–9, 182–3, 185, 186–7,
190, 192–3, 245–6, 277

and disorders, 182–3, 186,
188–9, 192, 195–6; and self-
protection, 190–1, 193–4, 216;
faith in Special Constabulary,
71–2, 184; prisoners, 192–3, 215

and parliamentary representation (N.I.), 28, 31–4, 35, 99, 100,
126–7, 135, 137, 138–9, 168–70,
171, 172, 173, 223–6, 227, 241;
(Westminster), 44, 109, 159; local
government representation, 223–4,
226, 227, 243, 245; demand secure
representation on public bodies,
6, 231–2, 237–41, 243–6; dislike
P.R., 38, 229–30, 231–2, 234;
British criticisms of, 113, 184,
199; *see also* U.U.C.; U.U.L.A.
Ulster Volunteer Force, 24, 181, 191,
192
Unbought Tenants' Association, 30,
224
Unemployment, 5, 30, 32, 33, 34,
52–3, 59, 64, 72, 83, 85, 88–9,
101–2, 157–8, 196, 203; and
1932 riots, 53, 158
Unemployment Funds, 85, 88–9,
93, 151, 152, 161
Unemployment Reinsurance Agree-

ments, 1926 and 1936, 93, 115
United Education Committee of the
Protestant Churches of Northern
Ireland, 62–3, 252–62
United States, 52, 108
Upcott, Sir (Charles) Gilbert, 94
Uprichard, Rev. W. O., 42

Vane-Tempest-Stewart, Charles Stewart
Henry, 7th Marquess of Londonderry (Minister of Education), 11,
14–15, 70–1, 124, 258; potentially broadening influence in N.I.,
15; and education, 15, 27, 247,
249–50; offended by Catholic hierarchy's attitude, 249; dislikes
Protestant agitators, 15; at first
resists Protestant demands to
amend 1923 Education Act,
250–3, but eventually concedes,
255–6; justifies change, 256

Wages, 155–6
Wales, 53, 55, 88, 102, 149, 161, 166,
167, 174
Wales, Prince of, 23
Waley, S. D., 77, 90–1, 92, 143
Watt, S. (Ministry of Home Affairs),
22, 25, 193, 205, 216, 218
Wattlebridge, 207
Waverley, Viscount, *see* Anderson,
Sir John
Wheatley, J., 165, 166, 168
Whiskard, G. G., 208
Whyte, Dr J., 278
Wickham, Lieutenant-Colonel G. C.
(R.I.C.; R.U.C.), 22, 23, 181, 190,
213
Williamson, J., 216–17
Wilson, Field-Marshal Sir Henry, 201
Woods, Lieutenant-Colonel P. J. (Inde-
pendent Unionist M.P.), 30
Workman, Clark & Co., 52, 66, 117,
153
World War (First), 15, 58, 88, 164,
249; (Second), 56, 86, 128, 147,
156, 164, 262
Worthington-Evans, Sir Laming, 82–3
Wright, D., 134
Wyse, A. N. Bonaparte (Ministry of
Education), 249, 260, 267

Yorkshire, 5